Communications
in Computer and Information Science   1399

Editorial Board Members

Joaquim Filipe ⓘ
  Polytechnic Institute of Setúbal, Setúbal, Portugal
Ashish Ghosh
  Indian Statistical Institute, Kolkata, India
Raquel Oliveira Prates ⓘ
  Federal University of Minas Gerais (UFMG), Belo Horizonte, Brazil
Lizhu Zhou
  Tsinghua University, Beijing, China

More information about this series at http://www.springer.com/series/7899

Donald Ferguson · Claus Pahl ·
Markus Helfert (Eds.)

Cloud Computing and Services Science

10th International Conference, CLOSER 2020
Prague, Czech Republic, May 7–9, 2020
Revised Selected Papers

 Springer

Editors
Donald Ferguson
Columbia University
New York, USA

Claus Pahl 🆔
Free University of Bozen-Bolzano
Bolzano, Italy

Markus Helfert
Maynooth University
Maynooth, Ireland

ISSN 1865-0929   ISSN 1865-0937 (electronic)
Communications in Computer and Information Science
ISBN 978-3-030-72368-2   ISBN 978-3-030-72369-9 (eBook)
https://doi.org/10.1007/978-3-030-72369-9

© Springer Nature Switzerland AG 2021
This work is subject to copyright. All rights are reserved by the Publisher, whether the whole or part of the material is concerned, specifically the rights of translation, reprinting, reuse of illustrations, recitation, broadcasting, reproduction on microfilms or in any other physical way, and transmission or information storage and retrieval, electronic adaptation, computer software, or by similar or dissimilar methodology now known or hereafter developed.
The use of general descriptive names, registered names, trademarks, service marks, etc. in this publication does not imply, even in the absence of a specific statement, that such names are exempt from the relevant protective laws and regulations and therefore free for general use.
The publisher, the authors and the editors are safe to assume that the advice and information in this book are believed to be true and accurate at the date of publication. Neither the publisher nor the authors or the editors give a warranty, expressed or implied, with respect to the material contained herein or for any errors or omissions that may have been made. The publisher remains neutral with regard to jurisdictional claims in published maps and institutional affiliations.

This Springer imprint is published by the registered company Springer Nature Switzerland AG
The registered company address is: Gewerbestrasse 11, 6330 Cham, Switzerland

Preface

The present book includes extended and revised versions of a set of selected papers from the 10th International Conference on Cloud Computing and Services Science (CLOSER 2020), held as a web-based event due to the Covid-19 pandemic, from 7–9 May 2020.

CLOSER 2020 received 69 paper submissions from 26 countries, of which 18% were included in this book. The papers were selected by the event chairs and their selection is based on a number of criteria that include the classifications and comments provided by the program committee members, the session chairs' assessment and also the program chairs' global view of all papers included in the technical program. The authors of selected papers were then invited to submit a revised and extended version of their papers having at least 30% innovative material.

The 10th International Conference on Cloud Computing and Services Science, CLOSER 2020, focused on the highly important area of Cloud Computing, inspired by some recent advances that concern the infrastructure, operations and available services through the global network. Further, the conference considered as essential the link to Services Science, acknowledging the service-orientation in most current IT-driven collaborations. The conference was nevertheless not about the union of these two (already broad) fields, but about Cloud Computing where we are also interested in how Services Science can provide theory, methods and techniques to design, analyze, manage, market and study various aspects of Cloud Computing.

The papers selected to be included in this book contribute to the understanding of relevant trends of current research on Cloud Computing and Services Science, including core concerns of cloud and service research such as resource management, performance engineering, orchestration and self-healing in cloud, edge, fog and network environments, but also addressing recent topics such as governance, the link to big data or software engineering practices such as microservices and DevOps up to a look into quantum computing and the cloud.

We would like to thank all the authors for their contributions and also the reviewers, who have helped to ensure the quality of this publication.

May 2020

Donald Ferguson
Claus Pahl
Markus Helfert

Organization

Conference Co-chairs

Markus Helfert	Maynooth University, Ireland
Claus Pahl	Free University of Bozen-Bolzano, Italy

Program Chair

Donald Ferguson	Columbia University, USA

Program Committee

Luca Abeni	Scuola Superiore Sant'Anna, Italy
Vasilios Andrikopoulos	University of Groningen, The Netherlands
Janaka Balasooriya	Arizona State University, USA
Marcos Barreto	Federal University of Bahia (UFBA), Brazil
Simona Bernardi	Universidad de Zaragoza, Spain
Nik Bessis	Edge Hill University, UK
Luiz F. Bittencourt	IC/UNICAMP, Brazil
Iris Braun	Dresden Technical University, Germany
Andrey Brito	Universidade Federal de Campina Grande, Brazil
Matteo Camilli	Università degli Studi di Milano, Italy
Claudia Canali	University of Modena and Reggio Emilia, Italy
Manuel Capel-Tuñón	University of Granada, Spain
Miriam Capretz	Western University, Canada
Eddy Caron	École Normale Supérieure de Lyon, France
John Cartlidge	University of Bristol, UK
Roy Cecil	IBM Portugal, Portugal
Richard Chbeir	Université de Pau et des Pays de l'Adour (UPPA), France
Augusto Ciuffoletti	Università di Pisa, Italy
Daniela Claro	Universidade Federal da Bahia (UFBA), Brazil
Thierry Coupaye	Orange, France
Mario Antonio Dantas	Federal University of Juiz de Fora (UFJF, Brazil
Sabrina De Capitani di Vimercati	Università degli Studi di Milano, Italy
Flávio de Oliveira Silva	Federal University of Uberlândia, Brazil
Yuri Demchenko	University of Amsterdam, The Netherlands
Giuseppe Di Modica	University of Bologna, Italy
Vincent Emeakaroha	Munster Technological University, Ireland
Tomás Fernández Pena	Universidad Santiago de Compostela, Spain
Somchart Fugkeaw	Thammasat University, Thailand

Fabrizio Gagliardi	Barcelona Supercomputing Centre, Spain
Antonio García Loureiro	University of Santiago de Compostela, Spain
Chirine Ghedira	IAE - University Jean Moulin Lyon 3, France
Hamada Ghenniwa	Western University, Canada
Sukhpal Gill	Queen Mary University of London, UK
Lee Gillam	University of Surrey, UK
Katja Gilly	Miguel Hernández University of Elche, Spain
Gabriel González-Castañé	University College Cork, Ireland
Antonios Gouglidis	Lancaster University, UK
Nils Gruschka	University of Oslo, Norway
Mohamed Hussein	Suez Canal University, Egypt
Ilian Ilkov	IBM Nederland B.V., The Netherlands
Anca Ionita	University Politehnica of Bucharest, Romania
Ivan Ivanov	SUNY Empire State College, USA
Martin Jaatun	University of Stavanger, Norway
Keith Jeffery	Independent Consultant (previously Science and Technology Facilities Council), UK
Meiko Jensen	Kiel University of Applied Sciences, Germany
Yiming Ji	Georgia Southern University, USA
Ming Jiang	University of Sunderland, UK
Carlos Juiz	Universitat de les Illes Balears, Spain
Attila Kertész	University of Szeged, Hungary
Carsten Kleiner	University of Applied Sciences & Arts Hannover, Germany
Ioannis Konstantinou	National Technical University of Athens, Greece
George Kousiouris	Harokopio University of Athens, Greece
József Kovács	MTA SZTAKI, Hungary
Nane Kratzke	Lübeck University of Applied Sciences, Germany
Adam Krechowicz	Kielce University of Technology, Poland
Kyriakos Kritikos	ICS-FORTH, Greece
Ulrich Lampe	TU Darmstadt, Germany
Riccardo Lancellotti	University of Modena and Reggio Emilia, Italy
Frank Leymann	University of Stuttgart, Germany
Shijun Liu	Shandong University, China
Xiaodong Liu	Edinburgh Napier University, UK
Francesco Longo	Università degli Studi di Messina, Italy
Denivaldo Lopes	Federal University of Maranhão, Brazil
Joseph Loyall	BBN Technologies, USA
Glenn Luecke	Iowa State University, USA
Mirco Marchetti	University of Modena and Reggio Emilia, Italy
Mauro Marinoni	Scuola Superiore Sant'Anna of Pisa, Italy
Fatma Masmoudi	University of Sfax, Tunisia
Ioannis Mavridis	University of Macedonia, Greece
Andreas Menychtas	BioAssist S.A., Greece
André Miede	Hochschule für Technik und Wirtschaft des Saarlandes, Germany

Monica Mordonini	University of Parma, Italy
Mirella Moro	Federal University of Minas Gerais (UFMG), Brazil
Kamran Munir	University of the West of England, Bristol, UK
Hidemoto Nakada	National Institute of Advanced Industrial Science and Technology (AIST), Japan
Philippe Navaux	UFRGS - Federal University of Rio Grande Do Sul, Brazil
Emmanuel Ogunshile	University of the West of England, Bristol, UK
Tolga Ovatman	Istanbul Technical University, Turkey
Alexander Paar	Duale Hochschule Schleswig-Holstein, Germany
Federica Paganelli	CNIT - National Interuniversity Consortium for Telecommunications, Italy
Michael Palis	Rutgers University, USA
Nikos Parlavantzas	IRISA, France
David Paul	The University of New England, Australia
Dana Petcu	West University of Timisoara, Romania
Laurent Philippe	Université de Franche-Comté, France
Agostino Poggi	University of Parma, Italy
Antonio Puliafito	Università degli Studi di Messina, Italy
Francesco Quaglia	Tor Vergata University of Rome, Italy
Cauligi Raghavendra	University of Southern California, Los Angeles, USA
Arcot Rajasekar	University of North Carolina at Chapel Hill, USA
Manuel Ramos Cabrer	University of Vigo, Spain
Christoph Reich	Furtwangen University, Germany
José Ignacio Requeno Jarabo	Verimag, Norway
Pedro Rosa	UFU - Federal University of Uberlândia, Brazil
António Rosado da Cruz	Instituto Politécnico de Viana do Castelo, Portugal
Belén Ruiz-Mezcua	Carlos III University, Spain
Elena Sanchez Nielsen	Universidad de La Laguna, Spain
Anderson Santana de Oliveira	SAP Research, France
Patrizia Scandurra	University of Bergamo, Italy
Erich Schikuta	Universität Wien, Austria
Lutz Schubert	Ulm University, Germany
Stefan Schulte	Technische Universität Darmstadt, Germany
Mohamed Sellami	Télécom SudParis, France
Wael Sellami	University of Sfax, Tunisia
Carlos Serrão	ISCTE - Instituto Universitário de Lisboa, Portugal
Keiichi Shima	IIJ Innovation Institute, Japan
Richard Sinnott	University of Melbourne, Australia
Frank Siqueira	Federal University of Santa Catarina, Brazil
Ellis Solaiman	Newcastle University, UK
Jacopo Soldani	Università di Pisa, Italy
Josef Spillner	Zurich University of Applied Sciences, Switzerland
Cosmin Stoica	Sintezis, Romania

Yasuyuki Tahara   The University of Electro-Communications, Japan
Cédric Tedeschi   IRISA - University of Rennes 1, France
Gilbert Tekli   Research and Development Consultant, Lebanon
Joe Tekli   Lebanese American University (LAU), Lebanon
Guy Tel-Zur   Ben-Gurion University of the Negev (BGU), Israel
Orazio Tomarchio   University of Catania, Italy
Slim Trabelsi   SAP, France
Francesco Tusa   University College London, UK
Yiannis Verginadis   ICCS, National Technical University of Athens, Greece
Mladen Vouk   North Carolina State University, USA
Karoline Wild   Institute of Architecture of Application Systems,
                            University of Stuttgart, Germany
Jan-Jan Wu   Academia Sinica, Taiwan, Republic of China
Faiez Zalila   CETIC, Belgium
Michael Zapf   Georg Simon Ohm University of Applied Sciences,
                            Germany
Chrysostomos Zeginis   ICS-FORTH, Greece
Wolfgang Ziegler   Fraunhofer Institute SCAI, Germany
Farhana Zulkernine   Queen's University, Canada

Additional Reviewers

Hamza Baniata   University of Szeged, Hungary
Zakaria Benomar   University of Messina, Italy
Sofiane Lounici   SAP Security Research, France
Andras Markus   University of Szeged, Hungary
Benedikt Pittl   University of Vienna, Austria
Elivaldo Lozer Ribeiro   UFBA, Brazil
Eduardo Roloff   UFRGS, Brazil
Salma Sassi   University of Jendouba, Tunisia
Giuseppe Tricomi   Università degli Studi di Messina, Italy

Invited Speakers

Domenico Talia   University of Calabria, Italy, and Fuzhou University,
                            China
Rajiv Ranjan   Newcastle University, UK
Frank Leymann   University of Stuttgart, Germany
Schahram Dustdar   Vienna University of Technology, Austria

Contents

Trusted Client-Side Encryption for Cloud Storage

Marciano da Rocha[1], Dalton Cézane Gomes Valadares[2,4],
Angelo Perkusich[3], Kyller Costa Gorgonio[4], Rodrigo Tomaz Pagno[1],
and Newton Carlos Will[1(✉)]

[1] Department of Computer Science, Federal University of Technology - Paraná,
Dois Vizinhos, Brazil
marciano@alunos.utfpr.edu.br, {rodrigopagno,will}@utfpr.edu.br
[2] Department of Mechanical Engineering, Federal Institute of Pernambuco,
Caruaru, Brazil
dalton.valadares@caruaru.ifpe.edu.br
[3] Department of Electrical Engineering, Federal University of Campina Grande,
Campina Grande, Brazil
perkusic@dee.ufcg.edu.br
[4] Department of Computer Science, Federal University of Campina Grande,
Campina Grande, Brazil
kyller@dsc.ufcg.edu.br

Abstract. Nowadays, users are delegating the data storage to cloud
services, due to the virtually unlimited storage, change history, broadband connection, and high availability. Despite the benefits and facilities,
it is necessary to pay extra attention to data confidentiality and users'
privacy, as numerous threats aim to collect such information in an unauthorized manner. An approach to ensure data confidentiality is the use
of client-side encryption, with the user taking control of the encryption
keys and defining which files or data will be encrypted. This scheme is
already explored by many applications on personal computers and also as
a native feature in some smartphone operating systems, but are still susceptible to certain types of attacks. Aiming to improve the security of the
client-side encryption approach, we propose to apply the Intel Software
Guard Extensions (SGX) to perform data sealing, creating a secure vault
that can be synchronized with any cloud storage service, while relying on
the SGX to protect the key handling. To validate our proposal, we build
a proof of concept based on the Cryptomator application, an open-source
client-side encryption tool specially designed for cloud storage services.
Our results show an overall performance better than the original Cryptomator application, with stronger security premises. Thus, our solution
proved to be feasible and can be expanded and refined for practical use
and integration with cloud synchronization services.

Keywords: Intel SGX · Data sealing · File encryption ·
Confidentiality · Integrity · Secure storage · Cloud storage

© Springer Nature Switzerland AG 2021
D. Ferguson et al. (Eds.): CLOSER 2020, CCIS 1399, pp. 1–24, 2021.
https://doi.org/10.1007/978-3-030-72369-9_1

1   Introduction

Data confidentiality is a central concern today, since the users are increasingly using cloud storage services to keep their files and access them from any device connected to the Internet. These files can contain sensitive data, such as financial and medical information, which makes governance and data security extremely important [38]. Following this trend, there is an increase in the cyber-attacks that aim to explore sensitive information from people and companies [26,31,51]. Companies faced an average of 25 new threats per day in 2006, up to 500,000 in 2016 [61], and 61% of the CEOs are concerned with the state of the cyber-security of their company [42].

When the user delegates data storage to a cloud provider, the security and privacy of such data must gain special attention, since a third party can get access to these files and information, and the confidentiality of sensitive data must be ensured. Cloud storage providers offer some mechanisms to protect the data, such as access control and encryption, but even so, data leaks are not uncommon [1,37,53]. Also, these storage providers do not always guarantee or respect the privacy of their users [8,15,19].

To add an extra layer of security, the user can perform data encryption before sending them to the cloud storage provider. This can be done by encrypting single files, the entire volume, or using secure vaults, ensuring the confidentiality of all sensitive data to be synchronized with a cloud service. This approach also puts the user in the control of the encryption keys, avoiding that a data leakage in the cloud provider compromises them.

Despite the user having total control of the data and the encryption procedure, this approach also brings some extra concerns. First of all, major encryption solutions use a password defined by the user to derive the encryption key, and such password is often weak and can be discovered using dictionary attacks, default passwords, rainbow tables, or even brute force [44]. Another factor is that commonly file and disk encryption solutions store the encryption key in the main memory and, even when the user chooses a strong password, a malicious application can recover the encryption key by performing a memory dumping or similar techniques.

Hardware-based mechanisms, such as Intel Software Guard Extensions (SGX) [28], can be used to generate and protect the encryption keys. SGX allows the creation of an encrypted area of memory to protect code and data from unauthorized access, even when the operating system or hypervisor is compromised. It also provides sealing, enabling the sensitive data to be securely stored in the permanent storage, without the need to handle the encryption keys [4].

In this context, we seek to improve the security of traditional file/disk encryption systems, while decreasing the user's need to trust the cloud service provider.

1.1   Contribution

In this paper, we propose the use of Intel SGX features to perform data sealing and processing more securely, since these operations are performed only inside an enclave, which is supposed to be protected even against adversaries with high privileges inside the operating system. We implemented, as a proof of concept, an application using the Cryptomator, an open-source client-side encryption tool used for the protection of cloud files. We modified the Cryptomator, integrating it with an Intel SGX application, to use the SGX data sealing feature, which is performed only inside an enclave. This way, the data encryption/decryption processes are performed more securely, extending this security also for the keys, since they are also handled inside the enclave.

The main contributions of this work are:

- The proposal to improve the security of the disk/file encryption process using Intel SGX;
- The implementation of such proposal considering an Intel SGX application integrated with the Cryptomator tool;
- The performance evaluation of a proof of concept, considering six different hardware combinations.

This paper is an extended version of our previous work entitled *Secure Cloud Storage with Client-Side Encryption Using a Trusted Execution Environment* [46], which has been presented at the *10th International Conference on Cloud Computing and Services Science (CLOSER)*. We expanded our former work with new performance results and comparisons, and a more accurate security assessment on the Intel SGX technology and our prototype. Moreover, we present a reviewed and expanded set of related works, also covering aspects of using Intel SGX in cloud environments.

1.2 Outline

The remainder of this paper is organized as follows: Sect. 2 provides background information about the cloud storage and disk encryption techniques, as well the Intel Software Guard Extensions technology; Sect. 3 presents previous research closely related to our proposal, in the field of cloud storage security, the use of Intel SGX in file encryption and in cloud storage services; Sect. 4 describes the solution proposed by this paper and the prototype developed in order to validate the proposed approach; Sect. 5 presents the performance evaluation of the prototype on six different hardware combinations; the threat model as well the security evaluation of the Intel SGX technology and the proposal solution are presented in Sect. 6; the limitations of our solution are described in Sect. 7; future work are described in Sect. 8 and, finally, Sect. 9 concludes the paper.

2 Background

This Section presents a brief description of important concepts used in this work, such as cloud storage, file/disk encryption, the Cryptomator software and Intel Software Guard Extensions.

2.1   Cloud Storage

Currently, due to the advance in networking technology and broadband communication, a wide range of systems are using cloud providers to store configuration and application data. Besides, users are using cloud storage services to keep personal files and data, as well as companies are delegating the storage of financial and commercial information also to the cloud. Cloud storage brings many benefits, such as virtually unlimited storage, version history for each file, and access to data at any time from any device connected to the Internet.

As the use of these services grows, the concern with the confidentiality of the stored data also becomes a central point, since these services become targets of cyber-criminals [54]. Encryption is largely used to ensure the confidentiality of sensitive data, and its techniques can be applied in two manners: client-side and server-side.

Server-side encryption delegates the encryption procedures and key management to the cloud storage provider. This approach can provide the isolation of users' data, but there are several risks of keeping the encryption key and data encrypted with it in the same place. Furthermore, the cloud provider still has access to users' files in plaintext.

On the other hand, in client-side encryption, the user is responsible for executing the encryption and handling the encryption keys, being a user-centric approach. This way, the data are sent to the cloud already encrypted, ensuring that the cloud provider cannot access the plaintext information, and the user can choose which data will be encrypted. Also, the user can store the encryption key in a token device, or derive it from a password.

Finally, both client-side and server-side encryption can be combined to provide extra layers of security to sensitive data.

2.2   File and Disk Encryption

Nowadays, many people and companies store a range of sensitive data to their cell phones and computers, which must have confidentiality ensured. Such data include personal documents, financial information, passwords, medical information, among others. All of this information may be susceptible to third party access, either physically via the device itself, or through network access, such as public WiFi connections at airports and other places. Setting a lock password in the device may be not sufficient to protect these data from unauthorized access. Thus, the use of file and disk encryption, such as Full Disk Encryption (FDE) mechanisms, became an important mechanism to ensure data confidentiality.

FDE aims to encrypt entire volumes and can be divided into two categories: hardware-based FDE and software-based FDE. In hardware-based FDE, the encryption is performed by the disk controller, which also handles the encryption keys. Besides, the MBR (Master Boot Record) is also encrypted, preventing manipulation attacks [36]. While avoiding a range of attack vectors with key manipulation, some implementations allow the stored data to be extracted from the drive without knowing the key used to perform the encryption [34].

On the other hand, software-based FDE intercepts all the operating system (OS) requests and encrypts the data before storage, or fetches encrypted data on the storage media and returns OS-readable information. The CPU performs the encryption/decryption, and the main memory stores the encryption keys. Commonly, these solutions use AES (Advanced Encryption Standard) as the default encryption algorithm [36]. Software-based encryption solutions are also frequently used to encrypt single files and to create secure vaults, which consists of an encrypted folder or a virtual file system where the sensitive files are stored.

2.3   Cryptomator

Cryptomator is a solution specially developed for encrypting files that are synchronized with cloud storage services, performing client-side encryption. It enables creating vaults locally, in a virtual hard drive, and syncing them to the cloud storage service. All files inside these vaults are encrypted individually in a transparent way, before being sent to the cloud. This approach ensures that the user's data are never unencrypted in the cloud and allows the cloud storage provider to maintain a file update history. Cryptomator also provides a directory structure obfuscation, ensuring higher data confidentiality [21].

The application is developed in Java and uses FUSE to create a file system in userspace. Cryptomator is divided into three main modules: **CryptoFS**, **CryptoLib** and **Graphical User Interface** (GUI). The **CryptoFS** implements the virtual file system, enabling the vault creation and offering a communication interface between the operating system and the encryption procedures. The **CryptoLib** provides encryption/decryption functions, being invoked by CryptoFS to perform these operations. Finally, the **GUI** enables the users to access their vaults.

The procedure performed by Cryptomator to read the file data, presented in Fig. 1, can be described in 12 steps:

1. The user requests the operating system to open a file;
2. The operating system requests FUSE for file data. FUSE allows that the userspace applications export a filesystem to the Linux kernel, with functions to mount the file system, unmount it and communicate with the kernel;
3. The FUSE forwards this request to the Cryptomator, using the CryptoFS library;
4. The Cryptomator requests the operating system to have the file data fetched from the storage device;
5. The operating system locates the data;
6. These data are loaded into the main memory;
7. The operating system provides these data to the Cryptomator;
8. The CryptoFS library sends the encrypted data to the CryptoLib library;
9. The CryptoLib library decrypts the received data and returns them to CryptoFS library;
10. The CryptoFS library sends the decrypted data to FUSE;
11. FUSE forwards such data to the operating system;
12. Finally, the operating system provides the user with the decrypted file.

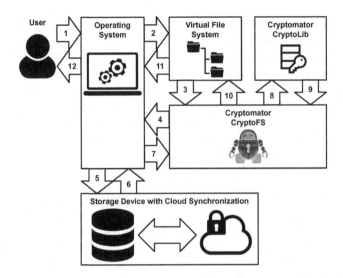

Fig. 1. Workflow for reading and decrypting stored data with Cryptomator [46].

The CryptoFS splits the file into blocks with 32 KB to send to the CryptoLib module, instead of encrypting the whole file at once. The data writing procedure is quite similar, with the plaintext file being sent first to the CryptoLib module before being written in the storage device. All the files stored in the vault can be synchronized with a cloud storage service, in its encrypted form, ensuring also the data confidentiality over the network.

2.4 Intel Software Guard Extensions Technology

Intel Software Guard Extensions (SGX) is an extension of the Intel CPU instruction set, that aims to protect sensitive information in an application, ensuring that these data cannot be modified or accessed by software running at a higher privilege level. The new instructions enable the developer to define private regions of memory, called *enclaves*, blocking any access to these data from outside the enclaves. The main goal of the SGX technology is to reduce the Trusted Computing Base (TCB) to a piece of hardware and software, as shown in Fig. 2.

The SGX blocks unauthorized accesses to data or code inside an enclave, generating access faults. The data inside the enclave memory are encrypted using a 128-bit time-invariant AES-CTR algorithm, and the CPU stores the encryption key, without access by external entities [5,29]. During the data transmission between the registers, the internal access control mechanisms, from the processor, avoid unauthorized access. Malware and even system code with higher privilege can't change the data inside the enclave, ensuring their confidentiality and integrity.

Intel SGX also provides mechanisms to detect if any part of the enclave was tampered with. Each enclave has an author self-signed certificate that enables

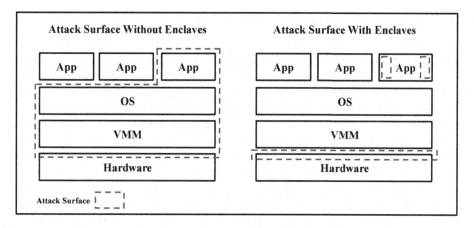

Fig. 2. Attack surface of a security-sensitive application without SGX enclaves and with SGX enclaves [52].

it to prove that it was correctly loaded to the memory and is trustworthy. The enclave is linked to the application that created it, which is open to any inspection and analysis [33].

To extend the data confidentiality and integrity primitives to a permanent storage device, Intel SGX provides the **sealing** feature. This mechanism allows the enclave to request a *sealing key*, which is an encryption key derived from the CPU and the enclave signature, and is used to *seal* the data before storing them. This key never goes out the boundaries of the CPU, and there is no need to store it for recovering (*unseal*) the data. The AES-GCM algorithm is used for data sealing and the AES-CMAC algorithm is used to generate the sealing key [4,5].

Enclaves are also able to share data with each other by using an attestation mechanism, which allows an enclave to prove that it is legitimate, has not been tampered with and was loaded correctly, allowing the creation of a secure channel for communication. Local attestation is used when both enclaves are running in the same platform, defining a symmetric key by a Diffie-Hellman key agreement procedure, authenticated by the hardware. This procedure ensures that both enclaves were loaded correctly and that all static measurements are valid. Remote attestation is also provided [4], allowing that a third-party ensures the application really runs on an SGX.

3 Related Work

This Section contains related works that also consider cloud storage security and privacy, disk encryption using the Intel SGX technology, and the use of Intel SGX in cloud storage.

3.1   Cloud Storage Security and Privacy

The security and privacy of files stored in the cloud are a central concern well explored in the literature. Zhou *et al.* [64] proposed trusted models to address the trustworthiness of cryptographic Role-Based Access Control (RBAC) schemes. With these trusted models, users can decide to join a specific role and decide what data will be accepted. Also, Wang *et al.* [59] proposed a scheme that combines Ciphertext-Policy Attribute-Based Encryption (CP-ABE) and blockchain to create a decentralized framework that provides full control to the data owner.

Different frameworks have been proposed aiming to ensure data security and privacy. An approach relies on a Trusted Third Party (TTP) to provide data confidentiality [22]. The TTP service performs encryption/decryption features and can be employed in the users' machine or on top of the cloud storage service. Another work uses a data slicing approach to achieve secure data storage in an enterprise environment, allowing the migration of application data to cloud environments while keeping the confidentiality [55]. Decomposition is used to split and store data in different cloud storage providers [7,41], while client-side AES encryption is used to increase data security and confidentiality [6].

Hardware-based security mechanisms are also applied to provide security and privacy in cloud storage services. Crocker and Querido [20] proposed an approach that uses a hardware token and the OAuth 2.0 protocol to build a two-factor encryption architecture, which can be used with any cloud storage provider. Valadares *et al.* [56] proposed an architecture that requires TEEs to decrypt and compute the sensitive data, in cloud/fog-based IoT applications, and applies authentication and authorization for the participants, increasing the security and privacy of the data.

3.2   File and Disk Encryption with Intel SGX

The use of Intel SGX to provide data confidentiality and integrity is explored in the literature. Karande *et al.* [30] proposed an approach to ensure the integrity of operating system log files by using data sealing, avoiding unauthorized modification. Condé *et al.* [16] also applied data sealing to improve the security of user authentication procedures in operating systems, ensuring the confidentiality of credential files.

In a generic way, Richter *et al.* [45] proposed the isolation of kernel modules into enclaves, preventing the spreading of vulnerabilities from one module to others, which could compromise the system. To validate the proposal, the authors created a Loadable Kernel Module (LKM) that registers a new mode inside the kernel encryption API, allowing the use of enclaves to perform disk encryption. Esteves *et al.* [25] also presented a stackable file system framework that uses the isolated execution provided by Intel SGX to extend the SafeFS architecture, a FUSE-based framework that enables the construction of secure distributed file systems. Data sealing is also combined with FUSE to protect in-memory and persistent storage [11].

Finally, Ahmad *et al.* [2] combined Intel SGX and Oblivious RAM (ORAM) to create a secure file system resistant to side-channel attacks. The file system runs in an enclave and all the requests are made by other application enclaves, by using a secure channel created through the attestation procedure. Another approach aims to create a tamper-resistant storage using a two-way authentication mechanism to transfer data from the SSD firmware to the SGX enclave, in a secure way [3].

3.3   Cloud Storage with Intel SGX

Intel SGX technology is also used to provide secure access control on cloud storage environments. Peterson *et al.* [40] used the remote attestation process to ensure data confidentiality and integrity in processing and storage, adding a protective layer that enables privacy assurance and access control. Contiu *et al.* [17] presented a cryptographic access control with zero knowledge, which used the Intel SGX to address the impracticality of the Identity-Based Broadcasting Encryption (IBBE), reducing the computational complexity. Another approach implements a cryptographic access control by using Anonymous Broadcast Encryption (ANOBE) scheme with Intel SGX, achieving scalability by using micro-services [18]. Finally, Djoko *et al.* [24] proposed a stackable file system approach that provides confidentiality and integrity, by using a client-side SGX enclave to handle the encryption keys.

4   Proposal

This work proposes the use of the sealing feature, provided by Intel SGX, to perform client-side encryption on files that will be synchronized with a cloud storage provider. This approach aims to enable strong data confidentiality and integrity properties, by using a Trusted Execution Environment (TEE), while keeping the user in control of the files. To this purpose, we chose to modify the Cryptomator application (Sect. 2.3), which is a modular and open-source solution for client-side file encryption, working with a wide range of cloud storage services.

Cryptomator is designed to support multiple encryption modes without any changes in the main architecture of the software. The CryptoLib module describes a set of methods that must be implemented to perform the encryption and decryption procedures. The original Cryptomator implementation brings only an AES encryption mode that uses default Java functions to perform the operations.

Our implementation consists of adding a new encryption mode, performing the operations within an enclave, and using the sealing key, generated by the CPU. We implement all the functions required by the CryptoLib, allowing the user to choose between the AES encryption or the SGX option. Since the enclave code is developed in C++ language, we use the Java Native Interface (JNI) to mediate the communication between the CryptoLib and the enclave.

Figure 3 presents the communication between the CryptoFS and CryptoLib modules. We can see the two encryption modes supported by the modified CryptoLib. When using the SGX mode, CryptoLib will communicate with the SGX enclave to send the data blocks. The shaded box indicates the SGX enclave, which manipulates the key and encrypts and decrypts the data blocks, in a trusted way. The communication flow is explained below:

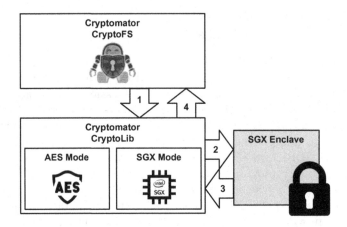

Fig. 3. Workflow performed for data encryption and decryption through the Cryptomator with the inclusion of data sealing feature provided by Intel SGX technology [46].

1. The CryptoFS library calls the encrypt/decrypt functions from the CryptoLib library, which contains AES and SGX modes;
2. In the SGX mode, the CryptoLib library creates an enclave and sends to it each data block to perform the encryption/decryption procedure;
3. The encrypted/decrypted blocks are sent back to the CryptoLib;
4. The encrypted/decrypted data are forwarded to the CryptoFS library.

5   Performance Evaluation

To evaluate the proposal based on the implemented proof of concept, we ran a set of performance tests in different hardware combinations, as well we compared our solution with the unmodified Cryptomator application and other disk/file encryption solutions.

5.1   Experimental Setup

We run tests in a custom PC with the following settings: motherboard with a Z390 chipset, 16 GB 2666 MHz RAM, SGX enabled with 128 MB PRM size, running Ubuntu 16.04.6 LTS, kernel 4.15.0-51-generic. We used the Intel SGX SDK 1.7 for Linux and set the stack size at 4 KB and the heap size at 1 MB.

To measure the CPU contribution to the performance impact of the encryption task, we used two distinct CPUs:

- **CPU 1:** Dual-core 3.8 GHz Intel Pentium G5500;
- **CPU 2:** Octa-core 3.6 GHz Intel i7 9700K.

We also used three distinct storage devices to perform the tests, each one containing different characteristics regarding performance for data reading and writing, as described below:

- **Device 1:** HDD Samsung ST1000LM024, 1 TB storage size, 5400 RPM spin speed, 145 MB/s maximum data transfer rate, 8 MB buffer DRAM size;
- **Device 2:** SSD SanDisk PLUS, 240 GB storage size, 530 MB/s sequencial read, 440 MB/s sequencial write;
- **Device 3:** SSD NVMe M.2 Samsung 970 EVO Plus, 250 GB storage size, 3500 MB/s sequencial read, 2300 MB/s sequencial write.

For all devices, we used an Ext4 filesystem partition. To achieve the highest read and write rates for each device, we used a *RAMDisk* as data destination and source for the read and write evaluations, respectively. Thus, there is no speed limitation by the source or destination of the data.

5.2   Methodology

The performance tests were carried out using five different solutions to read and write data:

- **Without Encryption:** Data read and write operations on the storage device without any type of encryption;
- **LUKS:** Data read and write operations on the storage device using native cryptographic mode in Ubuntu with LUKS (Linux Unified Key Setup);
- **VeraCrypt:** Data read and write operations on the storage device using VeraCrypt with encrypted containers;
- **Cryptomator:** Data read and write operations on the storage device using the original Cryptomator application;
- **Cryptomator-SGX:** Data read and write operations on the storage device using the implemented solution, which integrates the SGX data sealing with the Cryptomator application.

We choose LUKS [10] to perform the comparison since it is an in-kernel solution and it presents a low overhead. Also, VeraCrypt [27] is a multiplatform solution that uses a compiled binary to obtain high performance.

Two distinct scenarios were considered: the copy of a single file, and the copy of multiple files. We used the ISO image of the CentOS 7 [12] operating system to evaluate the transfer of a single file. Featuring the transfer of several files, we extracted the same image, using the recursive directory transfer mode, and used its files and folders. The RSync tool was used to transfer data.

To obtain stable results, Intel TurboBoost, SpeedStep, and HyperThread extensions were disabled. Besides, we executed the tests ten times for each scenario, clearing the system's cache before each execution, aiming to reduce variations from the operating system.

5.3   File Writing Performance

The first test aims to evaluate the performance of a single file writing. Figure 4 shows the results obtained by the different storage devices, when using the Intel Core i7 CPU. Figure 5 presents the results for the Intel Pentium CPU.

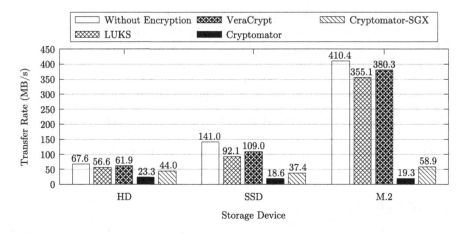

Fig. 4. Transfer rate writing a single file with Intel Core i7 9700K CPU.

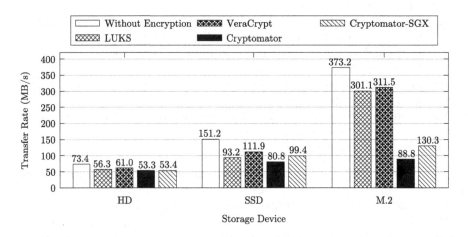

Fig. 5. Transfer rate writing a single file with Intel Pentium G5500 CPU.

Analyzing the results, we can note that LUKS and VeraCrypt, which use multithreading programming, achieve higher transfer rates, very close to the rates shown without any encryption feature. Since Cryptomator uses a single thread approach, its data transfer rate is lower than the other applications, mainly in storage devices with higher throughput. This characteristic is accentuated with the Intel Core i7 CPU use. In Intel Pentium CPU, the Cryptomator application achieves higher transfer rates, due to the higher processing clock. Besides, the difference between it and the other file encryption solutions is reduced, due to the smaller number of processing cores.

Our solution (Cryptomator-SGX) demonstrated higher transfer rates than the vanilla Cryptomator in this scenario, considering all six combinations of CPU and storage device. The better performance is achieved by the use of CPU instructions to perform the encryption, and by the optimized code in the SGX enclave. These optimizations suppress the overhead imposed by the data transfer operations through the JNI interface, the context changes, and communication with the enclave.

In the second scenario (writing several files of different sizes), we seek to identify the impact caused by the file indexing operations, performed by the file system to build the references to the files. Figure 6 shows the results in this scenario when using the Intel Core i7 CPU. We observe a performance drop, both in vanilla Cryptomator and in our solution, when compared to LUKS and VeraCrypt. Comparing the vanilla Cryptomator and the Cryptomator-SGX implementations, we can see that there is no significant difference in performance.

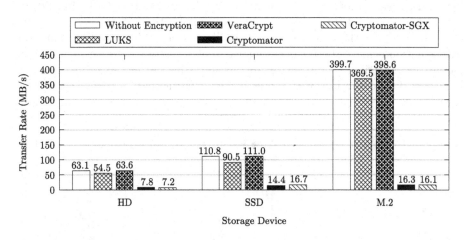

Fig. 6. Transfer rate writing multiple files with Intel Core i7 9700K CPU.

Figure 7 shows the results obtained using the Intel Pentium CPU for the same scenario. We can also notice that both Cryptomator and Cryptomator-SGX achieve a higher transfer rate when compared to the Intel Core i7 CPU. Comparing our solution with the original Cryptomator implementation, the results show a sensitive drop, especially in the M.2 storage device.

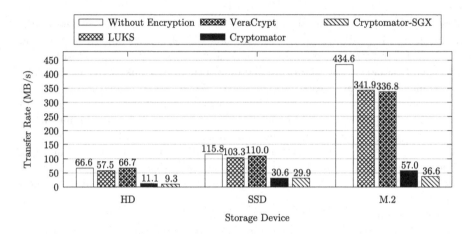

Fig. 7. Transfer rate writing multiple files with Intel Pentium G5500 CPU.

5.4 File Reading Performance

We also evaluated the overhead in reading operations. Figure 8 shows the result in the first scenario, reading a single file, using the Intel Core i7 CPU. In this scenario, we can see that the vanilla Cryptomator application achieves transfer rates close to or higher than LUKS, despite its limitations. Also, the Cryptomator-SGX solution achieves better performance in all the storage devices, when compared to the original Cryptomator application. This performance improvement is mainly due to the use of CPU decryption instructions, instead of the Java functions.

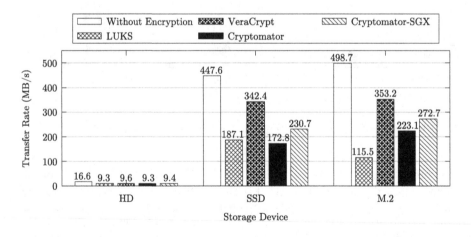

Fig. 8. Transfer rate reading a single file with Intel Core i7 9700K CPU.

Likewise, Fig. 9 presents the results in the same scenario using the Intel Pentium CPU. Our solution also achieves transfer rates very close to or better than the vanilla Cryptomator application. In the SSD and M.2 storage devices, our solution increases the transfer rates achieved by Cryptomator by 1.56×. When using the SSD storage device, we can notice even better performance than LUKS.

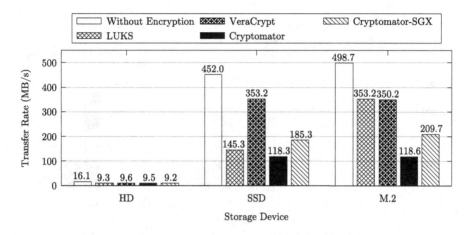

Fig. 9. Transfer rate reading a single file with Intel Pentium G5500 CPU.

In the second scenario, reading multiple files, our solution achieved good performance, mainly when compared with the original Cryptomator implementation. Figure 10 shows the result with the Intel Core i7 CPU. Our solution achieves higher transfer rates than the vanilla Cryptomator across all the storage devices. In the M.2 storage device, we can also see a better performance than LUKS.

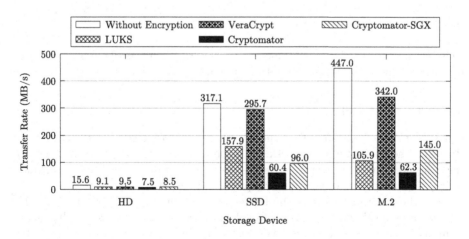

Fig. 10. Transfer rate reading multiple files with Intel Core i7 9700K CPU.

Figure 11 presents the results for the same scenario, but using the Intel Pentium CPU. We can also note that our solution achieves higher transfer rates than the original Cryptomator implementation, except when using the SSD storage device. Also, in the HD and SSD storage devices, our solution presents results very close to LUKS.

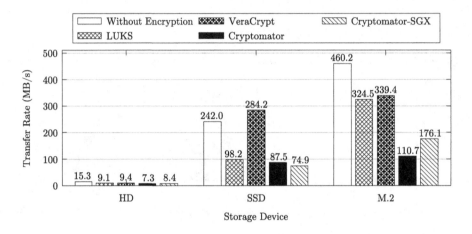

Fig. 11. Transfer rate reading multiple files with Intel Pentium G5500 CPU.

Finally, the overhead presented by our solution, when compared to VeraCrypt, is mainly due to the single thread architecture applied in the Cryptomator application. The effects of this design decision stand out mainly when performing the reading of multiple files, with these requests executed in a serialized way.

6 Security Assessment

This section presents the threat model, the security analysis of Intel SGX technology, and the security assessment of the implemented solution.

6.1 Threat Model

Our threat model considers that the adversaries aim to access confidential data stored on the computer's hard disk. To do this, they can have physical access to the computer, and can even remove the disk and install it on another machine. Doing this, they can use higher computational power to apply techniques to retrieve the password used in the key generation, or the encryption key itself. We also assume that they have installed some malicious software on the user's computer, trying to obtain the encryption key by a memory dumping, or the vault password by using a keylogger.

The adversaries can also monitor the network traffic, to obtain data transmitted between the user's computer and the storage provider. The storage provider may be deployed in an untrusted cloud, or even may be compromised. They can also obtain access to the storage provider and retrieve data, or the storage provider can leak its encryption keys or the data in plaintext.

6.2 Intel SGX Security Assessment

As described in Sect. 2.4, the main goal of Intel SGX is to keep the Trusted Computing Base (TCB) very small, being composed only by a small portion of hardware and software. This approach presents a reduced attack surface and raises the security level of the applications. Data inside the enclave are kept safe even when the operating system or the hypervisor is compromised.

Intel SGX aims to ensure data and code confidentiality and integrity when running inside enclaves. To achieve this, all the enclave data and code are put inside a protected region of memory, encrypted by a 128-bit AES-CTR algorithm, with the encryption key being randomly generated on each boot. Also, instructions and data are decrypted only by the CPU, and the encryption key never goes out its boundaries. The SGX sealing feature provides confidentiality and integrity for data stored outside the enclave, using a 128-bit AES-GCM algorithm. The encryption key is derived from the CPU and the enclave signature, and also never goes out the CPU boundaries [5].

One important point is that the development environment must be secure, otherwise, the enclave code can be compromised. In order to build secure enclaves, the API and SDK software must be installed from the official channels, keeping them updated with their most recent versions. Also, the developer must take precautions when manipulating data inside the enclave, to avoid leakage of sensitive data.

Despite the security mechanisms employed by the Intel SGX technology, it does not cover side-channel attacks. Wang et al. [60] presented four side-channel attack vectors that SGX offers no protection: power statistics, cache miss statistics, branch timing, and page accesses via page tables. Data access patterns and physical attacks against the CPU, such as fault injection or reprogramming of machine code functionalities, are also not covered by the SGX threat model [9,13].

Many works in the literature explore side-channel attacks in SGX applications [32,35,48,50,58], as well as propose several solutions to mitigate such attacks. Software-based solutions are commonly achieved through the use of Intel Transactional Synchronization Extensions (TSX) [14,49] and Oblivious RAM (ORAM) [2,43,47]. Bulck et al. [57] presented an analysis of the vulnerabilities and mitigations in shielding runtimes implementations, including SGX.

6.3 Cryptomator-SGX Security Assessment

To assess the security of our solution, we consider that the Intel SGX technology works properly, according to its specifications, and that the proposed solution development environment is reliable. We also consider that the Intel SGX technology is secure, focusing our validation only on the changes made in the Cryptomator.

The Intel SGX sealing feature allows using a CPU derived key to encrypt data and ensures that the key can only be retrieved in the same platform. Thus, when the data are copied to another machine, it will not be possible to recover the key used to perform the decryption, even using the enclave that encrypted the data, as the derivation of the key also depends on the CPU. The sealing operation is performed by a 128-bit AES-GCM algorithm, and even an attacker copying the data to a high-performance environment, the encryption breaking procedure will be very expensive, taking a long time. Also, to ensure that only the data owner has access to them on the platform where they were encrypted, we kept a second layer of security, in which the user defines a password to access the vault. This password is also used to encrypt the file names.

In case an attacker installs some malicious software to obtain the sealing key, through memory dumping or similar techniques, they will not be successful, since that key never leaves the CPU, being derived by it when necessary. Also, if an attacker has physical access to the machine, or successfully cracks the sealing key, they still need to recover the vault password or key, in order to obtain access to file names and the vault itself. Another approach is to implement a solution that uses the CryptoLib module to bypass the Cryptomator security mechanisms, but they will still need to input the vault password or key. This approach provides a second layer of security to the user's data.

On the other hand, if the cloud storage provider is compromised and leak the user data, or if attackers have access to the cloud infrastructure or cloud service, they will still need the vault key to retrieve the file names and the sealing key to retrieve the file data. This security level is ensured by the client-side encryption performed by our solution. The server-side encryption, performed by the cloud storage provider, will add an extra layer of security to the user data and will represent a new obstacle for an attacker to overcome.

Finally, if attackers listen to the network traffic, to obtain the plaintext data or some tip about the encryption keys, they will not have any success. All the data sent to the cloud storage provider are encrypted by the client, and no plaintext data or key are sent.

7   Limitations

The main limitation of our solution relies on the single thread architecture of the Cryptomator application, which results in lower performance in multi-core platforms, as shown in Sect. 5. We decided to add the SGX sealing feature without making changes to the Cryptomator architecture, to maintain the compatibility with the original project. Thus, only one enclave is created to perform the encryption/decryption procedures, and the operations are queued by the Cryptomator, which reduces the performance when compared with multithread solutions. A multithread version of the solutions requires major changes in the Cryptomator architecture and may be explored in future work.

Due to a limitation of the operating system, the sealing feature cannot be applied to encrypt the file names. Then, we keep the Cryptomator default encryption feature for this purpose. Thus, the user is still required to input a password to open the vault and generate an encryption key to cipher the file names. This limitation also adds an extra layer of protection in the solution: since the SGX sealing feature performs an authenticated encryption by using the AES-GCM algorithm, additional information is added to the encrypted data. As a result, the file size is increased by around 1.7%.

Besides, the data are only accessible in the machine in which they were sealed since the sealing key is derived from the CPU. To transfer the data to another machine, the remote attestation procedure can be added to the solution, to establish a secure channel between the two machines. Using this secure channel, data can be transferred to the destination machine, where they can be sealed with the key generated in this machine. In case the CPU used in the data encryption is lost, due to a malfunction or other occurrence, the data cannot be unsealed.

File sharing through the cloud storage provider also becomes difficult, because of the nature of the sealing key. This limitation can be circumvented with the remote attestation mechanism, or by using another CPU-independent key derivation scheme for file encryption. Since the data are encrypted in the client-side, cloud deduplication techniques may be ineffective; this situation is addressed by Yan et al. [63]. Finally, our solution does not ensure data confidentiality on the I/O devices. Dhar et al. [23], Peters et al. [39], and Weiser and Werner [62] present solutions to this problem.

8   Future Work

The use of data sealing, provided by the Intel SGX technology, has proven to be an efficient solution for encrypting sensitive files. However, due to the constant need to perform backups and remote access to data, the current solution can be improved to use the remote attestation feature, allowing the transfer of data from the containers between two machines, which are running the application through secure channels. To provide strong security guarantees, it is also possible to seal the Cryptomator configuration data. Such change requires adjustments to the CryptoFS library structure, which may remove compatibility with the main project.

The Intel SGX technology can also be applied to manipulate the encryption keys used by the cryptographic algorithms running within an enclave, removing the dependency of the CPU key. For this, it is necessary to use the same concept applied by Richter et al. [45]. In this scenario, security guarantees provided by the Intel SGX technology prevent an attack on the primary memory from obtaining the user's password or the key used by encryption, reducing the chances of a successful attack to allowing data migration to another platform.

9   Conclusion

In this paper, we proposed using the data sealing feature, provided by the Intel SGX, to ensure data confidentiality at the client-side, allowing the users to synchronize their sensitive data with cloud storage services in a secure way. We developed a proof of concept based on the Cryptomator application, a file encryption solution specially designed to work with a wide range of cloud storage services.

Experimental results demonstrated that, in most cases, our solution performs better than the original Cryptomator implementation, by using Intel SGX features and specific CPU instructions to perform data encryption/decryption. Compared with other solutions, our results show that significant changes are necessary for the Cryptomator design to obtain better transfer rates.

Our solution also provides an extra level of security, as discussed in Sect. 6, by combining the data sealing feature with a user-defined password to manage the vaults. Since the main memory does not store the sealing key, and all the sensitive operations are carried out inside the enclave, the probabilities of data or key leakage are reduced.

Finally, our solution proved to be feasible and extensible to be applied in many contexts. The source code is available at https://github.com/utfpr-gprsc/cryptomator-sgx.

References

1. Data breach report: cloud storage exposes 270,000 users' private information (2020). https://www.securitymagazine.com/articles/91985-data-breach-report-cloud-storage-exposes-users-private-information
2. Ahmad, A., Kim, K., Sarfaraz, M.I., Lee, B.: OBLIVIATE: a data oblivious file system for Intel SGX. In: Proceedings of the 25th Network and Distributed System Security Symposium. Internet Society, San Diego (2018). https://doi.org/10.14722/ndss.2018.23284
3. Ahn, J., et al.: DiskShield: a data tamper-resistant storage for Intel SGX. In: Proceedings of the 15th Asia Conference on Computer and Communications Security. ACM, Taipei (2020). https://doi.org/10.1145/3320269.3384717
4. Anati, I., Gueron, S., Johnson, S., Scarlata, V.: Innovative technology for CPU based attestation and sealing. In: Proceedings of the 2nd International Workshop on Hardware and Architectural Support for Security and Privacy. ACM, Tel-Aviv (2013)
5. Aumasson, J.P., Merino, L.: SGX secure enclaves in practice: security and crypto review. In: Proceedings of the Black Hat. Black Hat, Las Vegas (2016)
6. Babitha, M., Babu, K.R.R.: Secure cloud storage using AES encryption. In: Proceedings of the International Conference on Automatic Control and Dynamic Optimization Techniques, pp. 859–864. IEEE, Pune (2016). https://doi.org/10.1109/ICACDOT.2016.7877709
7. Branco Jr., E.C., Monteiro, J.M., Reis, R., Machado, J.C.: A flexible mechanism for data confidentiality in cloud database scenarios. In: Proceedings of the 18th International Conference on Enterprise Information Systems, pp. 359–368. SciTePress, Rome (2016). https://doi.org/10.5220/0005872503590368

8. Branscombe, M.: Has Microsoft been looking at user files to find the 75tb OneDrive hoarders? (2015). https://www.techradar.com/news/internet/cloud-services/has-microsoft-been-looking-at-user-files-to-find-the-75tb-onedrive-hoarders--1308186
9. Brasser, F., Müller, U., Dmitrienko, A., Kostiainen, K., Capkun, S., Sadeghi, A.R.: Software grand exposure: SGX cache attacks are practical. In: Proceedings of the 11th USENIX Workshop on Offensive Technologies. USENIX, Vancouver (2017). https://www.usenix.org/conference/woot17/workshop-program/presentation/brasser
10. Broz, M.: Linux Unified Key Setup (2020). https://gitlab.com/cryptsetup/cryptsetup/wikis/home
11. Burihabwa, D., Felber, P., Mercier, H., Schiavoni, V.: SGX-FS: hardening a file system in user-space with Intel SGX. In: Proceedings of the 10th IEEE International Conference on Cloud Computing Technology and Science. IEEE, Nicosia (2018). https://doi.org/10.1109/CloudCom2018.2018.00027
12. CentOS: The CentOS Project (2020). https://www.centos.org/
13. Chen, G., et al.: Racing in hyperspace: closing hyper-threading side channels on SGX with contrived data races. In: Proceedings of the 39th IEEE Symposium on Security and Privacy. IEEE, San Francisco (2018). https://doi.org/10.1109/SP.2018.00024
14. Chen, S., Zhang, X., Reiter, M.K., Zhang, Y.: Detecting privileged side-channel attacks in shielded execution with Déjà Vu. In: Proceedings of the ACM on Asia Conference on Computer and Communications Security, pp. 7–18. ACM, Abu Dhabi (2017). https://doi.org/10.1145/3052973.3053007
15. Clover, J.: Hackers using iCloud's find my iPhone feature to remotely lock macs and demand ransom payments (2017). https://www.macrumors.com/2017/09/20/hackers-find-my-iphone-remote-mac-lock/
16. Condé, R.C.R., Maziero, C.A., Will, N.C.: Using Intel SGX to protect authentication credentials in an untrusted operating system. In: Proceedings of the 23rd Symposium on Computers and Communications. IEEE, Natal (2018). https://doi.org/10.1109/ISCC.2018.8538470
17. Contiu, S., Pires, R., Vaucher, S., Pasin, M., Felber, P., Réveillère, L.: IBBE-SGX: cryptographic group access control using trusted execution environments. In: Proceedings of the 48th Annual International Conference on Dependable Systems and Networks, pp. 207–218. IEEE, Luxembourg City (2018). https://doi.org/10.1109/DSN.2018.00032
18. Contiu, S., Vaucher, S., Pires, R., Pasin, M., Felber, P., Réveillère, L.: Anonymous and confidential file sharing over untrusted clouds. In: Proceedings of the 38th Symposium on Reliable Distributed Systems, pp. 21–2110. IEEE, Lyon (2019). https://doi.org/10.1109/SRDS47363.2019.00013
19. Cox, J.: Hackers stole account details for over 60 million Dropbox users (2016). https://www.vice.com/en_us/article/nz74qb/hackers-stole-over-60-million-dropbox-accounts
20. Crocker, P., Querido, P.: Two factor encryption in cloud storage providers using hardware tokens. In: Proceedings of the Global Communications Conference Workshops. IEEE, San Diego (2015). https://doi.org/10.1109/GLOCOMW.2015.7414154
21. Cryptomator: Cryptomator system architecture (2019). https://cryptomator.org/security/architecture

22. Dahshan, M., Elkassas, S.: Framework for securing data in cloud storage services. In: Proceedings of the 11th International Conference on Security and Cryptography, pp. 267–274. SciTePress, Vienna (2014). https://doi.org/10.5220/0005043802670274

23. Dhar, A., Puddu, I., Kostiainen, K., Capkun, S.: ProximiTEE: hardened SGX attestation by proximity verification. In: Proceedings of the 10th Conference on Data and Application Security and Privacy, pp. 5–16. ACM, New Orleans (2020). https://doi.org/10.1145/3374664.3375726

24. Djoko, J.B., Lange, J., Lee, A.J.: NeXUS: practical and secure access control on untrusted storage platforms using client-side SGX. In: Proceedings of the 49th Annual International Conference on Dependable Systems and Networks, pp. 401–413. IEEE, Portland (2019). https://doi.org/10.1109/DSN.2019.00049

25. Esteves, T., et al.: TrustFS: an SGX-enabled stackable file system framework. In: Proceedings of the 38th International Symposium on Reliable Distributed Systems Workshops. IEEE, Lyon (2019). https://doi.org/10.1109/SRDSW49218.2019.00012

26. Huang, K., Siegel, M., Madnick, S.: Systematically understanding the cyber attack business: a survey. ACM Comput. Surv. **51**(4) (2018). https://doi.org/10.1145/3199674

27. IDRIX: VeraCrypt - free open source disk encryption with strong security for the paranoid (2020). https://www.veracrypt.fr/en/Home.html

28. INTEL: Intel Software Guard Extensions Programming Reference (2014). https://software.intel.com/sites/default/files/managed/48/88/329298-002.pdf

29. Intel: Intel Software Guard Extensions SDK for Linux OS Developer Reference. Intel Corporation (2016). https://01.org/sites/default/files/documentation/intel_sgx_sdk_developer_reference_for_linux_os_pdf.pdf

30. Karande, V., Bauman, E., Lin, Z., Khan, L.: SGX-Log: securing system logs with SGX. In: Proceedings of the Asia Conference on Computer and Communications Security. ACM, Abu Dhabi (2017). https://doi.org/10.1145/3052973.3053034

31. Khraisat, A., Gondal, I., Vamplew, P., Kamruzzaman, J.: Survey of intrusion detection systems: techniques, datasets and challenges. Cybersecurity **2** (2019). https://doi.org/10.1186/s42400-019-0038-7

32. Kim, D., et al.: SGX-LEGO: fine-grained SGX controlled-channel attack and its countermeasure. Comput. Secur. **82**, 118–139 (2019). https://doi.org/10.1016/j.cose.2018.12.001

33. McKeen, F., et al.: Innovative instructions and software model for isolated execution. In: Proceedings of the 2nd International Workshop on Hardware and Architectural Support for Security and Privacy. ACM, Tel-Aviv (2013). https://doi.org/10.1145/2487726.2488368

34. Meijer, C., van Gastel, B.: Self-encrypting deception: weaknesses in the encryption of solid state drives. In: Proceedings of the 40th Symposium on Security and Privacy, pp. 72–87. IEEE, San Francisco (2019). https://doi.org/10.1109/SP.2019.00088

35. Moghimi, A., Eisenbarth, T., Sunar, B.: *MemJam*: a false dependency attack against constant-time crypto implementations in SGX. In: Smart, N.P. (ed.) CT-RSA 2018. LNCS, vol. 10808, pp. 21–44. Springer, Cham (2018). https://doi.org/10.1007/978-3-319-76953-0_2

36. Müller, T., Freiling, F.C.: A systematic assessment of the security of full disk encryption. IEEE Trans. Dependable Secure Comput. **12**(5), 491–503 (2015). https://doi.org/10.1109/TDSC.2014.2369041

37. Muncaster, P.: Verizon hit by another Amazon S3 leak (2017). https://www. infosecurity-magazine.com/news/verizon-hit-by-another-amazon-s3/
38. Onwujekwe, G., Thomas, M., Osei-Bryson, K.M.: Using robust data governance to mitigate the impact of cybercrime. In: Proceedings of the 3rd International Conference on Information System and Data Mining. ACM, Houston (2019). https:// doi.org/10.1145/3325917.3325923
39. Peters, T., Lal, R., Varadarajan, S., Pappachan, P., Kotz, D.: BASTION-SGX: Bluetooth and architectural support for trusted I/O on SGX. In: Proceedings of the 7th International Workshop on Hardware and Architectural Support for Security and Privacy, pp. 1–9. ACM, Los Angeles (2018). https://doi.org/10.1145/3214292. 3214295
40. Peterson, R., et al.: Vallum: privacy, confidentiality and access control for sensitive data in cloud environments. In: Proceedings of the 11th International Conference on Cloud Computing Technology and Science. IEEE, Sydney (2019). https://doi. org/10.1109/CloudCom.2019.00026
41. Pottier, R., Menaud, J.: Privacy-aware data storage in cloud computing. In: Proceedings of the 7th International Conference on Cloud Computing and Services Science, pp. 405–412. SciTePress, Porto (2017). https://doi.org/10.5220/ 0006294204050412
42. PwC: global economic crime survey 2016: adjusting the lens on economic crime. Technical report, PwC (2016). https://www.pwc.com/gx/en/economic-crime-survey/pdf/GlobalEconomicCrimeSurvey2016.pdf
43. Rane, A., Lin, C., Tiwari, M.: Raccoon: closing digital side-channels through obfuscated execution. In: Proceedings of the 24th USENIX Security Symposium, pp. 431–446. USENIX Association, Washington, D.C. (2015). https://www.usenix.org/ conference/usenixsecurity15/technical-sessions/presentation/rane
44. Rawlings, R.: Here are the most popular passwords of 2019 (2019). https:// nordpass.com/blog/top-worst-passwords-2019/
45. Richter, L., Götzfried, J., Müller, T.: Isolating operating system components with Intel SGX. In: Proceedings of the 1st Workshop on System Software for Trusted Execution. ACM, Trento (2016). https://doi.org/10.1145/3007788.3007796
46. da Rocha, M., Valadares, D.C.G., Perkusich, A., Gorgonio, K.C., Pagno, R.T., Will, N.C.: Secure cloud storage with client-side encryption using a trusted execution environment. In: Proceedings of the 10th International Conference on Cloud Computing and Services Science, pp. 31–43. SciTePress, Prague (2020). https:// doi.org/10.5220/0009130600310043
47. Sasy, S., Gorbunov, S., Fletcher, C.W.: ZeroTrace: oblivious memory primitives from Intel SGX. In: Proceedings of the Network and Distributed System Security Symposium. Internet Society, San Diego (2018). https://doi.org/10.14722/ndss. 2018.23239
48. Schwarz, M., Weiser, S., Gruss, D., Maurice, C., Mangard, S.: Malware guard extension: abusing Intel SGX to conceal cache attacks. Cybersecurity 3(1) (2020). https://doi.org/10.1186/s42400-019-0042-y
49. Shih, M.W., Lee, S., Kim, T., Peinado, M.: T-SGX: eradicating controlled-channel attacks against enclave programs. In: Proceedings of the Network and Distributed System Security Symposium. Internet Society, San Diego (2017). https://doi.org/ 10.14722/ndss.2017.23193
50. Shinde, S., Chua, Z.L., Narayanan, V., Saxena, P.: Preventing page faults from telling your secrets. In: Proceedings of the 11th Asia Conference on Computer and Communications Security, pp. 317–328. ACM, Xi'an (2016). https://doi.org/10. 1145/2897845.2897885

51. Singh, M., Singh, M., Kaur, S.: Issues and challenges in DNS based botnet detection: a survey. Comput. Secur. **86** (2019). https://doi.org/10.1016/j.cose.2019.05.019

52. Sobchuk, J., O'Melia, S., Utin, D., Khazan, R.: Leveraging Intel SGX technology to protect security-sensitive applications. In: Proceedings of the 17th International Symposium on Network Computing and Applications. IEEE, Cambridge (2018). https://doi.org/10.1109/NCA.2018.8548184

53. Spring, T.: Insecure backend databases blamed for leaking 43 TB of app data (2017). https://threatpost.com/insecure-backend-databases-blamed-for-leaking-43tb-of-app-data/126021/

54. Sumathi, M., Sangeetha, S.: Survey on sensitive data handling—challenges and solutions in cloud storage system. In: Peter, J.D., Alavi, A.H., Javadi, B. (eds.) Advances in Big Data and Cloud Computing. AISC, vol. 750, pp. 189–196. Springer, Singapore (2019). https://doi.org/10.1007/978-981-13-1882-5_17

55. Trang, T.T.X., Maruyama, K.: Secure data storage architecture on cloud environments. In: Proceedings of the 11th International Joint Conference on Software Technologies, pp. 39–47. SciTePress, Lisbon (2016). https://doi.org/10.5220/0005974400390047

56. Valadares, D.C.G., da Silva, M.S.L., Brito, A.E.M., Salvador, E.M.: Achieving data dissemination with security using FIWARE and Intel software guard extensions (SGX). In: Proceedings of the 23rd Symposium on Computers and Communications. IEEE, Natal (2018). https://doi.org/10.1109/ISCC.2018.8538590

57. Van Bulck, J., Oswald, D., Marin, E., Aldoseri, A., Garcia, F.D., Piessens, F.: A tale of two worlds: assessing the vulnerability of enclave shielding runtimes. In: Proceedings of the Conference on Computer and Communications Security, pp. 1741–1758. ACM, London (2019). https://doi.org/10.1145/3319535.3363206

58. Van Bulck, J., Piessens, F., Strackx, R.: SGX-Step: a practical attack framework for precise enclave execution control. In: Proceedings of the 2nd Workshop on System Software for Trusted Execution, pp. 4:1–4:6. ACM, Shanghai (2017). https://doi.org/10.1145/3152701.3152706

59. Wang, S., Wang, X., Zhang, Y.: A secure cloud storage framework with access control based on blockchain. IEEE Access **7**, 112713–112725 (2019). https://doi.org/10.1109/ACCESS.2019.2929205

60. Wang, W., et al.: Leaky cauldron on the dark land: understanding memory side-channel hazards in SGX. In: Proceedings of the 24th ACM SIGSAC Conference on Computer and Communications Security. ACM, Dallas (2017). https://doi.org/10.1145/3133956.3134038

61. Weafer, V.: Report: 2017 threats prediction. Technical report, McAfee Labs (2016). https://www.mcafee.com/au/resources/reports/rp-threats-predictions-2017.pdf

62. Weiser, S., Werner, M.: SGXIO: generic trusted I/O path for Intel SGX. In: Proceedings of the 7th Conference on Data and Application Security and Privacy, pp. 261–268. ACM, Scottsdale (2017). https://doi.org/10.1145/3029806.3029822

63. Yan, H., Li, X., Wang, Y., Jia, C.: Centralized duplicate removal video storage system with privacy preservation in IoT. Sensors **18**(6) (2018). https://doi.org/10.3390/s18061814

64. Zhou, L., Varadharajan, V., Hitchens, M.: Trust-based secure cloud data storage with cryptographic role-based access control. In: Proceedings of the 10th International Conference on Security and Cryptography, pp. 62–73. SciTePress, Reykjavík (2013). https://doi.org/10.5220/0004508600620073

Relevance of Near-Term Quantum Computing in the Cloud: A Humanities Perspective

Johanna Barzen[1](✉) ⓘ, Frank Leymann[1] ⓘ, Michael Falkenthal[2] ⓘ, Daniel Vietz[1] ⓘ, Benjamin Weder[1] ⓘ, and Karoline Wild[1] ⓘ

[1] University of Stuttgart, Universitätsstraße 38, 70569 Stuttgart, Germany
`{johanna.barzen,frank.leymann,daniel.vietz,benjamin.weder,`
`karoline.wild}@iaas.uni-stuttgart.de`
[2] StoneOne AG, Keithstraße 6, 10787 Berlin, Germany
`michael.falkenthal@stoneone.de`

Abstract. As quantum computers are becoming real, they have the inherent potential to significantly impact many application domains. In this paper we outline the fundamentals about programming quantum computers and show that quantum programs are typically hybrid consisting of a mixture of classical parts and quantum parts. With the advent of quantum computers in the cloud, the cloud is a fine environment for performing quantum programs. The tool chain available for creating and running such programs is sketched. As an exemplary problem we discuss efforts to implement quantum programs that are hardware independent. A use case from quantum humanities is discussed, hinting which applications in this domain can already be used in the field of (quantum) machine learning. Finally, a collaborative platform for solving problems with quantum computers – that is currently under construction – is presented.

Keywords: Cloud computing · Quantum computing · Hybrid applications · Quantum humanities

1 Introduction

Quantum computing advanced up to a state that urges attention to the software community: problems that are hard to solve based on classical (hardware and software) technology become tractable in the next couple of years [54]. Quantum computers are offered for commercial use (e.g. IBM Q System One), and access to quantum computers are offered by various vendors like Amazon, IBM, Microsoft, or Rigetti via the cloud.

However, todays quantum computers are error-prone. For example, the states they store are volatile and decay fast (decoherence), the operations they perform are not exact (gate fidelity) etc. Consequently, they are "noisy". And their size (measured in Qubits – see Sect. 2.1) is of "intermediate scale". Together, todays quantum computers are Noisy Intermediate Scale Quantum (NISQ) computers [61]. In order to perform a quantum algorithm reliably on a NISQ machine, it must be limited in size [41].

Because of this, the overall algorithms are often hybrid. They perform parts on a quantum computer, other parts on a classical computer. Each part performed on a

© Springer Nature Switzerland AG 2021
D. Ferguson et al. (Eds.): CLOSER 2020, CCIS 1399, pp. 25–58, 2021.
https://doi.org/10.1007/978-3-030-72369-9_2

quantum computer is fast enough to produce reliable results. The parts executed on a classical computer analyze the results, compute new parameters for the quantum parts, and pass them on to a quantum part. Typically, this is an iteration consisting of classical pre-processing, quantum processing, and classical post-processing.

This iteration between classical parts and quantum parts reveals why the cloud is a solid basis for executing quantum applications: it offers classical environments as well as quantum computers (see before).

What are viable applications on NISQ computers? For example, simulation of molecules in drug discovery or material science is very promising [26], many areas of machine learning will realize significant improvements [18], as well as solving optimization problems [27].

The reminder of this paper is structured as following: Sect. 2 sketches the programming model of quantum computers. Quantum computing in the cloud is introduced in Sect. 3. How to remove hardware dependencies is addressed in Sect. 4. Section 5 outlines a use case from quantum humanities. A collaboration platform for developing and exploiting quantum applications is subject of Sect. 6. Section 7 concludes the paper.

This paper is based on [44] extended by a comprehensive use case for quantum machine learning from the digital humanities.

2 Programming Model

Next, we introduce the basics of the quantum programming model – see [55].

2.1 Quantum Registers

The most fundamental notion of quantum computing is the quantum bit or qubit for short. While a classical bit can have either the value 0 or 1 at a given time, the value of a qubit $|x\rangle$ is any combination of these two values: $|x\rangle = \alpha \cdot |0\rangle + \beta \cdot |1\rangle$ (to distinguish bits from qubits we write $|x\rangle$ instead of x for the latter). This so-called superposition is one source of the power of quantum computing.

The actual value of a qubit is determined by a so-called measurement. $|\alpha|^2$ and $|\beta|^2$ are the probabilities that – once the qubit is measured – the classical value "0" or "1", respectively, results. Because either "0" or "1" will definitely result, the probabilities sum up to 1: $|\alpha|^2 + |\beta|^2 = 1$.

Just like bits are combined into registers in a classical computer, qubits are combined into quantum registers. A quantum register $|r\rangle$ consisting of n qubits has a value that is a superposition of the 2^n values $|0\ldots0\rangle, |0\ldots01\rangle$, up to $|1\ldots1\rangle$. A manipulation of the quantum register thus modifies these 2^n values at the same time: this quantum parallelism is another source of the power of quantum computing.

2.2 Quantum Operations

Figure 1 depicts two qubits $\alpha|0\rangle + \beta|1\rangle$ and $\gamma|0\rangle + \delta|0\rangle$: because $|\alpha|^2 + |\beta|^2 = |\gamma|^2 + |\delta|^2 = 1$, each qubit can be represented as a point on the unit circle, i.e. as a vector of length 1. Manipulating a qubit results in another qubit, i.e. a manipulation U of qubits preserves the lengths of qubits as vectors. Such manipulations are called unitary transformations. A quantum algorithm combines such unitary transformations to manipulate qubits (or quantum registers in general). Since the combination of unitary transformations is again a unitary transformation, a quantum algorithm is represented by a unitary transformation too.

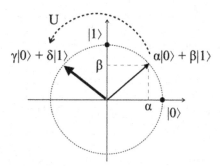

Fig. 1. Depicting a qubit and its manipulation (see [44] Fig. 1).

This geometric interpretation of qubits is extended to quantum registers: a quantum register with n qubits can be perceived as a unit vector in a 2^n-dimensional vector space. A quantum algorithm is then a unitary transformation of this vector space.

A quantum algorithm U takes a quantum register $|r\rangle$ as input and produces a quantum register $|s\rangle = U(|r\rangle)$ as output, with

$$|s\rangle = \sum_{i=1}^{2^n} \alpha_i |x_1^i \cdots x_n^i\rangle, x_j^i \in \{0, 1\}$$

The actual result of the algorithm U is determined by measuring $|s\rangle$. Thus, the result is $(x_1^i \cdots x_n^i) \in \{0, 1\}^n$ with probability α_i^2. Obviously, different executions of U followed by a measurement to determine U's result will produce different bit-strings according to their probability: A single execution of a quantum algorithm is like a random experiment. Because of this, a quantum algorithm is typically performed many times to produce a probability distribution of results (see Fig. 2 for an example) – and the most probable result is taken as "the" result of the quantum algorithm.

2.3   Quantum Algorithms

As shown in Fig. 3, the core of a quantum algorithm is a unitary transformation – which represents the proper logic of the algorithm. Its input register $|r\rangle$ is prepared in a separate step (which turns out to be surprisingly complex [60, 73, 76]). Once the unitary transformation produced its output $|s\rangle$, a separate measurement step determines its result.

Optionally, some pre-processing or some post-processing is performed in a classical environment turning the overall algorithm into a hybrid one. Especially, many successful algorithms in a NISQ environment make use of classical processing to reduce the

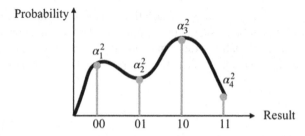

Fig. 2. Depicting a qubit and its manipulation (see [44] Fig. 2).

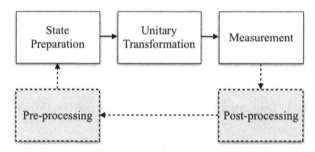

Fig. 3. Basis structure of a quantum algorithm (see [44] Fig. 3).

execution time on a quantum computer: the goal is to avoid decoherence and gate faults by spending only a short amount of time on a noisy quantum machine.

One example is a hybrid algorithm called Variational Quantum Eigensolver for determining eigenvalues [59]. This can be done by using a parameterized quantum algorithm computing and measuring expectation values, which are post-processed on a classical computer. The post-processing consists of a classical optimization step to compute new parameters to minimize the measured expectation values. The significance of this algorithm lies in the meaning of eigenvalues for solving many practical problems (see Sect. 5.3).

Another example is the Quantum Approximate Optimization Algorithm [24] that is used to solve combinatorial optimization problems. It computes a state on a quantum machine the expectation values of which relate to values of the cost function to be maximized. The state is computed based on a parameterized quantum algorithm, and these parameters are optimized by classical algorithms in a post-processing step as before. Since many machine learning algorithms require solving optimization problems, the importance of this algorithm is obvious too (see Sect. 5.3).

An overview on several fundamental (non-hybrid) algorithms can be found in the work by Montanaro [51].

2.4 Quantum Software Stack

Programming a quantum computer is supported by a software stack the typical architecture of which is shown in Fig. 4. LaRose describes incarnations of this stack by major vendors [39]. Also, Sect. 3 discusses details of some implementations.

The heart of the stack is a quantum assembler: it provides a textual rendering for key unitary transformations that are used to specify a quantum algorithm.

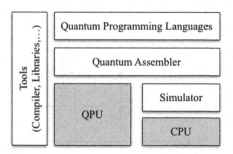

Fig. 4. Principle architecture of today's quantum software stack (see [44] Fig. 4).

Since a quantum assembler is very low level, quantum programming languages are offered that host the elements of the quantum assembler in a format more familiar to traditional programmers – but still, the assembler flavor is predominant. In addition, functions to connect to quantum machines (a.k.a. quantum processing unit QPU) and simulators etc. are provided.

Quantum programming languages also come with libraries that provide implementations of often used quantum algorithms to be used as subroutines.

A compiler transforms a quantum assembler program into an executable that can be run on a certain QPU. Alternatively, the compiler can transform the quantum assembler into something executable by a simulator on a classical CPU.

2.5 Sample Research Questions

The most fundamental question is about a proper engineering discipline for building (hybrid) quantum applications. For example: What development approach should be taken? How do quantum experts interact with software engineers? How are quantum applications tested and debugged?

3 Quantum as a Service

Since quantum algorithms promise to speed up known solutions of several hard problems in computer science, research in the field of software development for quantum computing has increased in recent years. In order to achieve speedup against classical algorithms, quantum algorithms exploit certain quantum-specific features such as superposition or entanglement [37]. The implementation of quantum algorithms is supported by the quantum software stack as shown in Fig. 4. In this section, we give an overview of current tools for the development of quantum software. We further discuss deployment, different service models, and identify open research areas.

3.1 Tooling

Several platforms implementing the introduced quantum computing stack have been released in recent years [39]. This includes platforms from quantum computer vendors, such as Qiskit [64] from IBM or Forest [62] from Rigetti, as well as platforms from third-party vendors such as ProjectQ [78] or XACC [48].

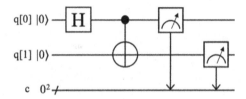

Fig. 5. Example of a quantum circuit (see [44] Fig. 5).

The quantum algorithms are described by so-called quantum circuits which are structured collections of quantum gates. These gates are unitary transformations on the quantum register (see Sect. 2.3). Each platform provides a universal set of gates that can be used to implement any quantum algorithm. Figure 5 shows a simple example of such a circuit. It uses two qubits (each represented as a horizontal line), both of which are initialized as $|0\rangle$. A classical two-bit register c is used for the results of measurement and depicted as one single line. The Hadamard gate (H), which creates an equal superposition of the two basis states $|0\rangle$ and $|1\rangle$, is applied to the qubit at quantum register position 0. Then, the Controlled Not gate (CNOT) is applied to the qubits at quantum register positions 0 and 1, whereby the former acts as control-bit and a NOT operation is applied to the second qubit iff the control qubit is $|1\rangle$. Finally, measurement gates are added to both qubits stating that these qubits will be measured and the resulting values will be stored in the classical bit register.

The different platforms support different quantum programming languages, which are embedded in classical host languages, such as PyQuil from Forest embedded in Python, or Qiskit embedded in Python, JavaScript, and Swift. The platforms provide libraries with methods for implementing a quantum circuit. The listing below shows a code snippet example of the creation and execution of the circuit from Fig. 5. The first line imports the library. Then, a circuit object is created to accumulate the gates in sequential order. Gate H is added to the circuit in line 4 and the CNOT gate is added to the circuit in line 5. Finally, measurement is added to the circuit in line 9. After the circuit is built, a concrete backend is chosen in line 11, which can be either a local simulator, a simulator in the cloud, or a QPU. The execution of the circuit is initiated in line 14. This execute method requires the circuit, the chosen backend, and the number of shots as input. As stated in Sect. 2.2, a quantum algorithm is normally executed multiple times and the number of executions can be configured using the shots parameter.

```
1    from SDK import lib
2    # create circuit and add gates
3    circuit = lib.Circuit()
4    circuit.H(0)
5    circuit.CNOT(0, 1)
6    # ...
7    # many more
8    # ...
9    Circuit.measure()
10   # choose QPU
11   Backend = lib.getBackend('...')
12   # compile circuit and send to QPU
13   result = lib.execute(circuit, backend, shots)
```

The circuit is then converted to quantum assembler language by the complier of the respective platform, e.g., to OpenQASM for QPUs of IBM, or Quil [77] for QPUs of Rigetti. In Sect. 4.4 quantum compilers are introduced in more detail. The compiled code is sent to the selected backend. The execution itself normally is job-based, meaning that it will be stored in a queue before it gets eventually executed. The result, as mentioned before, is a probability distribution of all measured register states and must be interpreted afterwards.

Although the vendor-specific libraries are embedded in high-level programming languages, the implementation of quantum algorithms using the universal sets of gates requires in-depth quantum computing knowledge. Therefore, libraries sometimes already provide subroutines for common quantum algorithms, such as the Variational Quantum Eigensolver, or Quantum Approximate Optimization Algorithm. LaRose [39] compares different libraries with regards to their provided subroutines. However, these subroutines can often not be called without making assumptions about their concrete implementation and the used QPU.

Currently, most platforms are provided by the quantum computer vendors and are, thus, vendor-specific. However, there are also vendor-agnostic approaches, such as ProjectQ or XACC that both are extensible software platforms allowing to write vendor-agnostic source code and run it on different QPUs. Section 4 gives more details on the hardware-agnostic processing of quantum algorithms.

3.2 Deployment and Quantum Application as a Service

Several quantum computer vendors provide access to their quantum computers via the cloud. This cloud service model can be called Quantum Computing as a Service (QCaaS) [65]. Also cloud providers, such as Amazon, Microsoft, or 1Qbit, have taken QCaaS offerings to their portfolio. The combination of quantum and traditional computing infrastructure is essential for the realization of quantum applications. As already shown in Fig. 3, a quantum computer is typically not used on its own but in combination with classical computers: the latter are still needed to store data, pre- and post-process data, handle user interaction etc. Therefore, the resulting architecture of a quantum application is hybrid consisting of both quantum and classical parts.

The deployment logic of the quantum part is currently included in the source code as shown in the code snippet from Sect. 3.1. For running a quantum application (i) the respective platform has to be installed on a classical computer, (ii) the circuit must be implemented, (iii) the backend has to be selected, and (iv) the circuit must be executed. Therefore, we propose another service model that we call Quantum Application as a Service (QaaS), which is depicted in Fig. 6. The QaaS offering wraps all application and deployment logic of a quantum application, including the quantum circuit as well as data pre- and post-processing, and provides an application programming interface (API) that can then be used for the integration with traditional applications, e.g., web applications or workflows.

The traditional application passes input data to the API. However, this input data must be properly encoded in order to initialize the quantum register for the following computation [40]. This data encoding, the construction of an appropriate quantum circuit, its compilation, and the deployment is all handled by the service. For the execution of the circuit itself a QCaaS offering can be used. A hardware-agnostic processing of quantum algorithms would also enable the flexible selection of different QCaaS as further discussed in Sect. 4. The result of this execution is interpreted by the quantum application and finally returned to the traditional application.

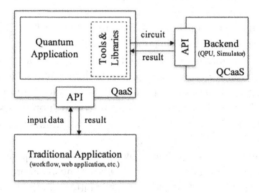

Fig. 6. Quantum Application as a Service (QaaS) and Quantum Computing as a Service (QCaaS) (see [44] Fig. 6).

This concept would enable to separate quantum applications from traditional applications, particularly with regard to their deployment. Furthermore, the integration of quantum computing features can be eased since QaaS enables to use common technologies of service-based architectures.

3.3 Sample Research Questions

To realize the proposed concept, the driving question is: How are hybrid quantum-classical applications deployed? In addition, the integration of quantum applications with traditional applications must be considered. This raises further questions. For example: What are the details of quantum algorithms, and especially their input and output formats? What are efficient encodings of input data? And for which parts of an application can a speedup be achieved?

4   Removing Hardware Dependencies

In this section, we motivate the need for removing the dependencies of quantum algorithms from quantum hardware and vendor-specific quantum programming languages. Afterwards, we present a method for the processing of hardware-independent quantum algorithms. Further, we sketch existing approaches to compile quantum algorithms to executables, optimize them, and show open research questions for selecting and distributing the quantum algorithms over suitable quantum and classical hardware.

4.1   Problem

Due to the rapid development and improvement of quantum computers [54], it is important to keep implementations of quantum algorithms as hardware-independent and portable as possible, to enable the easy exchange of utilized quantum machines. Novel quantum algorithms are mostly specified and published in the abstract quantum circuit representation [80]. Therefore, to execute them, they must be implemented using the quantum programming language of a specific vendor (see Sect. 3.1). However, the quantum programming languages are not standardized and are usually only supported by a small subset or even only one quantum hardware vendor [39]. Therefore, the implementation of a quantum algorithm utilizing a specific quantum programming language can lead to a vendor lock-in. To circumvent this problem, a standardized, machine-readable, and vendor-agnostic representation for quantum circuits is required, which can be automatically translated into the representations of the different vendor-specific quantum programming languages (see Sect. 2.4).

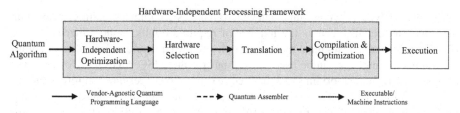

Fig. 7. Processing of hardware-independent quantum algorithms (see [44] Fig. 7).

Furthermore, after specifying a quantum algorithm using a certain quantum programming language, the utilized qubits and gates must be automatically mapped to qubits, gates, and measurements that are provided by the quantum machine to keep them independent of different quantum machines of a specific vendor [13].

4.2   Hardware-Independent Processing

In this section, we present a method for the processing of hardware-independent quantum algorithms, which is based on the works of Häner et al. [29] and McCaskey et al. [48]. First, the required steps are presented and afterwards the following sections introduce available research works that can be integrated into the approach and provide an overview of open research questions for the different steps.

The required processing steps for hardware-independent quantum algorithms are sketched in Fig. 7. The inputs and outputs of the different steps are depicted by the arrows connecting them. First, the quantum algorithm is defined utilizing a vendor-agnostic quantum programming language, which should be standardized and comprise all relevant parts of quantum algorithms [48]. Then, a hardware-independent optimization can be performed (see Sect. 4.5), which, e.g., deletes unnecessary qubits or gates [29].

Based on the optimized quantum algorithm, suitable quantum hardware is selected in the next step. For this, important properties characterizing the quantum algorithm, such as the required number of qubits or the utilized gate set, are retrieved [79]. Due to the limited quantum hardware in the NISQ era [61], this information is important and can be used to select a quantum computer that can successfully execute the quantum algorithm. Furthermore, this selection can be based on different metrics, such as the error-probability, the occurring costs, or the set of vendors that are trusted by the user [48].

After the selection of the quantum hardware to execute an algorithm, the algorithm must be translated from the vendor-agnostic quantum programming language to the quantum assembler of a vendor that supports the execution on the selected quantum hardware [48]. Next, it can be compiled to an executable for the selected quantum hardware. For this, the available vendors usually provide suitable compilers (see Sect. 4.4) [39]. During the compilation process, hardware-dependent optimizations are performed. Finally, the executable can be deployed and executed on the selected quantum machine (see Sect. 3.2).

4.3 NISQ Analyzer

The NISQ Analyzer [69] is a component which analyzes quantum algorithms and extracts the important details, such as the number of required qubits or the utilized gate set [79]. Therefore, the quantum algorithm specified in the hardware-independent quantum programming language can be used as an input for the NISQ Analyzer. However, the analysis of quantum algorithms and the precise estimation of resource requirements are difficult problems [71]. For example, the required gates for the initial data encoding [40] or the overhead due to required error correction codes [38] must be considered. Additionally, the resource requirements for oracle implementations are often ignored but lead to a large overhead that should be noted [70]. Thus, tooling support is required that extracts all relevant characteristics of quantum algorithms and provides them to the other components, such as the quantum compiler.

4.4 Quantum Compiler

The quantum compiler is in charge of performing the mapping from the quantum assembler representing a quantum algorithm to an executable for a concrete quantum computer [13, 30]. The mapping of gates and measurements that are physically implemented by a quantum computer can be performed directly. However, gates and measurements that are not physically available have to be mapped to a "subroutine" consisting of physical gates and measurements [30]. For example, if a measurement using a certain basis is not implemented, the quantum state must be transferred into a basis for which a measurement is provided by the quantum hardware and the measurement must be done in this basis. The utilized subroutines strongly influence the execution time and error probability of the calculation, as they add additional gates and measurements [35, 78]. Hence, suited metrics and algorithms to select the required subroutines are important to reduce the overhead of the mapping (see Sect. 4.5). Additionally, the qubits must be mapped to available physical qubits, which influences the quantum algorithm execution as well, due to different characteristics of the qubits, such as decoherence time or connectivity [87]. However, the available quantum compilers are mostly vendor-specific [39], and therefore, compile the quantum algorithm implementations defined in the quantum assembler of a certain vendor to the executable for concrete quantum hardware that is provided by this vendor. Other quantum compilers define their own quantum assembler language to specify quantum algorithms and map them to executables for a certain quantum computer as well [36]. Thus, the dependency on the vendor- or compiler-specific quantum assembler language cannot be removed by these kinds of quantum compilers. Hence, quantum compilers must be integrated into the approach for processing hardware-independent quantum algorithms (see Fig. 7).

4.5   Optimization of Quantum Algorithms

Quantum algorithms can be optimized in two ways: (i) hardware-independent or (ii) hardware-dependent [29]. For the hardware-independent optimization, general optimizations at the quantum circuit level are performed, according to a cost function, such as the circuit size or the circuit depth [80]. In contrast, hardware-dependent optimization takes hardware-specific characteristics, such as the available gate set of the target quantum computer or the decoherence time of different qubits, into account [34]. Hence, this optimization is often combined with the compilation to an executable for a certain quantum computer.

In the following, we sketch some existing works regarding the optimization of quantum algorithms. Heyfron and Campbell [30] propose a quantum compiler that reduces the number of T gates, while using the Clifford + T gate set. They show that the cost of the T gate is much higher than for the other Clifford gates, and therefore, they improve the circuit costs by decreasing the T count. Itoko et al. [34] present an approach to improve the hardware-dependent mapping from the utilized qubits and gates in the quantum algorithm to the provided qubits and gates of the quantum computer during the compilation process. Maslov et al. [47] propose an approach that is based on templates to reduce the circuit depth, which means the number of gates that are executed in sequence on the qubits. A template is a subroutine that can be used to replace functionally equivalent circuit parts by more efficient ones in terms of different metrics like cost or error probability. Hence, they introduce a method to detect and replace suitable circuit parts with templates.

4.6 Sample Research Questions

For the definition and processing of hardware-independent quantum algorithms and the selection of suitable quantum hardware, different research questions must be solved, some of which are presented in the following.

The definition of an abstract hardware-independent quantum programming language is important to remove the hardware dependencies of quantum algorithms. Therefore, sample research questions are: What elements are required to define quantum algorithms? How should suited modeling tooling support look like? What subroutines are important and should be provided as libraries?

To automatically select the best available quantum hardware for a quantum algorithm, suited tooling support must be developed. Hence, open research questions are: What characteristics of quantum algorithms are important for the hardware selection? How can these characteristics be retrieved automatically? What are suited metrics and algorithms for the hardware selection? What are the interesting optimization goals?

The hardware-dependent and -independent optimization of quantum algorithms are especially important in the NISQ era. Therefore, interesting research questions are: What are new or improved optimization algorithms? What data about quantum hardware is relevant for the optimization and how can it be obtained?

By comparing the performance of different quantum compilers, the compiler with the best optimization result or best execution time can be selected. Hence, sample research questions are: What are suited benchmarks for the comparison of quantum compilers? How can the optimality of the compiled executable be verified with respect to different optimization goals, like the number of required gates or the number of fault paths?

5 Quantum Humanities: A Use Case from Quantum Machine Learning

Determining how quantum computing can solve problems in machine learning is an active and fast-growing field called quantum machine learning [75]. In this section we give a use case from the digital humanities [10] that shows how quantum machine learning can be applied.

5.1 Quantum Humanities

As the following use case will stress, there are promising application areas for quantum computing not only in industry or natural science but also in the humanities. We coined the term *quantum humanities* for using quantum computing to solve problems in this domain [9]. It aims at exploiting the potentials offered by quantum computers in the humanities, raise research questions, and describe problems that may benefit from applying quantum computers. Figure 8 gives an overview of the process and algorithms (see Sect. 5.3–5.5) used to analyze the data from our project called MUSE.

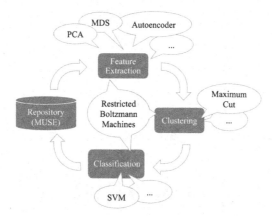

Fig. 8. MUSE data analysis (see [44] Fig. 9).

5.2 MUSE

MUSE [7, 52] aims at identifying costume patterns in films. Costume patterns are abstract solutions of how to communicate certain stereotypes or character traits by e.g. the use of specific clothes, materials, colors, shapes, or ways of wearing. To determine the conventions that have been developed to communicate for example a sheriff or an outlaw, MUSE developed a method and a corresponding implementation to support the method to capture and analyze costumes occurring in films.

The method consists of five main steps: (1) defining the domain by an ontology, (2) identifying – based on strict criteria – the films having most impact within the domain, (3) capturing all detailed information about costumes in films in the MUSE repository, (4) analyzing this information to determine costumes that achieve a similar effect in communicating with the recipient, and (5) abstracting these similarities to costume patterns [4, 7]. This method has been proven to be generic by applying it in our parallel project MUSE4Music [6].

Ontology. To structure costume parameters that have a potential effect on the recipient of a film a detailed ontology was developed [4, 5]. As a basis for this ontology, several taxonomies have been devised, which structure sub-domains such as kinds of clothing, materials, functions or conditions. An example of such a taxonomy can be seen in Fig. 9: The taxonomy of colors structures a relevant subset of colors in hierarchical form (see Sect. 5.4 on how these taxonomies contribute to determine of similarity measures between costumes).

The ontology brings these taxonomies together and adds relations (e.g. worn above, tucked inside, wrapped around etc.) on how base elements (e.g. trousers, shirts, boots etc.) are combined into an overall outfit. The 3151 nodes of the ontology induce the schema of the MUSE repository. The repository facilitates the structured capturing of all relevant information about the films, their characters and their costumes.

Data Set. The MUSE data set currently (July 2020) contains more than 4,900 costumes out of 58 films, consisting of more than 27,000 base elements, 60,000 primitives (e.g. collar, sleeves, buttons, etc.), 151,000 color selections and 171,000 material selections.

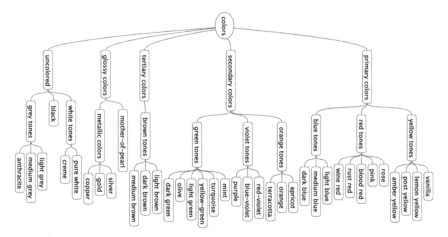

Fig. 9. Taxonomy of colors (based on [5]).

In the sense of the open data initiative, this data set is freely available to be used and analyzed [53]. It provides a well-structured and labelled data set that allows several analysis techniques to be applied.

Data Analysis. As a first approach to analyze the data to identify those significant elements a costume designer uses to achieve a certain effect, a two-step analysis process was introduced [19]. The first step applies data mining techniques – mainly association rule mining – to determine hypotheses about which elements are used to communicate a certain stereotype, for example. The second step aims at refining and verifying such hypotheses by using online analytical processing (OLAP) techniques [23] to identify indicators for costume patterns.

To improve the process of building hypotheses that hint to potential costume patterns we are currently extending the analysis of the MUSE data by various techniques from machine learning. Each costume is described by a huge number of properties. Simply mapping each property of a costume to a feature, the resulting feature space would be of huge dimension. Therefore, feature extraction, namely principle component analysis (PCA), multidimensional scaling (MDS) and autoencoders, are applied to reduce the dimension of the feature space without losing important information. To group those costumes together, that achieve the same effect, different cluster algorithms, such as maximum cut, k-means etc. are applied and evaluated. As there are new costumes frequently stored into the database the usage of classification algorithms is investigated to enable classifying these costumes.

Currently, this approach is implemented on a classical computer with classical machine learning algorithms. But since quantum computing can contribute to solve several problems in machine learning – as shown in the following section – it is promising to improve the approach accordingly [8].

5.3 Potential Improvements

Several machine learning algorithms require the computation of eigenvalues or apply kernel functions: these algorithms should benefit from improvements in the quantum domain. Many machine learning algorithms are based on optimization, i.e. improvements in this area like Quantum Approximate Optimization Algorithm QAOA should imply improvements of those machine learning algorithms.

Whether or not such improvements materialize is discussed in several papers that compare sample classical and quantum machine learning algorithms, e.g. [11, 14, 28].

Data Preparation. The data captured in MUSE are categorical data mostly. Since most machine learning algorithms assume numerical data, such categorical data must be transformed accordingly: this is a complex problem.

For example, the different colors of pieces of clothes could be assigned to integer numbers. But the resulting integers have no metrical meaning as required by several machine learning algorithms. Instead of this, we exploited the taxonomy that structures all of our categorical data by applying the Wu and Palmer metric [85] to derive distances between categorial data (for more details see Sect. 5.4).

As described above, costumes have a large number of features, thus, this number must be reduced to become tractable. We experiment with feature extraction based on restricted Boltzmann machines [31, 32] as well as with principal component analysis, embeddings and autoencoders (see Sect. 5.5). Feature selection based on deep Boltzmann machines [81] may also be used.

Eigenvalues. Principal component analysis strives towards combining several features into a single feature with high variance, thus, reducing the number of features. For example, in Fig. 10 the data set shown has high variance in the A axis, but low variance in the B axis, i.e. A is a principal component. Consequently, the X and Y features of the data points are used to compute A values as a new feature, reducing the two features X and Y into a single feature A.

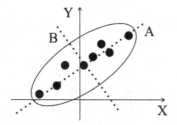

Fig. 10. Principal component of a data set (see [44] Fig. 8).

The heart of this analysis is the calculation of the half axes and their lengths of the ellipse "best" surrounding the data set. This is done by determining the eigenvalues of the matrix representing the ellipse. Computing eigenvalues can be done on a quantum computer much faster than classically by means of quantum phase estimation and variational quantum eigensolvers. Thus, Quantum principal component analysis [45] is an algorithm we will use in our use case.

Quantum Boltzmann Machines. Zhang, Li and Zhu [86] provided a quantum algorithm of a quantum restricted Boltzmann machine. In a use case, it has shown performance superior to a classical restricted Boltzmann machine.

Similarly, Amin et al. et al. [2] described an approach for both, quantum Boltzmann machines as well as quantum restricted Boltzmann machines. They report that the quantum restricted Boltzmann machine outperforms the classical restricted Boltzmann machine for small size examples.

Thus, quantum Boltzmann machines are candidates for our use case, especially because they can be exploited in clustering and classification tasks.

Clustering. Several quantum clustering algorithms and their improvements over classical algorithms are presented by Aimeur, Brassard and Gambs [1]. Since clustering can be achieved by solving Maximum Cut problems, some attention has been paid to solve MaxCut on quantum computers.

For example, Crooks [17] as well as Zhou et al. [88] use QAOA to solve MaxCut problems on NISQ machines. A similar implementation on a Rigetti quantum computer has been described by Otterbach et al. [58]. Thus, quantum clustering is promising.

Classification. Support vector machines (SVM) are established classifiers. Rebentrost, Mohseni and Lloyd [66] introduce quantum support vector machines and show an exponential speedup in many situations.

Schuld, Sinayskiy and Petruccione [74] present a quantum version of the k-nearest neighbor algorithm, and an implementation of a classifier on IBM Quantum Experience [72]. A hybrid classifier has been introduced by Schuld and Killoran [73].

The use of kernels in machine learning is well-established [33] and kernels are used in case non-linear separable data must be classified. A hybrid classifier that makes use of kernels is given by Schuld and Killoran [73]. Ghobadi, Oberoi and Zahedinejhad [25] describe classically intractable kernels for use even on NISQ machines. Thus, quantum classifiers are promising.

5.4 Categorical Data

Before the potential improvements of quantum machine learning outlined above can be applied to our use case, we need to address the problem of categorical data, since most of the MUSE data is categorical and the relevant algorithms use numerical data. As our use case can be seen as paradigmatic for further use cases from quantum humanities, addressing the problem of categorical data will be discussed in more detail in this section.

Categorical data is data with a finite set of values, e.g. enumerations of strings. If it has a canonical order it is called ordinal data, otherwise it is called nominal data. Ordinal data can be compared with "greater than" or "less than", for example, while nominal data only support comparisons with "equal" and "not equal". Calculations on categorical data, even if it is numerical, have in general no meaning. For example, what is the maximum value of a set of colors? What is the sum of ZIP codes? What is the average of the two dress sizes M and XXL?

As stated above, many algorithms in machine learning expect metrical data as input, i.e. numerical data that support calculations and comparisons in a meaningful manner.

For example, the average of a set of salaries can be computed, its mean value etc. and the result has a well-understood semantics. Such calculations are often performed to compute the distance of data points in a feature space, e.g. to determine clusters of data points or whether a new data point belongs to a known cluster.

Thus, to benefit from corresponding algorithms, categorical data has to be transformed into metrical data. A very basic transformation may assign a natural number to a categorical data item like "red $\mapsto$ 1" and "blue $\mapsto$ 5". But algorithms would then infer that "red < blue" which is not meaningful. There are transformations that avoid such problems (like one-hot-encoding) by assigning each different values of a categorical parameter to a new dimension in a feature space. As a consequence, if a parameter (like ZIP code) has many different values or if many categorical parameters must be processed, such encodings create feature spaces with very high dimensions—which demand huge processing power.

Embeddings try to solve this problem by mapping a high-dimensional feature space F into a significantly lower-dimensional space. The latter space is the normed vector space $(\mathbb{R}^n, \| \cdot \|)$, where n $\ll$ dim F and $\| \cdot \|$ is any proper norm on $\mathbb{R}^n$. The embedding is a map: F $\rightarrow$ $\mathbb{R}^n$ such that the distance $\|x - y\|$ between two points $x = \varphi(a)$ and $y = \varphi(b)$ approximately corresponds to the similarity of the original data points a, b $\in$ F.

Measuring Similarity of Parameters with Tree-Structured Domains
Definition: For a finite set M a *similarity measure on M* is a map $s : M \times M \rightarrow \mathbb{R}$ with the following properties:

i. $s(i, j) = s(j, i)$ (symmetry)
ii. $s(i, i) \geq s(j, i)$ (maximal similarity)
iii. $s(i, j) \geq 0$ (positivity)
iv. $s(i, i) = 1$ (self-identity)

where i, j are arbitrary elements in M. Often, s_{ij} is written instead of $s(i, j)$.   □

For example, when analyzing text corpora, the cosine similarity is typically used that assigns the cosine between two vectors each of which represents a document [46] as similarity of two documents. In case the domain of a categorical parameter is structured by means of a taxonomy (or more general, by means of a tree) the Wu-Palmer similarity measure [85] can be used. To define this measure, we remind three definitions.

Definition: A finite graph $G = (N, E)$ is called a *tree* iff the following holds:
i.   G is directed
ii. card E = card N − 1
iii. $\exists! w \in N : d_{in}(w) = 0$

The node w is called *root* of G ($d_{in}(n)$ is the number of incoming edges of node n, i.e. the root w has no incoming edges).   □

The Wu-Palmer similarity measure is based on length of paths in the tree structuring the domain of a categorical parameter.

Definition: Let x, y $\in$ N be two nodes of a tree G. A *path* $p_{x,y}$ *from x to y* is a set of edges $\{(x_0, x_1), (x_1, x_2) \ldots, (x_{n-1}, x_n)\} \subseteq E$ with $x = x_0$ and $x_n = y$. A path is often specified as $p_{x,y} : x = x_0 \rightarrow x_1 \rightarrow \ldots \rightarrow x_{n-1} \rightarrow x_n = y$ and the number of edges of a path is called the *length* of the path $L(p_{x,y})$.   □

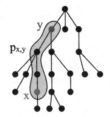

Fig. 11. A path between the nodes x and y in a tree.

Figure 11 depicts a tree and highlights the path $p_{x,y}$ in the tree between nodes x and y. The length $L(p_{x,y})$ of this path is 3: $L(p_{x,y}) = 3$. Note, that the direction of edges of a tree are often not explicitly drawn because their direction is assumed to be from top to bottom.

Definition: Let $G = (N, E)$ be a tree, w its root, $x, y \in N$, and let $p_{x,w}$: $x = x_0 \rightarrow x_1 \rightarrow \ldots \rightarrow x_{n-1} \rightarrow x_n = w$ and $p_{y,w}$: $y = y_0 \rightarrow y_1 \rightarrow \ldots \rightarrow y_{m-1} \rightarrow y_m = y$ be the paths from x to w and from y to w, respectively. The uniquely defined $v \in N$ with the properties

i. $v \in \{x_0, x_1, \ldots, x_{n-1}, x_n\} \cap \{y_0, y_1, \ldots, y_{m-1}, y_m\}$
ii. $\forall (v, v') \in E : v' \notin \{x_0, \ldots, x_n\} \cap \{y_0, \ldots, y_m\}$

is called the *lowest common ancestor* of x and y.   □

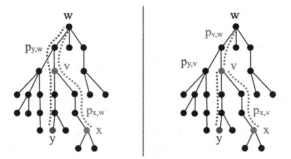

Fig. 12. The lowest common ancestor of two nodes in a tree, and paths used to determine the Wu-Palmer similarity measure.

The lowest common ancestor v of the two nodes x and y are depicted in Fig. 12. The two paths $p_{x,w}$ and $p_{y,w}$ from x and y to the root are shown in the left side of the figure, and v is the lowest common ancestor of x and y. In the right hand side of the figure, the paths $p_{x,w}$ and $p_{y,w}$ are split into paths $p_{x,v}$ and $p_{y,v}$ from x and y to their lowest common ancestor v, and another path $p_{v,w}$ from v to w. These paths are used next to finally define the Wu-Palmer similarity measure [85] as follows:

__Definition:__ Let $G = (N, E)$ be a tree, w its root, $x, y \in N$, and v the lowest common ancestor of x and y. Then,

$$\omega(x, y) := \frac{2 \cdot L(p_{v,w})}{L(p_{x,v}) + L(p_{y,v}) + 2 \cdot L(p_{v,w})}$$

is called the *Wu-Palmer similarity* of x and y.   □

Note, that the path $p_{x,w}$ can be written as $p_{x,w} : p_{x,v} \to p_{v,w}$, i.e. as the composite path from x to v followed by the path from v to w (see Fig. 12), and similar for the path $p_{y,w}$. With this it is obvious that the Wu-Palmer similarity can be computed as

$$\omega(x, y) = \frac{2 \cdot L(p_{v,w})}{L(p_{x,w}) + L(p_{y,w})}$$

The following can be seen directly from the definition of a similarity measure:

__Proposition:__ The Wu-Palmer similarity ω is a similarity measure on the node set of a tree G.   ∎

Thus, categorical parameters the domains of which are structured by a tree (e.g. by a taxonomy) can be measured with respect to their similarity. As an example, the similarity of x and y in Fig. 12 is

$$\omega(x, y) = 2 \cdot \frac{L(p_{v,w})}{L(p_{x,v}) + L(p_{y,v}) + 2 \cdot L(p_{v,w})} = 2 \cdot \frac{2}{3 + 3 + 2 \cdot 2} = \frac{2}{5}$$

Similarity of Set-Valued Categorical Parameters. A categorical parameter may be set-valued. E.g. a shares portfolio may contain shares from different companies. Any similarity measure s on a given set N can be extended to a similarity measure on the powerset of N, $\wp(N)$. Thus, categorical parameters with set-valued domains can be measured in terms of their similarity if the (single) domain the members of the set come from are equipped with a similarity measure.

__Definition:__ Let $G = (N, E)$ be a tree, $A, B \subseteq N$, and s be a similarity measure on N. Then,

$$\sigma(A, B) := \frac{1}{2} \left(\frac{1}{card A} \cdot \sum_{a \in A} \max_{b \in B} s(a, b) + \frac{1}{card B} \cdot \sum_{b \in B} \max_{a \in A} s(a, b) \right)$$

defines a map $\sigma : (\wp(N) \backslash \emptyset) \times (\wp(N) \backslash \emptyset) \to \mathbb{R}$.   □

The following follows from the fact, that s is a similarity measure:

__Proposition:__ σ is a similarity measure.   ∎

Figure 13 shows two sets $A \subseteq N$ and $B \subseteq N$. The similarity values of pair from $A \times B$ are given as annotations of the dashed lines indicating the proper pairs, e.g. s(a, y) = 0.3. The maximum value of the pairs with the same first component are noted close to the first component. Based on this the similarity $\sigma(A, B)$ of the two sets A and B is computed as

$$\sigma(A, B) = \frac{1}{2}\left(\frac{1}{3} \cdot (0.7 + 0.9 + 0.8) + \frac{1}{2} \cdot (0.8 + 0.9)\right) = \frac{1}{2}(0.8 + 0.85) \approx 0.825$$

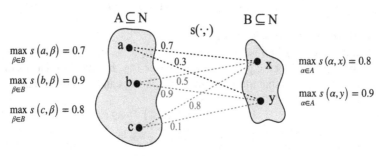

Fig. 13. Comparing set-valued categorical parameters.

Especially, if a domain N is structured by a tree, the Wu-Palmer similarity measure induces a similarity measure on $\wp(N)$. This can be extended to tuples of set-valued parameters:

<u>Definition:</u> Let N_i be sets with similarity measure s_i, and let σ_i be the similarity measure on $\wp(N_i)$ induced by s_i. Then,

$$\mu((A_1, \cdots, A_m), (B_1, \cdots, B_m)) := \frac{1}{m}\sum_{i=1}^{m}\sigma_i(A_i, B_i)$$

defines a map

$$\mu : \prod_{i=1}^{m}(\wp(N_i)\backslash\emptyset) \times \prod_{i=1}^{m}(\wp(N_i)\backslash\emptyset) \to \mathbb{R}.$$

$\square$

Directly from the definitions, the following is implied:

<u>Proposition:</u> μ is a similarity measure.   ∎

Costume Similarity Matrix. The data from the MUSE database are mostly categorical. Based on the taxonomies of the costume parameters that are used to capture all relevant information about a certain costume (see Sect. 5.2) the similarity of the costumes and their base elements can be determined as described above.

Often, algorithms are more conveniently formulated based on the distance of data than based on similarity. For this purpose, the notion of distance must be defined.

5.5 Distance Measures and Feature Extraction

Definition: Let M be a finite set. A *distance measure* (a.k.a. *dissimilarity measure*) *on M* is a map $t : M \times M \rightarrow \mathbb{R}$ with the following properties:

i. $t(i, j) = t(j, i)$ (symmetry)
ii. $t(i, j) \geq 0$ (positivity)
iii. $t(i, j) = 0 \Leftrightarrow i = j$ (definiteness)
     where i, j are arbitrary elements in M. Often, t_{ij} is written instead of $t(i, j)$. In case t in addition has the property.
iv. $t(i, j) \leq t(i, k) + t(k, j)$ (triangle inequality)

for arbitrary elements i, j, k in M, t is called a *metric* on M.   □

A categorical parameter the domain of which is structured by a tree has a distance measure defined that can be derived from the Wu-Palmer similarity measure. This is because similarity measures induce distance measures and vice versa:

Proposition: If s is a similarity measure on M, then

$$t(i,j) = \sqrt{s(i, i) + s(j, j) - 2s(i, j)}$$

is a distance measure on M. If t is a distance measure on M, then

$$s(i,j) = \frac{1}{1 + t(i,j)}$$

is a similarity measure on M.   ∎

For example, in Fig. 12 the similarity of x and y is $\omega(x, y) = 2/5$. Thus, their distance based on the induced distance measure from the proposition is $t(x, y) = \sqrt{6/5}$. Note, that there are different ways to turn a similarity measure into a distance measure and vice versa. The proposition only gives two straightforward ways.

Figure 14 depicts a distance matrix for the color and genre values of 21 random chosen costumes from the database using the Wu-Palmer similarity measure. As most of the costumes have more than one color or genre value the similarity of set-valued categorical parameters is used. The color code in Fig. 14 corresponds to the degree of distance of two costumes and is described on the right side of the figure: dark blue corresponds to a distance value of 0, i.e. the two elements are equal, and dark red, with a distance value of 1, indicates maximum dissimilarity. Based on distance measures the concept of an embedding can now be precisely defined.

Definition: Let M be a finite set and t be a distance measure on M. A map $\varphi: (M, t) \rightarrow (\mathbb{R}^n, d)$ with the property $d(\varphi(i), \varphi(j)) \approx t(i, j)$ for all i, j ∈ M is called an *embedding*. Here, d is any appropriate metric on $\mathbb{R}^n$.   □

Several algorithms are known to compute embeddings. Especially when data sets should be visualized, embeddings in two- or three-dimensional space (i.e. n = 2 or n = 3) are desirable. For this purpose, multidimensional scaling (MDS) algorithms [16] are used to compute embeddings. Figure 15 depicts the result of an embedding. If $M \subseteq \mathbb{R}^m$ and m ≫ n, an embedding is a feature extraction technique for dimensionality reduction to make processing data in machine learning tractable.

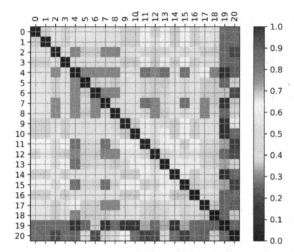

Fig. 14. Distance matrix for color and genre values of 21 random chosen costumes. (Color figure online)

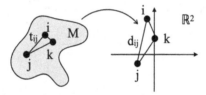

Fig. 15. An embedding of a set with distance metric into $\mathbb{R}^2$ with Euclidian metric.

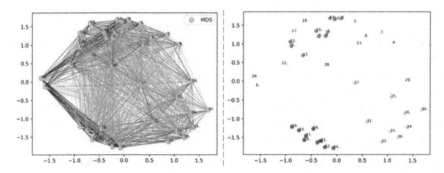

Fig. 16. Multidimensional scaling (left side) and clustering (right side).

As an example of MDS applied to the presented use case, Fig. 16 (left side) depicts the embedding of the color and genre values of 40 randomly selected costumes and their distances into the two-dimensional space with the Euclidean metric.

This embedding allows to run different cluster algorithms to determine those costumes that have the same effect. Figure 16 (right side) gives an example on how such costume clusters may look like. The algorithm used is the OPTICS (Ordering Points to Identify the Clustering Structure) clustering algorithm that creates an augmented ordering of the neighboring points representing its density-based clustering structure [3].

As can be seen in this example, not all costumes (depicted as numbers) can be classified as part of the identified clusters (colored circles). By taking a closer look at the individual clustered costumes they indicate candidates of costume patterns, e.g. the cluster in the lower left corner (red circles) reveals that in the Western genre one of the dominant colors of the costumes is black. The candidate clusters require verification by a broader data set.

Classical and Hybrid Autoencoder. Besides PCA or embeddings, there are several other algorithms to perform feature extraction, e.g. autoencoders. In the following, we show how an autoencoder is used in a quantum-inspired environment to analyze the MUSE data.

An autoencoder is a neural network performing the task of reconstructing the original input data as output data. The strength of this approach is to reduce the dimensions of a feature space by learning a representation of the input training data set. Romero, Olson and Aspuru-Guzik [67] introduce a quantum autoencoder for efficient compression of quantum data. Based on this, we have implemented a quantum-classical hybrid autoencoder in Qiskit [64] and TensorFlow Quantum (TFQ) [83]. The quantum autoencoder performs five main steps: (i) prepare the input data, (ii) learn how to preserve the quantum information of the input data with a reduced number of qubits (corresponding to the dimensions to the feature space) by an encoder, (iii) reset the qubits that are supposed to be compressed to $|0\rangle$, (iv) reconstruct the quantum states of the input data as output by a decoder, and (v) measure the quantum states.

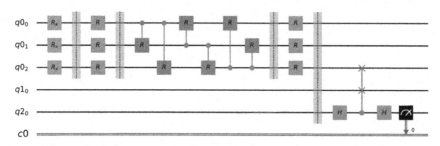

Fig. 17. Training sup-part of a quantum autoencoder circuit.

Figure 17 depicts the sub-part of the implemented circuit run on Qiskit performing the training of the neural net. All five qubits are initialized to $|0\rangle$. The first three qubits $q0_i$ represent three dimensions. The second two qubits $q1_0, q2_0$ are ancillae qubits that are used to perform a SWAP test. The R_x gates represent rotations around the x-axis to achieve an angle encoding of the input data [41, 84]. The other R gates are rotations, which are parameterized by three values. Those values are initially randomly chosen and then modified via gradient decent in each iteration. Some of these rotations (pink) are controlled rotations. The final SWAP test determines how much the two quantum states $q0_2$ and $q1_0$ differ.

An autoencoder can be trained by minimizing the reconstruction error, i.e. the difference between the original input and the reconstructed output. In our use case we compared the reconstruction error of classical and hybrid autoencoders. During the first step a classical autoencoder was used to reduce all color values of the MUSE dataset to a three-dimensional feature space, while in the second step (i) classical autoencoders and (ii) quantum autoencoders were used to further reduce the dimension to two.

In Fig. 18, the reconstruction error is visualized on the y-axis, and the performed number of iterations is depicted on the x-axis (average of 10 passes). The following autoencoders have been used: in our classical implementation we used (1) PyTorch [63] (orange line) and (2) TensorFlow [82] (green line); our hybrid implementation used (3) Qiskit and PyTorch (blue line) and (4) TFQ (yellow line). As several tests indicated that already the required SWAP test is highly error-prone due to the decoherence of the qubits and the fidelity of the gates on the quantum device, we have chosen a simulator to perform our hybrid encoder implemented with Qiskit and PyTorch.

The results depicted by Fig. 18 show that the reconstruction error of the hybrid autoencoders are both smaller compared to the classical autoencoders (error rate per autoencoder: (1) 0.0698, (2) 0.0696, (3) 0.0681, (4) 0.0665) and require much fewer iterations than the classic autoencoders. However, the downside of our hybrid autoencoders, especially the autoencoder implemented in Qiskit and PyTorch, is their longer training time compared to the classical autoencoders (time in seconds per autoencoder: (1) 1,8, (2) 3,7, (3) 2660, (4) 28,9). Nevertheless, the hybrid implementations are preferable because their results are quantum states, i.e. they can be immediately processed by further quantum algorithms, e.g. quantum cluster algorithms, benefitting from the potential improvements by using the quantum computer (see Sect. 5.3) accessible via a cloud (see Sect. 3).

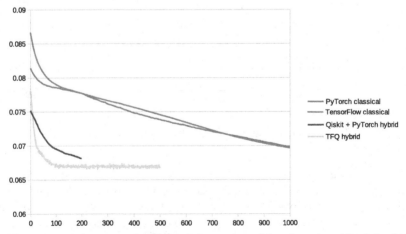

Fig. 18. Reconstruction errors (y-axis) and the number of iterations (x-axis) of classical and hybrid autoencoders. (Color figure online)

5.6 Sample Research Questions

The most essential and fundamental question for quantum humanities is to evaluate which existing and new problems from the humanities can be addressed by quantum computers. Especially, which problems are best solved by classical, hybrid, or quantum algorithms? Besides speedup, which algorithms result in higher precision? Which language allows to communicate between many disciplines (e.g. mathematics, physics, computer science, and the different areas from the humanities)? Are there completely new questions from the humanities that are only addressable based on a quantum computer?

6 Collaborative Quantum Application Platform

Driven by the continuous improvement of quantum hardware, specialists in various fields have developed new quantum algorithms and applications in recent years. The use of these quantum applications requires in-depth knowledge of theory and practice, which is often lacking in small and medium-sized companies. A major challenge today is to facilitate the transfer of knowledge between research and practice to identify and fully exploit the potential of new emerging technologies. To prepare a body of knowledge for quantum computing reasonably and make it usable for different stakeholders, a collaborative platform where all participants come together is essential [43]. For this purpose, the quantum application platform must cover the entire process from the development of quantum algorithms to their implementation and execution. The diversity of stakeholders and their different objectives lead to a variety of requirements for such a quantum platform.

Building upon the stakeholders identified by Leymann, Barzen and Falkenthal [43], we firstly identify key entities, which serve as an anchor for the knowledge on a quantum platform, secondly identify essential requirements for their expedient implementation and, finally, show a general extendable architecture for a collaborative quantum software platform.

6.1 Key Entities

To foster a clear structuring of the knowledge created on a quantum software platform the following key entities can be used. They allow different experts to hook into the platform and enable to share and contribute knowledge.

Quantum Algorithm. As mentioned before, quantum algorithms are developed and specified typically by experts with in-depth quantum physics background. Thus, for a quantum software platform it is essential to capture quantum algorithms as artefacts. Besides generally sharing them, further valuable information can be attached to quantum algorithms, such as discussions among experts regarding resource consumption of an algorithm, its speedup against classical algorithms, or its applicability to NISQ computers.

Algorithm Implementation. Besides the representation of quantum algorithms in their conceptual form, i.e., as mathematical formulas or abstract circuits, the heterogeneous field of quantum hardware demands to capture vendor- and even hardware-specific implementations of quantum algorithms. This is because, implementations for a particular quantum computer offering of a vendor requires the use of a vendor-specific SDK. Thus, implementations of an algorithm for quantum computers offered by different vendors ends up in different code or even the usage of completely different quantum programming languages. Thus, enabling sharing of different algorithm implementations on a quantum software platform stimulates knowledge transfer and reduces ramp-up especially for unexperienced users.

Data Transformator. Since quantum algorithms rely on the manipulation of quantum states they do not operate directly on data as represented in classical software. Instead, the data to be processed must be encoded in such a way that they can be prepared into a quantum register. Different problem classes such as clustering or classification have specific requirements for the data to be processed. It can be of great benefit to identify general transformation and coding strategies for relevant problem classes. Such strategies can then be represented and discussed on the platform as data transformations.

Hybrid Quantum Application. Since only the quantum parts of an algorithm are executed on a quantum computer, they must be delivered together with classical software parts that run on classical computers. To exploit the full potential of quantum algorithms, they often have to be properly integrated into an already running system landscape, which includes proper data preparation and transformation. This is why solutions that are rolled out in practice are typically hybrid quantum applications (see Sect. 3.2). Therefore, knowledge transfer about applicable software solutions for particular use cases at hand is bound to hybrid quantum applications.

Quantum Pattern. Software patterns are widely used to capture proven solution principles for recurring problems in many fields in computer science. Thus, quantum patterns seem to be a promising approach to also capture proven solutions regarding the design of quantum algorithms, their implementation and integration in existing systems. First patterns for developing quantum algorithms have already been published [40] and an entire pattern language on architecting quantum applications can be an object of investigation on the intended platform.

6.2   Requirements

The essential challenge to create and provide a reasonable body of knowledge on quantum algorithms and applications involves the collaboration among several stakeholders. In contrast to traditional software engineering, quantum algorithms are typically not specified by computer scientist rather than by quantum physicists. Furthermore, to understand and implement those algorithms a different mindset is required because the key buildings blocks of algorithms are no longer loops, conditions, or procedure calls but quantum states and their manipulation via unitary operators.

By involving all participants identified by Leymann, Barzen and Falkenthal [43] in the platform, added value can be created, both for experienced quantum specialists and inexperienced customers. For this, the following listed requirements must be met.

Knowledge Access. Often only certain specialists and scientists have the required expertise for developing quantum algorithms and their implementation. To identify and exploit the use cases of quantum computing in practice, companies must be empowered to gather knowledge and to exchange with experts (developer, service provider, consultants, and so on) [50]. Additionally, due to the high level of research activities in this area, the exchange between experts is important in order to share and discuss new findings with the community at an early stage.

Best Practices for Quantum Algorithm Development. The development of new algorithms requires in-depth knowledge and expertise in theory and practice. Documented, reusable best practices for recurring problems, i.e. patterns, can support and guide people in the development of new quantum algorithms.

Decision-Support for Quantum Applications and Vendors. A two-stage decision-support is required to identify appropriate solutions for real-world use cases. First, quantum algorithms that prove to provide a solution for a given problem have to be identified. Second, the appropriate implementation and quantum hardware have to be selected for integration and execution. For the second stage the resource consumption of algorithms and implementations on different quantum hardware are of main interest (see Sect. 4.2).

Vendor-Agnostic Usage of Quantum Hardware. Currently, various algorithm implementations from different vendors are available via proprietary SDKs that have been developed specifically for their hardware. To avoid vendor lock-in the quantum algorithm must be portable between different vendors which can be achieved by a standardized quantum programming language (see Sect. 3.1 and 4.2).

Data Transformation for Quantum Algorithms. Especially for machine learning and artificial intelligence data of sufficient quality is essential. This applies to both, classical and quantum algorithms. Such data have to be made available and respectively encoded for the quantum algorithm [49].

Quantum Application as a Service (QaaS). The hybrid architecture of quantum applications consisting of classical and quantum parts increases the complexity of their deployment. Quantum applications provided "as a Service" via a self-service portal ease the utilization of the new technology (see Sect. 3.2).

6.3 Architecture

In Fig. 19 the architecture of the collaborative quantum software platform is depicted. In essence, the platform consists of two parts: The analysis and development platform as depicted on the left of the figure for collecting, discussing, analyzing, and sharing knowledge, and the marketplace as depicted on the right that offers solutions in the form of quantum applications and consulting services.

The analysis and development platform addresses the needs of specialists and researchers in the field of quantum computing and software engineering. In a first step, knowledge in the form of publications, software artifacts, datasets, or web content can be placed on the platform – either manually via a user interface or automatically using a crawler. This knowledge can originate from various sources, such as arXiv.org or github.com. In a first step it can be stored as raw data in the QAlgo & data content store. Content of interest has to be extracted from these raw data, such as a quantum algorithm described in a journal article. To facilitate collaboration among different disciplines and to create a common understanding, the representation of quantum circuits and mathematical expressions must be normalized. A qualified description of the knowledge artifact with metadata is also essential to find and link relevant knowledge. Therefore, metadata formats must be normalized and enriched. The knowledge artifacts are then stored and provided via an expert portal to specialists and scientists and via a customer portal to users looking for solutions for their use cases and the community of interested people.

Specialists and scientists can discuss, evaluate, and improve the different key entities on the platform. Algorithms and their implementations can be linked and evaluated based on defined metrics using the NISQ Analyzer (see Sect. 4.3). Identified best practices, e.g., for creating entanglement, can then be stored as quantum patterns in a Quantum Computing Pattern Repository. These patterns ease the development of new algorithms as they provide proven solutions for frequently occurring problems at the design of quantum algorithms. Patterns solving specific problems can then be combine and applied for realizing a broader use case [20–22]. However, best practices are not only relevant for the development, but also for data preparation as input for quantum algorithms and the integration of quantum algorithms with classical applications. Data preparation is essential, and must especially be considered in the NISQ era.

Since most quantum algorithms are hybrid algorithms, execution of quantum applications means a distributed deployment of hybrid quantum applications among classical and quantum hardware. Such applications can be stored for reuse in the Hybrid-App-Repository. For the quantum part, the quantum computer vendor and more specific a single QPU has to be selected, depending on the QPU properties, the algorithm implementation, and the input data. The platform automates this selection and provides a vendor-agnostic access to quantum hardware. For the deployment, technologies for classical computing are evaluated to provide an integrated deployment automation toolchain. Standards such as the Topology and Orchestration Specification for Cloud Applications (TOSCA) [56] have been developed precisely for this purpose to enable portability, interoperability, and the distribution across different environments [68, 69]. Thus, TOSCA as an international standard offers good foundation for an integration of classical and quantum deployment.

While the expert portal is tailored to provide a sufficient user interface and toolchain addressing the needs of quantum computing experts the marketplace on the right of Fig. 19 enables service providers and further stakeholders, such as consultants, to offer solutions. Customers can place requests for solutions for certain problems or use cases at hand. It is further intended to also allow consulting services to be offered in addition to hybrid quantum applications and their deployments. This means that also business models besides the development and distribution are enabled by the interplay of the marketplace and the analysis and development platform. For example, hybrid quantum applications can be provided as a service, which is enabled through the automated

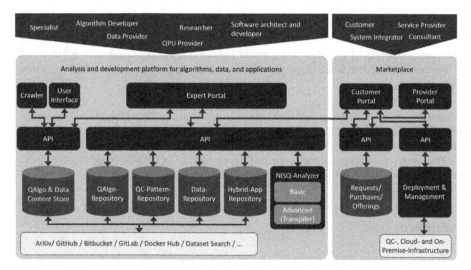

Fig. 19. Architecture for a collaborative quantum software platform ([44] Fig. 10).

deployment capabilities by means of a TOSCA orchestrator such as OpenTOSCA [12, 57] or Cloudify [15]. Further, the selection of quantum algorithms fitting to specific constraints of quantum hardware can be supported by the NISQ Analyzer and the discussions of experts. With the help of the marketplace, knowledge and software artifacts, such as quantum algorithm implementations and hybrid quantum applications, can be monetized. Every turnover on the platform leads to incentives for participating experts to make further knowledge available on the platform.

6.4 Sample Research Questions

The platform provides the basis for the technical realization of the research questions already discussed. However, further questions are raised: What are best practices for data preparation as input for quantum algorithms? What are best practices for integrating quantum algorithms with classical applications? How to combine the best practices in quantum computing with other domains such as cloud computing? Which metadata is required to adequately describe the key entities on the platform?

7 Conclusions

New possibilities to solve classically intractable problems based on quantum computing is at the horizon. Quantum computers appear as part of the cloud infrastructure, and based on the hybrid nature of quantum-based applications, cloud computing techniques will contribute to the discipline of building them. Lots of new research questions appeared.

To evaluate promising application areas, we presented a use case from quantum humanities in which quantum machine learning techniques were used to derive insights from a comprehensive data set.

We are about to build the collaborative quantum application platform, and exploit it for several use cases, especially in the area of machine learning. A pattern language for quantum computing as well as tooling support [42, 84] are under construction. Research on the removal of hardware dependencies including deployment of hybrid quantum applications is ongoing.

Acknowledgements. We are grateful to Marie Salm and Manuela Weigold for discussing several subjects of this paper. Also, our thanks go to Philipp Wundrack, Marcel Messer, Daniel Fink and Tino Strehl for their valuable input and implementing several aspects of our use case.

This work was partially funded by the BMWi project PlanQK (01MK20005N) and the Terra Incognita project Quantum Humanities funded by the University of Stuttgart.

References

1. Aimeur, E., Brassard, G., Gambs, S.: Quantum clustering algorithms. In: Proceedings of the 24th International Conference on Machine Learning, Corvallis, OR (2007)
2. Amin, M.A., Andriyash, E., Rolfe, J., Kulchytskyy, B., Melko, R.: Quantum Boltzmann machine. Phys. Rev. X **8**, 021050 (2018)
3. Ankerst, M., Breunig, M.M., Kriegel, H., Sander, J.: OPTICS: ordering points to identify the clustering structure. In: ACM SIGMOD International Conference on Management of Data. ACM Press (1999)
4. Barzen, J.: Wenn Kostüme sprechen – Musterforschung in den Digital Humanities am Beispiel vestimentärer Kommunikation im Film. Dissertation University Cologne (2018). (in German)
5. Barzen, J.: Taxonomien kostümrelevanter Parameter: Annäherung an eine Ontologisierung der Domäne des Filmkostüms. Technical report, University Stuttgart, no. 2013/04 (2013). (in German)
6. Barzen, J., Breitenbücher, U., Eusterbrock, L., Falkenthal, M., Hentschel, F., Leymann, F.: The vision for MUSE4Music. Applying the MUSE method in musicology. Comput. Sci. Res. Dev. **32**, 323–328 (2017). https://doi.org/10.1007/s00450-016-0336-1. Proceedings of SummerSoC 2016
7. Barzen, J., Falkenthal, M., Leymann, F.: Wenn Kostüme sprechen könnten: MUSE - Ein musterbasierter Ansatz an die vestimentäre Kommunikation im Film. In: Bockwinkel, P., Nickel, B., Viehhauser, G. (eds.) Digital Humanities. Perspektiven der Praxis, Frank & Timme (2018). (in German)
8. Barzen, J., Leymann, F.: Quantum humanities: a first use case for quantum-ML in media science. In: ISAAI 2019 Proceedings—Artificial Intelligence (2020). Digitale Welt **4**(1)
9. Barzen, J., Leymann, F.: Quantum humanities: a vision for quantum computing in digital humanities. SICS Softw.-Intensive Cyber-Phys. Syst. **35**(1–2), 153–158 (2019). https://doi.org/10.1007/s00450-019-00419-4
10. Berry, D. (ed.): Understanding Digital Humanities. Palgrave, London (2012)
11. Biamonte, J., Wittek, P., Pancotti, N., Rebentrost, P., Wiebe, N., Lloyd, S.: Quantum machine learning. Nature **549**, 195–202 (2017)
12. Binz, T., et al.: OpenTOSCA – a runtime for TOSCA-based cloud applications. In: Basu, S., Pautasso, C., Zhang, L., Fu, X. (eds.) ICSOC 2013. LNCS, vol. 8274, pp. 692–695. Springer, Heidelberg (2013). https://doi.org/10.1007/978-3-642-45005-1_62
13. Booth Jr., J.: Quantum compiler optimizations (2012). arXiv:1206.3348
14. Ciliberto, C., et al.: Quantum machine learning: a classical perspective. Proc. Roy. Soc. A **474** (2018). https://doi.org/10.1098/rspa.2017.0551

15. Cloudify (2020). https://cloudify.co/. Accessed 07 Sept 2020
16. Cox, T.F., Cox, M.A.A.: Multidimensional Scaling. Chapman and Hall, London (2001)
17. Crooks, G.E.: Performance of the quantum approximate optimization algorithm on the maximum cut problem (2018). arXiv:1811.08419v1
18. Dunjko, V., Taylor, J.M., Briegel, H.J.: Quantum-enhanced machine learning. Phys. Rev. Lett. **117**, 130501 (2016)
19. Falkenthal, M., et al.: Pattern research in the digital humanities: how data mining techniques support the identification of costume patterns. Comput. Sci. Res. Dev. **32**, 311–321 (2016). https://doi.org/10.1007/s00450-016-0331-6. Proceedings of SummerSoC 2016
20. Falkenthal, M., Barzen, J., Breitenbücher, U., Fehling, C., Leymann, F.: Effective pattern application: validating the concept of solution implementation in different domains. Int. J. Adv. Softw. **7**(3&4), 710–726 (2014)
21. Falkenthal, M., et al.: Leveraging pattern applications via pattern refinement. In: Proceedings of the International Conference on Pursuit of Pattern Languages for Social Change (PURPLSOC), pp. 38–61. epubli GmbH (2016)
22. Falkenthal, M., Barzen, J., Breitenbücher, U., Leymann, F.: Solution languages: easing pattern composition in different domains. Int. J. Adv. Softw. **10**(3&4), 263–274 (2017)
23. Falkenthal, M., et al.: Datenanalyse in den Digital Humanities – Eine Annäherung an Kostümmuster mittels OLAP Cubes. In: Datenbanksysteme für Business, Technologie und Web (BTW), 16. Fachtagung des GI-Fachbereichs "Datenbanken und Informationssysteme" (2015). (in German)
24. Farhi, E., Goldstone, J., Gutmann, S.: A quantum approximate optimization algorithm. MIT-CTP/4610 (2014)
25. Ghobadi, R., Oberoi, J.S., Zahedinejhad, E.: The power of one qubit in machine learning (2019). arXiv:1905.01390v2
26. Grimsley, H.R., Economou, S.E., Barnes, E., Mayhall, N.J.: An adaptive variational algorithm for exact molecular simulations on a quantum computer. Nat. Commun. **10** (2019). Article number: 3007
27. Guerreschi, G.G., Smelyanskiy, M.: Practical optimization for hybrid quantum-classical algorithms (2017). arXiv:1701.01450v1
28. Havenstein, Ch., Thomas, D., Chandrasekaran, S.: Comparisons of performance between quantum and classical machine learning. SMU Data Sci. Rev. **1**(4), 11 (2018)
29. Häner, T., Steiger, D.S., Svore, K., Troyer, M.: A software methodology for compiling quantum programs. Quantum Sci. Technol. **3**(2), 020501 (2018)
30. Heyfron, L.E., Campbell, E.T.: An efficient quantum compiler that reduces T count. Quantum Sci. Technol. **4**(1), 015004 (2018)
31. Hinton, G.E., Salakhutdinov, R.R.: Reducing the dimensionality of data with neural networks. Science **313**(5786), 504–507 (2006)
32. Hinton, G.E.: A practical guide to training restricted Boltzmann machines. In: Montavon, G., Orr, G.B., Müller, K.-R. (eds.) Neural Networks: Tricks of the Trade. LNCS, vol. 7700, pp. 599–619. Springer, Heidelberg (2012). https://doi.org/10.1007/978-3-642-35289-8_32
33. Hofmann, Th., Schölkopf, B., Smola, A.J.: Kernel methods in machine learning. Ann. Stat. **36**(3), 1171–1220 (2008)
34. Itoko, T., Raymond, R., Imamichi, T., Matsuo, A.: Optimization of quantum circuit mapping using gate transformation and commutation. Integration **70**, 43–50 (2020)
35. Javadi-Abhari, A., Nation, P., Gambetta, J.: Qiskit – write once, target multiple architectures (2019). https://www.ibm.com/blogs/research/2019/11/qiskit-for-multiple-architectures/. Accessed 07 Sept 2020
36. Javadi-Abhari, A., et al.: ScaffCC: scalable compilation and analysis of quantum programs. Parallel Comput. **45**, 2–17 (2015)

37. Jozsa, R., Linden, N.: On the role of entanglement in quantum-computational speed-up. Proc. Roy. Soc. Lond. Ser. A Math. Phys. Eng. Sci. **459**(2036), 2011–2032 (2003)
38. Laflamme, R., Miquel, C., Paz, J.P., Zurek, W.H.: Perfect quantum error correcting code. Phys. Rev. Lett. **77**(1), 198 (1996)
39. LaRose, M.: Overview and comparison of gate level quantum software platforms (2019). arXiv:1807.02500v2
40. Leymann, F.: Towards a pattern language for quantum algorithms. In: Feld, S., Linnhoff-Popien, C. (eds.) QTOP 2019. LNCS, vol. 11413, pp. 218–230. Springer, Cham (2019). https://doi.org/10.1007/978-3-030-14082-3_19
41. Leymann, F., Barzen, J.: The bitter truth about gate-based quantum algorithms in the NISQ era. Quantum Sci. Technol. **5**, 044007 (2020)
42. Leymann, F., Barzen, J.: Pattern atlas (2020). arXiv:2006.05120
43. Leymann, F., Barzen, J., Falkenthal, M.: Towards a platform for sharing quantum software. In: 2019 Proceedings of the 13th Advanced Summer School on Service Oriented Computing. IBM Research Division (2019)
44. Leymann, F., Barzen, J., Falkenthal, M., Vietz, D., Weder, B., Wild, K.: Quantum in the cloud: application potentials and research opportunities. In: Proceedings of the 10th International Conference on Cloud Computing and Services Science (CLOSER 2020), pp. 9–24. SciTePress (2020)
45. Lloyd, S., Mohseni, M., Rebentrost, P.: Quantum principal component analysis. Nat. Phys. **10**, 631 (2014)
46. Manning, C., Raghavan, P., Schütze, H.: An Introduction to Information Retrieval. Cambridge University Press, Cambridge (2009)
47. Maslov, D., Dueck, G.W., Miller, D.M., Negrevergne, C.: Quantum circuit simplification and level compaction. IEEE Trans. Comput. Aided Des. Integr. Circ. Syst. **27**(3), 436–444 (2008)
48. McCaskey, A.J., Lyakh, D., Dumitrescu, E., Powers, S., Humble, T.S.: XACC: a system-level software infrastructure for heterogeneous quantum classical computing. Quantum Sci. Technol. **5**, 024002 (2020)
49. Mitarai, K., Kitagawa, M., Fujii, K.: Quantum analog-digital conversion. Phys. Rev. A **99**(1), 012301 (2019). American Physical Society
50. Mohseni, M., Read, P., Neven, H.: Commercialize early quantum technologies. Nature **543**(7644), 171–175 (2017)
51. Montanaro, A.: Quantum algorithms: an overview. npj Quantum Inf. **2** (2016). Article number: 15023
52. MUSE (2020). https://www.iaas.uni-stuttgart.de/forschung/projekte/muse/. Accessed 07 Sept 2020
53. MUSE GitHub (2020). https://github.com/Muster-Suchen-und-Erkennen/muse-docker. Accessed 07 Sept 2020
54. National Academies of Sciences, Engineering, and Medicine: Quantum Computing: Progress and Prospects. The National Academies Press, Washington, DC (2019)
55. Nielsen, M.A., Chuang, I.L.: Quantum Computation and Quantum Information. Cambridge University Press, Cambridge (2016)
56. OASIS: TOSCA simple profile in YAML version 1.2. OASIS (2019). Accessed 07 Sept 2020
57. OpenTOSCA (2020). https://www.opentosca.org/. Accessed 07 Sept 2020
58. Otterbach, J.S., et al.: Unsupervised machine learning on a hybrid quantum computer (2017). arXiv:1712.05771
59. Peruzzo, A., et al.: A variational eigenvalue solver on a photonic quantum processor. Nat. Commun. **5** (2014). Article number: 4213
60. Plesch, M., Brukner, Č: Quantum-state preparation with universal gate decompositions. Phys. Rev. A **83**, 032302 (2011)

61. Preskill, J.: Quantum computing in the NISQ era and beyond. Quantum **2**, 79 (2018)
62. PyQuil (2020). https://github.com/rigetti/pyquil. Accessed 07 Sept 2020
63. PyTorch (2020). https://pytorch.org/. Accessed 07 Sept 2020
64. Qiskit (2020). https://qiskit.org/. Accessed 07 Sept 2020
65. Rahaman, M., Islam, M.M.: A review on progress and problems of quantum computing as a service (QcaaS) in the perspective of cloud computing. Glob. J. Comput. Sci. Technol. **15**(4) (2015)
66. Rebentrost, P., Mohseni, M., Lloyd, S.: Quantum support vector machine for big data classification. Phys. Rev. Lett. **113**, 130503 (2014)
67. Romero, J., Olson, J.P., Aspuru-Guzik, A.: Quantum autoencoders for efficient compression of quantum data (2017). arXiv:1612.02806v2
68. ʻSaatkamp, K., Breitenbücher, U., Kopp, O., Leymann, F.: Method, formalization, and algorithms to split topology models for distributed cloud application deployments. Computing **102**(2), 343–363 (2019). https://doi.org/10.1007/s00607-019-00721-8
69. Saatkamp, K., Breitenbücher, U., Kopp, O., Leymann, F.: Topology splitting and matching for multi-cloud deployments. In: Proceedings of the 7th International Conference on Cloud Computing and Service Science (CLOSER 2017), pp. 247–258. SciTePress (2017)
70. Salm, M., Barzen, J., Breitenbücher, U., Leymann, F., Weder, B., Wild, K.: A roadmap for automating the selection of quantum computers for quantum algorithms (2020). arXiv:2003.13409
71. Scherer, A., Valiron, B., Mau, S.-C., Alexander, S., Van den Berg, E., Chapuran, T.E.: Concrete resource analysis of the quantum linear-system algorithm used to compute the electromagnetic scattering cross section of a 2D target. Quantum Inf. Process. **16**(3) (2017). Article number: 60 https://doi.org/10.1007/s11128-016-1495-5
72. Schuld, M., Fingerhuth, M., Petruccione, F.: Implementing a distance-based classifier with a quantum interference circuit (2017). arXiv:1703.10793
73. Schuld, M., Killoran, N.: Quantum machine learning in feature Hilbert spaces. Phys. Rev. Lett. **122**, 040504 (2019)
74. Schuld, M., Sinayskiy, I., Petruccione, F.: Quantum computing for pattern classification. In: Pham, D.-N., Park, S.-B. (eds.) PRICAI 2014. LNCS (LNAI), vol. 8862, pp. 208–220. Springer, Cham (2014). https://doi.org/10.1007/978-3-319-13560-1_17
75. Schuld, M., Sinayskiy, I., Petruccione, F.: An introduction to quantum machine learning. Contemp. Phys. **56**(2), 172–185 (2015)
76. Shende, V.V., Markov, I.L.: Quantum circuits for incompletely specified two-qubit operators. Quantum Inf. Comput. **5**(1), 049–057 (2005)
77. Smith, R.S., Curtis, M.J., Zeng, W.J.: A practical quantum instruction set architecture (2016). arXiv:1608.03355
78. Steiger, D.S., Haner, T., Troyer, M.: ProjectQ: an open source software framework for quantum computing. Quantum **2**, 49 (2018)
79. Suchara, M., Kubiatowicz, J., Faruque, A., Chong, F.T., Lai, C.-Y., Paz, G.: QuRE: the quantum resource estimator toolbox. In: 2013 IEEE 31st International Conference on Computer Design (ICCD), pp. 419–426. IEEE (2013)
80. Svore, K.M., Aho, A.V., Cross, A.W., Chuang, I., Markov, I.L.: A layered software architecture for quantum computing design tools. Computer **39**(1), 74–83 (2006)
81. Taherkhania, A., Cosmaa, G., McGinnity, T.M.: Deep-FS: a feature selection algorithm for Deep Boltzmann Machines. Neurocomputing **322**, 22–37 (2018)
82. TensorFlow (2020). https://www.tensorflow.org/. Accessed 07 Sept 2020
83. TensorFlow Quantum (2020). https://www.tensorflow.org/quantum. Accessed 07 Sept 2020
84. Weigold, M., Barzen, J., Breitenbücher, U., Falkenthal, M., Leymann, F., Wild, K.: Pattern views: concept and tooling for interconnected pattern languages (2020). arXiv:2003.09127

85. Wu, Z., Palmer, M.: Verb semantics and lexical selection. In: Proceedings of the 32nd Annual Meeting of the Associations for Computational Linguistics, Las Cruces, New Mexico (1994)
86. Zhang, P., Li, S., Zhou, Y.: An algorithm of quantum restricted Boltzmann machine network based on quantum gates and its application. Shock Vibr. **2015** (2015). Article ID 756969. https://doi.org/10.1155/2015/756969
87. Zhang, Y., Deng, H., Li, Q., Song, H., Nie, L.: Optimizing quantum programs against deco-herence: delaying qubits into quantum superposition. In: 2019 International Symposium on Theoretical Aspects of Software Engineering (TASE), pp. 184–191. IEEE (2019)
88. Zhou, L., Wang, S.-T., Choi, S., Pichler, H., Lukin, M.D.: Quantum approximate optimization algorithm: performance, mechanism, and implementation on near-term devices (2019). arXiv: 1812.01041v2

A Framework for Comparative Evaluation of High-Performance Virtualized Networking Mechanisms

Gabriele Ara[1]([✉])[iD], Leonardo Lai[1][iD], Tommaso Cucinotta[1][iD], Luca Abeni[1][iD], and Carlo Vitucci[2]

[1] Scuola Superiore Sant'Anna, Pisa, Italy
{gabriele.ara,leonardo.lai,tommaso.cucinotta,luca.abeni}@santannapisa.it
[2] Ericsson, Stockholm, Sweden
carlo.vitucci@ericsson.com

Abstract. This paper presents an extension to a software framework designed to evaluate the efficiency of different software and hardware-accelerated virtual switches, each commonly adopted on Linux to provide virtual network connectivity to containers in high-performance scenarios, like in Network Function Virtualization (NFV). We present results from the use of our tools, showing the performance of multiple high-performance networking frameworks on a specific platform, comparing the collected data for various key metrics, namely throughput, latency and scalability, with respect to the required computational power.

Keywords: Kernel bypass · DPDK · Netmap · NFV · Containers · Cloud computing

1 Introduction

Over the last decade, many applications shifted from centralized approaches to distributed computing paradigms, thanks to the widespread availability of high-speed Internet connections. As a result, cloud computing services experienced a stable growth in the past few years, both in sheer size and the number of services provided to their end-users. Their success is mostly due to their high level of flexibility in resource management, especially for those applications that may be subject to significant service demand variations over time.

Cloud systems also gained the interest of network operators, intending to replace traditional physical networking infrastructures with more flexible cloud-based systems. To achieve this goal, highly specialized networking devices will be progressively replaced with equivalent software-based implementations that can be dynamically instantiated and relocated inside a cloud-based infrastructure, called Virtualized Network Functions (VNFs). This approach represents the core idea behind Network Function Virtualization (NFV), which has gained popularity in recent years. Given the nature of the services usually deployed in

© Springer Nature Switzerland AG 2021
D. Ferguson et al. (Eds.): CLOSER 2020, CCIS 1399, pp. 59–83, 2021.
https://doi.org/10.1007/978-3-030-72369-9_3

NFV infrastructures, these systems must be characterized by high performance in terms of throughput and latency among VNFs. These services are typically deployed in long service chains; for this reason, it is imperative to maintain the cost of individual components interactions as small as possible, to avoid high end-to-end costs across the whole chain. These requirements are so tight that the NFV industry is now considering Operating System (OS) containers to deploy VNFs in cloud infrastructures, rather than traditional Virtual Machines (VMs), following the rise of popularity of container solutions like LXC or Docker. These solutions exhibit similar performance as deploying VNF applications directly on the host OS [7,9], by partially sacrificing isolation among virtualized components.

Thanks to containers' superior performance, the research focus is now into further reducing communication overheads. Many high-performance I/O frameworks have been developed in the past decade to reduce by several orders of magnitude the cost for user-space application to send and receive packets with respect to traditional networking stacks.

1.1 Contributions

This paper shows the characteristics of a benchmarking framework for comparing system performance when adopting high-performance I/O solutions to interconnect VNF components deployed in a private cloud infrastructure using OS containers. In particular, this tool eases the creation of a virtual network infrastructure using software-based networking solutions or even leveraging special features in network devices that support the Single-Root I/O Virtualization (SR-IOV) specification. It can then be used to deploy on that infrastructure a set of benchmarking applications that measure system performance under various working conditions. We present experimental results collected using this framework and compare the performance of various virtual switching solutions (either software-based or hardware-accelerated) when subject to synthetic workloads.

This work constitutes an extended version of the paper already appeared in [4]. Details on this will follow at the end of Sect. 5.

2 Background

Application components or services deployed in OS containers inside a cloud infrastructure can choose among several network primitives to communicate with each other or with the external world. Usually, these primitives use network virtualization techniques to provide a set of gateways to exchange data over a virtual network infrastructure. Choosing the right communication primitives to use when connecting multiple encapsulated components may significantly impact the overall application performance and latency, but some of them require a special set-up from the infrastructure provider that limits the flexibility in deployment typical of cloud environments.

In this work, we focus on the following solutions: **(i)** *kernel-based network-ing*, **(ii)** *kernel-based networking with network stack bypass* (e.g. Netmap), **(iii)** *software-based user-space networking*, **(iv)** *hardware-accelerated user-space net-working*. In the following, we summarize the main characteristics of each of these techniques when adopted in NFV scenarios to interconnect OS containers within a private cloud infrastructure. We will focus on the performance attained when adopting each solution on general-purpose computing machines running Linux.

2.1   Kernel-Based Networking and VNFs

Most operating systems, including Linux, provide abstractions that can be used to create and assign virtual Ethernet ports to VMs or OS containers. Each virtual port has no corresponding hardware interface; they are purely implemented in software as endpoints for networked communications within the same host by emulating the behavior of real Ethernet ports. Typically, these virtual ports are created as directly connected pairs: this means that each port in the pair is always directly connected with the other one as if connected by a virtual cable.

Using standard techniques provided by the Linux kernel, containers or other virtualized environments can be interconnected by assigning one end of the vir-tual Ethernet pair each. This operation usually hides the selected port from the host networking devices[1], allowing applications in the VM or container to send packets to the virtual port on the other end of the connection.

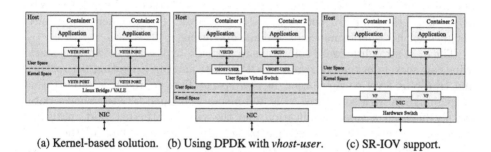

(a) **Kernel-based solution.**   (b) Using DPDK with *vhost-user*.   (c) SR-IOV support.

Fig. 1. Different approaches to inter-container networking. Adapted from [4].

To connect more than two virtualized environments to the virtual network or to connect a VM or container to the actual physical Network Interface Controller (NIC), a virtual implementation of a L2 switch is required, to forward packets

---

[1] OS containers in Linux achieve isolation employing cgroups and namespaces. With these tools, virtual Ethernet ports assigned to a container will no longer be visible or accessible outside the assigned cgroup/namespace, but it will still be part of the host network stack. In this sense, OS containers do not introduce any overhead when encapsulated applications exchange packets over the virtual network.

from each virtualized environment to the desired destination, be it another virtual port or the outside world. For this purpose, the Linux kernel implements a virtual switch called *"linux-bridge"*. It allows VNFs to communicate on the same host with other containerized VNFs or with other hosts via forwarding through actual Ethernet ports present on the machine, as shown in Fig. 1a.

Virtual Ethernet ports can be accessed via blocking or nonblocking system calls, for example using the standard POSIX Socket API, exchanging packets via send() and recv() (or their more general forms sendmsg() and recvmsg()). With this approach, at least two system calls are required to exchange each UDP datagram over the virtual network; therefore, overheads grow proportionally with the number of packets exchanged. In addition, each packet traverses various network stack layers in the Linux kernel, to be properly processed and delivered.

The recent introduction of batch system calls in the kernel API enables partial amortization of the cost of a system call over a *burst* of packets. The sendmmsg()/ recvmmsg() system calls handle multiple packets in a single call, reducing the number of system calls required to exchange huge traffic volumes. However, this only reduces the ratio between the number of packets and the number of system calls needed to exchange each packet over the local virtual network, but packets still need to traverse the whole kernel network stack, going through additional copies, even when transmitted locally on a machine.

2.2 Bypassing the Kernel's Networking Stack

Several solutions can be adopted inside the Linux kernel to bypass (entirely or partially) the standard networking stack, in favor of more efficient pipelines designed for high-performance data plane operations.

The most straightforward solution is to partially bypass the networking stack using raw sockets instead of regular UDP sockets and implementing networking and transport-level encapsulation in user-space. This approach is often taken in combination with zero-copy APIs and memory-mapped I/O to transfer data quickly between a single application and the virtual Ethernet port, partially reducing the time needed to send a packet [21]. This way, part of the high-level processing required on the kernel side can be skipped, leaving the kernel the only burden of forwarding raw Ethernet frames from an Ethernet port to another one, at the expense of handling upper networking stack layers (UDP, IP, etc.) inside the user-space application itself. For this purpose, some efficient user-space implementations of the network stack exist [13,26]. Finally, applications using raw sockets require exclusive access to the virtual network interface, preventing other applications in the same virtualized environment to access it; this is not a relevant problem in most NFV scenarios, since each container usually encapsulates exactly one VNF application.

Another solution is to change the *linux-bridge* component into another in-kernel software switch that is more optimized for the traffic expected from the VNFs. A representative example of this solution is Open vSwitch (OVS) [18], a flexible general-purpose virtual switch implemented as a kernel module focused on high-performance scenarios. The implementation of OVS is optimized to handle traffic generated by virtualized environments, employing caching techniques throughout its implementation, especially in its packet classifier.

Another advantage of using a replacement for *linux-bridge* inside the kernel is that VNF applications do not need to be rewritten or customized for different sets of APIs or system calls. However, there are situations in which this approach cannot achieve the required performance levels. If we analyze the overhead required for UDP or raw sockets, about 50% of total processing time is spent on the system calls [21]. This consideration indicates that send(), recv(), and similar APIs are not efficient mechanisms to exchange data between the userspace application and the kernel. This consideration can lead to two distinct approaches to tackle this problem: (i) redesign the way user-space applications interact and exchange data with the Linux kernel itself; (ii) bypass the Linux kernel entirely and build new APIs and communication mechanisms in userspace, so that there is no need to pay the cost of executing a system call at all. The former is the approach taken by Netmap, while the latter is the one of many solutions that rely on kernel bypass techniques described in Sect. 2.3.

Netmap [22] is a networking framework for high-performance I/O developed for FreeBSD and Linux. Netmap has a custom APIs allowing applications to send and receive multiple packets per system call, without any need for data copies between user and kernel space[2]. Netmap achieves high performance removing three main packet processing costs [21], namely system call overheads (amortized over large packet bursts), per-packet dynamic memory allocation (pre-allocating fixed-size packet buffers and descriptors during interfaces initialization phase), and expensive data copies (providing user-space applications direct access to in-kernel packet buffers). These features are provided by leveraging standard memory mapping and protection mechanisms for device registers and other kernel memory areas to enforce protection among processes.

FreeBSD already includes Netmap kernel support by default since version 11, while Netmap can be installed on Linux by patching a set of standard NIC drivers and loading some additional custom modules[3]. The driver patches introduce a new mode for the various network device drivers in the Linux kernel, called Netmap mode. Unlike the NIC default operating mode, in which packets are exchanged from and to each NIC through the standard kernel's networking stack, devices in Netmap mode no longer communicate with the default networking stack. Rather, their ring buffers are connected to Netmap-defined ring buffers, implemented in a shared memory area. Netmap data structures provide device-independent yet efficient access to data, providing a representation that closely resembles NICs' typical ring-based internal structures [21].

An application that wants to leverage Netmap features can either use a modified version of libpcap [20], which supports network devices in Netmap mode, or directly use Netmap's custom API. In the latter case, the application

---

[2] However, data copies across multiple processes are still required for security reasons, especially when interacting components do not trust each other, like VNFs.

[3] https://github.com/luigirizzo/netmap.

first obtains a reference to Netmap's in-kernel data structures from user-space, including packet buffers; it can then start filling them with packets to send or consuming the received packets. Synchronization between user and kernel space is achieved using either blocking system calls (using either `select()` or `poll()` to send or receive packets), or non-blocking ones (using `ioctl()` for both sending and receiving operations). The non-blocking alternative checks if there are empty packet buffers for new outgoing packets (for send operations) or if there are packets ready to be processed (for receiving ones) [22].

Notice that, contrary to traditional `sendmsg()`/`recvmsg()` and similar system calls, Netmap uses system calls only as synchronization mechanisms, no data copies are issued between user and kernel space during the execution of each system call. Also, Netmap provides other features to achieve high performance for both local and remote communications, including support for multiple hardware queues, and zero-copy data transfer with supported interfaces [22].

2.3   Inter-container Communications with Kernel Bypass

Significant performance improvements over traditional networking between containers can be achieved also bypassing the kernel entirely. This removes the costs associated with system calls, context switches and unneeded data copies as much as possible. Various I/O frameworks undertake such approach, recurring to a set of kernel bypassing techniques to exchange batches of packets among applications without requiring a single system call. Typically, they require using different kinds of virtualized or para-virtualized network interfaces that can be managed from the user-space.

One notable example of these kinds of ports is introduced by the *virtio* standard [24]: it defines a new kind of para-virtualized ports which rely on shared memory to achieve high-performance networking among applications running on the same host (even across containers), a fairly common situation in NFV scenarios. These interfaces expose "virtual queues" for incoming/outgoing packets that can be shared among different guests on the same hosts or connected to software implementations of network switches, allowing the implementation of efficient host-to-guest and guest-to-guest communications. While *virtio* interfaces are typically implemented by hypervisors (e.g. QEMU, KVM), a user-space implementation of the *virtio* specification, called *vhost-user*, has been defined.

Notice that while *virtio* ports can effectively improve significantly same-host communication performance with respect to fully virtualized Ethernet ports, they cannot be used to directly access the physical network without any user-space software implementation of a network switch, which is necessary to achieve both dynamic and flexible communications among independently deployed VNFs.

Data Plane Development Kit (DPDK)[4] is an open source framework for fast packet processing implemented entirely in user-space, characterized by a

---

[4] https://www.dpdk.org/.

high portability across multiple platforms. Initially developed by Intel for its own family of network devices, it now provides a flexible high-level programming abstraction, called Environment Abstraction Layer (EAL) [1], that provides applications an efficient access point to low-level resources from user-space without depending on specific hardware devices. Data Plane Development Kit (DPDK) uses various techniques to reduce the gap between applications and network interfaces, including non-blocking access to packet rings, batch packet transfers between memory and interfaces, and the use of resident huge pages of memory to hold memory buffers.

Other than several physical interfaces from multiple vendors, DPDK supports *virtio*-based networking via its own implementation of *vhost-user* interfaces. Hence, DPDK APIs can be used to exchange data efficiently both locally and with applications residing on remote hosts, in complete transparency for the user applications: for local communications, *vhost-user* ports can be used, while for remote ones the efficient user-space implementation of real Ethernet device drivers provided by DPDK can be leveraged. For this reason, DPDK has become extremely popular over the past few years to develop high-performance networking applications.

2.4 High-Performance Switching Among Containers

High-performance virtual networking infrastructures can be implemented by employing a combination of software and/or hardware tools. There are essentially three main ways to achieve this goal: **(i)** by assigning each container a virtual Ethernet port and connecting each of port to an efficient implementation of an in-kernel software switch (Fig. 1a); **(ii)** by assigning each container a *virtio* port, using *vhost-user* to bypass the kernel, and then connect each port to a software implementation of a virtual switch running in user-space on the same host (Fig. 1b); **(iii)** by leveraging special capabilities of certain NIC devices that allow concurrent access from multiple applications and that can be accessed in user-space by using DPDK drivers (Fig. 1c). The virtual switch instance used on each host (either software or hardware) is then connected to the physical network via the actual NIC interface present on the host.

Many software implementations of L2/L3 switches are available, each implementing their own packet processing logic responsible for packet forwarding. Some of them can be used in combination with DPDK, Netmap or other networking frameworks to improve the performance over standard networking APIs. For these reasons, performance may differ significantly across implementations.

A common characteristic of most software virtual switches is a non-negligible amount of processing power required to achieve very high network performance. On the other hand, special NIC devices that support the SR-IOV specification allow traffic offloading to a hardware switch embedded in the NIC itself, which applications can access concurrently without interfering with each other.

Below, we briefly describe the most common software virtual switches in the NFV industrial practice, and the characteristics of network devices compliant with the SR-IOV specification.

VALE [23] is an implementation of an efficient virtual Ethernet switch that can be used instead of the default host networking stack to connect applications that use ports in Netmap mode on the same host or to connect virtual Netmap ports with the physical NIC present on the host. In principle, VALE acts like a traditional L2 learning switch, associating each port with a list of L2 addresses by inspecting the source field of each incoming Ethernet frame. VALE is specialized to manage Netmap's ring buffers and it implements a multi-stage forwarding process that leverages packet batching and cache prefetching instructions to speed up memory accesses. While it does not support zero-copy of data from one port to another, even on the same host, for isolation purposes between different applications [23], it does not require any data copy between user and kernel space (thanks to Netmap API design).

DPDK Basic Forwarding Sample Application[5] is a sample application provided by DPDK that can be used to connect DPDK-compatible ports, either virtual or physical, in pairs: this means that each application using a given port can only exchange packets with a corresponding port chosen during system initialization. For this reason, this software does not perform any packet processing operation, hence it cannot be used in real use-case scenarios.

Open vSwitch (OVS)[6] is an open source virtual switch for general-purpose usage with enhanced flexibility thanks to its compatibility with the *OpenFlow* protocol [18]. Recently, OVS has been updated to support DPDK and *virtio*-based ports, which accelerated considerably packet forwarding operations by performing them in user-space rather than within a kernel module [2]. This is the preferred solution when the focus is on data-plane performance, rather than deploying OVS as an alternative to the default network stack inside the Linux kernel (see Sect. 2.2).

FD.io Vector Packet Processing (VPP)[7] is an extensible framework for virtual switching released by the Linux Foundation Fast Data Project (FD.io). Since it is developed on top of DPDK, it can run on various architectures and it can be deployed in VMs, containers or bare metal environments. It uses Cisco VPP that processes packets in batches, improving the performance thanks to the better exploitation of instruction and data cache locality [5].

Snabb[8] is a packet processing framework that can be used to provide networking functionality in user-space. It allows for programming arbitrary packet processing flows [17] by connecting functional blocks in a Directed Acyclic Graph (DAG).

While not being based on DPDK, it has its own implementation of *virtio* and some NIC drivers in user-space, which can be included in the DAG.

Single-Root I/O Virtualization (SR-IOV) [8] is a specification that allows a single NIC device to appear as multiple PCIe devices, called Virtual Functions

---

[5] https://doc.dpdk.org/guides/sample_app_ug/skeleton.html.

[6] https://www.openvswitch.org.

[7] https://fd.io/.

[8] https://github.com/snabbco/snabb.

(VFs), that can be independently assigned to VMs or containers and move data through dedicated buffers within the device.

VMs and containers can directly access dedicated VFs and leverage the L2 hardware switch embedded in the NIC for either local or remote communications (Fig. 1c).

Using DPDK APIs, applications within containers can access the dedicated VFs bypassing the Linux kernel, removing the need of any software switch running on the host; however, a DPDK daemon is needed on the host to manage the VFs.

3 Proposed Framework

This section presents the framework we realized for the purpose of evaluating and comparing the performance and efficiency of different virtual networking solutions. The framework can be easily installed and configured on any desired number of interconnected general-purpose servers running an Ubuntu-based Linux distribution; it can be used to instantiate and deploy a number of OS containers, each running a custom high-performance benchmarking application. This application, also developed for this framework, serves the dual purpose to generate/consume synthetic network traffic, simulating real NFV applications, and to collect statistics to evaluate system performance in the given configuration.

The purpose of this framework is to carry out a number of experiments from multiple points of view, depending on the investigation focus, while varying testing parameters (e.g. packet size, sending rate, etc.) and system configuration. Each test defines which networking solution is to be used to interconnect the benchmarking applications, how many instances for each machine should be instantiated, and what are the characteristics of the network traffic that should be generated. After each individual distributed test is done, the framework collects and stores the system performance measured by each benchmarking application and moves on to the next configuration in the list. This way, multiple tests can be performed consecutively, without any additional user intervention. When all tests are finished, a summary of the collected statistics is presented to the user.

The software is open-source and it is freely available on GitHub, under a GPLv3 license, at: https://github.com/gabrieleara/nfv-testperf . It can be conveniently extended by researchers or practitioners, should they need to write further customized testing applications. Figure 2 depicts the software architecture of the framework, which includes a number of software tools, both readily available or custom-made, and Bash scripts. The latter ones are used to install system dependencies, configure and customize installation, set up and run performance evaluations, and collect statistic data.

The framework dependencies include the DPDK framework (including its Basic Forwarding Sample Application), Netmap (and its own virtual switch, VALE), and the other user-space virtual switches described in Sect. 2.4: the user-space implementation of OVS (compiled with DPDK support), VPP, and

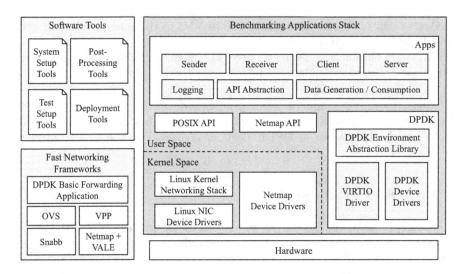

Fig. 2. Main elements of the proposed framework. Adapted from [4].

Snabb. Each virtual switch is configured to act as a simple learning L2 switch, with the only exception represented by the DPDK Basic Forwarding Sample Application, which does not have this functionality. In addition, OVS, VPP, and VALE can be connected to physical Ethernet ports to perform tests for inter-machine communications.

Figure 2 shows the internal structure of the custom benchmarking application included in the framework. This can be configured to act either as traffic generator and/or consumer (depending on the kind of VNF application that is emulated) to evaluate system performance from the following points of view:

Throughput: Many VNFs generate or consume huge volumes of network traffic per second: for this reason, it is of utmost importance to evaluate the maximum forwarding performance provided by each networking solution, varying system parameters, in relationship with the required computational resources. For this purpose, the benchmarking application can be configured to act as a pure sender or pure receiver application, to generate/consume unidirectional traffic (from each sender to a designated receiver application).

Latency: In general, in NFV infrastructures it is crucial to strive for the minimum latency possible for individual interactions, in order to reduce the end-to-end latency between components across long service chains. For this purpose, a client/server application pair is used to generate bidirectional traffic to evaluate the average round-trip latency for each packet when multiple packets are transmitted in bursts over the virtual network infrastructure. To do so, the server application will send back each packet it receives to its corresponding client.

Scalability: Evaluations from this point of view are orthogonal with respect of the two previous dimensions, in particular with respect to throughput: since full utilization of a computing infrastructure is achieved only when multiple VNFs are deployed on each host, it is extremely important to evaluate how the networking performance of multiple concurrent applications are affected when increasing the number of applications deployed on the each host. For this purpose there are no dedicated applications: multiple instances of each designated application can be deployed concurrently to evaluate how that affects global system performance.

The benchmarking applications are implemented in C and they are built over a custom API that masks the differences between POSIX, DPDK, or Netmap frameworks; this way, they can be used to evaluate system performance using each of the approaches described in Sect. 2 to realize the virtual network infrastructure. When POSIX APIs are used to exchange packets, raw sockets can also be used rather than regular UDP sockets to bypass partially the Linux networking stack, building Ethernet, IP and UDP packet headers in user-space.

Each application emulates a specific kind of VNF application, namely a sender, a receiver, a server, or a client application. In each case, the application accepts a number of parameters that determine the kind of traffic that is generated/consumed, including the sending/receiving rate, packet size, burst size, etc. To maximize application performance, the applications are developed to use always non-blocking APIs and measurements of elapsed time are performed by checking the TSC register instead of less precise timers provided by Linux APIs.

During each test, each application is deployed within a LXC container on the targeted machines and automatically connected to the other designated application in the pair, according to the provided configuration. The Linux distribution that is used to realize each container is based on a simple *rootfs* built from a basic *BusyBox* and it contains only the necessary resources to run the benchmarking applications. Depending on the networking solution selected for the current test, the framework takes care of all the setup necessary to interconnect the deployed applications with the desired networking technology, being it *linux-bridge*, VALE, another software-based virtual switch (using *virtio* and *vhost-user* ports), or a SR-IOV Ethernet adapter; again, each scenario is depicted in Fig. 1. In any case, deployed applications use polling to exchange network traffic over the selected ports. For tests involving multiple hosts, only OVS, VPP, or VALE can be used among software-based virtual switches to interconnect the benchmarking applications; otherwise, it is possible to assign to each container a dedicated VF and leverage the embedded hardware switch in the SR-IOV network card to forward traffic from one host to another.

The proposed framework can be easily extended to include more low-level networking frameworks, alongside DPDK and Netmap's APIs, or more virtual switching solutions that can be used to interconnect the containerized applications. From this perspective, the inclusion of other *virtio*-based virtual switches is straightforward, and it does not require any modification of the existing test applications. In contrast, other low-level networking frameworks not considered in this work that rely on custom port type/programming paradigms may require the extension of the API abstraction layer to adapt it to the new low-level components. Other high-level testing applications generating or consuming different types of synthetic workloads can also be easily introduced on top of the existing API. Further details about the framework's extensibility can be found at https://github.com/gabrieleara/nfv-testperf/wiki/Extending.

4   Experimental Results

This section reports experimental results obtained with the framework just introduced above. The goal of the experiments is to test the functionality of the framework and compare the performance of the various virtual switching solutions described in this paper.

We performed all experiments on two identical hosts: the first has been used for all local inter-container communications tests, while both hosts have been used for multi-host communication tests (using containers as well). The two hosts are two Dell PowerEdge R630 V4 servers, each equipped with two Intel® Xeon® E5-2640 v4 CPUs at 2.40 GHz, 64 GB of RAM, and an Intel® X710 DA2 Ethernet Controller for 10 GbE SFP+ (used in SR-IOV experiments and multi-host scenarios). The two Ethernet controllers have connected directly with a 10 Gigabit Ethernet cable. Both hosts are configured with Ubuntu 18.04.3 LTS, Linux kernel version 4.15.0-54, DPDK version 19.05, OVS version 2.11.1, Snabb version 2019.01, VPP version 19.08, and Netmap for Linux (September 2020). To maximize results reproducibility, the framework carries out each test disabling CPU frequency scaling (governor set to performance and Turbo Boost disabled). Finally, the various components of the framework have been configured to avoid using hyperthreads simultaneously.

4.1   Testing Parameters

The framework's configuration depends on the parameters used to instantiate the containers containing the benchmarking applications, set up the virtual network,

Table 1. List of parameters used to run performance tests with the framework. Adapted from [4].

Parameter	Symbol	Description
Test dimension	D	The test evaluates *throughput* or *latency* performance
Hosts used	L	The test performs only communications on a single host (shown as *"local"*) or between different hosts (*"remote"*)
Containers set	S	The number of container pairs deployed on the host for the test duration; this is expressed as "$NvsN$"—e.g. "$1vs1$" means that there are two containers in a pair, while "$4vs4$" means four pairs of containers are deployed
Virtual switch	V	The virtual switch used to connect the containers; can be one among *linux-bridge*, *basicfwd* (for the Basic Forwarding Sample Application), *ovs*, *snabb*, *sriov*, *vpp*, *vale*
Packet size	P	The size of each packet, in bytes; includes the content of the whole Ethernet frame
Sending rate	R	The desired packet sending/receiving rate, expressed in packets per second
Burst size	B	The number of packets that are grouped in each burst

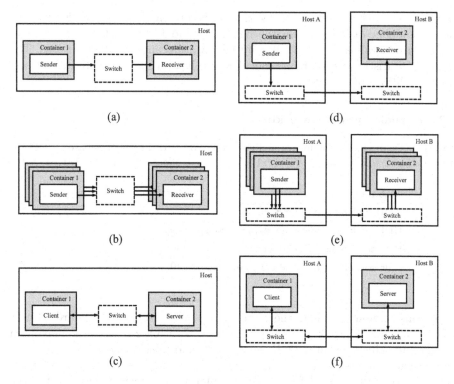

Fig. 3. Different testing scenarios used for our evaluations. In particular, (a), (b), and (c) refer to single-host scenarios, while (d), (e), and (f) to scenarios that consider multiple hosts. From [4].

and instruct the applications to generate traffic with specific characteristics. The number of test cases is significant; hence, we show only relevant results for each different perspective.

To identify each test, we use the following notation, where a tuple uniquely identifies each test in the following form:

$$(D, \ L, \ S, \ V, \ P, \ R, \ B)$$

Table 1 describes each parameter in detail. Then, referring to the results of multiple tests at the same time, we omit from this notation the parameters that are free to vary within a predefined set of values. For example, to show some tests performed while varying the sending rate, the R parameter may not be included in the tuple.

For each test, the framework automatically deploys the applications on one or both hosts, grouped in pairs (i.e. sender/receiver or client/server), and it runs the desired test for a fixed amount of time. The scenarios that we considered in our experiments are summarized in Fig. 3. Each test uses only a fixed set of parameters and runs for 1 minute. Upon completion, we compute the average value of the desired metric (either throughput or latency), after discarding a certain number of values from the beginning and the end of the experiment; the discarded values are related to initial warm-up and shutdown phases. The resulting statistics are therefore calculated only over values related to steady-state conditions of the system.

4.2 Kernel-Based Networking

Table 2. From [4]. Maximum throughput achieved for various socket-based solutions: ($D = throughput$, $L = local$, $S = 1vs1$, $V = linux\text{-}bridge$, $P = 64$, $R = 1M$, $B = 64$).

Technique	Max throughput (kpps)
UDP sockets using `send/recv`	338
UDP sockets using `sendmmsg/recvmmsg`	409
Raw sockets using `send/recv`	360
Raw sockets using `sendmmsg/recvmmsg`	440

In this section, we show the performance achieved using standard POSIX system calls and Linux kernel's networking stack. Table 2 reports the maximum throughput achieved using POSIX socket APIs and *linux-bridge* to interconnect a pair of sender and receiver application, both deployed on the same host (Fig. 3a). With this configuration, the maximum throughput is achieved when most of the networking stack is bypassed, using raw sockets, with a maximum throughput of 0.440 Mpps. As we will show in the following sections, using Netmap or techniques that entirely bypass the Linux kernel, it is possible to achieve well over 2 Mpps in similar set-ups. Given their inferior performance compared to the other frameworks, in all the results that will follow standard POSIX system calls and *linux-bridge* will not be considered anymore.

4.3 Throughput Evaluations

This section evaluates throughput performance between two applications in a single pair, deployed either on the same host or multiple directly connected machines, varying the desired sending rate, packet, and burst sizes using high-performance networking frameworks. In all our experiments, we noticed that varying the burst size from 32 to 256 packets per burst did not affect throughput performance; thus, we will always refer to the case of 32 packets per burst in further reasoning, if not explicitly indicated otherwise. In all our experiments, we considered 1 Gbps exactly equal to 10^9 bits per second.

Same-Host Throughput Results. First, we deployed a single pair of sender and receiver applications on a single host (Fig. 3a), and we connected them each time with one among the various high-performance frameworks available:

$$(D = throughput, \; L = local, \; S = 1vs1)$$

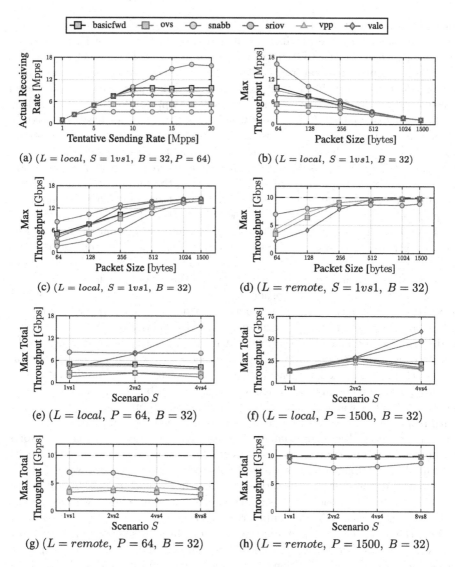

Fig. 4. Throughput performance obtained varying system configuration and virtual switch used to connect sender/receiver applications deployed in LXC containers.

In these tests, we varied the packet sending rate from 1 to 20 Mpps and the packet size from 64 to 1500 bytes. The two applications are configured to generate and consume each exchanged packet's content, respectively, simulating an actual application's behavior.

Figure 4a shows that each networking solution matches the desired throughput in each of our tests until a certain plateau is reached, which varies depending on the capabilities of each virtual port/switch combination. In our evaluations, this maximum throughput strongly depends on the packet size; thus, from now on, we consider only the maximum achievable throughput for each networking framework when the size of each packet varies in our desired range.

The maximum receiving rates achieved in our tests between two containers on the same host are shown in Figs. 4b and 4c. Each plot shows the achieved receiving rate (y-axis), expressed respectively in Mpps and Gbps, as a function of the size of each packet (x-axis), for which a logarithmic scale has been used. In both figures, the behavior shown by each solution is similar: with an increase in the packet size, the throughput in terms of Mpps decreases progressively, while in terms of Gbps it grows logarithmically with the packet size (Fig. 4c). From these results, we can see that while the maximum throughput in terms of Mpps is achieved with the smallest of the selected packet sizes (64 bytes), in terms of Gbps it is better to use the biggest packet size (1500 bytes).

From both figures, it is clear that the maximum performance is attained by offloading network traffic to the SR-IOV device, exploiting its embedded hardware switch. Instead, the second-best solution varies depending on the packet size selected: while for smaller packet sizes both the Basic Forwarding Sample Application and VPP dominate the other solutions, as the packet size increases over 128 bytes, VALE outperforms them both, almost resulting en-par with SR-IOV offloading. The overall high performance of the Basic Forwarding Sample Application is expected since it does not implement any actual switching logic. The minimal performance gap between VPP and the latter solution indicates that the batch packet processing features that characterize VPP can effectively distribute packet processing overheads among incoming bursts of packets. Finally, OVS and Snabb, which lack similar optimizations, obtain inferior performance with respect to the other solutions. Comparing its performance with other evaluations present in literature that used Snabb only to connect directly two ports without a switching component in-between [3], we were able to conclude that its internal L2 switching component represents the major bottleneck for Snabb.

In general, these figures show that the efficiency of each port/switch pair has a more significant impact when smaller packets are exchanged over the virtual network, and hence a higher number of packets is processed by each virtual switch: the performance gap among the various solutions is very small for packets whose size is 1 kB and beyond. From this, we can conclude that for bigger packet sizes, the system's major bottleneck becomes the capability of the CPU and the memory subsystem to move data from one CPU core to another, which is mostly equivalent for any implementation. Given also the slightly superior performance achieved by SR-IOV, especially for smaller packet sizes, we also concluded that its hardware switch is more efficient at moving a large number of packets between CPU cores than the software implementations that we tested.

Note that the authors of VALE reported a performance peak of 27 Mpps in [14], however the sender/receiver application they used is simpler than ours, that scans through every byte of sent and received packets, calculating a very simple CRC, for the purpose of emulating better the effect on the overall experiment of possible limits arising from the limited memory bandwidth available.

Therefore, the performance attainable with our framework is expected to be lower, albeit more representative of what would be achievable by a realistic application that has to prepare the packets to send and process the received ones. Additionally, in our experimentation, a non-particularly fast CPU was used, clocked at 2.4 GHz, while in the experiments in [14] a 4 GHz CPU was used. Finally, they employed VMs rather than OS containers to perform the experiment, In that configuration, Netmap applications can leverage some optimizations that forward system calls to a pool of threads running on the host machine [15], which may lead to increased performance compared to bare-metal deployments.

Multiple Hosts. We repeated these evaluations deploying the receiver application on a separate host (Fig. 3d), using the only virtual switches able to forward traffic between multiple hosts[9]:

$$(D = throughput, \; L = remote, \; S = 1vs1, \; V \in \{ovs, sriov, vpp, vale\})$$

Figure 4d shows the maximum receiving rates achieved for a burst size of 32 packets. In this scenario, results depend on the exchanged packets' size: for smaller packet sizes, the dominating bottleneck is still represented by the CPU for all software-based virtual switches, while for bigger packets, the Ethernet line rate limits the total throughput achievable by any virtual switch to only 10 Gbps. From these results, we concluded that when the expected traffic is characterized by relatively small packet sizes (up to 256 bytes), deploying a component on a directly connected host does not impact system performance negatively when using OVS, VPP, or VALE. Also, we noticed that in this scenario, there is no clear best virtual switch with respect to the others: while SR-IOV is more efficient for smaller packet sizes, software-based virtual switches perform better for bigger ones.

4.4   Throughput Scalability Evaluations

The scalability of system performance is a critical factor in NFV since the full utilization of system resources can be achieved only by deploying multiple components on each host. That is why we repeated all our throughput evaluations deploying multiple application pairs on the same host (Fig. 3b), up to 4 sender/receiver pairs:

$$(D = throughput, \; L = local, \; S \in \{1vs1, 2vs2, 4vs4\})$$

From our previous evaluations, we highlighted that the throughput capability of most networking solutions varies greatly depending on the size of the packets exchanged over the local network. For this reason, we show in Figs. 4e and 4f the relationship between the number of application pairs deployed simultaneously and the maximum total throughput achieved (i.e. the maximum sum

---

[9] The Basic Forwarding Sample Application does not implement any switching logic, while Snabb was not compatible with our selected SR-IOV Ethernet controller.

of throughput values registered simultaneously by all sender/receiver pairs) for packets of 64 and 1500 bytes respectively.

Figure 4e highlights a significant difference between VALE and the other network solutions considered in this work. While most virtual switches do not achieve higher total throughput when increasing the number of application pairs transmitting 64 bytes per packet, VALE's throughput increases almost linearly with the number of application pairs. Most virtual switches have a fixed amount of processing power at their disposal, distributed among all the packet flows traversing them[10]. On the other hand, VALE operates directly inside the Linux kernel: each sender process is responsible for forwarding its packets to their destination. In a scenario where N processes send packets simultaneously over the local network, VALE can use virtually N times the processing power than with a single sender. The effectiveness of this approach is evident when the scalability of the system is taken into account, albeit it does consume part of the processing power of each process to do packet processing operations. The resulting performance is only penalized when only one packet flow is present on the system ($1vs1$), while the other software/hardware virtual switches cannot keep up once more network flows are added.

The situation is slightly different when we increase the packet size, up to 1500 bytes per packet. Figure 4f shows that for bigger packets, SR-IOV also shows a similar almost-linear behavior with the increase of the number of participants: in this case, VALE and SR-IOV can sustain 4 senders with only a per-packet performance drop of about 0% and 17.8%, respectively. On the contrary, *virtio*-based switches can still only distribute the same amount of resources over a more significant number of network flows.

From these results, we concluded that the number of packets mostly represents the major limitation of our SR-IOV NIC exchanged on the local network. In contrast, the most significant limitation of *virtio*-based switches is the capability of the CPU to move data from one application to another, which depends on the overall amount of bytes exchanged. Finally, VALE is affected by the same limitation of the other software-based virtual switches, but thanks to its distributed implementation it is possible to sustain higher traffic volumes without consuming an unreasonable amount of processing power (see also Sect. 4.6 for more details about performance and processing power).

Repeating scalability evaluations on multiple hosts ($L = remote$), we deployed up to 8 application pairs ($S = 8vs8$) transmitting data from one host to the other one (Fig. 3e). Figures 4g and 4h show that the selected packet size strongly influences the outcome. Similarly to single-flow remote test results, the system's major bottleneck is represented by the limited throughput of the Ethernet line rate when bigger packets are used (256 bytes and above). When exchanging smaller packets, the CPU becomes unable to efficiently move big numbers

---

[10] This limitation corresponds to the processing power reserved for each worker thread they spawn for software virtual switches, while for SR-IOV devices, it is an intrinsic characteristic of their hardware implementation.

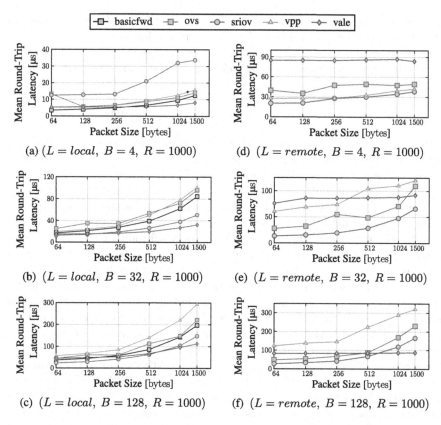

Fig. 5. Average round-trip latency obtained varying system configuration and virtual switch used to connect client/server applications deployed in LXC containers. Plots on the left refer to tests performed on a single-host, while plots on the right involve two separate hosts.

of packets from and to the NIC, especially when software-based solutions are adopted.

4.5 Latency Performance Evaluations

For the latency dimension, we evaluated the round-trip latency between a pair of client and server applications, depending on the network traffic and the network infrastructure, to estimate the per-packet processing overhead introduced by each different solution. In particular, our focus is to evaluate how each technology distributes its packet processing costs over multiple packets when increasing the number of packets in each burst. To carry out these experiments, we deployed a single pair ($S = 1vs1$) of client/server applications on either a single ($L = local$) or multiple hosts ($L = remote$). In each test, benchmark applications use a relatively low packet sending rate, enough so that there can be no interference between the processing of a burst of packets and the following one.

First, we deployed both the client and the server on the same host (Fig. 3c), varying the burst size from 4 to 128 packets per burst and the packet size from 64 to 1500 bytes:

$$(D = latency, \ L = local, \ S = 1vs1, \ R = 1000)$$

In all our tests, the performance that we registered for Snabb was considerably worse than the ones achieved by other solutions; for example, the minimum average latency registered for Snabb is about 64 μs, even when other solutions in similar working conditions averaged well under 40 μs. Since this behavior is repeated in all our tests, regardless of which network parameters are applied, Snabb will not be discussed further.

Figures 5a to 5c show that SR-IOV is the only solution that cannot provide single-digit microsecond round-trip latency even for small packet and burst sizes, achieving at best about 12.4 μs. Increasing the burst size to 32 packets per burst improves its performance, enabling SR-IOV to outperform all *virtio*-based virtual switches, although VALE remains the most lightweight solution. From these results, we inferred that the variation of the burst size has a lower influence on the SR-IOV and VALE performance; for this reason, they are both suitable solutions that can be used with more bursty traffic.

We repeated the same evaluations by deploying the server application on a separate host ($L = remote$, Fig. 3f). In this new scenario, SR-IOV unsurprisingly always outperforms OVS and VPP, as shown in Figs. 5d to 5f; in fact, software-based virtual switches introduce two new levels of indirection with respect to directly offloading all network traffic to the NIC: the two software instances, each running in their respective hosts, perform additional packet processing operations that contribute to the overall latency of each packet exchanged to the ones already performed in hardware by the very same SR-IOV device. On the other hand, VALE's performance is less subject to change when varying packet or burst sizes, achieving consistently around 85 μs round-trip latency on average.

4.6   Performance and Computational Requirements

Finally, we compared the cost of these high-performance networking solutions in terms of computational power required. For this purpose, during our throughput evaluations we configured the sender and receiver applications to measure the consumed computational power, by comparing the CPU time executed by the process against the actual time.

For most of these scenarios the overall CPU utilization can be obtained by some simple considerations. First of all, both DPDK and Netmap achieve maximum performance when applications continuously poll the network driver. For this reason, each sender/receiver application consumes exactly 100% of the CPU time when running at maximum capacity. Software-based user-space virtual switches (i.e. DPDK Basic Forwarding Sample Application, OVS, Snabb,

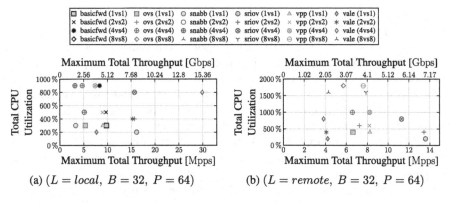

Fig. 6. Total CPU utilization vs maximum throughput measured varying the number of network flows and type of virtual switch used to connect sender/receiver applications deployed in LXC containers.

and VPP) are each implemented as a user-space process which also continuously polls network drivers for maximum performance. Hence, they each consume an entire CPU for each worker thread they spawn. On the contrary, SR-IOV and VALE do not require additional CPUs, albeit for two very different reasons: SR-IOV does not utilize any CPU at all, since it is an hardware offload solution; VALE runs inside each sender/receiver process, moving packets whenever an application executes a system call, as mentioned in Sect. 4.4.

Experimental results confirm these formulations, as shown in Fig. 6. Since for each of our tests the total CPU utilization for each solution depends only on the number of participants required by the test (e.g. 1vs1, 2vs2, and so on), we show only the maximum throughput performance registered during each test with the associated CPU utilization. It is implicit that given a certain system configuration, sending a smaller number of packets per second would result in worse throughput performance, but it would not affect CPU utilization when polling techniques are used. Figure 6 shows the clear advantage in terms of CPU costs of SR-IOV and VALE against the other switching technologies: in each system configuration, they always require one less CPU than the others for local and two less CPUs for multi-host communications.

It must be noted that most of these solutions support some form of interrupt coalescing techniques, similarly to the Linux New API (NAPI) [25], to reduce the overall CPU utilization at the cost of reduced throughput/latency performance. For example, Netmap API provides blocking access to NICs, allowing processes to suspend while waiting for the device to be ready again, thus reducing CPU utilization [22]. DPDK can also be used in combination with interrupts [11], but before sending or receiving packets the program must switch back to polling mode. This reduces CPU utilization during idle times, at the cost of greater latency when interrupts must be disabled to revert to polling mode, when the first packet of a burst is received.

As a final note, both OVS and VPP support multi-threaded packet forwarding by spawning multiple worker threads on separate cores and assigning each worker thread a subset of the virtual switch ports. When using this mode, benchmarking performance is directly influenced by the placements of the various applications. If the same worker thread manages multiple sender applications, performance is the same as shown in Figs. 4e and 4f, at the cost of consuming additional CPUs if assigning their receivers to other continuously polling worker threads. On the other hand, when spreading each sender application to a separate worker thread, both OVS and VPP can scale the total traffic linearly with network flows. The placement of receiver applications is entirely irrelevant from this perspective. However, it must be noted that using this mode has a considerable cost in terms of computational requirements since each worker thread consumes the totality of a CPU core, imposing a hard limit on the number of VNFs that can be deployed on a single machine.

5   Related Work

The proliferation of different technologies to exchange packets among applications deployed in virtualized environments has created the need for new tools to evaluate virtual switching solutions' performance with respect to throughput, latency, and scalability. For this reason, various works in the research literature addressed the problem of network performance optimization for VMs and containers, often analyzing the problem from different points of view.

A comparison among standard POSIX sockets and more modern *kernel bypass* frameworks like DPDK and Remote Direct Memory Access (RDMA)[11] focusing on round-trip latency between two directly connected hosts [11] showed that both DPDK and RDMA significantly outperform POSIX UDP sockets. In the study, DPDK and RDMA were the only ones able to achieve single-digit microsecond latency, with the drawback that applications must continuously poll the physical devices for incoming packets, leading to high CPU utilization.

Another work [14] compared qualitatively and quantitatively common high-performance networking setups, including SR-IOV, Snabb, OVS (with DPDK), and Netmap, measuring throughput and relative CPU utilization when deploying two VMs on either a single or two multiple directly connected hosts. Their evaluations concluded that, in their setups, Netmap could reach up to 27 Mpps (when running on a 4 GHz CPU), outperforming SR-IOV, due to the limited bandwidth of its hardware switch.

A previous comparison among high-performance networking technologies [10] analyzed the performance of three different frameworks: DPDK, Netmap, and PF_RING[12]. The analysis showed that two major bottlenecks may limit networking performance between two hosts: CPU capacity and NIC maximum transfer rate. Characteristics of network traffic (like packet or burst sizes) can influence whether one or the other represents the dominating bottleneck: when the

---

[11] http://www.rdmaconsortium.org.

[12] https://www.ntop.org/products/packet-capture/pf_ring/.

per-packet processing cost is kept low, the NIC maximum transfer rate is what imposes a cap on performance; on the other hand, as processing cost increases the CPU becomes increasingly more loaded, until it reaches a maximum packet processing rate. DPDK achieved the highest throughput in terms of packets per second, independently from the burst size; on the contrary, Netmap reached its highest throughput only when at grouping least 128 packets in each burst, and even then, it could not reach performance similar to DPDK or PF_RING.

The authors of a more recent work addressed the scalability of various virtual switching solutions against the number of VMs deployed on the same host [19], comparing VPP and OVS against SR-IOV. From their evaluations, they concluded that SR-IOV could sustain a more significant number of VMs with respect to its software-based counterparts, achieving almost linear throughput scalability for the number of VMs. Both OVS and VPP were only able to scale the total throughput up to a certain plateau, which depended on the number of CPU resources reserved for each virtual switch: the global resources allocated to each virtual switch were distributed equally among VMs, with a per-VM performance degradation that increased with the number of parallel VMs.

The same authors of this paper presented a preliminary work [3] that compared various virtual switching techniques based on *kernel bypass* for inter-container communications. That evaluation was limited to techniques that bypass the Linux kernel and only a single unidirectional packet flow on a single host. The results indicated that offloading traffic to the SR-IOV interface was the most suitable among the tested solutions. Another work comparing a much broader number of test cases and working conditions has also been presented by the same authors [4], deploying benchmarking applications on either one or multiple machines and presenting a new set of tools useful to repeat the experiments in other scenarios conveniently.

This paper constitutes an extension of our prior work [4] just described above. In this paper, we provided a more in-depth description of high-performance networking frameworks, including also Netmap, that does not rely entirely on *kernel bypass* mechanisms. We described how the original framework has been extended to support also Netmap and its virtual switch VALE as suitable inter-container communication mechanisms. With the new extended framework, we now provided a broader comparative analysis of the obtained networking performance, including VALE in our experiments. Finally, we also analyzed the computational requirements of each of the networking solutions included in the framework, which was missing from [4].

6   Conclusions and Future Work

This paper presented an extension to a software framework for the comparative evaluation of virtual networking solutions commonly used in the NFV industrial practice. With the extended framework, we evaluated the performance and computational demands of interconnecting VNFs, both on a single or multiple hosts. Results obtained on our reference machine show that SR-IOV or Netmap's virtual switch, VALE, obtain superior performance against the competition when networking on a single host; this is true not only in terms of throughput, latency, and scalability of the virtual network but also in terms of the processing power needed to perform packet forwarding at high rates. For inter-host communications, the CPU's limitations or the limited throughput of the underlying physical layer represent the major bottleneck for each of the tested solutions, at least on our reference hardware.

In the future, we plan to support additional virtual networking solutions, like SoftNIC [12] or PF_RING, as well as other virtual switches, like FastClick [6] or BESS [12]. Finally, we plan to implement support for one or more high-performance networking frameworks to real state-of-the-art NFV applications, like the ones developed for the OpenAirInterface project [16], and evaluate the potential performance improvements of these frameworks for real industrial applications, rather than emulating their behavior.

Acknowledgements. The authors would like to thank professor Giuseppe Lettieri from the University of Pisa for the timely help provided during the integration of Netmap in the framework.

References

1. Impressive packet processing performance enables greater workload consolidation. White Paper, Intel (2012). https://media15.connectedsocialmedia.com/intel/06/13251/Intel_DPDK_Packet_Processing_Workload_Consolidation.pdf
2. Open vSwitch enables SDN and NFV transformation. White Paper, Intel 2015. https://networkbuilders.intel.com/docs/open-vswitch-enables-sdn-and-nfv-transformation-paper.pdf
3. Ara, G., Abeni, L., Cucinotta, T., Vitucci, C.: On the use of kernel bypass mechanisms for high-performance inter-container communications. In: Weiland, M., Juckeland, G., Alam, S., Jagode, H. (eds.) ISC High Performance 2019. LNCS, vol. 11887, pp. 1–12. Springer, Cham (2019). https://doi.org/10.1007/978-3-030-34356-9_1
4. Ara, G., Cucinotta, T., Abeni, L., Vitucci, C.: Comparative evaluation of kernel bypass mechanisms for high-performance inter-container communications. In: Proceedings of the 10th International Conference on Cloud Computing and Services Science. SCITEPRESS - Science and Technology Publications (2020)
5. Barach, D., Linguaglossa, L., Marion, D., Pfister, P., Pontarelli, S., Rossi, D.: High-speed software data plane via vectorized packet processing. IEEE Commun. Mag. **56**(12), 97–103 (2018)
6. Barbette, T., Soldani, C., Mathy, L.: Fast userspace packet processing. In: Proceedings of the Eleventh ACM/IEEE Symposium on Architectures for Networking and Communications Systems, ANCS 2015, USA, pp. 5–16 (2015)
7. Barik, R.K., Lenka, R.K., Rao, K.R., Ghose, D.: Performance analysis of virtual machines and containers in cloud computing. In: 2016 International Conference on Computing, Communication and Automation (ICCCA). IEEE, April 2016
8. Dong, Y., Yang, X., Li, J., Liao, G., Tian, K., Guan, H.: High performance network virtualization with SR-IOV. J. Parallel Distrib. Comput. **72**(11), 1471–1480 (2012)
9. Felter, W., Ferreira, A., Rajamony, R., Rubio, J.: An updated performance comparison of virtual machines and Linux containers. In: IEEE International Symposium on Performance Analysis of Systems and Software (ISPASS), March 2015

10. Gallenmüller, S., Emmerich, P., Wohlfart, F., Raumer, D., Carle, G.: Comparison of frameworks for high-performance packet IO. In: ACM/IEEE Symposium on Architectures for Networking and Communications Systems (ANCS), May 2015
11. Géhberger, D., Balla, D., Maliosz, M., Simon, C.: Performance evaluation of low latency communication alternatives in a containerized cloud environment. In: IEEE 11th International Conference on Cloud Computing (CLOUD), July 2018
12. Han, S., Jang, K., Panda, A., Palkar, S., Han, D., Ratnasamy, S.: SoftNIC: A software NIC to augment hardware. Technical Report UCB/EECS-2015-155, EECS Department, University of California, Berkeley, May 2015
13. Jeong, E., et al.: mTCP: a highly scalable user-level TCP stack for multicore systems. In: 11th USENIX Symposium on Networked Systems Design and Implementation, pp. 489–502 (2014)
14. Lettieri, G., Maffione, V., Rizzo, L.: A survey of fast packet I/O technologies for network function virtualization. In: Kunkel, J.M., Yokota, R., Taufer, M., Shalf, J. (eds.) ISC High Performance 2017. LNCS, vol. 10524, pp. 579–590. Springer, Cham (2017). https://doi.org/10.1007/978-3-319-67630-2_40
15. Maffione, V., Rizzo, L., Lettieri, G.: Flexible virtual machine networking using netmap passthrough. In: 2016 IEEE International Symposium on Local and Metropolitan Area Networks (LANMAN). IEEE, June 2016
16. Nikaein, N., Marina, M.K., Manickam, S., Dawson, A., Knopp, R., Bonnet, C.: OpenAirInterface. ACM SIGCOMM Comput. Commun. Rev. **44**(5), 33–38 (2014)
17. Paolino, M., Nikolaev, N., Fanguede, J., Raho, D.: SnabbSwitch user space virtual switch benchmark and performance optimization for NFV. In: IEEE Conference on Network Function Virtualization and Software Defined Network, November 2015
18. Pfaff, B., et al.: The design and implementation of Open vSwitch. In: 12th USENIX Symposium on Networked Systems Design and Implementation, pp. 117–130 (2015)
19. Pitaev, N., Falkner, M., Leivadeas, A., Lambadaris, I.: Characterizing the performance of concurrent virtualized network functions with OVS-DPDK, FD.IO VPP and SR-IOV. In: Proceedings of the 2018 ACM/SPEC International Conference on Performance Engineering - ICPE 2018. ACM Press (2018)
20. Rizzo, L.: Netmap: A novel framework for fast packet I/O. In: 2012 USENIX Annual Technical Conference (USENIX ATC 12), Boston, MA, pp. 101–112. USENIX Association (2012)
21. Rizzo, L.: Revisiting network I/O APIs: the Netmap framework. Queue **10**(1), 30 (2012)
22. Rizzo, L., Landi, M.: Netmap: memory mapped access to network devices. ACM SIGCOMM Comput. Commun. Rev. **41**(4), 422 (2011)
23. Rizzo, L., Lettieri, G.: VALE, a switched ethernet for virtual machines. In: Proceedings of the 8th International Conference on Emerging Networking Experiments and Technologies - CoNEXT 2012. ACM Press (2012)
24. Russell, R., Tsirkin, M.S., Huck, C., Moll, P.: Virtual I/O Device (VIRTIO) Version 1.0. Standard, OASIS Specification Committee (2015)
25. Salim, J.H., Olsson, R., Kuznetsov, A.: Beyond Softnet. In: Annual Linux Showcase & Conference, vol. 5, pp. 18–18 (2001)
26. Yasukata, K., Honda, M., Santry, D., Eggert, L.: StackMap: low-latency networking with the OS stack and dedicated NICs. In: USENIX Annual Technical Conference (USENIX ATC 16), Denver, CO, pp. 43–56, June 2016

Cloud Computing for Enabling Big Data Analysis

Loris Belcastro[1] , Fabrizio Marozzo[1,2] , Domenico Talia[1,2(✉)] ,
and Paolo Trunfio[1]

[1] DIMES, University of Calabria, Rende, Italy
{lbelcastro,fmarozzo,talia,trunfio}@dimes.unical.it
[2] DtoK Lab Srl, Rende, CS, Italy

Abstract. Every day billions of people access web sites, blogs, and social media. Often they use their mobile devices and produce huge amount of data that can be effectively exploited for extracting valuable information concerning human dynamics and behaviors. Such data, commonly referred as Big Data, contains rich information about user activities, interests, and behaviors, which makes it intrinsically suited to a very large set of applications. For getting valuable information and knowledge from such data in a reasonable time, novel scalable frameworks and data analysis techniques on Cloud systems have been developed. This paper aims at describing some recent Cloud-based frameworks and methodologies for Big Data processing that can be used for developing and executing several data analysis applications, including trajectory mining and sentiment analysis. The paper is organized in two main parts. The first part focuses on tools for developing and executing scalable data analysis applications on Clouds. The second part presents data analysis methodologies for extracting knowledge from large datasets.

Keywords: Cloud computing · Big data analysis · Sentiment analysis · Trajectory mining · Social data analysis

1 Introduction

In the last years the ability to produce and gather data has increased exponentially. In the Internet of Things' era, huge amounts of digital data are generated by and collected from several sources, such as sensors, mobile devices, web applications and services. Moreover, with the large use of mobile devices, every day billions of people access web sites, blogs and social media producing a massive amount of digital data that can be effectively exploited to extract valuable information concerning many events, facts, human dynamics and behaviors. Such data, commonly referred as Big Data, contains valuable information about user activities, interests, and behaviors, which makes it intrinsically suited to a very large set of applications [6]. The huge amount of data generated, the speed at which it is produced, and its heterogeneity in terms of format, represent a challenge to the current storage, process and analysis capabilities. To extract value

© Springer Nature Switzerland AG 2021
D. Ferguson et al. (Eds.): CLOSER 2020, CCIS 1399, pp. 84–109, 2021.
https://doi.org/10.1007/978-3-030-72369-9_4

from such kind of data, novel distributed and Cloud-based frameworks and scalable data analysis techniques have been developed for capturing and analyzing complex and/or high velocity data.

In this scenario, high performance computers, such as many and multi-core systems, Clouds, and multi-clusters, paired with parallel and distributed algorithms are commonly used by data analysts to tackle Big Data issues and get valuable information and knowledge in a reasonable time. In particular, Cloud computing systems provide large-scale computing infrastructures for complex high-performance applications, such as those that use advanced data analytics techniques for extracting useful information from large, complex datasets [29]. However, combining Big Data analytics techniques with scalable computing systems allows for obtaining new insights from data in a shorter time.

This paper aims at presenting some recent Cloud-based frameworks and methodologies for Big Data processing that can be used for developing and executing several data analysis applications, including trajectory mining and sentiment analysis. The paper is organized in two main parts. The first part focuses on tools for developing and executing scalable data analysis applications on Cloud. The second part presents data analysis methodologies for extracting knowledge from large datasets.

In particular, the paper is structured as follows. Section 2 presents the Data Mining Cloud Framework designed for developing and executing distributed data analytics applications as workflows of services. In such environment data sets, analysis tools, data mining algorithms and knowledge models are implemented as single services that can be combined through a visual programming interface for designing distributed workflows to be executed on Clouds. Section 3 describes a high-level library for developing parallel data mining applications based on the extraction of useful knowledge from large dataset gathered from social media. The library aims at reducing the programming skills needed for implementing scalable social data analysis applications.

Section 4 presents Nubytics, a Software-as-a-Service (SaaS) system that exploits Cloud facilities to provide efficient services for analyzing large datasets. The system allows users to import their data to the Cloud, extract knowledge models using high performance data mining services, and exploit the inferred knowledge to predict new data and behaviors. Section 5 describes SMA4TD, a methodology for discovering behavior and mobility patterns of users attending large-scale public events, by analyzing social media posts.

Section 6 presents a novel Region-of-Intererest (RoI) mining technique that exploits the information contained in geotagged social media items (e.g. tweets, posts, photos or videos with geospatial information) to discover RoIs with high accuracy. Section 7 presents a methodology for discovering the polarization of social media users during election events characterized by the competition of political factions. The methodology uses an automatic incremental procedure based on neural networks for analyzing the posts published by social media users. Finally, Sect. 8 concludes the paper.

2   Data Mining Cloud Framework (DMCF)

The Data Mining Cloud Framework (DMCF) [24] is a software system for design-ing and executing data analysis workflows on Clouds. DMCF supports a large variety of data analysis processes, including single-task applications, parame-ter sweeping applications [23], and workflow-based applications. A Web-based user interface allows users to compose their applications and submit them for execution to a Cloud platform, according to a Software-as-a-Service approach.

The DMCF's architecture has been designed to be implemented on differ-ent Cloud systems, so as to take advantage of main cloud computing features, such as elasticity of resources provisioning. In DMCF, at least one Virtual Web Server runs continuously in the Cloud, as it serves as user front-end. In addition, users specify the minimum and maximum number of Virtual Compute Servers, which are in charge of executing the data mining tasks. The DMCF can exploit the auto-scaling features that allows dynamic spinning up or shutting down Vir-tual Compute Servers, based on the number of tasks ready for execution in the DMCF's Task Queue. Since storage is managed by the Cloud platform, the number of storage servers is transparent to the user.

2.1   Workflow Formalisms

Workflows may encompass all the steps of discovery based on the execution of complex algorithms and the access and analysis of scientific data. In data-driven discovery processes, knowledge discovery workflows can produce results that can confirm real experiments or provide insights that cannot be achieved in laboratories. In particular, DMCF allows to program workflow applications using two languages:

1. *VL4Cloud* (Visual Language for Cloud), a visual programming language that lets users develop applications by programming the workflow components graphically [26].
2. *JS4Cloud* (JavaScript for Cloud), a scripting language for programming data analysis workflows based on JavaScript [25].

Both languages use two key programming abstractions:

1. *Data* elements denote input files or storage elements (e.g., a dataset to be analyzed) or output files or stored elements (e.g., a data mining model).
2. *Tool* elements denote algorithms, software tools or service performing any kind of operation that can be applied to a data element (data mining, filtering, partitioning, etc.).

In particular, three different types of Tools can be used in a DCMF workflow:

1. A *Batch Tool* is used to execute an algorithm or a software tool on a Virtual Compute Server without user interaction. All input parameters are passed as command-line arguments.

2. A *Web Service Tool* is used to insert into a workflow a Web service invocation.
3. A *MapReduce Tool* is used to insert into a workflow the execution of a MapReduce algorithm or application running on a cluster of virtual servers [7].

For each Tool in a workflow, a *Tool descriptor* includes a reference to its executable, the required libraries, and the list of input and output parameters. Each parameter is characterized by *name, description, type,* and can be *mandatory* or *optional.* As an example, a MapReduce Tool descriptor is composed by two groups of parameters: *generic parameters,* which are parameters used by the MapReduce runtime, and *applications parameters,* which are parameters associated to specific MapReduce applications. In the following, we list a few examples of generic parameters:

- *mapreduce.job.reduces*: the number of reduce tasks per job;
- *mapreduce.job.maps*: the number of map tasks per job;
- *mapreduce.input.fileinputformat.split.minsize*: the minimum size of chunk that map input should be split into;

Another common element is the task concept, which represents the unit of parallelism in our model. A *task* is a Tool included in a workflow, which is intended to run in parallel with other tasks on a set of Cloud resources. According to this approach, VL4Cloud and JS4Cloud implement a *data-driven task parallelism.* This means that, as soon as a task does not depend on any other task in the same workflow, the runtime asynchronously spawns it to the first available virtual machine. A task T_j does not depend on a task T_i belonging to the same workflow (with $i \neq j$), if T_j during its execution does not read any data element created by T_i.

In VL4Cloud, workflows are directed acyclic graphs whose nodes represent data and tools elements. The nodes can be connected with each other through direct edges, establishing specific dependency relationships among them. When an edge is being created between two nodes, a label is automatically attached to it to express the kind of relationship between the two nodes. Data and Tool nodes can be added to the workflow singularly or in array form. A data array is an ordered collection of input/output data elements, while a tool array represents multiple instances of the same tool.

In early versions, DMCF has exploited the default storage provided by public cloud infrastructures for any I/O operations. This implies that DMCF's I/O performance was limited by the performance of the storage provided by cloud providers. In work [27] it has been discussed how to use the Hercules system within DMCF for storing temporary data generated by workflow-based applications. Hercules is a highly scalable, in-memory, distributed storage system [18]. In a later work [22], we also used a data-aware scheduling runtime that exploits data locality during the execution of workflows. An experimental evaluation was carried out to evaluate the advantages of these strategies and to demonstrate the effectiveness of the solution. Using the proposed data-aware strategy and Hercules as a temporary storage service, I/O overhead was reduced by 55% compared to standard Azure storage-based execution, leading to a 20% reduction in total execution of the workflow.

2.2   Workflow Examples

Figure 1 shows an example of data analysis workflow developed using the visual workflow language of DMCF.

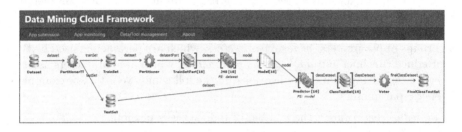

Fig. 1. Example of data analysis application designed using VL4Cloud.

In JS4Cloud, workflows are defined with a JavaScript code that interacts with Data and Tool elements through three functions:

1. *Data Access*, for accessing a Data element stored in the Cloud;
2. *Data Definition*, to define a new Data element that will be created at runtime as a result of a Tool execution;
3. *Tool Execution*, to invoke the execution of a Tool available in the Cloud.

Once the JS4Cloud workflow code has been submitted, an interpreter translates the workflow into a set of concurrent tasks by analysing the existing dependencies in the code. The main benefits of JS4Cloud are:

1. It extends the well-known JavaScript language while using only its basic functions (arrays, functions, loops);
2. It implements both a data-driven task parallelism that automatically spawns ready-to-run tasks to the Cloud resources, and data parallelism through an array-based formalism;
3. These two types of parallelism are exploited implicitly so that workflows can be programmed in a totally sequential way, which frees users from duties like work partitioning, synchronization and communication.

Figure 2 shows the script-based workflow version of the visual workflow shown in Fig. 1. In this example, parallelism is exploited in the for loop at line 7, where up to 16 instances of the J48 classifier are executed in parallel on 16 different partitions of the training sets, and in the for loop at line 10, where up to 16 instances of the Predictor tool are executed in parallel to classify the test set using 16 different classification models.

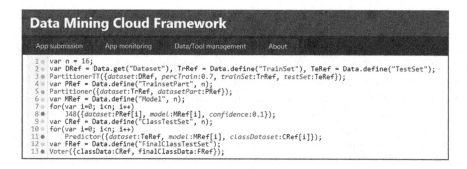

Fig. 2. Example of data analysis application designed using JS4Cloud.

Figure 2 shows a snapshot of the parallel classification workflow taken during its execution in the DMCF's user interface. Beside each code line number, a colored circle indicates the status of execution. This feature allows a user to monitor the status of the workflow execution. Green circles at lines 3 and 5 indicate that the two Partitioners have completed their execution; the blue circle at line 8 indicates that J48 tasks are still running; the orange circles at lines 11 and 13 indicate that the corresponding tasks are waiting to be executed.

2.3 Workflow Study Cases

DMCF has been used to implement several Big Data analytics applications, including a workflow for discovering patterns and rules from trajectory data [2]. Figure 3 shows the VL4Cloud workflow that define the steps of such application. Experimental evaluation has been carried out on GPS datasets tracing the movement of taxies in the urban area of Beijing. The results showed that, due to the high complexity and large volumes of data involved in the application scenario, the trajectory pattern mining process takes advantage from the scalable execution environment offered by DMCF in terms of both execution time, speed-up and scale-up.

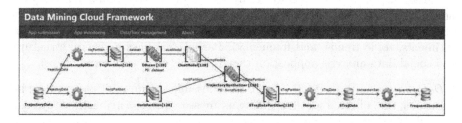

Fig. 3. Trajectories workflow composed and executed in the Data Mining Cloud Framework (DMCF).

DMCF has also been used to implement a Cloud-based computing infrastructure for the analysis of SNP microarray data [1]. It was possible to define a software tool (Cloud4SNP) for the parallel preprocessing and statistical analysis of pharmacogenomics SNP microarray data. Experimental evaluation shows efficient execution times and very good scalability. Moreover, the system implementation shows how the exploitation of a Cloud platform allows researchers and professionals to face in an elastic way the requirements of small as well as very large pharmacogenomics studies.

DMCF also supports data classification workflows that include MapReduce computations. As an example, in [8] DMCF has been used to implement a MapReduce data analysis application for predicting flight delays. Every year approximately 20% of airline flights are delayed or canceled mainly due to bad weather, carrier equipment, or technical airport problems. The goal of that application is to implement a predictor of the arrival delay of scheduled flights due to weather conditions. To run the workflow, we used a Hadoop cluster composed of 1 head node and 8 worker nodes, over the cloud servers used by the DMCF environment. With this setting, the turnaround time decreased from about 7 h by using 2 workers, to about 1.7 h by using 8 workers, with a speedup that is very close to linear values.

3   Parallel Social Data Analysis (ParSoDA)

Several developers and researches are working on the design and implementation of tools and algorithms for extracting useful information from data gathered from social media. In most cases the amount of data to be analyzed is so big that high-performance computers, such as many and multi-core systems, Clouds, and multi-clusters, paired with parallel and distributed algorithms, are used by data analysts to reduce response time to a reasonable value [9]. Several research projects consider not only the data analysis task, but also procedures including other data processing tasks needed for building social data applications. In particular, these projects aim at helping scientists to implement all the steps that compose social data mining applications without the need to implement common operations from scratch.

ParSoDA (Parallel Social Data Analytics) [12] is a Java library that includes algorithms widely used to process and analyze data gathered from social media with the goal of extracting different kinds of information (e.g., user mobility, user sentiments, topic trends, and frequency). ParSoDA defines a general structure for a social data analysis application that is formed by the following steps:

- *Data acquisition*: during this step, it is possible to run multiple crawlers in parallel; the collected social media items are stored on a distributed file system (HDFS [28]).
- *Data Filtering*: this step filters the social media items according to a set of filtering functions.
- *Data Mapping*: this step transforms the information contained in each social media item by applying a set of map functions.

- *Data Partitioning*: during this step, data is partitioned into shards by a primary key and then sorted by a secondary key.
- *Data Reduction*: this step aggregates all the data contained in a shard according to the provided reduce function.
- *Data Analysis*: this step analyzes data using a given data analysis function to extract the knowledge of interest.
- *Data Visualization*: at this final step, a visualization function is applied on the data analysis results to present them in the desired format.

For each of these steps, ParSoDA provides a predefined set of functions. For example, for the data acquisition step, ParSoDA provides crawling functions for gathering data from some of the most popular social media platforms (e.g., Twitter and Flickr), while for the data filtering step, ParSoDA provides functions for filtering geotagged items based on their position, time of publication, and contained keywords. Users are free to extend this set of functions with their owns.

3.1 Reference Architecture and Execution Flow

Figure 4 presents the reference architecture and execution flow of a ParSoDA application that runs on the Hadoop [30] or Spark [31] framework. In such way, it is possible to implement several parallel and distributed data mining applications with high scalability. As shown in Fig. 4(a), user applications can utilize ParSoDA and other libraries (e.g., Mahout[1], MLlib[2]). Applications can be executed on Hadoop or Spark, using YARN as resource manager and HDFS as distributed storage system. Figure 4(b) provides details on how applications are executed on a Hadoop or a Spark cluster. The cluster is formed by one or more master nodes, and multiple worker nodes. Once a user application is submitted to the cluster, its steps are executed according to their order (i.e., data acquisition, data filtering, etc.).

On a Hadoop cluster, some steps are inherently MapReduce-based, namely: *data filtering*, *data mapping*, *data partitioning* and *data reduction*. This means that all the functions used to perform these steps are executed within a MapReduce job that runs on a set of worker nodes. In particular, the data filtering and data mapping steps are wrapped within Hadoop Map tasks; the data partitioning step corresponds to Hadoop Split and Sort tasks; the data reduction step is executed as a Hadoop Reduce task. The remaining steps (data acquisition, data analysis, and data visualization) are not necessarily MapReduce-based. This means that the functions associated with these steps could be executed in parallel on multiple worker nodes, or alternatively they could be executed locally by the master node(s). The latter case does not imply that execution is sequential, because a master node can make use of some other parallel runtime (e.g., MPI).

On a Spark cluster, the main steps are executed into two Spark stages that run on a set of worker nodes. A *stage* is a set of independent tasks executing

---

[1] https://mahout.apache.org/.
[2] https://spark.apache.org/mllib/.

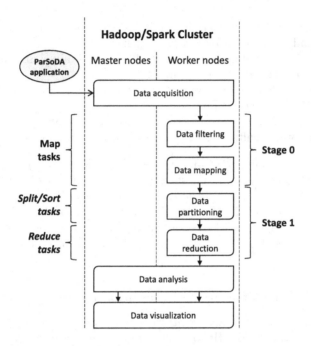

Fig. 4. Reference architecture and execution flow.

functions that do not need to perform data shuffling (e.g., transformation and action functions). Specifically: data filtering and mapping are executed at the first stage (*Stage 0*), while data partitioning and reduction are executed at the second stage (*Stage 1*). Concerning the remaining steps (data acquisition, data analysis, and data visualization), the same considerations made for Hadoop apply to Spark.

3.2 Usability and Scalability Evaluation

Writing a parallel data analysis application from scratch usually requires deep programming skills and the writing of many lines of code. In fact, designing and implementing such kind of applications pose a number of challenges to developers such as parallelization of complex algorithms, reduction of communication costs, and optimization of memory usage. As demonstrated in [13], the use of ParSoDA leads to a drastic reduction of lines of code. In particular, ParSoDA allows programmers to save hundred lines of code in the main (as the programmer needs to specify only the functions to be used and their parameters), in the data acquisition and data partition steps (where built-in functionalities are exploited), as well as in the data filtering, mapping, and reduction steps (where the programmer needs only to define the function logic). For the data analysis and visualization steps, we used the same code to invoke external libraries, which does not lead to a gain in terms of lines of code. However, for these steps, Par-

SoDA ensures many advantages in terms of usability. In fact, in the application main defined through ParSoDA, all the MapReduce jobs created for the different steps, such as the ones in the analysis and visualization steps, are automatically chained. This means that the output of a job is automatically used as input to the next step. In contrast, without ParSoDA, programmers need to manually control the execution flow among different jobs.

The scalability of ParSoDA has been evaluated by running the data analysis applications on a private cloud infrastructure with 300 cores and 1.2 TB of RAM. In the experiments we run, the Spark version of ParSoDA has been preferred, since, as demonstrated in [10], it resulted to be faster than the Hadoop version of that library.

4 Nubytics

Nubytics [16] is another system we developed to exploit Cloud facilities to provide scalable services in the analysis of very large datasets. The system allows users to import their data to the Cloud, extract knowledge models using high performance data mining services, and use the inferred knowledge to predict new data. Nubytics provides data classification and regression services that can be used in a variety of scientific and business applications. Scalability is ensured by a parallel computing approach that fully exploits the resources available on the Cloud. In addition, Nubytics is provided in accordance with the Software-as-a-Service (SaaS) model. This means that no installation is required on the user's machine: the Nubytics interface is offered by a web browser, so it can be run from most devices, including desktop PCs, laptops, and tablets. This is a key feature for users who need ubiquitous and seamless access to scalable data analysis services, without needing to cope with the installation and system management issues of traditional analytics tools.

Nubytics differs from general purpose data analysis frameworks like Azure ML, Hadoop and Sparks, or data-oriented workflow management systems like ClowdFlows and DMCF, as it provides specialized services for data classification and prediction. These services are provided by a Web interface that allows designers and analysts to focus on the data analysis process without worrying on low level programming details. This approach is similar to that adopted by BigML. However, Nubytics also focuses on scalability, by implementing an ad hoc parallel computing approach that fully exploits the distributed resources of a Cloud computing platform.

4.1 Architecture

The Nubytics architecture includes storage and compute components. The storage components are:

- *Data Folder* that contains data sources and the results of data analysis, and *Tool Folder* that contains algorithms for data analysis and prediction.

- *Data Table*, *Tool Table* and *Task Table* that contain metadata information associated with data, tools, and tasks.
- *Task Queue* that contains the tasks to be executed.

The compute components are:

- *Virtual Compute Servers* that execute the data analysis tasks.
- *Virtual Web Servers* that host the system front end, i.e., the Nubytics web interface.

The architecture manages submission and execution of data analysis tasks by the following steps:

1. Using the services provided by the front end, a user can configure and submit the desired data analysis task (e.g., training a classification model from a dataset).
2. Exploiting a data parallel approach, the system models the task as a set of parallel sub-tasks that are inserted into the Task Queue for processing.
3. Each idle Virtual Compute Server picks a sub-task from the Task Queue and concurrently starts its execution.
4. Each Virtual Compute Server gets the part of data assigned to it from the Data Folder where the original dataset is stored.
5. After sub-task completion, each Virtual Compute Server puts the result on the Data Folder.
6. The front end notifies the user as soon as the task has completed, and allows her/him to access the results.

4.2   Services

The Nubytics front end is divided into three sections - *Datasets*, *Tasks* and *Models* - corresponding to the three groups of services provided by the system: dataset management, task management and model management.

Datasets of a user are stored in a Cloud storage space associated to the user's account. The *Datasets* section provides several data management services, including: importing (uploading) a dataset from the user's terminal; exporting (downloading) a dataset to the user's terminal; listing and searching the available datasets; modifying the metadata of a dataset; creating a copy, deleting, or restoring a dataset.

The *Tasks* section provide services for configuring, submitting and managing data analysis tasks. Two classes of tasks can be submitted: training tasks and prediction tasks.

A training task takes as input a dataset and produces a classification or regression model from it. The goal of classification is to derive a model that classifies the instances of a dataset into one or more classes. Using a classification model, we can predict the membership of a new data instance to a given class from a set of predefined classes. The goal of regression is to build a model that associates a numerical value to the instances of a dataset. Therefore, a regression model can be used to forecast a quantitative value starting from the field values of a new data instance.

The configuration of a training task is made by selecting the input dataset, the class field (which is categorical in case of classification and numerical in case of regression), and the predictive fields that must be considered for the analysis (they can be all - or a subset of - the original dataset fields). A parallel computing approach is used to speedup the execution of training tasks. This is done using a data parallel approach that divides the original task in sub-tasks, assigns a sub-task to a different virtual compute server on the Cloud, and joins the partial results computed by multiple servers into a single model.

A prediction task takes two input elements: a model generated by a training task, and a new dataset whose instances must be classified or regressed. As a result, the new dataset will include a new field containing the predicted class label (in case of classification) or numerical value (in case of regression) of each tuple. Also in this case, parallelism is exploited by performing the prediction task in parallel on multiple Cloud servers.

Multiple tasks can be submitted to the system, and the user can monitor the status of each one through a task management interface, as shown by the screenshot in Fig. 5. For each task, the interface shows the task type (prediction or training), some information about execution (start, end, and elapsed time), and the current status. Additional details on a task can be seen by selecting the corresponding row. For instance, the figure shows Input Dataset and Output Model of the second task, which is a Training task.

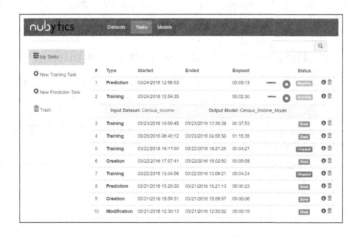

Fig. 5. Screenshot of the Tasks section.

5   SMA4TD

SMA4TD (Social Media Analysis for Trajectory Discovery) [17] is a methodology aimed at discovering behavior rules, correlations and mobility patterns of visitors attending large-scale events, trough the analysis of a large number of social media posts. In particular, the main goals of the methodology are as follows.

1. *Discovery of Most Visited Places and Most Attended Events.* We analyze the collected data to discover the places that have been most visited by users, and the events that have been most attended by visitors during the observed period.
2. *Discovery of Most Frequent Sets of Visited Places and Most Frequent Sets of Attended Events.* We extract the sets of places that are most frequently visited together by users, and the events that have been most attended by visitors during the observed period.
3. *Discovery of Most Frequent Mobility Patterns among Places and Most Frequent Sequences of Attended Events.* We analyze the collected data to discover mobility behaviors among the places, and to extract useful knowledge (i.e. patterns, rules and regularities) about the attended events.
4. *Discovery of the Origin and Destination of Visitors.* We study the mobility flows of people attending the events, evaluating which countries visitors came from and which countries they moved after the events. In some cases, this information can give some insights about the touristic impact on the local territory.

The methodology is composed of seven steps: i) identification of the set of events; ii) identification of places-of-interests where the events take place; iii) collection of geotagged items related to events and pre-processing; iv) identification of users who published at least one of the geotagged items; v) pre-processing and creation of the input dataset; vi) data analysis and trajectory mining; and vii) results visualization.

5.1 Steps 1-2: Definition of Events and Places-of-Interest

The first two steps aim at defining the events $\mathcal{E}$ and the corresponding places-of-interest $\mathcal{P}$. Specifically, during step 1, each event is described by the id of the place-of-interest (PoI) where it is located, starting/ending time of the event, and other optional data (e.g., free/paid event, type of event, etc.). Step 2 is aimed at defining the geographical boundaries of the PoIs in $\mathcal{P}$. This can be done in two ways: i) *manually* defining the boundaries of the PoIs (e.g., as polygons on a map); ii) *automatically*, using external services (e.g., cadastral maps [19]), or public web services providing the geographical boundaries of a place given its name (e.g., OpenStreetMap[3]).

5.2 Steps 3-4-5: Collection and Pre-processing of Geotagged Items, Identification of Users and Creation of the Input Dataset

The goal of step 3 is to collect all the geotagged items $\mathcal{G}$ posted during each event $e_i \in \mathcal{E}$ from the place p_i where e_i was held. Data collection is done by using the

---

[3] https://www.openstreetmap.org/.

publicly available APIs provided by most social media platforms. The $\mathcal{G}$ dataset is pre-processed in order to clean, select and transform data to make it suitable for analysis. In particular, we first clean the collected data by removing all items with unreliable positions (e.g., items with coordinates that have been manually set by users or applications). Then, we proceed by selecting only the geotagged items posted by users who actually attended an event, by removing replies and favorites posted by other users. Finally, we transform data by keeping one item per user per event, because we are interested to know only if a user attended an event or not. The identification of users is the goal of step 4. This is done by extracting the set $\mathcal{U}$ of distinct users who published at least one geotagged item in $\mathcal{G}$.

Step 5 creates the input datasets $\mathcal{D} = \{d_1, d_2, ...\}$, where d_i is a tuple $<u_i, \{e_{i1}, e_{i2}, ..., e_{ik}\}, optFields>$ in which e_{ij} is the jth event attended by user u_i, and $optFields$ are optional descriptive fields (e.g., nationality, interests).

5.3 Step 6-7: Data Mining and Results Visualization

After having built the input dataset $\mathcal{D}$, it is analyzed for discovering behaviour and mobility patterns of users attending the large-scale event under investigation. Specifically, we perform both *associative* and *sequential analysis*, as described in the following.

Associative analysis is exploited with the goal of discovering (inside data) the item values that occur together with a high frequency. The mechanisms of association allow identifying the conditions that tend to occur simultaneously, or the patterns that repeat in certain conditions. Applied to dataset $\mathcal{D}$, we perform two associative mobility mining tasks: (*i*) *frequent event sets discovery*, aimed at extracting the sets of events (places) that are most frequently attended (visited) together by visitors during the whole observed large-scale event; and (*ii*) *frequent event rules extraction*, devoted to discover frequent associative rules among the events.

On the other hand, *sequential analysis* algorithms are intended to discover the sequences of elements that occur most frequently in the data. Unlike associative analysis, in sequential analysis are fundamental the time dimension and the chronological order in which the values appear in the data. In our case, this type of analysis is useful to discover the most frequent mobility patterns among the places, and/or the most frequent sequences of attended events. Moreover, if the observed period is extended to some days (or weeks) before/after the event time, we can also discover the origin/destination (i.e., country, city) of visitors and which countries visitors came from/move after the event (i.e., to infer touristic insights).

Finally, results visualization is performed by the creation of info-graphics aimed at presenting the results in a way that is easy to understand to the general public, without providing complex statistical details that may be hard to understand to the intended audience. The graphic project is grounded on some of the most acknowledged and ever-working principles underpinning a 'good' info-graphic piece.

5.4   Study Cases: FIFA World Cup 2014 and EXPO 2015

In this section we present the results obtained by analyzing geotagged posts of social media users attending the FIFA World Cup 2014 and EXPO 2015.

FIFA World Cup 2014. During the FIFA World Cup 2014, we monitored the Twitter users attending the 64 matches played during the football competition and analyzed such data through the SMA4TD methodology to discover behaviors and frequent movements of fans [14]. In this case study, the places-of-interest are the stadiums in which the World Cup matches have been played. The corresponding RoIs have been manually defined from a map as the smallest rectangles fully containing the boundaries of each stadium. For each match, we considered only the tweets posted from coordinates falling within the above defined RoIs during the matches. Totally, the number of tweets that have been collected (from June 12 to July 13, 2014) amounted to about 526,000. We have made several analyzes on user behavior. For example, we described how the number of people attending the matches changed over time. To do that, we report in Fig. 6 trends and numbers *(i)* of Twitter users we tracked attending at the matches during the World Cup, and *(ii)* of attendees officially published by the FIFA website[4]. Specifically, Fig. 6 shows a time plot of the collected attendance data, in which the number of attendees is plotted versus the number of matches.

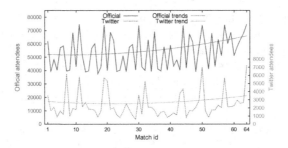

Fig. 6. Number of attendees per match, comparing Twitter users and official attendee numbers.

It clearly shows that there are several peaks of participation during the competition, probably corresponding to some matches that have attracted more attention with respect to other ones. Interestingly, in some cases Twitter data peaks are equivalent to the official attendance ones. We also studied the participation of fans to the matches. The results show that 71.3% of the fans attended a single match, 16% attended two matches, 6% attended three matches, and only 6.7% attended four or more matches. We also studied the most frequent paths of fans who attended two or three matches of the same team during the group stage.

---

[4] http://www.fifa.com/worldcup/archive/brazil2014.

For example, the most frequent 2-match-set was ⟨*Colombia-Greece, Colombia-Cote d'Ivoire*⟩, followed by ⟨*Brazil-Mexico, Croatia-Mexico*⟩, and by ⟨*Argentina-Bosnia, Argentina-Iran*⟩, i.e., matches likely attended by fans of Colombia, Mexico and Argentina. Looking at their nationality, spectators were likely fans of Mexico, Brazil and Australia.

EXPO 2015. For the second study case we monitored Instagram users who visited the EXPO 2015 pavilions aiming at discovering mobility patterns inside the exhibition area, correlations among visits to pavilions, and the main flows of origin/destination of visitors [15]. EXPO 2015[5] was a Universal Exposition held under the theme "Feeding the Planet, Energy for Life", which was hosted in Milan, Italy, from May 1st to October 31st, 2015. Exhibitors were individual countries, international organizations, civil society organizations and companies, for a total of 188 exhibition spaces. Some of the exhibitors were hosted inside individual (self-built) pavilions, while others were hosted inside shared pavilions. For the sake of uniformity, in this paper we will use the term pavilion to indicate both an individual pavilion and a distinct area (assigned to a given exhibitor) of a shared pavilion. Cumulatively, about 22.2 million people visited the EXPO area and its pavilions during the six months of the whole exposition, making it the world-wide largest event of the year 2015. Visitors at EXPO used various social network to share their experience with friends and followers.

The set of events $\mathcal{E}$ considered for this scenario is composed by the showcases (each one organized by a country or organization/company) exhibited in the exposition spaces (generally referred as pavilions in the following). Specifically, let us consider $\mathcal{E} = \{e_1, e_2, ..., e_{188}\}$, where each e_i is described by the following properties:

$$e_i = \langle p_i, [t_i^{begin}, t_i^{end}] \rangle$$

where p_i is the pavilion, t_i^{begin} is May 1st and t_i^{end} is October 31st.

The places-of-interest to be considered are the pavilions. Specifically, we defined the PoI set $\mathcal{P} = \{p_1, p_2, ..., p_{188}\}$, where each p_i is a pavilion that has been used as exhibition area during the EXPO 2015. For each PoI, we drew its corresponding RoI as a rectangle bounding the pavilion area.

Figure 7 shows a comparison between trends and numbers of the Instagram visitors we tracked, and the official visitors published on the EXPO website (see Footnote 5). The observed period is August 1st–October 31st, but official numbers have been published only for the period starting in August, thus the corresponding curve has been traced only for the last three months. We used different scales for Instagram visitor numbers and the EXPO visitor ones: on the right is the scale of the formers, while on the left is the scale of the latter ones. In particular, Fig. 7(a) shows a time plot of the daily visits to EXPO. The trends are quite evident: initially (May and June) the visitors are relatively few; then, they grow significantly during the months of September and October. Moreover,

---

[5] http://www.expo2015.org/.

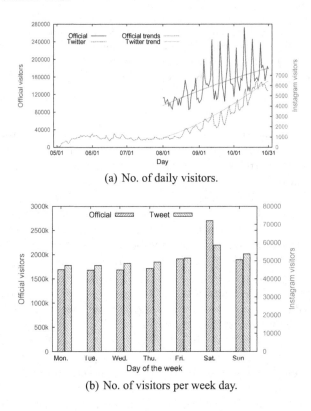

(a) No. of daily visitors.

(b) No. of visitors per week day.

Fig. 7. Statistics about visitors, comparing Instagram users and official attendee numbers.

there are several peaks of attendance, corresponding to visits occurred during the week-end days. By looking at the trends in the figure, it can be noted a strong correlation (Pearson coefficient 0.7) between official visitor numbers and those obtained from our analysis, which confirms the reliability of the results we obtained. Figure 7(b) compares Instagram and official visitor numbers, aggregated by the week day (Pearson correlation 0.94). The results clearly show that during the week-end days there is a peak of visits, with the highest number of people registered on Saturdays.

6 RoI Mining

Geotagged data gathered from social media can be used to discover interesting locations visited by users called Places-of-Interest (PoIs). Since a PoI is generally identified by the geographical coordinates of a single point, it is hard to match it with user trajectories. Therefore, it is useful to define an area, called *Region-of-Interest (RoI)*, to represent the boundaries of the PoI's area. *RoI mining* techniques are aimed at discovering Regions-of-Interest from PoIs and other data.

G-RoI [11] is a novel RoI mining technique that exploits the indications contained in geotagged social media items (e.g. tweets, posts, photos or videos with geospatial information) to discover the RoI of a PoI with a high accuracy. Given a PoI p identified by a set of keywords, a geotagged item is associated to p if its text or tags contain at least one of those keywords. Starting from the coordinates of all the geotagged items associated to p, *G-RoI* calculates an initial convex polygon enclosing all such coordinates, and then iteratively reduces the area using a density-based criterion. Then, from all the convex polygons obtained at each reduction step, *G-RoI* adopts an area-variation criterion to choose the polygon representing the RoI for p.

Let a PoI $\mathcal{P}$ be identified by one or more keywords $K = \{k_1, k_2, ...\}$. Let G_{all} be a set of geotagged items. Let $G = \{g_0, g_1, ...\}$ be the subset of G_{all}, obtained by applying a *G-RoI preprocessing* procedure that selects from G_{all} only the geotagged items associated to $\mathcal{P}$, i.e., the text or tags of each $g_i \in G$ contains at least one keyword in K. Let $C = \{c_0, c_1, ...\}$ be a set of coordinates, where c_i represents the coordinates of $g_i \in G$. Thus, every $c_i \in C$ represents the coordinates of a location from which a user has created a geotagged item referring to $\mathcal{P}$. Let cp_0 be a convex polygon enclosing all the coordinates in C, obtained by running the convex hull algorithm [3] on C, described by a set of vertices $\{v_0, v_1, ...\}$.

To find the RoI $\mathcal{R}$ for $\mathcal{P}$, the G-RoI algorithm uses two main procedures:

- *G-RoI Reduction.* Starting from cp_0, it iteratively reduces the area of the current convex polygon by deleting one of its vertex. A density-based criterion is adopted to choose the next vertex to be deleted. The density of a polygon is the ratio between the number of geotagged items enclosed by the polygon, and its area. At each step, the procedure deletes the vertex that produces the polygon with highest density, among all the possible polygons. The procedure ends when it cannot further reduce the current polygon, and returns the set of convex polygons $CP = \{cp_0, ..., cp_n\}$ obtained after the n steps that have been performed.
- *G-RoI Selection.* It analyses the set of convex polygons CP returned by the *G-RoI reduction* procedure, and selects the polygon representing RoI $\mathcal{R}$ for PoI $\mathcal{P}$. An area-variation criterion is adopted to choose $\mathcal{R}$ from CP. Given CP, the procedure identifies two subsets: a first subset $\{cp_0, ..., cp_{cut-1}\}$ such that the area of any cp_i is significantly larger than the area of cp_{i+1}; a second subset $\{cp_{cut}, ..., cp_n\}$ such that the area of any cp_i is not significantly larger than the area of cp_{i+1}. The procedure returns cp_{cut} as RoI $\mathcal{R}$. This corresponds to choosing cp_{cut} as the corner point of a discrete *L-curve* [20] obtained by plotting the areas of all the convex polygons in CP on a Cartesian plane, as detailed later in this section.

6.1   Methodology

Without going into algorithmic details that can be found at [11], we briefly describe how the *G-RoI reduction* and *selection* procedures work through a real

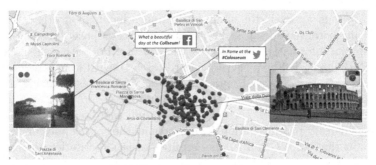

(a) Collection of geotagged items.

(b) Initial convex polygon cp_0.   (c) Generating cp_1 by deleting one vertex from cp_0.   (d) Final convex polygon cp_{cut}.

Fig. 8. G-RoI reduction and selection on Colosseum's geotagged items.

example. Starting from a small sample of 200 geotagged items from different social media, referring to the *Colosseum* in Rome and posted at a maximum distance of 500 m from it.

In their posts and photos, social media users identify the *Colosseum* with different keywords, such as *Coliseum, Coliseo, Colisée*, and synonymous such as *Flavian Amphitheatre* or *Amphitheatrum Flavium*. All the geotagged items in our sample contain at least one of such keywords. From these posts, the 200 coordinates shown in Fig. 8(a) have been extracted. Given the coordinates, the *G-RoI reduction* procedure calculates the initial convex polygon cp_0 (shown Fig. 8(b)), and then iteratively reduces the area. Figure 8(c) shows polygon cp_1 obtained after the first step by deleting one of the vertices from cp_0. The *G-RoI reduction* procedures iterates until it cannot further reduce the current polygon. The output of the procedure is the set of convex polygons $CP = \{cp_0, cp_1, ..., cp_n\}$ obtained at each step.

The *G-RoI selection* procedure identifies the point p_{cut} that is located at the maximum distance ($dist^{max}$) from the *reference line* joining the first point and the last point under analysis (p_0 and p_n). If the set of points $\{p_{cut}, ..., p_n\}$ follows a linear trend, i.e., there is no point below a *threshold line* at distance th from the reference line joining the points p_{cut} and p_n, then the procedure returns the polygon corresponding to p_{cut} as RoI $\mathcal{R}$ (see Fig. 8(d)). Otherwise, the *G-RoI selection* procedure iterates by finding a new cut-off point from the set of points on the right of p_{cut}.

We experimentally evaluated the accuracy of G-RoI in detecting the RoIs associated to a set of PoIs. The analysis was carried out on 24 PoIs located in the center of Rome (St. Peter's Basilica, Colosseum, Circus Maximus, etc.) using about 1.2 millions geotagged items published in Flickr from January 2006 to May 2016 in the areas under analysis. Specifically, we made several preliminary tests to find parameter values that perform effectively in that scenario, taking into account that the various PoIs are characterized by significant variability of shape, area and density (number of Flickr photos divided by area). In particular, the threshold *th* was set to 0.27. The experimental results showed also that G-RoI is able to detect RoIs with high accuracy. Over a set of 24 PoIs in Rome, G-RoI achieved a mean precision of 0.78, a mean recall of 0.82, and a mean F_1 score of 0.77.

7   Iterative Opinion Mining Using Neural Networks

IOM-NN (*Iterative Opinion Mining using Neural Networks*) [5] is a new methodology for estimating the polarization of public opinion on political events characterized by the competition of factions or parties. It can considered as an alternative technique to traditional opinion polls, since it is able to capture the opinion of a larger number of people more quickly and at a lower cost. In particular, IOM-NN uses an automatic incremental procedure based on feed-forward neural networks for analyzing the posts published by social media users. Starting from a limited set of classification rules, created from a small subset of hashtags that are notoriously in favor of specific factions, our methodology iteratively generates new classification rules. A classification rule allows to determine if a post is in favor of a faction based on the words/hashtags it contains. Then, such rules are used to determine the polarization of social media users - who wrote posts about the political event - towards a faction. As shown in Fig. 9, the proposed methodology consists of three main steps:

1. *Collection of Posts*: posts are collected by using a set of keywords related to the selected political event.
2. *Classification of Posts*: the collected posts are then classified by using an incremental procedure implemented through neural networks.
3. *Polarization of Users*: the classified posts are analyzed for determining the polarization of users towards a faction.

Collection of Posts. A political event $\mathcal{E}$ is characterized by the rivalry of different factions $F = \{f_1, f_2, ..., f_n\}$. Examples of political events and relative factions are: *i*) municipal election, in which a faction supports a mayor candidate; *ii*) parliament election, in which a faction supports a party; *iii*) presidential election, in which a faction supports a presidential candidate [21]. The posts are collected by using the keywords that people commonly use to refer the political event $\mathcal{E}$ on social media. Such keywords K can be divided in two groups:

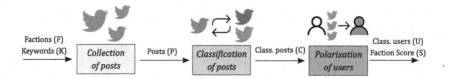

Fig. 9. Execution flow of IOM-NN.

- $K_{context}$, which contains generic keywords that can be associated to $\mathcal{E}$ without referring to any specific faction in F.
- $K_F^\oplus = K_{f1}^\oplus \cup ... \cup K_{fn}^\oplus$, where $K_{fi}^\oplus$ contains the keywords used for supporting $f_i \in F$ (positive faction keywords).

The keywords in K are given as input to public APIs provided by social media platforms, which permit to *collect* posts containing one or more keywords.

The collected posts are *pre-processed* before the analysis. The output of this step is a collection of posts P. In particular, they are modified and filtered as follows:

- The text of posts is normalized by transforming it to lowercase and replacing accented characters with regular ones (e.g., IOVOTOSI or iovotosí → iovotosi).
- Words are stemmed for allowing matches with declined forms (e.g., vote or votes or voted → vot).
- Stop words are removed from text by using preset lists.
- All the posts written in a language different from the one(s) spoken in the nation(s) hosting the considered political event are filtered out.

Classification of Posts. The input of the algorithm for the classification of posts is composed of: the posts P generated in the previous step, the set of positive faction keywords $K_F^\oplus$, the maximum number of iterations max_{iters}, the minimum increment of the classified posts *eps* at each iteration, and a threshold *th*. Instead, the output is a collection of posts C that have been classified in favor of a faction.

As discussed in [4], the algorithm is divided in two parts. The fist part performs the preliminary iteration (iteration 0). At this iteration, IOM-NN exploits the set of positive faction keywords ($K_F^\oplus$) for classifying a part of the posts. Specifically, it classifies a post in favor of a faction if it contains only positive keywords for such faction. In general, at the end of this iteration, only a small part of posts are classified, since not all users use keywords in $K_F^\oplus$ for declaring their support to factions. The second part iteratively generates new classification rules for classifying other posts. At each iteration, such rules are inferred by exploiting the posts that have been classified at the previous iterations.

Polarization of Users. This algorithm is used for determining the polarization of users. The input is composed of: a collection of classified posts C, a filtering function $filter$ with its parameters par_f, and a polarization function $polarize$ with its parameters par_p. The output is composed of a collection of classified users U and a faction score (S) containing the polarization percentages for each faction. As first step, the classified posts are aggregated by user to produce a dictionary (C_U), which contains the list of classified posts P_u for each user u. Two empty variables are initialized for storing the output. On each pair $\langle u, P_u \rangle$ of C_U, the algorithm performs the following operations:

- It filters out all the pairs that do not match the criteria defined by the $filter$ function. For example, users who published a number of posts below a given threshold are skipped.
- Using the classified posts P_u, it computes v_s^u a vector containing the score of user u for each faction. The score vector is calculated by using the function $polarize$.
- It adds the pair $\langle u, v_s \rangle$ to U.

Then, the algorithm calculates the overall faction score S as the normalized sum of the user vector scores $\langle u, v_s^u \rangle$. Finally, the output is returned.

7.1 Case Study: The 2016 US Presidential Election

In this section we describe and analyze a case study: the 2016 US presidential election, which was characterized by the rivalry between Hillary Clinton and Donald Trump. The analysis has been performed on data collected for ten US Swing States: Colorado, Florida, Iowa, Michigan, Ohio, New Hampshire, North Carolina, Pennsylvania, Virginia, and Wisconsin. Overall about 2.5 million of tweets, posted by 521,291 users, have been collected from October 10, 2016 to November 7, 2016 (the day before the election). From such data we filtered out all the tweets posted by users with a not defined location or with a location that does not belong to any of the considered states. In particular, for each faction f_i we defined three set of keywords $K_{f_i}^{\oplus}$, $K_{f_i}^{\ominus}$ and $K_{f_i}^{\circ}$ that are respectively positive, negative and neutral keywords for faction f_i. For example, for the *Hillary Clinton* faction $K_{Clinton}^{\oplus}$ contains keywords used to clearly support her party (e.g., *#voteHillary*), $K_{Clinton}^{\ominus}$ contains keywords to speak negatively about her (e.g., *#neverhillary*), $K_{Clinton}^{\circ}$ contains neutral keywords (e.g., *clinton* or *democrats*). *IOM-NN* exploits only positive faction keywords $(K_{f_i}^{\oplus})$ for classifying posts and then for determining the polarization of users.

For such study case, the *filter* and *polarize* functions have been configured as follows. Specifically, a user u is considered only if he/she fulfills the following criteria: *i*) u posted at least $minPosts$ on the political event of interest; *ii*) it exists a faction f for which u has published more than 2/3 of his/her posts. For each user u, the *polarize* function returns a vector score as follows: the percentage of posts written by u in favor of preferred faction f, 0 for the other factions.

Figure 10 shows how the user polarization algorithm works on some classified posts. For each user, the posts if favor of Clinton and Trump are counted. Users

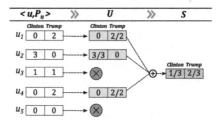

Fig. 10. Example of how the *user polarization* algorithm works.

who fulfill the criteria of filter function are considered and added to the set of classified users U. Then U is combined and normalized to obtain the vector S containing the overall polarization percentages.

As shown in Fig. 11, IOM-NN was able to correctly identify the winning candidate in 8 out of 10 cases, outperforming the opinion polls that correctly classifies 6 out 10 states.

Fig. 11. Comparison among the real winning candidate and that identified by IOM-NN and opinions polls. The *Democratic Donkey* symbolizes the party of Hillary Clinton, while the *Republican Elephant* that of Donald Trump.

8   Conclusions

In science and business, scientists and professionals analyze huge amounts of data, commonly called Big Data, to extract information and knowledge useful for making new discoveries or for supporting decision processes. This can be done by exploiting Big Data analytics techniques and tools. In this scenario, Cloud computing represents a compelling solution for Big Data analytics, allowing faster data analysis, that means more timely results and then prompt data value. This paper presented some Cloud-based frameworks and methodologies for Big Data processing that we recently developed. They can be used for developing and executing different kinds of real-world data analysis applications. In particular, in the first part of the paper we presented some tools for developing and running Big Data application on Clouds (i.e., DMCF, ParSoDA, and Nubytics).

To complete the view, in the second part of the paper we presented innovative methodologies for extracting useful information about mobility behaviors (i.e., SMA4TD and G-RoI) and political sentiment of social media users (i.e., IOM-NN).

References

1. Agapito, G., Cannataro, M., Guzzi, P., Marozzo, F., Talia, D., Trunfio, P.: Cloud4SNP: distributed analysis of SNP microarray data on the cloud, pp. 468–475 (2013). https://doi.org/10.1145/2506583.2506605
2. Altomare, A., Cesario, E., Comito, C., Marozzo, F., Talia, D.: Trajectory pattern mining for urban computing in the cloud. IEEE Trans. Parallel Distrib. Syst. **28**(2), 586–599 (2017). https://doi.org/10.1109/TPDS.2016.2565480
3. Barber, C.B., Dobkin, D.P., Huhdanpaa, H.: The quickhull algorithm for convex hulls. ACM Trans. Math. Softw. **22**(4), 469–483 (1996)
4. Belcastro, L., Cantini, R., Marozzo, F., Talia, D., Trunfio, P.: Discovering political polarization on social media: a case study, pp. 182–189 (2019). https://doi.org/10.1109/SKG49510.2019.00038
5. Belcastro, L., Cantini, R., Marozzo, F., Talia, D., Trunfio, P.: Learning political polarization on social media using neural networks. IEEE Access **8**, 47177–47187 (2020). https://doi.org/10.1109/ACCESS.2020.2978950
6. Belcastro, L., Marozzo, F., Talia, D.: Programming models and systems for big data analysis. Int. J. Parallel Emerg. Distrib. Syst. **34**(6), 632–652 (2019). https://doi.org/10.1080/17445760.2017.1422501
7. Belcastro, L., Marozzo, F., Talia, D., Trunfio, P.: Programming visual and script-based big data analytics workflows on clouds. Adv. Parallel Comput. **26**, 18–31 (2015). https://doi.org/10.3233/978-1-61499-583-8-18
8. Belcastro, L., Marozzo, F., Talia, D., Trunfio, P.: Using scalable data mining for predicting flight delays. ACM Trans. Intell. Syst. Technol. **8**(1) (2016). https://doi.org/10.1145/2888402
9. Belcastro, L., Marozzo, F., Talia, D., Trunfio, P.: Big data analysis on clouds. In: Zomaya, A.Y., Sakr, S. (eds.) Handbook of Big Data Technologies, pp. 101–142. Springer, Cham (2017). https://doi.org/10.1007/978-3-319-49340-4_4
10. Belcastro, L., Marozzo, F., Talia, D., Trunfio, P.: Appraising SPARK on large-scale social media analysis. In: Heras, D.B., Bougé, L. (eds.) Euro-Par 2017. LNCS, vol. 10659, pp. 483–495. Springer, Cham (2018). https://doi.org/10.1007/978-3-319-75178-8_39
11. Belcastro, L., Marozzo, F., Talia, D., Trunfio, P.: G-RoI: automatic region-of-interest detection driven by geotagged social media data. ACM Trans. Knowl. Discov. Data **12**(3) (2018). https://doi.org/10.1145/3154411
12. Belcastro, L., Marozzo, F., Talia, D., Trunfio, P.: ParSoDA: high-level parallel programming for social data mining. Soc. Netw. Anal. Min. **9**(1), 1–19 (2018). https://doi.org/10.1007/s13278-018-0547-5
13. Belcastro, L., Marozzo, F., Talia, D., Trunfio, P.: A high-level programming library for mining social media. In: Post-Proceedings of the High Performance Computing Workshop 2018, Cetraro, Italy. Advances in Parallel Computing, vol. 34, pp. 3–21. IOS Press, 2–6 July 2019

14. Cesario, E., et al.: Following soccer fans from geotagged tweets at FIFA World Cup 2014. In: Proceedings of the 2nd IEEE Conference on Spatial Data Mining and Geographical Knowledge Services, Fuzhou, China, pp. 33–38, July 2015. https://doi.org/10.1109/ICSDM.2015.7298021

15. Cesario, E., et al.: Analyzing social media data to discover mobility patterns at EXPO 2015: methodology and result. In: The 2016 International Conference on High Performance Computing & Simulation (HPCS 2016), Innsbruck, Austria, pp. 230–237, July 2016. https://doi.org/10.1109/HPCSim.2016.7568340

16. Cesario, E., Iannazzo, A., Marozzo, F., Morello, F., Talia, D., Trunfio, P.: Nubytics: scalable cloud services for data analysis and prediction. In: 2nd International Forum on Research and Technologies for Society and Industry (RTSI 2016), Bologna, Italy, pp.1–6, September 2016. https://doi.org/10.1109/RTSI.2016.7740643

17. Cesario, E., Marozzo, F., Talia, D., Trunfio, P.: SMA4TD: a social media analysis methodology for trajectory discovery in large-scale events. Online Soc. Netw. Media **3–4**, 49–62 (2017). https://doi.org/10.1016/j.osnem.2017.10.002

18. Duro, F.R., Blas, J.G., Carretero, J.: A hierarchical parallel storage system based on distributed memory for large scale systems. In: Proceedings of the 20th European MPI Users' Group Meeting, pp. 139–140 (2013)

19. de Graaff, V., de By, R.A., van Keulen, M., Flokstra, J.: Point of interest to region of interest conversion. In: Proceedings of the 21st ACM SIGSPATIAL International Conference on Advances in Geographic Information Systems, SIGSPATIAL 2013, pp. 388–391. ACM, New York (2013)

20. Hansen, P.C.: Analysis of discrete ill-posed problems by means of the L-Curve. SIAM Rev. **34**(4), 561–580 (1992)

21. Marozzo, F., Bessi, A.: Analyzing polarization of social media users and news sites during political campaigns. Soc. Netw. Anal. Min. **8**(1), 1–13 (2017). https://doi.org/10.1007/s13278-017-0479-5

22. Marozzo, F., Rodrigo Duro, F., Garcia Blas, J., Carretero, J., Talia, D., Trunfio, P.: A data-aware scheduling strategy for workflow execution in clouds. Concurrency Comput. **29**(24) (2017). https://doi.org/10.1002/cpe.4229

23. Marozzo, F., Talia, D., Trunfio, P.: A cloud framework for parameter sweeping data mining applications. In: Proceedings of the 3rd IEEE International Conference on Cloud Computing Technology and Science (CloudCom 2011), Athens, Greece, pp. 367–374. IEEE Computer Society Press, December 2011. https://doi.org/10.1109/CloudCom.2011.56

24. Marozzo, F., Talia, D., Trunfio, P.: A cloud framework for big data analytics workflows on azure. Adv. Parallel Comput. **23**, 182–191 (2013). https://doi.org/10.3233/978-1-61499-322-3-182

25. Marozzo, F., Talia, D., Trunfio, P.: Js4Cloud: script-based workflow programming for scalable data analysis on cloud platforms. Concurrency Comput. **27**(17), 5214–5237 (2015). https://doi.org/10.1002/cpe.3563

26. Marozzo, F., Talia, D., Trunfio, P.: A workflow management system for scalable data mining on clouds. IEEE Trans. Serv. Comput. **11**(3), 480–492 (2018). https://doi.org/10.1109/TSC.2016.2589243

27. Rodrigo Duro, F., Marozzo, F., Garcia Blas, J., Talia, D., Trunfio, P.: Exploiting in-memory storage for improving workflow executions in cloud platforms. J. Supercomput. **72**(11), 4069–4088 (2016). https://doi.org/10.1007/s11227-016-1678-y

28. Shvachko, K., Kuang, H., Radia, S., Chansler, R.: The hadoop distributed file system. In: 2010 IEEE 26th symposium on Mass storage systems and technologies (MSST), pp. 1–10. IEEE (2010)

29. Talia, D., Trunfio, P., Marozzo, F.: Data analysis in the cloud: models. Tech. Appl. (2015). https://doi.org/10.1016/C2014-0-02172-7
30. White, T.: Hadoop: The Definitive Guide. O'Reilly Media, Inc., Sebastopol (2012)
31. Zaharia, M., et al.: Apache spark: a unified engine for big data processing. Commun. ACM **59**(11), 56–65 (2016)

A Multi-cloud Parallel Selection Approach for Unlinked Microservice Mapped to Budget's Quota: The PUM^2Q

Juliana Carvalho[1]($^{(\boxtimes)}$) (iD), Fernando Trinta[2]($^{(\boxtimes)}$) (iD), and Dario Vieira[3]($^{(\boxtimes)}$) (iD)

[1] University Federal of Piauí - UFPI, Picos, Brazil
`julianaoc@ufpi.edu.br`
[2] University Federal of Ceará - UFC, Fortaleza, Brazil
`fernando.trinta@dc.ufc.br`
[3] EFREI-Paris, Paris, France
`dario.vieira@efrei.fr`

Abstract. The world is facing a complicated moment in which social isolation is necessary. Therefore, to minimize the problems of companies, remote work is being widely adopted, which is only possible because of existing technologies, including cloud computing. Choosing the providers to host the business applications is a complex task, as there are many providers and most of them offer various services with the same functionality and different capabilities. Thus, in this paper, we propose an approach, called PUM^2Q, for selecting providers to host a distributed application based on microservices that have little communication between them. PUM^2Q is a provider selection approach based on multi-criteria, and it copes with the needs of microservices individually and in parallel. The proposed approach extends our previous one, UM^2Q, and should be incorporated by PacificClouds. Besides, we carry out a performance evaluation by varying the number of requirements, microservices, and providers. We also compare PUM^2Q and UM^2Q. The results presented by PUM^2Q are better than those given by UM^2Q, showing not only its viability but also expanding the number of approaches adopted by PacificClouds. As a result, PUM^2Q making the tasks of the software architect, who is the user of PacificClouds, more flexible.

Keywords: Multi-criteria decision-making method · Microservices · Multi-cloud parallel selection

1 Introduction

Despite existing for a long time, remote work was not widely adopted. In the face of a pandemic in which social isolation is essential, many companies have started using it. Many remote jobs are only possible due to the existence of several technologies, and one of them being cloud computing. According to Flexera[1],

---

[1] https://info.flexera.com/SLO-CM-REPORT-State-of-the-Cloud-2020.

© Springer Nature Switzerland AG 2021
D. Ferguson et al. (Eds.): CLOSER 2020, CCIS 1399, pp. 110–132, 2021.
https://doi.org/10.1007/978-3-030-72369-9_5

30% of companies are adopting more cloud computing than predicted before the pandemic. Flexera[2] also points out that 84% of companies with more than 1,000 employees have as a strategy for the use of multiple clouds. Given this context, we can see the importance of cloud computing and, more specifically, of a multi-cloud environment in the current and future scenario.

The use of multiple clouds brings many advantages, as it consolidates the benefits obtained by cloud computing, allowing the user to choose the services that best meet their needs regardless of the provider. Effectively, using multiple providers and multiple cloud services per provider to compose a distributed application has several challenges, including those described by Flexera (see Footnote 2), such as cloud cost management, governance, security, compliance, lack of resources/expertise, multiple clouds management and cloud migration.

In this paper, we propose an approach for selecting multiple providers to host an application based on microservices from the software architect's perspective. The applications considered in this work have little interaction between microservices so we disregarded them. The proposed approach, named PUM^2Q, selects providers considering the requirements of availability, response time and cost. PUM^2Q treats the provider selection for a microservice regardless of another microservice. For this, a software architect needs to define an application budget quota for each microservice. The proposed approached extends the work published in [4], in which we propose the UM^2Q approach. The two approaches differ because the one proposed in this work parallels each provider selection for each microservice. Thus, PUM^2Q increases the number of scenarios served by UM^2Q, as the selection time decreases, and it supports scenarios with a more significant amount of microservices, providers and services per provider. To demonstrate this, we propose a performance evaluation as well as a comparison between the two proposals described in Sect. 5.

PacificClouds [5] is a platform that aims to manage the deployment and execution of an application based on microservices distributed in a multi-cloud environment. The multi-cloud environment aims to mitigate vendor lock-in and also allows the software architect to distribute an application to take the advantages offered by cloud computing. Also, PacificClouds uses microservices as the architectural style because they provide support to build applications in which each part is independently scalable and deployed. To achieve its goals, PacificClouds must select the providers and services to host all application microservices.

PacificClouds intends to incorporate several provider selection approaches in order to address a higher number of scenarios and, consequently, the software architect's needs. We propose other selection approaches besides the one described in [4], which meet different scenarios. The method proposed in [2] obtains the best solution, but it is limited in the input size, that is, in the number of microservices of an application and the amount of available providers. The approach proposed in [3] obtains a viable solution and accepts a large entry, that is, an application with a large number of microservices and providers.

---

[2] https://www.flexera.com/blog/cloud/2019/02/cloud-computing-trends-2019-state-of-the-cloud-survey/.

The UM^2Q introduced in [4] gets an optimal local solution and accepts a large entry, but smaller than the proposal in [3]. The purpose of PUM^2Q is to take advantage of UM^2Q and expand the size of the entrance. Therefore, PUM^2Q is an approach that contributes to increase the number of scenarios served by PacificClouds.

Once this approach focuses on applications based on microservices distribute in a multi-cloud environment, we adopted the definition for multi-cloud [5], which is a delivery model where there is no agreement between the providers involved. We use the definition of microservices described in [5], followed by an approach example in Sect. 2. In Sect. 3 we present a formulation for the model; and, in Sect. 4 the PUM^2Q approach description.

Other works in the literature deal with the selection process in cloud computing, but as described in [4], they focus on different aspects. In [4], as presented in Sect. 6, we describe some works that focus on the user's perspective and propose a taxonomy called providers and services granularity (PSG), which classifies the papers according to the number of providers and services used both in the selection phase and in the application. Further, we present other works that use parallel approaches to address the selection of cloud providers, and we also compared them to PUM^2Q.

According to the aspects described in this section, the main contributions of this work are as follows:

1. We propose a provider selection process for an application microservice regardless of another microservice in the same application. For this, a software architect must define an application budget quota for each microservice;
2. We propose a parallel selection of providers to host an application's microservices;
3. We describe a formal description of the proposed approach;
4. We present a tool that implements the proposed approach;
5. We assess a performance evaluation to verify the PUM^2Q feasibility. Furthermore, we compare PUM^2Q and UM^2Q.

2   Example for PUM^2Q

The main objective of PUM^2Q is to choose providers in parallel to host an application based on microservices from the software architect's perspective, in a manner that, the approach selects a single provider for each microservice. For this, a software architect needs to provide PUM^2Q with the requirements of each application's microservice and the available providers' capabilities. In this section, we present a simplified example for PUM^2Q.

The example shows an application with three microservices represented by MS1, MS2 and MS3, illustrated in Fig. 1a. MS1 requires three cloud services, represented by S11, S21 and S31. Figure 1a also shows the services of the provider Cloud1, which has 6 services represented by CS11, CS21, CS31, CS41, CS51 and CS61. Figures 1b, 1c and 1d show the selection of candidate services from the provider Cloud1 that meet each cloud services required to compose MS1.

(a) Microservices' Application and Available Provider.

(b) Candidate Services for S11 from MS1.

(c) Candidate Services for S21 from MS1.

(d) Candidate Services for S31 from MS1.

Fig. 1. Examples for candidate services for PUM^2Q.

Figure 2 shows the candidate combinations to serve MS1, according the provider Cloud1 capabilities. Next, PUM^2Q selects the provider combination Cloud1 for MS1 that has the highest score. The approach calculates the score by the weighted average between the values for availability, response time and cost and the weight of each one. The weight represents the priority of the requirement. PUM^2Q repeats the process on all available providers for MS1. In the end, there is a set of candidate combinations for MS1, one for each provider. Again, the approach selects the best candidate among providers by looking at their score. PUM^2Q performs the entire process for all microservices in parallel.

Fig. 2. Candidate combinations for PUM^2Q.

Now, let's assume that the budget defined for the application is 12 and that the budget quota for MS1 is 4, for MS2 is 5 and for MS3 is 3. Figure 3 shows the set of candidate combinations for each application microservice containing the score, the cost and the provider to which it belongs. We can observe that combination 3 for MS1 has the highest score, and it does not exceed the budget's quota for MS1. We can also notice that combination 3 for MS2 has the highest score, but it does exceed the budget's quota. So PUM^2Q must select combination 2 for MS2, as shown in Fig. 4. Its happens similarly with MS3 and the approach selects combination 2 to fit the budget, even though combination 3 has the highest score.

Microservice	Combination	Quota	Score	Cost	Provider
MS1	1	4	0.6	2	P1
	2		0.7	3	P2
	3		0.8	4	P3
MS2	1	5	0.5	2	P5
	2		0.7	4	P4
	3		0.8	7	P3
MS3	1	3	0.6	1	P2
	2		0.7	3	P5
	3		0.8	8	P1

Fig. 3. All candidate combinations for PUM^2Q.

Microservice	Combination	Quota	Score	Cost	Provider
MS1	1	4	0.6	2	P1
	2		0.7	3	P2
	3		0.8	4	P3
MS2	1	5	0.5	2	P5
	2		0.7	4	P4
	3		0.8	7	P3
MS3	1	3	0.6	1	P2
	2		0.7	3	P5
	3		0.8	8	P1

Fig. 4. Combinations selection for PUM^2Q.

3   Formulation

The proposed selection approach refers to the cloud providers selection from the software architect's perspective before an application deployment. The software architect must define their requirements for an application, and set a budget' quota for each application microservice. We consider that the provider's capabilities are available since this is an other challenge and we do not treat in this paper. In this section, we present a formal description for PUM^2Q through definitions, and the optimization of availability, response time and cost requirements.

As we can observe in Sect. 2, the required cloud services to compose a microservice have different requirements and the providers offer many services with the same functionalities but different capabilities. Even though our approach can handle as many requirements as needed, in this paper, we consider three user requirements: (i) response time (execution time + communication delay), (ii) availability, and (iii) application execution cost, but other requirements can be included in our model easily. We use three user's requirements that are enough to understand our proposed selection process. However, the software architect can define several other user requirements without significant changes in the code.

According to the previously described providers' selection process, and as in [4], we propose:

- Definition 1: **cloud service model** - as S(S.rt, S.a, S.c), in which S.rt, S.a, and S.c stand for response time, availability, and cost, respectively.
- Definition 2: **cloud services class** - as $SC_l = \{S_{l1}, S_{l2}, \ldots, S_{lo}\}$, in which $S_{l1}, S_{l2}, \ldots, S_{lo}$ are services of the same provider with same functionalities but different capabilities.
- Definition 3: **services provider model** - as $SP_k = \{SC_{k1}, SC_{k2}, \ldots, SC_{kp}\}$, in which $SC_{k1}, SC_{k2}, \ldots, SC_{kp}$ are services classes.
- Definition 4: **cloud provider set** - as CP $= \{SP_1, SP_2, \ldots, SP_q\}$, in which $SP_1, SP_2, \ldots, SP_q$ are services providers.
- Definition 5: **microservice model** - as $MS_i = \{S_{i1}^{k_1}, S_{i2}^{k_2}, \ldots, S_{ir}^{k_r}\}$, in which $S_{i1}^{k_1}, S_{i2}^{k_2}, \ldots, S_{ir}^{k_r}$ are cloud services indispensable to execute a microservice, and they should be of different cloud service classes. Each service required to compose the microservice i can belong to different classes of services from a cloud provider. Thus, $1 \leqslant k_r \leqslant o$, in which o is the maximum number of classes for a cloud provider.
- Definition 6: **application model** - as AP $= \{MS_1, MS_2, \ldots, MS_t\}$, in which $MS_1, MS_2, \ldots, MS_t$ are microservices.

All definitions described for the cloud selection process must follow the model of definition 1. Example: Definition X is modelled as X (X.rt, X.a, X.c).

3.1 Availability Requirement

The cloud availability for an application must meet at least the user-defined threshold, so that each application microservice meets the same threshold. We define MinAvbty as the user-defined minimum availability threshold. In Eq. 1, we define AP.a as the application availability, which is assigned to be defined as the lowest availability value among its microservices, and it must be greater than or equal to MinAvbty. Also, in Eq. 2, $MS_i.a$ represents the microservice availability i, which is assigned to be the lowest availability value among cloud services that compose MS_i and it must be greater than or equal to MinAvbty. We represent the cloud availability for a service by $S_{ij}^{k_j}.a$ in Eq. 2, which is the service j from provider K for the microservice i.

$$AP.a = \min_{1 \leqslant i \leqslant t} (MS_i.a) \geqslant MinAvbty, \forall MS_i \mid MS_i \in AP \tag{1}$$

$$MS_i.a = \min_{1 \leqslant j \leqslant r} (S_{ij}^{k_j}.a) \geqslant MinAvbty,$$
$$\forall S_{ij}^{k_j} \mid S_{ij}^{k_j} \in MS_i, MS_i \in AP, 1 \leqslant i \leqslant t \tag{2}$$

3.2 Response Time Requirement

The response time for an application must meet the user-defined threshold, so that each application microservice meets the same threshold. We define MaxRT as the user-defined maximum response time threshold, and `MaxRT` is the maximum execution time threshold (`MaxExecTime`) plus the maximum delay threshold (`MaxDelay`) defined by the user, as in Eq. 3. In Eq. 4, we define `AP.rt` as the response time of the application, which is assigned the highest response time value among their microservices, and that must be less than or equal to `MaxRT`. In addition, in Eq. 5, $MS_i.rt$ represents the response time of microservice `i`, which is assigned to be the highest response time value among their services and that must not be less than `MaxRT`. We represent the response time for a service by $S_{ij}^{k_j}.rt$ in Eq. 5, which is the service `j` from provider `k` for the microservice `i`.

$$MaxRT = MaxExecTime + MaxDelay \tag{3}$$

$$AP.rt = \max_{1 \leqslant i \leqslant t} (MS_i.rt) \leqslant MaxRT, \forall MS_i \mid MS_i \in AP \tag{4}$$

$$MS_i.rt = \max_{1 \leqslant j \leqslant r} (S_{ij}^{k_j}.rt) \leqslant MaxRT,$$
$$\forall S_{ij}^{k_j} \mid S_{ij}^{k_j} \in MS_i, MS_i \in AP, 1 \leqslant i \leqslant t \tag{5}$$

3.3 Cost Requirement

The application execution cost should not be higher than the cost threshold defined by the user (`Budget`). In Eq. 6, we define `AP.c` as the application execution cost, which is assigned as the sum of all its microservices' costs, and that must be less than or equal to the provided Budget.

$$AP.c = \sum_{i=1}^{t} MS_i.c \leqslant Budget, \forall MS_i \mid MS_i \in AP \tag{6}$$

In this work, an application has `t` as the microservices maximum, and a microservice has `r` as the services maximum. We do not address the services capabilities model from the provider perspective because this work focuses on the software architect perspective. We only verify if the service capabilities offered by a cloud provider meet the user requirement.

4 PUM^2Q Approach

We can observe in the previous sections that there are various available cloud providers, and each of them offers several services. An application can consist of many microservices, and each of them must require several cloud services to meet its tasks' requirements. Therefore, selecting cloud providers to host a distributed application in multiple clouds is complex. In this section, we propose PUM^2Q, a multi-cloud parallel selection approach to host the unlinked microservices mapped to quota's budget. The proposed parallel selection model refers to the cloud providers selection from the software architect's perspective before an application deployment.

In PUM^2Q, as in UM^2Q [4], we select multi-cloud providers to host each application microservice and each one of them is hosted by a single provider, considering only the microservice and software architect requirements. PUM^2Q hosts a microservice in a single provider so that its tasks do not exchange information among services from different providers. This approach presents three selection levels as in UM^2Q. In both, UM^2Q and PUM^2Q approaches, we execute the levels sequentially, but while in UM^2Q, the provider selection process for each microservice is sequential, in PUM^2Q is in parallel. The three levels will be described next.

4.1 First Level: Determine Candidate Services for a Microservice

We select the services of each provider that meet all software architect requirements, which results in a candidate services set from each provider for one microservice. Next, we rank all candidate services in each provider. We use the Simple Additive Weighting (SAW) technique as in [16], which has two phases: scaling and weighting.

Scaling Phase. First, a matrix $R = (R_{ij}; 1 \leqslant i \leqslant n; 1 \leqslant j \leqslant 3)$ is built by merging the requirement vectors of all candidate services. For this, the user requirements are numbered from 1 to 3, where 1 means availability, 2 means response time, and 3 means cost. These candidate services refer to the same service of the microservice. We must perform the entire process for each service of the microservice. Each row R_i corresponds to a cloud service S_{ij} and each column R_j corresponds to a requirement. Next, the requirements should be ranked using one of the two criteria described in Eqs. 7 and 8. Also, $R_j^{Max} = Max(R_{ij}), R_j^{Min} = Min(R_{ij}), 1 \leqslant i \leqslant n$.

Negative: the higher the value, the lower the quality.

$$V_{ij} = \begin{cases} \frac{R_j^{Max} - R_{ij}}{R_j^{Max} - R_j^{Min}} & \text{if } R_j^{Max} - R_j^{Min} \neq 0 \\ 1 & \text{if } R_j^{Max} - R_j^{Min} = 0 \end{cases} \tag{7}$$

Positive: the higher the value, the higher the quality.

$$V_{ij} = \begin{cases} \frac{R_{ij} - R_j^{Min}}{R_j^{Max} - R_j^{Min}} & \text{if } R_j^{Max} - R_j^{Min} \neq 0 \\ 1 & \text{if } R_j^{Max} - R_j^{Min} = 0 \end{cases} \tag{8}$$

Weighting Phase. The overall requirements score is computed for each candidate cloud service (Eq. 9).

$$Score(S_i) = \sum_{j=1}^{3} (V_{ij} * W_j) \mid W_j \in [0,1], \sum_{j=1}^{3} W_j = 1 \tag{9}$$

At the end of the first level, we have a set of all candidate services for one microservice from all available providers.

4.2   Second Level: Determine a Candidate Combination from All Providers

We must select all required services to compose each microservice in each provider from the candidate services selected in the first level. For this, we consider that the software architects define a budget quota for each microservice of an application. Thus, in Eq. 10, we define $MS_i.c$ as the microservice execution cost, which must be less than or equal to $(Budget * Quota_i)$. We define $Quota_i$ as the application execution budget quota defined for microservice i, and Budget as the application execution cost threshold. Next, in Eq. 11, we define that each $Quota_i$ must be between 0 and 1, and that the sum of all $(Budget * Quota_i)$ must be equal to the Application Budget. In addition, in Eq. 12, we define that the cost sum of all services of microservice i must be less than or equal to the execution cost of microservice i.

$$MS_i.c \leqslant Budget * Quota_i, \forall MS_i \mid MS_i \in AP \tag{10}$$

$$Quota_i \in]0,1], \sum_{i=1}^{t} Budget * Quota_i = Budget \tag{11}$$

$$\sum_{j=1}^{r} S_{ij}^{k_j}.c \leqslant Budget * Quota_i, \forall S_{ij}^{k_j} \mid S_{ij}^{k_j} \in MS_i, 1 \leqslant i \leqslant t \tag{12}$$

In order to compose a microservice, we need to combine all candidate services and check the execution cost for these services combinations. First, we must combine the candidate services that come from the same microservice and are offered by the same provider, which is represented by $(S_{ij_1}^k, ..., S_{ij_r}^k)$ in Eq. 13. Each element of the candidate combination $S_{ij}^{k_j}$ represents the candidate service j of provider k to the microservice i, in which $1 \leqslant j \leqslant r$ and r indicates the number of services to microservice i. Next, we calculate the combination execution cost and verify if it is less than or equal to $(Budget * Quota_i)$ as shown in Eq. 13, which is in accordance to Eqs. 10, 11, and 12. Each microservice has a maximum r services.

$$(S_{i1}^{k_1}, ..., S_{ir}^{k_r}) \mid (S_{i1}^{k_1}.c + ... + S_{ir}^{k_r}.c) \leqslant Budget * Quota_i \tag{13}$$

Next, we must choose a combination among candidate services combinations in each provider for each microservice. For this, our approach calculates the average score for each services combination, which is represented by aSC_{SP_k} in Eq. 14. SP_k is the provider k that belongs to a set of providers (CP), and CP has a maximum q providers. Besides, $Score(S_{i1}^{k_1}) + Score(S_{i2}^{k_2}) + ... + Score(S_{ir}^{k_r})$ represents the sum of all service scores of a combination, $S_{ir}^{k_r}$ is a candidate service of a combination, and r is a maximum of microservice services. We must choose the combination with the highest score average.

$$aSC_{SP_k} = \frac{Score(S_{i1}^{k_1}) + Score(S_{i2}^{k_2}) + ... + Score(S_{ir}^{k_r})}{r} \tag{14}$$

If multiple combinations have the highest score average, one of them must be selected based on one of the three requirements defined by a software architect, but according to his priorities.

At the end of the second level, there must be a candidate provider set (CSP_i) for the MS_i of an application, as shown in Eq. 15. SP_{ki} represents the candidate provider k for microservice i, and it has a candidate service combination chosen for a microservice i. An application has a maximum t microservices, and a microservice has a maximum q_i candidate providers.

$$CSP_i = \{SP_{1i}, SP_{2i}, \ldots, SP_{q_i i}\} \mid 1 \leqslant i \leqslant t,$$
$$t = size\,of(AP), q_i = size\,of(CSP_i) \tag{15}$$

4.3   Third Level: Determine a Combination for a Microservice

We select one provider for a microservice. First, we check the microservice execution cost for each candidate provider, which was calculated in the second level, as shown in Eq. 16. In this equation, $SP_{ki}.c$ indicates the execution cost of the microservice i for candidate provider k. We define that $SP_{ki}.c$ is the service costs sum of the candidate combination of provider k. In Eq. 16, $S_{ij}^{kj}.c$ is the service j cost of microservice i in candidate provider k.

$$SP_{ki}.c = \sum_{j=1}^{r}(S_{ij}^{kj}.c) \mid S_{ij}^{kj} \in SP_{ki}, SP_{ki} \in CSP_i, \tag{16}$$

$$1 \leqslant k \leqslant q_i, 1 \leqslant i \leqslant t$$

Next, we check the CSP from the Second Level for the microservice to obtain the SP that presents the average microservice execution cost, and we use Eqs. 17, 18 and 19. In Eq. 17, $Max(MS_i.c)$ returns the highest microservice execution cost among the candidate providers for microservice i. Next, in Eq. 18, $Min(MS_i.c)$ returns the lowest microservice execution cost among the candidate providers for microservice i. In addition, in Eq. 19, $Average(MS_i.c)$ returns the average microservice execution cost among the candidate providers for microservice i.

$$Max(MS_i.c) = \max_{1\leqslant k \leqslant s_i}(SP_{ki}.c) \mid \forall SP_{ki} \in CSP_i,$$
$$1 \leqslant i \leqslant t, q_i = size\,of(CSP_i) \tag{17}$$

$$Min(MS_i.c) = \min_{1\leqslant k \leqslant s_i}(SP_{ki}.c) \mid \forall SP_{ki} \in CSP_i$$
$$1 \leqslant i \leqslant t, q_i = size\,of(CSP_i) \tag{18}$$

$$Average(MS_i.c) = \frac{Max(MS_i.c) + Min(MS_i.c)}{2} \tag{19}$$

If there is more than one provider with the same average execution cost, we select the one with highest availability or performance, observing the priority defined by a system architect. We use Eqs. 20 and 21 to calculate the availability and response time for each candidate provider, respectively. Equation 20 defines $SP_{ki}.a$ as the cloud availability of one provider k for microservice i, which is assigned the lowest candidate service availability for microservice i. Equation 21 defines $SP_{ki}.rt$ as the response time of provider k for microservice i, which is assigned the highest candidate service response time of microservice i. Next, we use Eqs. 22 and 23 to calculate the highest value for availability and the lowest value for response time in each candidate provider based on Eqs. 20 and 21, respectively.

$$SP_{ki}.a = \min_{1 \leqslant j \leqslant r} (S_{ij}^{k_j}.a) \mid S_{ij}^{k_j} \in SP_{ki}, SP_{ki} \in CSP_i,$$
$$1 \leqslant k \leqslant q_i, 1 \leqslant i \leqslant t \tag{20}$$

$$SP_{ki}.rt = \max_{1 \leqslant j_x \leqslant r} (S_{ij_x}^{k}.rt) \mid S_{ij_x}^{k} \in SP_{ki}, SP_{ki} \in CSP_i,$$
$$1 \leqslant k \leqslant q_i, 1 \leqslant i \leqslant t \tag{21}$$

$$Max(MS_i.a) = \max_{1 \leqslant k \leqslant s_i} (SP_k.a) \mid \forall SP_k \in CSP_i \tag{22}$$

$$Max(MS_i.rt) = \min_{1 \leqslant k \leqslant s_i} (SP_k.rt) \mid \forall SP_k \in CSP_i \tag{23}$$

We execute the three levels sequentially for a microservice and in parallel for the microservices.

5   Performance Assessment

In this section, we describe the scenarios configuration, the tool, the experiments, and the outcomes of PUM^2Q and UM^2Q, and we present an analysis of the results.

5.1   Tool Description

We developed a tool to evaluate the PUM^2Q and UM^2Q selection process. The tool was implemented using Python 3.7, and we used the JSON format as input and output. The tool has two JSON files as input: one contains the service providers capabilities and the other has the application requirements. Figure 5 shows a JSON example for application and provider. In Fig. 5a, we can observe the definition of the requirements 'values, the budget's quota and the microservice capabilities for an application. In Fig. 5b, we can notice the definition of classes, services and the capabilities of a microservice for a provider. Each provider capability is organized by service classes and each class has its services. We consider three classes: computing, storage, and database. Each service must contain its functional and non-functional capabilities. As described in Sect. 4, PUM^2Q considers availability, response time, and cost as nonfunctional capabilities.

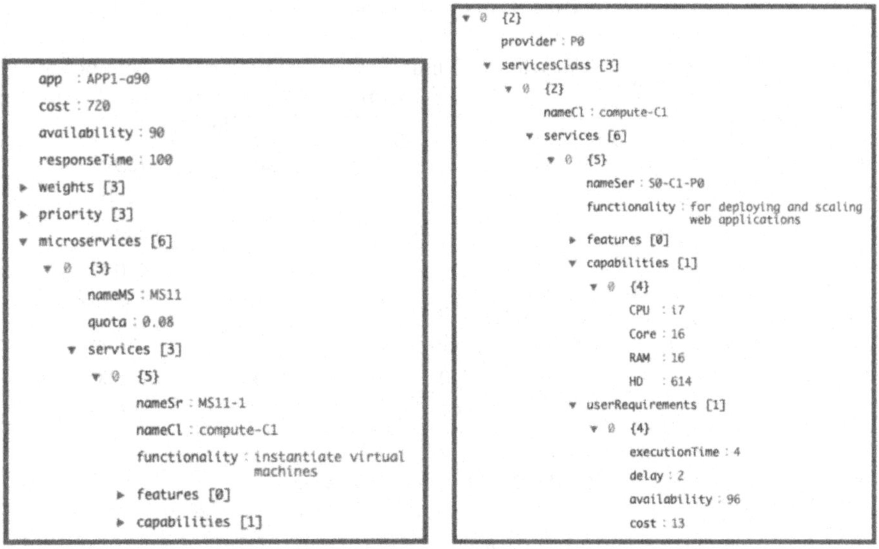

(a) Application.

(b) Provider.

Fig. 5. JSON examples.

Application information involves name, minimum availability, maximum response time, maximum budget, weight and priority of each user requirement, which are the same for each microservice. Besides, an application also contains microservice information, and there must be a description of the name and the total budget quota as in Eq. 10. The tool returns a JSON file, which contains the providers that will host the microservices as well as the services that will be used and each providers' cost.

5.2 Setting Scenarios

According to [8], there are few available datasets in the research domain. In this manner, in 50% of the works referenced by [8], the authors use a dataset configured randomly. So, we randomly configured eight sets of providers, and each provider has three services classes: compute, storage, and database. The first four provider sets differ from one another by the number of providers, and the last four ones by number of services per provider. We define these numbers of providers per set because we can demonstrate through them the flexibility of scenarios for the proposed solutions. Table 1 presents the number of sets, the amount of providers of each set, the number of services by class, the amount of services by providers and the number of services in each set.

Also, we configured the requirements for microservices-based applications. Each microservice contains one service of each class: compute, storage, and database. We set each application by microservice. Availability, response time,

Table 1. Set of providers.

Number of sets	Number of providers by sets	Number of services by class	Number of services by provider	Number of services by set
4	200	30	90	18000
	300			27000
	400			36000
	500			45000
4	200	20	60	12000
		30	90	18000
		40	120	24000
		50	150	30000

Table 2. Set of applications.

Applications	Carcterístics	
	Number of microservice	Number of services by application
App1	5	15
App2	6	18
App3	8	24
App4	10	30
App5	12	36
App6	14	42
App7	15	45
App8	16	48
App9	18	54
App10	20	60
App11	22	66
App12	25	75
App13	30	90
App14	35	105
App15	40	120
App16	45	135
App17	50	150

and cost requirements vary depending on the type of assessment that should be performed. Table 2 illustrates all applications used in the experiments. We define these applications to show the flexibility of PUM^2Q.

Each experiment was performed 30 times to reach the normal distribution [9]. We made the experiments on a Xenon processor Quad Core, 4 GB of RAM and a 256 GB SSD.

5.3   Experiments for PUM^2Q

We evaluated the performance of PUM^2Q using the tool described in Sect. 5.1. For this, we carried out seven experiments which vary the number of providers, number of services per provider, number of microservices per application, varying each requirement individually and then all they at the same time. Thus, we check for the possible variations that may influence the performance. For performing the experiments, we used the scenarios, according to Subsect. 5.2, which described 8 sets of providers and the requisites of 17 applications.

In all seven experiments, the y-axis represents the average selection time in seconds (s), the rows represent the applications, and the x-axis shows each experiment. The first and second experiments use the first and last four providers sets, respectively, described in Sect. 5.2, illustrated by Figs. 6a and 6b. Availability, response time, and cost requirements were not modified during the two experiments, maintaining the same value across all sets. Figures 6a and 6b show that increasing the number of providers and services respectively influence the average selection time. We can notice the increase in the number of services has more considerable influence than the increase in the number of provider.

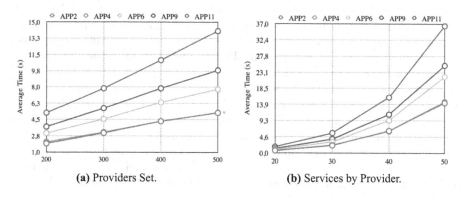

(a) Providers Set.   (b) Services by Provider.

Fig. 6. Experiments based on number of providers and services for PUM^2Q.

Observing the results of the first two experiments presented in Figs. 6a and 6b, we use the set of providers with 200 providers and 30 services per class of provider, with a total of 90 services per provider, for the other experiments because they represent intermediate values.

The third experiment illustrated in Fig. 7 has an objective observing the behaviour of the approach with the increase of the number of microservice and services by an application. We configure requirements of availability, response time, and cost with of intermediary values and use the set of providers with 200 providers, the first set of providers in Table 1. The results show that the average selection time is viable for 50 microservices or 150 services by the application using the intermediary values for the requirements.

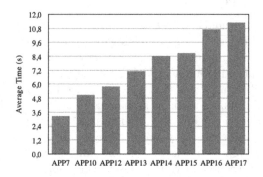

Fig. 7. The experiment based on microservice by application for PUM^2Q.

Figure 8 presents the other four experiments, which were performed using a set of two hundred providers, and each application was set to four different values. In Fig. 8a), the lowest one, 92%, indicates that all provider services must have this minimum value to meet application requirements, and the highest one, 98%, indicates that only cloud services with values between 98 and 100 meet this application requirement, which is in agreement with Eqs. 1 and 2. We set response time and cost requirements to values that can be met by most providers. The results show that the average time decreases with the increasing availability requirement value in each application.

Figure 8b shows the experiment in which we vary the response time's values. Thus, the lower the response time value, the fewer the cloud services that meet the requirement. We set availability and cost requirements to values that can be achieved by most providers. Figure 8b shows the selection time increases with the increase of the response time requirement in every application. We created budget classes for the experiment in Fig. 8c, in which each class has different budget values for each application, but all applications have the same value per service in each class. The results show that the average selection time increases as the budget class increases.

Figure 8d shows the experiment in which we vary the three requirements, in a manner that when the availability requirement increases, the cost and response time requirements decrease. We can notice that the average selection time decreases with the requirements restriction increase. This outcome shows that the requirements restriction increase reduces the number of providers that meet all requirements.

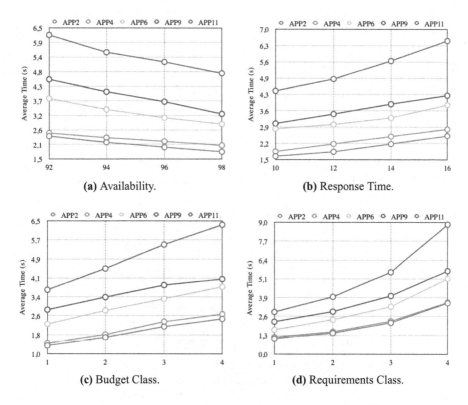

Fig. 8. Experiments based on requirements for PUM^2Q.

5.4 Experiments for UM^2Q

We performed the same PUM^2Q experiments with the UM^2Q to compare their response. We described the UM^2Q approach in [4], and the main difference between PUM^2Q and UM^2Q is that the former makes the selection in parallel and the latter in sequence. Thus, we carried out seven experiments and used the scenarios, according to the experiments for PUM^2Q.

We performed the seven experiments, the graphics shows in this paper represent the results, and their y-axis represents the average selection time in milliseconds (s), the rows represent the applications, and the x-axis shows each experiment. Figure 9a illustrates the experiment, which we vary the number of providers by set. We can observe that increasing the number of providers influences the average selection time. Figure 9b shows the experiment, in which we vary the number of services by the provider, and the average selection time increases with the growth in the number of services per provider. We can see in Figs. 9a and 9b, that the variation in the number of services has a more considerable influence than in the number of providers.

Figure 10 illustrates the experiment, which varies the number of microservice by application, and we configured the requirements of availability, response

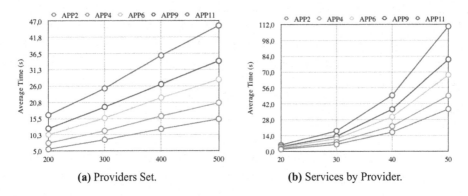

(a) Providers Set.   **(b)** Services by Provider.

Fig. 9. Experiments based on number of providers and services for UM^2Q.

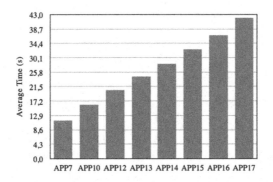

Fig. 10. The experiment based on microservice by application for UM^2Q.

time and cost with the intermediary values. We can observe that the number of microservices' influences the average selection time.

Figure 11 presents the other four experiments, which we performed using a set of 200 providers, and set each application to four different values. We can notice that in Fig. 11a, the values start with 92%, and end with 98%. We set response time and cost requirements to values that can be met by most providers. The results show that the average selection time decreases with the increasing availability requirement value in each application.

Figure 11b shows the experiment in which we vary the response time values. We set availability and cost requirements to values that can be achieved by most providers. We can observe in Fig. 11b that the selection time increases with the increase of the response time requirement in every application. In Fig. 11c, we created budget classes for the experiment; each class has different budget values for each application, and all applications have the same value per service. The results show that the average selection time increases as the budget class increases.

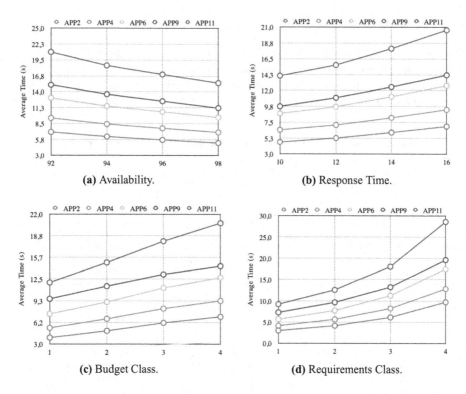

Fig. 11. Experiments based on requirements for UM^2Q.

In the last experiment, we vary the three requirements in a manner that when the availability requirement increases, the cost and response time requirements decrease, as illustrated by Fig. 11d. We can observe that the average selection time decreases with the requirements restriction increase.

5.5   Comparison Between PUM^2Q and UM^2Q

According to the experiments presented in Subsects. 5.3 and 5.4, we can notice that the applications have the same behaviour. The experiments differ in the aspect that the applications with fewer microservices in the PUM^2Q approach have a very close average selection time, while in UM^2Q the selection time between these applications is longer. The main difference is in the average selection time in all experiments in a comprehensive way. The PUM^2Q approach is 70% faster than the UM^2Q approach. The difference between them can be even more significant if performed on machines with a larger number of cores. Therefore, the PUM^2Q approach is more flexible than UM^2Q, as it allows for great scenarios, in which applications may have a higher number of microservices and services, as well as providers, may have a more substantial amount of classes and services per class.

6   Images/Related Work

Several works address the cloud selection problem, but each of them worries about different issues because there are several open ones. In Table 3, which contains seven columns, describe some research works that lead with the selection problem from the user perspective. The first column presents the work

Table 3. Summary of the related work characteristics based on [4].

Related work	Characteristics					
	PSG			Method	User-defined threshold	Goals
	(1)	(2)	(3)			
[6]	1	1	Service composition	Pareto set model, VOO	No	QoS dependency-aware service composition
[10]	1	1	Service composition	HPS	No	Cloud service composition
[13]	1	1	Service composition	SLO	Yes	Sequential service composition
[16]	1	1	Service composition	Hybrid GA	Yes	QoS-aware service composition
[12]	1	1	Service composition	PMMAS-CL	No	The service composition considering service correlation based on the library
[19]	1	1	Service composition	PDPSO	No	Cloud service selection
[7]	n	1	Service	CSRP	No	Ranking of top-k similar Service
[11]	n	1	Service	Grey Technique, TOPSIS, AHP	No	Ranking of Service
[18]	n	m	Resources	TOPSIS, AHP	No	Selection of cloud federation provider to execute a user requisition
[15]	n	m	Tasks	Defined by Authors	No	Independent task scheduling in cloud federation
[17]	n	m	Service	Defined by Authors	No	Selection and configuration of multi-cloud for microservices-based applications
[1]	n	m	Service	PROMETHEE	No	Selection QoS aware services for a service Composition
[14]	n	m	Service	FCA	no	Service composition in multi-cloud that focus on the communication cost
[20]	n	m	Service Composition	MPsaDABC	Yes	Large-scale service composition for cloud manufacturing
UM^2Q [4]	n	m	Microservices	SAW, Defined by Authors	Yes	Multi-cloud selection for an application microservices
PUM^2Q	n	m	Microservices	SAW, Defined by Authors	Yes	Multi-cloud parallel selection for an application microservices

PSG-Providers and Services Granularity, (1) Provider Granularity in the Selection Process, (2) Provider Granularity in the Selection Result, (3) Service Granularity per Provider reference, and the second, third, and fourth ones refer to a taxonomy to identify the work focus that deals with the cloud providers selection regarding the number of providers and services used by them in each phase, which we named providers and services granularity (PSG) and described in [4]. The second column shows the number of providers in the selection process, the third one shows the number of selected providers, the fourth one indicates the granularity per selected provider, the fifth one presents the methods used to solve the selection problem, the sixth one shows whether or not the user defines the requirements threshold, and in the last one presents the goals of the work. In Table 3, n indicates the number of providers in the selection process, which must be greater than 1, while m indicates the number of selected providers, and it must be greater than 1 and lower than or equal to n.

Note in Table 3 that the first four works use a single cloud provider and address the service composition problem. [6], in the first table line, studied dependency-aware service composition considering multiple QoS attributes to maximize the profit but they did not discover the services, while [10], in the second table line, proposed a strategy of cloud service composition evolution based on QoS, and the QoS values are calculated based on a four-structure model. [13] proposed an approach for QoS-aware cloud service composition that allows the user to define the QoS constraints and its preferences. Since microservices are composed of various services, we can consider them as a service composition. Therefore, PUM^2Q differs from the [13] because we address several service composition in parallel, one for each microservice, and we select a service composition among every service composition of all available providers to host a microservice. In the fourth table line, [16] also addresses QoS-aware cloud service, and this work differs both from the [13] and PUM^2Q because of the method used to solve the problem.

In 5 and 6's table lines works also use a single provider, but these works lead with the service composition in parallel. In [12], the authors propose a model to address the QoS correlation problem to optimize the service composition in cloud manufacturing. Besides, they offer an algorithm named Parallel Max-min Ant System based on the case library (PMMA-CL) to streamline the service composition, the algorithm uses ant colony that maintains the divergence of the population and then a learning strategy is adopted simultaneously to accelerate the convergence rate through particular ants based on dynamic database lists named library. [19] proposes an optimization algorithm for cloud service selection using parallel discrete particle swarm optimization (PDPSO), which uses the map/reduce mechanism to perform parallelization. The authors define each group of services as a particle, and each particle is a thread. They evaluated a fixed number of services as well as combinations. The proposed algorithm is efficient for a sequence of services, whereas PUM^2Q has at least one sequence for each microservice. Also, as PUM^2Q we deal with a multi-cloud environment, there are several candidate services as well as many candidate combinations.

We can observe in the seventh and eighth table lines, that the works of [7] and [11] address the service ranking. They differ from one another by the method used to rank the services. Besides, they differ from UM^2Q because they do not select various services in multiple providers. In the seventh and eighth table lines, [18] and [15] use cloud federation to execute a user requisition that cannot be executed for selected providers, which makes them only use multiple clouds when necessary.

In table line 11, [17] proposes an automated approach for the selection and configuration of cloud providers for multi-cloud microservices-based applications. The approach uses a domain specific language to describe the application's multi-cloud requirements and the authors provide a systematic method for obtaining proper configurations that comply with the application's requirements and the cloud providers' constraints. In table line 12, [1] proposes an algorithm to select a cloud with more number of service files and then we applied PROMETHEE, a multi criteria decision making method that selects the best service based on QoS criteria from optimal cloud combinations. In table line 13, [14] proposes a multi-cloud service composition (MCSC) approach based on Formal Concept Analysis (FCA). The authors use FCA to represent and combine information on multiple clouds. FCA is based on the concept of lattice, which is a powerful mean to classify clouds and services information. The authors first model the multi-cloud environment as a set of formal contexts. Next, they extract and combine candidate clouds from formal concepts. Finally, they select the optimal cloud combination and transform the MCSC into a classical service composition problem. [1,17], and [14] use multiple clouds in both the selection and execution processes as PUM^2Q, but they select services over various clouds while PUM^2Q selects microservices. In addition, these works do not allow the user to define the requirements thresholds. Further, PUM^2Q is more complex and more flexible, and it has a low communication cost because the microservices are independent.

Lastly, in table line 14, [20] propose a multi-population parallel self-adaptive differential artificial bee colony (MPsaDABC) algorithm for composite cloud manufacturing (CMfg) optimal service selection (CCSOS). The proposed algorithm adopts multiple parallel subpopulations, each of which evolves according to different mutation strategies borrowed from the differential evolution (DE) to generate perturbed food sources for foraging bees, and the control parameters of each mutation strategy are adapted independently. Moreover, the size of each subpopulation is dynamically adjusted based on the information derived from the search process. The algorithm proposed focuses on selecting one candidate service from each corresponding candidate service set to form the composite service while ensuring the overall QoS is optimal, whereas PUM^2Q deals with discovery candidate service to service composition. To validate the algorithm MPsaDABC, the authors use candidate service set scales, whereas in PUM^2Q we made the discovery services then took the candidate services. The number of candidate services in PUM^2Q vary according to the number of providers and services per providers.

7   Conclusion

The use of multi-cloud is interesting for both the academy and the industry, since it can help take the advantages offered by cloud computing by using the most suitable services for an application. The services selection is a complex task, because the providers offer many services with the same functionalities and different capabilities.

To facilitate the decision making by a software architect, PacificClouds intends to manage the deploying and executing process a microservice-based application in multi-cloud environments. One of the first steps for PacificClouds is to select providers and their services to host an application microservices. Thus, in this work, we propose PUM^2Q, which extends UM^2Q [4]. The PUM^2Q approach selects providers to host the application's microservices in parallel. The outcomes show that the requirements, the number of microservices and the number of providers and services per provider influence the average selection time. The results also indicate that PUM^2Q is more flexible than UM^2Q because it allows for substantially larger scenarios.

The PUM^2Q has the same limitation of the UM^2Q, which is the difficulty of the software architect to determine a budget quota for each application microservice. Besides, as future work, we intend to implement a recommendation system to suggest better settings than those requested by the user, which would be available with a little more investment.

References

1. Bhushan, S.B., Reddy, C.H.P.: A QoS aware cloud service composition algorithm for geo-distributed multi cloud domain. Int. J. Intell. Eng. Syst. **9**(4), 147–156 (2016). https://doi.org/10.22266/ijies2016.1231.16
2. Carvalho, J., Vieira, D., Trinta, F.: Dynamic selecting approach for multi-cloud providers. In: Luo, M., Zhang, L.-J. (eds.) CLOUD 2018. LNCS, vol. 10967, pp. 37–51. Springer, Cham (2018). https://doi.org/10.1007/978-3-319-94295-7_3
3. Carvalho, J., Vieira, D., Trinta, F.: Greedy multi-cloud selection approach to deploy an application based on microservices. In: PDP 2019 (2019). https://doi.org/10.1109/PDP.2019.00021
4. Carvalho, J., Vieira, D., Trinta, F.: UM2Q: multi-cloud selection model based on multi-criteria to deploy a distributed microservice-based application, pp. 56–68 (2020). https://doi.org/10.5220/0009338200560068
5. de Carvalho, J.O., Trinta, F., Vieira, D.: PacificClouds: a flexible MicroServices based architecture for interoperability in multi-cloud environments. In: CLOSER 2018 (2018)
6. Chen, Y., Huang, J., Lin, C., Shen, X.: Multi-objective service composition with QoS dependencies. IEEE Trans. Cloud Comput. **7**(2), 537–552 (2016). https://doi.org/10.1109/TCC.2016.2607750. http://ieeexplore.ieee.org/document/7563862/
7. Ding, S., Wang, Z., Wu, D., Olson, D.L.: Utilizing customer satisfaction in ranking prediction for personalized cloud service selection. Decis. Support Syst. **93**, 1–10 (2017). https://doi.org/10.1016/j.dss.2016.09.001

8. Hayyolalam, V., Kazem, A.A.P.: A systematic literature review on QoS-aware service composition and selection in cloud environment. J. Netw. Comput. Appl. **110**, 52–74 (2018). https://doi.org/10.1016/j.jnca.2018.03.003

9. Fischer, H.: A History of the Central Limit Theorem: From Classical to Modern Probability Theory. Sources and Studies in the History of Mathematics and Physical Sciences. Springer, New York (2011). https://doi.org/10.1007/978-0-387-87857-7

10. Hongzhen, X., Limin, L., Dehua, X., Yanqin, L.: Evolution of service composition based on QoS under the cloud computing environment. In: Proceedings of ICOACS 2016, pp. 66–69 (2016)

11. Jatoth, C., Gangadharan, G.R., Fiore, U., Buyya, R.: SELCLOUD: a hybrid multicriteria decision-making model for selection of cloud services. Soft. Comput. **23**(13), 4701–4715 (2018). https://doi.org/10.1007/s00500-018-3120-2

12. Jian, L., Youling, C., Long, W., Lidan, Z., Yufei, N.: An approach for service composition optimisation considering service correlation via a parallel max-min ant system based on the case library. Int. J. Comput. Integr. Manuf. **31**(12), 1174–1188 (2018). https://doi.org/10.1080/0951192X.2018.1529435

13. Liu, Z.Z., Chu, D.H., Song, C., Xue, X., Lu, B.Y.: Social learning optimization (SLO) algorithm paradigm and its application in QoS-aware cloud service composition. Inf. Sci. **326**, 315–333 (2016). https://doi.org/10.1016/j.ins.2015.08.004

14. Mezni, H., Sellami, M.: Multi-cloud service composition using formal concept analysis. J. Syst. Softw. **134**, 138–152 (2017). https://doi.org/10.1016/j.jss.2017.08.016

15. Panda, S.K., Pande, S.K., Das, S.: Task partitioning scheduling algorithms for heterogeneous multi-cloud environment. Arab. J. Sci. Eng. **43**(2), 913–933 (2017). https://doi.org/10.1007/s13369-017-2798-2

16. Seghir, F., Khababa, A.: A hybrid approach using genetic and fruit fly optimization algorithms for QoS-aware cloud service composition. J. Intell. Manuf. **29**(8), 1773–1792 (2016). https://doi.org/10.1007/s10845-016-1215-0

17. Sousa, G., Rudametkin, W., Duchien, L.: Automated setup of multi-cloud environments for microservices-based applications. In: 9th IEEE International Conference on Cloud Computing (2016). https://doi.org/10.1109/CLOUD.2016.49

18. Thomas, M.V., Chandrasekaran, K.: Dynamic partner selection in Cloud Federation for ensuring the quality of service for cloud consumers. Int. J. Model. Simul. Sci. Comput. **08**(03), 1750036 (2017). https://doi.org/10.1142/S1793962317500362. http://www.worldscientific.com/doi/abs/10.1142/S1793962317500362

19. Yimin, Z., Guojun, S., Xiaoguang, Y.: Cloud service selection optimization method based on parallel discrete particle swarm optimization. In: Proceedings of the 30th Chinese Control and Decision Conference, CCDC 2018, pp. 2103–2107 (2018). https://doi.org/10.1109/CCDC.2018.8407473

20. Zhou, J., Yao, X.: Multi-population parallel self-adaptive differential artificial bee colony algorithm with application in large-scale service composition for cloud manufacturing. Appl. Soft Comput. J. **56**, 379–397 (2017). https://doi.org/10.1016/j.asoc.2017.03.017

Live Migration Timing Optimization Integration with VMware Environments

Mohamed Esam Elsaid[1]([✉])(iD), Mohamed Sameh[2](iD), Hazem M. Abbas[2](iD), and Christoph Meinel[1](iD)

[1] Internet Technologien und Systeme, Hasso-Plattner Institut, Potsdam University, Potsdam, Germany
{Mohamed.Elsaid,Meinel}@HPI.de
[2] Department of Computer and Systems Engineering, Ain Shams University, Cairo, Egypt
mohamedsamehkhalil@gmail.com, Hazem.Abbas@eng.asu.edu.eg

Abstract. Live migration is an essential feature in virtual infrastructure and cloud computing datacenters. Using live migration, virtual machines can be online migrated from a physical machine to another with negligible service interruption. Load balance, power saving, dynamic resource allocation, and high availability algorithms in virtual data-centers and cloud computing environments are dependent on live migration. Live migration process has six phases that result in live migration overhead. Currently, virtual datacenters admins run live migrations without an idea about the migration cost prediction and without recommendations about the optimal timing for initiating a VM live migration especially for large memory VMs or for concurrently multiple VMs migration. Without cost prediction and timing optimization, live migration might face longer duration, network bottlenecks and migration failure in some cases. The previously proposed timing optimization approach is based on using machine learning for live migration cost prediction and the network utilization predict ion of the cluster. In this paper, we show how to integrate our machine learning based timing optimization algorithm with VMware vSphere. This integration deployment proves the practicality of the proposed algorithm by presenting the building blocks of the tools and backend scripts that should run to implement this timing optimization feature. The paper shows also how the IT admins can make use of this novel cost prediction and timing optimization option as an integrated plug-in within VMware vSphere UI to be notified with the optimal timing recommendation in case of a having live migration request.

Keywords: Cloud computing · Virtual · Live migration · Timing · VMware · vMotion · Modeling · Overhead · Cost · Datacenter · Prediction · Machine learning

1 Introduction

Datacenter resource virtualization is commonly used by IT administrators during the last decade. Running virtual or software defined machines has shown

© Springer Nature Switzerland AG 2021
D. Ferguson et al. (Eds.): CLOSER 2020, CCIS 1399, pp. 133–152, 2021.
https://doi.org/10.1007/978-3-030-72369-9_6

higher availability, rapid scaling, better resource utilization and more cost efficiency. Live migration of virtual machines is a key feature in virtual environments and cloud computing datacenters. Using live migration, virtual machines can be moved from a physical host to another while the applications are running online. This is because live migration causes negligible service interruption during the migration process. Servers load balance, power saving, fault tolerance and dynamic virtual machines allocation are all dependent on live migration. During the live migration process, the VM CPU cache, memory pages and IO buffers contents are migrated. However the storage content is shared between the source and the target servers, so storage content is not migrated. Live migration traffic is sent over the TCP/IP network that interconnects the virtualized cluster. During the live migration process, the memory, the CPU cache and system buffers content. However the memory content is the major content to be migrated.

Virtualized clusters load balance, power saving, dynamic resource management and fault tolerance depend on live migration feature.

- For load balance, live migration is used to update the allocation mapping between the VMs and the physical machines from time to time. This update is based on the physical machines utilization to keep all the cluster physical servers utilization balanced by avoiding system bottlenecks.
- In power saving, live migration is used to concatenate the VMs within less number of physical machines during the low utilization hours and so to minimize the number of active physical servers and switching the other idle servers into sleep mode.
- Fault tolerance also relies on live migration between two physical servers at least with keeping two copies of the VM; one at the source host and another copy at the target host. So in case of failure in the primary VM at the primary host, the secondary VM on the secondary host will takeover and act as a new primary VM.

Live migration has three different types; Pre-copy, Post-copy and Hybrid-copy [16]. As discussed in [16], Pre-copy Live migration is the commonly used type due to its robustness against VMs crash during the migration. So, Pre-copy migration is used by almost all hypervisors in the market; VMware ESXi, Microsoft Hyper-V, Xen and KVM.

As discussed before, VMs live migration is an essential feature in cloud computing and virtual datacenter environments, however live migration cost can not be ignored. The cost includes migration time, down time, network, CPU and power consumption overhead. The definition and the root cause of each cost parameter are as following:

1. *Migration Time*: Migration time is the period between the VM migration request initialization and having the VM activated at the destination server. This time can take from seconds to minutes depending on the VM memory content size, the network transmission rate during the migration and the dirty pages rate.

2. *Down Time*: This is the time consumed in the stop and copy phase, when the VM stopping condition applies and the last iteration of the migration copy should start and then the VM networking being attached to the target server and until being activated. Down time should typically be in the range of milli-seconds and so the applications and the users do not feel interruption, however in some cases it takes several seconds [17].

3. *Network Throughput Overhead*: Network average rate is the average throughput at which data was transmitted from the physical host NIC card during the migration time interval. This represents the consumed bandwidth of the network in Bps for live migration process. Live migration process is managed by the cluster manager server which uses the Transmission Control Protocol/Internet Protocol (TCP/IP) in the networks layers 3 and 4 for the live migration management and the iterative copies of memory pages.

4. *Power Consumption Overhead*: Live migration process consumes CPU cycles from the source and the target servers [27]. This overhead parameter should not be ignored especially when live migration is used for data-centers power saving algorithms. Live migration transmission rate is the dominant parameter that controls the power consumption during the migration process [30].

5. *CPU Overhead*: VMs live migration consumes also from the source and target servers CPU resources due to handling the iterative copy phase; as a CPU intensive phase of the migration[34]. Meanwhile, the more available CPU resources, the less migration time in case of having available network bandwidth.

Live migration cost is covered by different researchers, we list many of them in Table 1 and classify the articles based on research focus if it is cost prediction or just analysis, the validated hypervisors and the cost parameters that are considered.

We proposed empirical modeling techniques in [14] for VMs live migration in VMware environments to characterize live migration time, network rate and power consumption overhead. The proposed modeling is based on applying the regression techniques on the obtained test results to present a linear or non-linear regression based models for these migration cost parameters. In Reference [19], an analysis of live migration time and downtime is provided and then a comparison between Xen, KVM, Hyper-V and VMware vSphere hypervisors is presented in terms of storage migration and live migration time and downtime. A comparison between Xen and VMware live migration time and downtime is also presented in [28] with more investigation on the parameters that control the live migration time and downtime duration. The authors [9] show the impact of a VM live migration on the running applications performance from client side. The performance degradation of the application from client side was measured in operations per second. The impact of live migration on Internet Web 2.0 applications performance is discussed in [33]. This is important for environments with SLA requirements. For this purpose, a test-bed is built in [33] where the running Web 2.0 workload is Olio application, combined with Faban load

Table 1. Summary of related work.

Paper	Research scope	Mig. time	Down time	CPU	Network	Power	Testing env.
[14]	Regression Modeling	X	–	–	X	X	VMware
[19]	Perf. Comparison	X	X	–	–	–	All
[28]	Analysis and Comparison	X	X	–	–	–	Xen VMware
[33]	Perf. Evaluation	X	X	–	–	–	Xen
[22]	Analysis on Apps Perf.	X	X	–	–	–	Xen
[12]	Multi-VMs Scheduling	X	–	–	–	–	VMware
[25]	Analytical & Regression based Modeling	X	X	–	X	X	Xen
[24]	Analysis and Model Checker	X	–	–	–	–	Xen
[10]	Analytical Modeling	X	X	–	–	–	All
[13]	Cost Analysis	X	–	–	–	X	KVM
[31]	Cost Prediction	X	X	–	–	X	Xen
[32]	Cost Prediction	X	–	–	–	X	KVM
[6]	Cost Prediction	–	–	X	X	X	KVM
[35]	Prediction	X	–	–	–	–	VMware but not vMotion
[8]	Prediction	–	–	X	X	X	Oracle Virtual Box
[23]	Prediction	X	X	X	X	–	All
[5]	Prediction	X	X	–	–	–	Xen
[29]	Prediction	X	X	–	–	–	VMware/ Xen/ KVM
[21]	Prediction	X	–	X	–	–	Xen
[18]	Markov Model Prediction	–	–	X	–	–	CloudSim
[26]	Prediction	X	–	–	–	–	Xen
[15]	ML based Prediction	X	–	–	X	X	VMware
[11]	Analytical Modeling	X	X	–	X	–	All
[20]	Cost modeling	–	–	–	–	X	Xen

generator that access the Apache 2.2.8 Web server with MySQL database. In [12] the authors propose a scheduling weighted based approach for Multi-VMs live migration requests in VMware. The objective of the proposed technique is to minimize the total migration time for Multi-VMs. The weight assigned to each request is based on the memory usage and the network bandwidth and the article shows the impact of scheduling the migration requests using this weight on the total migration time of the VMs. Article [25] studies the impact of virtualization technology and live migration on multi-tier workloads as well as the migration performance. Experimental tests show that virtualization technology does not have significant overhead on Multi-Tier applications, however live migration causes performance decrease due to the migration cost and down time. This performance degradation is more significant with memory intensive multi-tier workloads.

The authors in [7] use Probabilistic Model Checking (PMC) and Markov Decision Process (MDP) to study the impact of VM size, page size, dirty pages rate, network rate and pre-copy iterations threshold on the live migration time and down time. The proposed approach uses numerical analysis and the results should be valid for any pre-copy based live migration. In [24], the authors build a performance model for live migration using several migration tests in a Xen hypervisor based test bed and then use Probabilistic Symbolic Model Checker (PRISM) for modelling verification. The proposed approach is used to model live migration time for single and multiple concurrent VMs migration. In [10], analytical modeling is also used to formalize live migration time and down time for single and multiple VMs. Then a Markov model is build for inter-DC network to study the impact of network bandwidth, number of migration requests rate and the number of interconnected DCs on the blocking probability for migration requests.

In [13], the author studies the relationship between live migration cost parameters; namely the migration time, the network bandwidth, the power consumption and their correlation with the size of the VM memory. Testing results show that the migration time exponentially decreases as the network rate increases. The average power usage of the source as well as the destination server linearly increases as the network rate increases. The migration time and the energy consumption linearly increase as the size (memory content) of the virtual machine increases. The models presented in this paper are experimental models that are obtained using KVM Hypervisor based test-bed.

In [15], we proposed a machine learning based cost prediction technique for live migration in VMware environments and in [16], we have proposed a novel timing optimization algorithm for VMs live migration that is based on [15] and on using datacenter network utilization prediction technique [16]. In this paper. we integrate the algorithm proposed in [16] as a plug-in with VMware vSphere UI that helps the IT admins for VMware clusters to predict live migration cost and to get a recommendation for the optimal timing to run live migration for the specified VM. For integration with VMware vSphere, JAVA, HTML, VMware PowerCLI and Python tools are used.

The rest of this paper is organized as following; in Sect. 2 we discuss the background on networking in VMware clusters and the research challenge to predict the optimal time for live migration. In Sect. 3, we present the timing optimization algorithm proposed in [16] to be integrated with VMware vSphere. In Sect. 4, we show the contribution of this paper which is the integration details of the timing optimization algorithm with VMware. This integration helps the IT admins to use the timing optimization feature for VMware environment as an example of a commonly used platform for virtual datacenter and cloud environments management portals. The integration results will be presented in Sect. 5 and then we conclude the paper in Sect. 6.

2   Background

As proposed in [16], live migration timing optimization depends on two main techniques; the first one is the cost prediction for live migration of the VMs [15], and the second approach is the datacenter network utilization prediction [16]. In this section, we present in depth the technical details of live migration configurations and virtual networking in VMware as a required background to show how live migration can impact the LAN or WAN scale networks throughput.

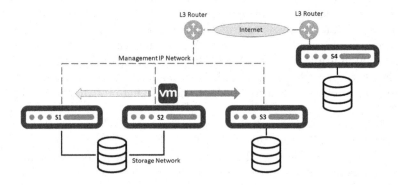

Fig. 1. Live migration configurations.

2.1   Live Migration Configurations

Live migration can be used also by different configurations; as shown in Fig. 1 that show the flexibility to live migrate a VM in LAN or WAN scale, with or without a share storage.

– The first scenario is to migrate the VM compute resources to another physical host without the VM storage virtual disk migration. This can be applied only under the condition of having a shared storage environment between the source and the target servers. In this case, mainly the memory content is migrated. For example the VM in Fig. 1 can be migrated with this scenario only between S1 and S2 hosts through the management IP network of the cluster.

- The second scenario is to migrate the compute and storage resources of the VM from a source to a target host through the management IP network of the cluster. In this case the memory and the virtual disk storage content should be migrated. So the VM in Fig. 1 can be migrated from S1 or S2 to S3 host or vice versa.
- The third scenario is to migrate the compute and storage resources of the VM from the source to the target host through the WAN or the Internet network. This scenario is mainly useful for datacenter migrations or disaster recovery solutions between datacenters in different locations. So to migrate the VM in Fig. 1 from S1, S2 or S3 to S4
- The fourth scenario of live migration is to have multiple VMs migration simultaneously. The number of simultaneous VMs to be migrated has a maximum limit. This limit is defined by the source host of the migration that is responsible for resources allocation and migration success verification process. Referring to Fig. 1, in multiple simultaneous VMs migration, there can be many VMs in different hosts that can be migrated from any of the hosts to another.

2.2   VMware Virtual Networking Configuration

Virtual networking in VMware is structured such that, each VM has one or more virtual Network Interface Cards (vNICs). Each vNIC at least one virtual port (vPort) and each vPort is assigned to a vSwitch. There are two types of vSwitch; a local switch inside the physical host only and a virtual Distributed Switch (vDS). The local vSwitch connects the VMs within this host, however the vDS connects between the VMs within this cluster. Each vSwitch has one or more uplink port which forwards and receives the traffic to and from a physical switch port.

Figure 2 shows an example of two physical hosts that are interconnected to a shared storage through a FC-SAN network and connected to the an IP network through an Ethernet switch. The solid lines show the physical connections and the dotted lines show the virtual connections for the virtual distributed switch. As shown in Fig. 2 a storage array is shared between the cluster servers using FC-SAN network; which is a common configuration in datacenters. Live migration utilizes the TCP/IP protocol and so it uses the IP network. From best practice point of view, each VM should have at least 2 NICs and each physical host should have at least 2 physical NICs [2]. A virtual distributed switch connects between the VMs in the cluster are connected. Using port groups, the IO traffic of the VMs can be isolated. There are two types of port groups in VMware; VM network distributed port group and VMkernel distributed port group. VM network port group manages the production traffic of the applications. VMkernel port group manages the special classes of traffic such as management, vMotion, NFS, Fault tolerance, iSCSI, replication traffic and VMware vSAN as a Software Defined Storage (SDS) traffic [3].

Physical machines NICs ports are represented to the distributed switch as uplink ports; which is responsible for the in-going and the out-going traffic into and from the distributed switch. Each port group should have at least one uplink port from each physical host. An uplink port can be shared between one or more port groups. For vMotion traffic, it is recommended to create a separate VMkernel port group across the VMs in the cluster. This vMotion port group must have one or more uplink ports from each physical host [2]. This uplink port function is not only for vMotion port group, but can be also for other VMkernel port group. From physical port point of view, vMotion traffic is physically isolated on the server port level abort from the applications traffic. However, it depends on the back-end networking topology, as vMotion and workload traffic might share and compete on the back-end network bandwidth.

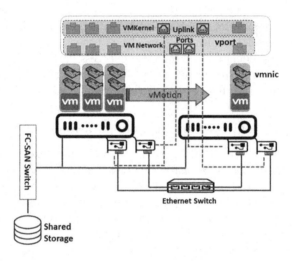

Fig. 2. Network topology for VMware vMotion [16].

3   Cost Prediction Algorithm and Timing Optimization

3.1   The Research Problem

For the best of our knowledge, the IT admins are currently running the live migrations of the VMs without an estimation about the migration cost and with no idea if the migration start time that they use is actually the optimal time or not. Missing this information might lead to resources bottlenecks, more migration cost and migration failures. So, the problem that we solve in this paper is how to help the IT admins to know the optimal timing for a VM live migration and to have a prediction about this migration cost.

In order to resolve this research problem, we have proposed the machine learning based cost prediction approach in [15] and the live migration timing optimization algorithm in [16].

In this paper, we extend on the previously achieved work and show how to integrate these algorithms with VMware vSphere UI as an added plug-in that can be optionally used before a live migration request. This is to prove that the cost prediction and the timing optimizing techniques proposed in [15] and [16] can be practically implemented and used by VMware clusters' admins.

3.2   Cost Prediction Algorithm

From these papers, the following empirical models could be proposed for live migration time, data rate and power consumption after applying the regression techniques:

- The relation between the network rate and the active memory size can be modelled as an exponential relation; as shown in Eq. (1).

$$R_s = \alpha e^{V_{Mem}} + \beta \tag{1}$$

R_s: is the source host network overhead in kBps.
V_{mem}: is the active memory size in kB of the source host when the live migration should start.
α and β: are the equation constants. From Eq. (1).
- Migration Time: A linear relationship is obtained between the migration time and the division of the memory size over the transmission rate; as represented in Eq. (2).

$$T_{mig} = a.(\frac{V_{mem}}{R_s}) + b \tag{2}$$

T_{mig} is the duration of the migration time in seconds.
a and b are the equation constants.
- Peak power consumption overhead has linear relation with the transmission rate; as represented in Eq. (3).

$$P_{mig} = \frac{dE_{mig}}{dt} = c\,\frac{dV_{mig}}{dt} = c\,R_s \tag{3}$$

P_{mig} is the peak power overhead in Watt, and c is constant. From Eq. (3).

In our previous papers, the above models could be used for cost analysis but not for cost prediction. This is because of the equations constants. These constants depend on the cluster hardware configuration like CPU specs, so they change from a cluster environment to another. So in order to determine these constants and achieve higher accuracy in cost prediction, we propose a machine learning framework to predict the live migration cost. the above models could be used for cost analysis but not for cost prediction. This is because of the equations constants. These constants depend on the cluster hardware configuration like CPU specs, so they change from a cluster environment to another. So in order to determine these constants and achieve higher accuracy in cost prediction, we propose a machine learning framework to predict the live migration cost.

The cost prediction algorithm is as proposed in Fig. 3. The training phase starts when the VMware PowerCLI script connects to the cluster vCenter Server

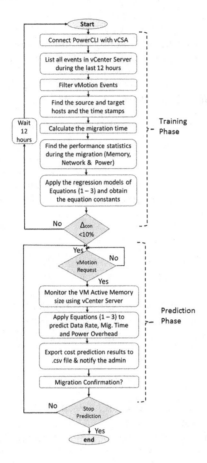

Fig. 3. Live migration cost prediction framework [15].

Appliance (vCSA). Then data collection starts with listing all the events happened in the cluster during the last 12 h. This 12 h cycle can be changed based on the cluster admin preference. From the collected events, vMotion events are filtered out. These vMotion events details like the source host, target host and time stamp are captured. Then the script calculates the complete and start time differences in order to get the migration time of each vMotion request. The performance logs of vCSA are collected at the start and the completion times at the vMotion events in order to get the active memory size of the migrated VMs in kB, the network overhead in kBps and the peak power change in Watt.

From the above data of each vMotion event, we use the regression models in Eqs. (1–3) to calculate the equations constants after doing several substitution and considering the minimum Root Mean Square Error (RMSE); Eq. (4).

$$RMSE = \sqrt{\frac{1}{N}\Sigma_{i=1}^{N}(d_i - f_i)^2} \qquad (4)$$

where N is the number of sample points collected during the last 12 h. d_i is the measured performance value and f_i is the regression equation value.

If the change in all the constants value became greater than 10% of the last 12 h cycle, the script waits for more 12 h and run again to continue in the training phase. If these changes became less than 10% of the last 12 h, so we consider the training phase of this cluster is finished, and the script then moves to the prediction phase. The time consumed until reaching this 10% convergence depends on the changes that happen in the VMs active memory size; which depends on the running workload. This sequence of data collection and models training makes the algorithm can fit at any vCenter Server cluster and adapt its models based on the cluster configuration in order to provide cost prediction.

In the prediction phase when a vMotion request is sent by the cluster admin, the active memory size is captured by the script before proceeding with live migration. Once the active memory size is known, Eq. (1) is used to predict the source host network throughput. Then Eq. (2) is used to predict the migration time, and finally Eq. (3) is used to predict the peak power consumption. The prediction data is exported to a .csv file that the cluster admin can read, and decide to proceed with this migration or not.

3.3   Timing Optimization Algorithm

In [16], we proposed a live migration timing optimization technique that is presented in Fig. 4 flowchart. The algorithm starts with establishing the connection with VMware vCenter Server Appliance (vCSA) [4] using PowerCLI client [1]. The developed PowerCLI script runs on the VMware cluster that is management by this vCSA. The next step is to train the live migration cost model based on the past 12 h events; as discussed in Fig. 3. Network traffic utilization prediction model uses the Hidden Markov Model algorithm proposed in [36] such that every 30 s a sample is captured of the VMware VMkernel network traffic history of the past day. These 2880 points are used as the dataset training. By finishing this step, the training phase should be finished and the algorithm is ready to predict.

In the prediction phase, When a vMotion request is issued for a specific VM or for Multi-VMs migration, the migration traffic rate and migration time are predicted by calling the machine learning technique proposed in Fig. 3. In this step, the migration time and network rate are estimated. Then the cluster network utilization prediction; proposed in [36] is used to estimate the network traffic volume of the VMkernel network for every 30 s during the next 1 h. By finishing this step, the prediction phase of the network traffic volume, the live migration time and the migration transmission rate is finished and timing optimization check should start.

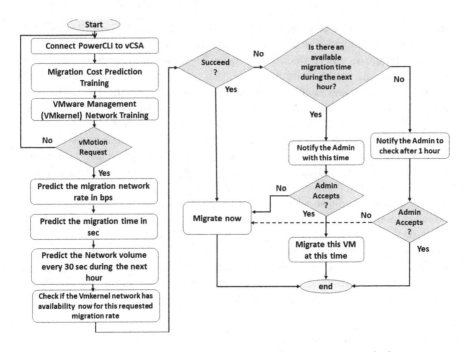

Fig. 4. Timing optimization approach for VM migration [16].

For optimal migration timing, the algorithm checks if the current time; when the vMotion request is received is a good time for initiating the vMotion process. For this check, the script runs Eq. (3) that estimates the network utilization during the estimated migration time interval.

$$R_{busy} = \frac{\sum_{n=0}^{N_{mig}} V_n}{T_{mig}}$$

$$R_{Avail.} = BW - R_{busy} \tag{5}$$

R_{busy} is the network traffic volume in bps that will be utilized by other VMkernel network traffic such as vSAN, management,..etc.

n is the 30 s based sample number in integer.

N_{mig} is the last sample that ends with the estimated migration time.

V_n is the traffic volume prediction in bytes for each sample.

$R_{Avail.}$ is the available throughput in bps for vMotion traffic.

BW is the VMkernel network bandwidth in bps.

The success check point in the flow chart verifies basically checks the below condition in Eq. (4)

$$R_{Avail.} > R_s * (1 + P_{Acc.}) \tag{6}$$

Where $P_{Acc.}$ is the prediction accuracy for the live migration network throughput. So Eq. (4) checks if the available network rate for VMkernel network $R_{Avail.}$ can meet the estimated migration transmission rate requirement with considering the prediction accuracy that is mentioned in [15]. if this check-point result is (Yes), live migration will start immediately. If the result is (No), the algorithm starts a new phase which is finding the optimal time for the VMs migration process initiation. In the case of (No), the algorithm checks for the optimal timing during the next hour from network availability stand point. So with 30 s interval, Eq. (4) is applied for the next hour prediction samples. If another optimal time is found, the network admin will be notified. If the admin accepts, the VMs migration will be postponed to the new time automatically. If the admin rejects the proposed new time recommendation, the migration will be start immediately. In case of not finding a better time during the next hour, the admin will be notified as well to request the migration again after 1 h. If the admins accepts, the algorithm stops. If the admin rejects that, the migration starts momentarily.

Figure 5 shows an example for a live migration process with and without timing optimization. As shown, the migration time can be minimized by using the timing optimization technique due to the higher transmission rate.

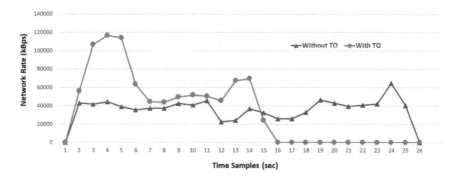

Fig. 5. Migration time decrease and rate increase due to optimal timing of live migration [16].

4 Integration with VMware vSphere

In this section, we present how the timing optimization algorithm proposed in [16] could be integrated with VMware User Interface (UI) using the testing lab discussed in Sect. 6. The integration with VMware UI as an extension work on [16] shows that the proposed timing optimization feature can be practically implemented and used by the IT admins.

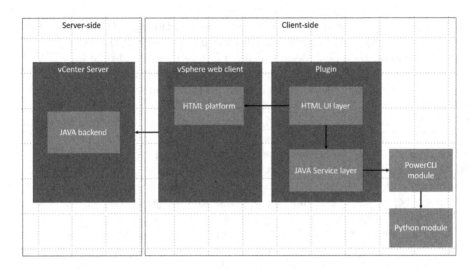

Fig. 6. Integration with VMware plug-in components structure.

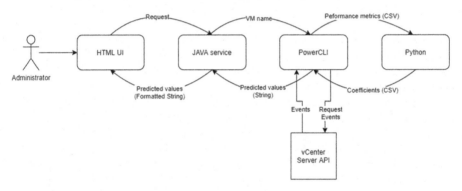

Fig. 7. Integration with VMware plugin data-flow.

VMware provides a software development kit for building plugins for the VMware vSphere client. The structure of the plugin is shown in Fig. 6 and it consists of the following components:

– HTML UI layer: this layer handles the way the plugin looks in the Web client. It allows adding menu options and navigation items.
– JAVA service layer: this layer is based on the Spring MVC and the OSGI framework, it represents the backend of the plugin. This layer communicates with the PowerCLI and Python modules to perform the coefficients calculation and provide the estimation.

- PowerCLI module: This component handles the live data collection through the PowerShell PowerCLI APIs. It collects data about the migrations that occurred in the last 12 h. The collected data is then processed by the Python module and returned to the JAVA service layer.
- Python module: This component processes the data using the Algorithm described by this paper and outputs the value for the coefficients α, β, a, b, and c to predict the expected duration for the migration, the expected power consumption, and the expected network usage.

Based on the integration of the above platforms and tools with VMware and the algorithms charts in Fig. 3 and Fig. 4, the steps we have used to integrate the proposed timing optimization algorithm with VMware vSphere are:

1. A shown in Fig. 7 The user interacts with the vSphere client UI, which contains the HTML layer added for the plugin, and requests the predicted migration overhead for a VM. This step is possible because the vSphere client software development kit allows developers to alter the user interface of the vSphere client to add new custom features.
2. The JAVA service layer receives the request from the UI layer and then forwards the request to the PowerCLI module.
3. The PowerCLI module gathers all the events run in the vCenter Server during the last 12 h and filter the vMotion events. The script identifies the source and target hosts of each vMotion event and the start and end time stamp of each migration. Based on that, the performance statistics of each migration is collected and passed to the next step in CSV format.
4. The Python module then takes in the collected data set and for each pair of data items it calculates the coefficients. Once the script finds Two successive coefficients with less than 10% difference in value it stops the search and returns this value in a CSV format to the PowerCLI module.
5. The equations from (1), (2), (3) are then used to predict the duration, power consumption, and required network bandwidth of the migration.
6. These results are returned to the JAVA service layer as a string of characters and then returned to The HTML UI layer after formatting the string and shown to the user as in Fig. 8.

In the next section, we show the result of using these scripting tools and following the above steps to integrate the cost prediction and timing optimization algorithms with VMware vSphere UI.

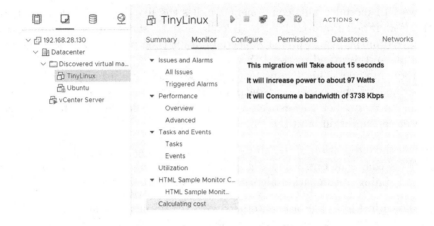

Fig. 8. Added icon: cost prediction plug-in.

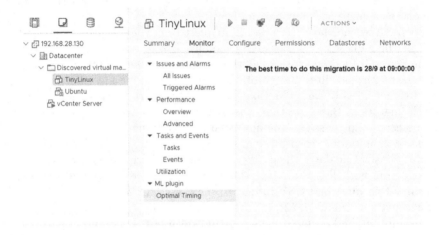

Fig. 9. Added icon: optimal timing plug-in.

5   Testing Results

The result of the integration with VMware vSphere UI is as shown in Fig. 8 and Fig. 9. As shown in Fig. 8, this newly added plugin in the UI of the VMware vSphere allow getting insights about the migration time, network rate and power consumption before initiating a VM migration and by using the data collected from the live migration history within the VMware cluster and with monitoring the VM active memory size. This allow the datacenter admins to make educated decisions about VMware vMotion events before committing the migration.

After determining the expected network rate of a VM live migration and using this integration method, it is also possible to create a more sophisticated migration system using the Hidden Markov model [36] in Fig. 4. Such a system would predict how the network bandwidth will change in the future and thus inform the datacenter administrator of the optimal time to do the migration in order to decrease the load on the network infrastructure. Figure 9 shows how this system would look to the administrator. To implement such a system the following changes would be made:

– The PowerCLI module needs to periodically collect network data to be used by the Python module for training.
– the Hidden Markov model needs be implemented in the Python module. This model will be able to predict the network state in the future and thus guess the best time for a certain VM to migrate.
– When the user requests a migration, the UI will show the user the best predicted time to do the migration after running the model from the previous step.

As a result of using live migration cost prediction and timing optimization techniques, the live migration time of the VMs can be saved by just shifting the migration start time of the same VM to the recommended optimal time. Table 2 show average and the maximum migration time increase without using timing optimization as normalized values versus using the timing optimization techniques. As shown in Table 2, for memory stress benchmark the average increase in the migration time without timing optimization is 1.45 versus with using timing optimization. This average increase is 1.26 for network stress applications. From the peak increase in the migration time point of view, the maximum migration time increase for memory stress benchmark without timing optimization is 2.05 versus with using the timing optimization. This maximum increase is 1.36 for network stress benchmark. The results mentioned in Table 2 show how significantly the timing optimization can save the migration time cost for VMs live migrations.

Table 2. Timing optimization performance [16].

	Mem stress	Net stress
Average mig. time %	145	126
Max. mig. time %	205	136

6   Conclusion

Virtual datacenters and cloud computing environments depend on the live migration feature for dynamic management of the infrastructure compute resources, power saving and system load balance. It is common to find tens or may be hundreds of live migration events per day in enterprises' datacenters. The cost of the live migration process includes the migration time, the network throughput overhead and the power consumption cost.

The challenge that the IT admins face is running the live migration sessions without an idea about the expected cost of each migration request of a VM. This might lead to resources bottlenecks, increase in the migration cost and higher failure probability of the VM copy, especially for large memory VM migration or for multiple concurrent VMs migrations.

In our last papers, we have proposed a machine learning based live migration cost prediction approach and a migration timing optimization technique that can resolve this challenge. In this paper, we provide an extension work on the previously proposed techniques in [16] and [15] and show a practical solution for this problem that could integrate the cost prediction and timing optimization algorithms with VMware vSphere UI; as an added plug-in to the UI. We show in this paper the building blocks of the software tools and platforms that should be used to achieve this integration and explain how this new feature work in the system back-end to facilitate this cost prediction and timing optimization as optional service for VMware clusters' IT admins.

References

1. https://code.vmware.com/tool/vmware-powercli/6.5
2. VMware Virtual Distributed Switch. https://docs.vmware.com/en/VMware-vSphere/6.0/com.vmware.vsphere.networking.doc/GUID-3147E090-D9BF-42B4-B042-16F8D4C92DE4.html
3. VMware VMkernel. https://docs.vmware.com/en/VMware-vSphere/6.7/com.vmware.vsphere.networking.doc/GUID-D4191320-209E-4CB5-A709-C8741E713348.html
4. www.vmware.com/products/vcenter-server.html
5. Akoush, S., Sohan, R., Rice, A., Moore, A.W., Hopper, A.: Predicting the performance of virtual machine migration. In: Proceedings of the 2010 IEEE International Symposium on Modeling, Analysis and Simulation of Computer and Telecommunication Systems, MASCOTS 2010, pp. 37–46. IEEE Computer Society, Washington, DC (2010). https://doi.org/10.1109/MASCOTS.2010.13
6. Aldossary, M., Djemame, K.: Performance and energy-based cost prediction of virtual machines live migration in clouds. In: Proceedings of the 8th International Conference on Cloud Computing and Services Science, CLOSER 2018, Funchal, Madeira, Portugal, 19–21 March 2018, pp. 384–391 (2018). https://doi.org/10.5220/0006682803840391
7. Bashar, A., Mohammad, N., Muhammed, S.: Modeling and evaluation of pre-copy live VM migration using probabilistic model checking. In: 2018 12th International Conference on Signal Processing and Communication Systems (ICSPCS), pp. 1–7 (2018)
8. Berral, J.L., Gavaldà, R., Torres, J.: Power-aware multi-data center management using machine learning. In: Proceedings of the 2013 42nd International Conference on Parallel Processing, ICPP 2013, pp. 858–867. IEEE Computer Society, Washington, DC (2013). https://doi.org/10.1109/ICPP.2013.102
9. Bezerra, P., Martins, G., Gomes, R., Cavalcante, F., Costa, A.: Evaluating live virtual machine migration overhead on client's application perspective. In: 2017 International Conference on Information Networking (ICOIN), pp. 503–508, January 2017. https://doi.org/10.1109/ICOIN.2017.7899536

10. Cerroni, W.: Multiple virtual machine live migration in federated cloud systems. In: 2014 IEEE Conference on Computer Communications Workshops (INFOCOM WKSHPS), pp. 25–30 (2014)

11. Cerroni, W.: Network performance of multiple virtual machine live migration in cloud federations. J. Internet Serv. Appl. **6**(1), 6:1–6:20 (2015). https://doi.org/10.1186/s13174-015-0020-x

12. Chen, Y., Liu, I., Chou, C., Li, J., Liu, C.: Multiple virtual machines live migration scheduling method study on VMware vMotion. In: 2018 3rd International Conference on Computer and Communication Systems (ICCCS), pp. 113–116 (2018)

13. Dargie, W.: Estimation of the cost of VM migration. In: 23rd International Conference on Computer Communication and Networks, ICCCN 2014, Shanghai, China, 4–7 August 2014, pp. 1–8. IEEE (2014). https://doi.org/10.1109/ICCCN.2014.6911756

14. Elsaid, M.E., Meinel, C.: Live migration impact on virtual datacenter performance: VMware vMotion based study. In: 2014 International Conference on Future Internet of Things and Cloud, pp. 216–221, August 2014. https://doi.org/10.1109/FiCloud.2014.42

15. Elsaid, M.E., Abbas, H.M., Meinel, C.: Machine learning approach for live migration cost prediction in VMware environments. In: Proceedings of the 9th International Conference on Cloud Computing and Services Science, CLOSER 2019, Heraklion, Crete, Greece, 2–4 May 2019, pp. 456–463 (2019). https://doi.org/10.5220/0007749204560463

16. Elsaid., M.E., Abbas., H.M., Meinel., C.: Live migration timing optimization for VMware environments using machine learning techniques. In: Proceedings of the 10th International Conference on Cloud Computing and Services Science - Volume 1: CLOSER, pp. 91–102. INSTICC, SciTePress (2020). https://doi.org/10.5220/0009397300910102

17. Salfner, F., Tröger, T., Polze, A.: Downtime analysis of virtual machine live migration. In: The Fourth International Conference on Dependability (DEPEND 2011), France, pp. 100–105 (2011). ISBN 978-1-61208-149-6

18. Farahnakian, F., Liljeberg, P., Plosila, J.: LiRCUP: linear regression based CPU usage prediction algorithm for live migration of virtual machines in data centers. In: 2013 39th Euromicro Conference on Software Engineering and Advanced Applications. IEEE, September 2013. https://doi.org/10.1109/seaa.2013.23

19. Hu, W., et al.: A quantitative study of virtual machine live migration. In: Proceedings of the 2013 ACM Cloud and Autonomic Computing Conference, CAC 2013, pp. 11:1–11:10. ACM, New York (2013). https://doi.org/10.1145/2494621.2494622

20. Huang, Q., Gao, F., Wang, R., Qi, Z.: Power consumption of virtual machine live migration in clouds. In: 2011 Third International Conference on Communications and Mobile Computing, pp. 122–125 (2011)

21. Huang, Q., Shuang, K., Xu, P., Liu, X., Su, S.: Prediction-based dynamic resource scheduling for virtualized cloud systems. J. Netw. **9**, 375–383 (2014)

22. Jiang, X., Yan, F., Ye, K.: Performance influence of live migration on multi-tier workloads in virtualization environments. In: CLOUD 2012 (2012)

23. Jo, C., Cho, Y., Egger, B.: A machine learning approach to live migration modeling. In: Proceedings of the 2017 Symposium on Cloud Computing, SoCC 2017, pp. 351–364. ACM, New York (2017). https://doi.org/10.1145/3127479.3129262

24. Kikuchi, S., Matsumoto, Y.: Performance modeling of concurrent live migration operations in cloud computing systems using prism probabilistic model checker. In: 2011 IEEE 4th International Conference on Cloud Computing, pp. 49–56 (2011)

25. Liu, H., Xu, C.Z., Jin, H., Gong, J., Liao, X.: Performance and energy modeling for live migration of virtual machines. In: HPDC (2011)

26. Patel, M., Chaudhary, S.: Survey on a combined approach using prediction and compression to improve pre-copy for efficient live memory migration on Xen. In: 2014 International Conference on Parallel, Distributed and Grid Computing, pp. 445–450 (2014)

27. Rybina, K., Schill, A.: Estimating energy consumption during live migration of virtual machines. In: 2016 IEEE International Black Sea Conference on Communications and Networking (BlackSeaCom), pp. 1–5 (2016)

28. Salfner, F., Tröger, P., Polze, A.: Downtime analysis of virtual machine live migration. In: The Fourth International Conference on Dependability, pp. 100–105. IARIA (2011)

29. Salfner, F., Tröger, P., Richly, M.: Dependable estimation of downtime for virtual machine live migration. Int. J. Adv. Syst. Meas. **5**, 70–88 (2012). http://www.iariajournals.org/systems_and_measurements/tocv5n12.html

30. Strunk, A., Dargie, W.: Does live migration of virtual machines cost energy? In: 2013 IEEE 27th International Conference on Advanced Information Networking and Applications (AINA), pp. 514–521 (2013)

31. Strunk, A.: Costs of virtual machine live migration: a survey. In: Proceedings of the 2012 IEEE Eighth World Congress on Services, SERVICES 2012, pp. 323–329. IEEE Computer Society, Washington, DC (2012). https://doi.org/10.1109/SERVICES.2012.23

32. Strunk, A.: A lightweight model for estimating energy cost of live migration of virtual machines. In: 2013 IEEE Sixth International Conference on Cloud Computing, pp. 510–517 (2013)

33. Voorsluys, W., Broberg, J., Venugopal, S., Buyya, R.: Cost of virtual machine live migration in clouds: a performance evaluation. In: Jaatun, M.G., Zhao, G., Rong, C. (eds.) CloudCom 2009. LNCS, vol. 5931, pp. 254–265. Springer, Heidelberg (2009). https://doi.org/10.1007/978-3-642-10665-1_23

34. Wu, Y., Zhao, M.: Performance modeling of virtual machine live migration. In: 2011 IEEE 4th International Conference on Cloud Computing, pp. 492–499(2011)

35. Zhao, M., Figueiredo, R.J.: Experimental study of virtual machine migration in support of reservation of cluster resources. In: Proceedings of the 2nd International Workshop on Virtualization Technology in Distributed Computing, VTDC 2007, pp. 5:1–5:8. ACM, New York (2007). https://doi.org/10.1145/1408654.1408659

36. Chen, Z., Wen, J., Geng, Y.: Predicting future traffic using hidden Markov models. In: 2016 IEEE 24th International Conference on Network Protocols (ICNP), pp. 1–6, November 2016. https://doi.org/10.1109/ICNP.2016.7785328

Using Self-Organizing Maps for the Behavioral Analysis of Virtualized Network Functions

Giacomo Lanciano[2,1(✉)], Antonio Ritacco[1], Fabio Brau[1], Tommaso Cucinotta[1], Marco Vannucci[1], Antonino Artale[3], Joao Barata[4], and Enrica Sposato[3]

[1] Scuola Superiore Sant'Anna, Pisa, Italy
{antonio.ritacco,fabio.brau,tommaso.cucinotta,
marco.vannucci}@santannapisa.it
[2] Scuola Normale Superiore, Pisa, Italy
giacomo.lanciano@sns.it
[3] Vodafone, Milan, Italy
{antonino.artale,enrica.sposato2}@vodafone.com
[4] Vodafone, Lisbon, Portugal
joao.oliveira3@vodafone.com

Abstract. Detecting anomalous behaviors in a network function virtualization infrastructure is of the utmost importance for network operators. In this paper, we propose a technique, based on Self-Organizing Maps, to address such problem by leveraging on the massive amount of historical system data that is typically available in these infrastructures. Indeed, our method consists of a joint analysis of system-level metrics, provided by the virtualized infrastructure monitoring system and referring to resource consumption patterns of the physical hosts and the virtual machines (or containers) that run on top of them, and application-level metrics, provided by the individual virtualized network functions monitoring subsystems and related to the performance levels of the individual applications. The implementation of our approach has been validated on real data coming from a subset of the Vodafone infrastructure for network function virtualization, where it is currently employed to support the decisions of data center operators. Experimental results show that our technique is capable of identifying specific points in space (i.e., components of the infrastructure) and time of the recent evolution of the monitored infrastructure that are worth to be investigated by human operators in order to keep the system running under expected conditions.

Keywords: Self-organizing maps · Machine learning · Network function virtualization

1 Introduction

The novel *Network Function Virtualization (NFV)* paradigm [25] has been nowadays adopted by all the major network service providers in response to the

© Springer Nature Switzerland AG 2021
D. Ferguson et al. (Eds.): CLOSER 2020, CCIS 1399, pp. 153–177, 2021.
https://doi.org/10.1007/978-3-030-72369-9_7

increasingly demanding requirements they have to meet, in particular, in terms of performance, flexibility and resiliency. Indeed, traditional approaches that rely on the deployment of network functions on top of proprietary *specialized* physical appliances – typically sized for the peak-hour and very costly to maintain – are no more sustainable in the complex, fast-paced scenarios that can be found in modern telecommunication systems. Thanks to the amazing advances in the *cloud computing* space, having on-demand access to a diverse set of virtualized resources (computing, storage, networking, etc.) – running on commodity hardware – has never been so easy and convenient. In the context of NFV, this kind of virtualization technologies is leveraged according to the *private cloud computing* model, where general-purpose computing, networking and storage resources owned by the operator can be dynamically and automatically managed and orchestrated, to fit the needs of time-varying workloads. This allows for cutting costs and energy consumption, as well as shortening development cycles and time-to-market [16]. For example, a virtualized network infrastructure can be easily adapted to adequately support new products of an organization or, if customers request new network functions, all it takes to handle such requests is to spin up new VMs that can be rapidly decommissioned when the functions are no longer needed. In this way, network functions can be completely decoupled from the underlying physical appliances they are deployed onto and can be effectively developed as distributed, elastic, resilient software applications. For NFV data centers, the choice of private cloud infrastructures – as opposed to the use of public cloud services – is also corroborated by latency-related concerns. Indeed, since such service-chains are highly delay-sensitive (e.g., LTE, 4G), it is unpractical to rely on public cloud infrastructures, that are usually shared among multiple tenants and non-necessarily deployed according to the network operator needs.

In order to guarantee scalability, robustness to failure, high availability, low latency, virtualized network functions (VNFs) are typically designed as large-scale distributed systems [27], often partitioned and replicated among many geographically dislocated data centers. The larger the scale, the more operations teams have to deal with complex interactions among the various components, such that diagnosis and troubleshooting of possible issues become incredibly difficult tasks [12]. Also, the capacity of such systems is designed according to some technical and economical considerations, in order to support the *standard load* conditions under which the VNFs perform well, ensuring a number of diverse kinds of Service Level Agreements (SLAs) between network operators and their customers. However, when extraordinary events or cascade failures occur, the network is typically overloaded and the allocated resources are not sufficient anymore to process all the incoming flows. Monitoring the status of the data center through an efficient distributed monitoring infrastructure that continuously gathers system-level metrics from all the different levels of the architecture (e.g., physical hosts metrics, virtual machines metrics, application-level key performance indicators, event logs) is a necessary step in order to build a pro-active system capable of detecting signals of system overload in advance. Such data usually drives the decisions of human operators, for instance, in terms of which actions must be taken to restore the expected conditions of the system after an outage has occurred, or how the available components should be reconfigured to prevent possible SLA violations in case of an unexpected increase in the workload.

One of the major problems of data center operators is *anomaly detection*, i.e., pinpointing unexpected and/or suspect behaviors of the system whenever it significantly deviates from the normal conditions. Indeed, recognizing characteristic patterns of resource consumption in early stages can be crucial to avoid resource exhaustion and to redirect critical traffic peaks so to minimize the risk of SLA violations (i.e., such that human experts can focus their efforts on the most critical activities), or at least to alert the staff to prepare the remediation/mitigation procedures in advance. Even though the amount of data usually produced by NFV infrastructures is huge, most of it is not explicitly labeled by specialized personnel, so that *unsupervised* machine learning (ML) algorithms (i.e., clustering or vector quantization techniques) are the easiest ones to use, especially for anomaly detection purposes. The objective of these algorithms is to group data with a similar trend in macro-categories and allow operators to keep tens or hundreds of virtual machines under control at the same time.

1.1 Contributions

In this paper, we propose to use *Self-organizing Maps (SOMs)* to perform a behavioral pattern analysis of VM metrics aiming at providing a comprehensive overview of the major behavioral patterns and detecting possible anomalies in a data center for NFV. The technique can be used to perform a joint analysis of *system-level metrics* available from the infrastructure monitoring system and *application-level metrics* available from the individual VNFs. It aims at supporting data center operations and specifically capacity and performance monitoring, by providing insightful information on the behavioral patterns, in terms of resource consumption and exhibited performance, of the analyzed VNFs. In our approach, the SOM-based behavioral analysis is leveraged to deliver a sophisticated alerting subsystem, whose output can be directly consumed by human operators or could be used as a trigger for automated remediation procedures.

This paper constitutes an extended version of our prior work [6], where we added related background concepts and technical details on our technique, describing for the first time the non-Euclidean distance we adopted and the automated alerting system that we built downstream of the SOM-based analysis, and discussing additional experimental results obtained with the proposed approach.

1.2 Paper Organization

This paper is organized as follows. After discussing the related literature in Sect. 2 and some fundamental background concepts in Sect. 3, we present our approach in Sect. 4, along with the data processing workflow we designed for the massive data set available in the Vodafone infrastructure. In Sect. 5, we discuss some obtained experimental results that validate the approach and highlight its practical relevance. Section 6 concludes the paper with our final remarks and ideas for future research in the area.

2   Related Work

In this section, we briefly review some of the most related works that are found in the research literature on using ML, and SOMs in particular, for classification and anomaly detection in cloud and NFV data centers.

Anomaly detection can be framed as the problem of pinpointing unexpected and/or suspect behaviors of a system whenever it significantly deviates from the normal conditions. Similar problems can be found in other fields and applications such as, for instance: intrusion detection in cyber-security, machinery fault [30] and product quality issues detection [1] in industrial contexts, or fraud detection in finance [22]. It is important to stress that anomaly detection is, in general, an inherently imbalanced problem due to the scarcity of anomalous observations with respect to the ones related to the normal conditions of a system. In order to tackle this kind of challenges, a huge amount of solutions has been proposed that, depending on the scenario and the nature of the data to be processed, pose their foundations on well-established techniques coming, for instance, from the research fields of information theory and statistics.

In the recent years, ML techniques have been gaining more and more traction in the context of anomaly detection applications because of their proven effectiveness in many of the aforementioned scenarios. This is mainly due to the versatility of this kind of methods and the increasing availability of data from which they can learn from, in a continuous manner [3]. Most of the approaches to anomaly detection address the associated challenges by feeding ML models with counters like CPU utilization, memory contention and network-related metrics [12,31,34]. Others include also system-level and/or application-level event logs in the analysis to increase the amount of features and facilitate the extraction of relevant patterns [8,35]. Embedding textual information has been in fact made easier by the advancements in Natural Language Processing (NLP) research [2]. Few existing works also consider the need of assisting human operators in conducting root-cause analysis to be a highly desirable feature of anomaly detection systems [14,28].

One of the major roadblocks that can be encountered when applying ML for solving a task is the scarcity, or the complete absence, of labelled data, a very common scenario in many practical applications. Such issues can be overcome by employing so-called *unsupervised* learning techniques that, as the definition suggests, are designed to operate without a ground truth (i.e., annotated data). It is worth noticing that this characteristic of such class of learning algorithms has the side effect of increasing the amount of data that can be used for training an ML model. The principal application of unsupervised techniques is *clustering* that consists in the formation of groups (the *clusters*) of data samples that are similar, where similarity is defined according to the employed distance function.

A SOM is a particular kind of neural network that leverages on the *competitive learning* approach for cluster formation [17]. In this context, when a new sample is presented to the SOM during the training, the Best Matching Unit (BMU) – the closest neuron to the data sample according to the employed distance function – is selected and BMU and its neighbors are rewarded by updating their weights so to make them more similar to the selected sample. The iteration of this process leads to the formation of the clusters that are represented by the associate SOM neurons. SOMs are designed for mapping high-dimensional data into a lower-dimensional (typically 2-dimensional) space. One of the main characteristics of the obtained clustering is that it preserves the *topology* and *distribution* of training data, at clusters-level. In practice, it means that more clusters will be located in the more dense regions of the original domain (distribution) and that similar data samples will be associated to the same cluster or to neighbor clusters (topology).

In the context of anomaly detection, such approaches usually operate by building, starting from training data, a set of clusters of samples that are representative of the expected – normal – conditions of a system. After training, such model can be exploited to compare new patterns to known behaviors according to a predefined distance metric, in order to infer whether the observations are anomalous or not. In these applications, the above mentioned properties of retention of the original data topology and distribution give the SOM the capability of creating a suitable number of clusters for the most representative situations: this distribution of clusters allows for a more reliable characterization of anomalous patterns due to the higher granularity reserved to more common situations.

Since early 90s, SOMs – as a *neural* approach to clustering – have achieved remarkable results at processing industrial data [15] in different fields. In [7], a SOM–based system for the visualization of complex process dynamics is proposed. In this application, topology conservation enables a smooth visualization of non-linear process transitions in a 2–dimensional map and favors the understanding of the influence of process parameters on process behavior. Similar approaches that exploit dimensional reduction and visualization on an easy-to–interpret 2D map are used also in [10] for process monitoring purposes and in [11] where the aspects of visualization of the evolution of process conditions are handled. In [4], SOMs are used for the grouping of electrical components based on a wide set of features that are efficiently mapped in a low dimensional space. In [33], it is shown how a SOM–based system can be used for detecting anomalies within a steel plant as far as the process faults and product defects are concerned. In this case, SOM clusterization is used to group similar process conditions or product features that are subsequently labelled according to experimental tests. The ability of SOMs to yield a distribution of the clusters in the problem domain that faithfully reflects the observed phenomenon behavior allows the generation of more specific clusters in the denser regions of the domain. The capability of SOMs of managing high–dimensional data and mapping them into a lower dimensional one have been exploited in medicine as well.

In [5], sonographic signals are processed and grouped in order to characterize those ones associated to breast cancer diagnosis. Another SOM-based approach was used in [32] to allow the analysis of complex cytometry data that is hard from a point of view of human experts due to the huge amount of variables to be taken simultaneously into consideration.

For what concerns NFV applications, the existing literature reports that ML techniques have been effectively used to solve different problems. In particular, in [13] a set of ML techniques are tested for an anomaly detection application. In this case, though, only supervised methods are considered and their performance is compared on data sets containing NFV features associated to different types of faults. Similarly, in [24], a *supervised* SOM-based method is proposed for fault detection. Here, a SOM is used to cluster *labelled* data, annotated by human experts to state which clusters correspond to faulty conditions, related to NFV performance indicators. In [26], SOM-based and other general clustering techniques are used for the same purpose in a small test-bed in the context of NFV. Likewise, in [20], the popular K–means algorithm is used to cluster cells traffic data in order group cells with similar through–time behavior and enable optimizations in the use of resources.

3   Background Concepts

3.1   Self-Organizing Maps

A SOM is an unsupervised vector quantization technique, used to produce a topology-preserving map using a competitive learning algorithm. The aim of the SOM training algorithm is to encode a data manifold (e.g., a sub-manifold $V \subseteq \mathbb{R}^N$) into a finite set $W = \{w_1, \cdots, w_M\}$ of reference vectors where $w_i \in \mathbb{R}^N$ is called *codebook*. Formally, a SOM is defined by a pair of maps (w, b). $w : \mathcal{L} \to \mathbb{R}^N$ is a discrete map from a two-dimensional lattice into a finite vector space, a.k.a., *features space*. Recall that a two-dimensional lattice of dimensions $H \times K$ is a discrete set

$$\mathcal{L} = \{hA + kB \mid h < H, \, k < K, \, h, k \in \mathbb{N}\} \subseteq \mathbb{R}^2$$

where $A, B \in \mathbb{R}^2$ determine its shape (e.g., $A = (1, 0)$ and $B = (0, 1)$ produce a *rectangular* grid, whereas $A = (\frac{1}{2}, \frac{\sqrt{3}}{2})$ and $B = (1, 0)$ produce an *hexagonal* grid). For the sake of simplicity, $\mathcal{L}$ is indexed with a lexicographical order (from 1 to $H \times K$), its elements $r_i \in \mathbb{R}^2$ are called *units* or also *neurons* and the images $w_i = w(r_i)$ of the neurons in the features space are called *weights*. Given a sample vector $x \in V$, $b : \mathbb{R}^N \to \mathcal{L}$ returns the *best-matching-unit* (BMU) i.e., the unit whose weight is closest to the input sample (or any such units, if multiple ones exist) depending on a distance d in the feature space.

$$b(x) \in \underset{r \in \mathcal{L}}{\arg \min} \, d(x, w(r)) \tag{1}$$

A common choice for the distance d is the Euclidean distance, albeit alternative choices are possible (e.g., see the discussion later in Sect. 4.3).

For each training epoch t, an update to the SOM weights is performed, for each input sample, as follows. At each iteration t', an *input data* x is fetched (using either a random or a sequential scheduling) and its associated best matching neuron $b(x)$ is computed. Then, the weights of *all neurons* are updated according to (2), where h is called *neighborhood function* and is defined as (3) (assumed to be a Gaussian in what follows).

$$w_k^{(t'+1)} = w_k^{(t')} + \alpha(t)h(b(x), r_k, t)(x - w_k^{(t')}) \quad \forall k \tag{2}$$

$$h(r, s, t) = -\exp\left(\frac{\|r - s\|^2}{\delta(t)}\right) \quad \forall r, s \in \mathcal{L} \tag{3}$$

Here, $\alpha(t')$ and $\delta(t')$ are respectively the learning rate and the radius of the neighborhood function, which depend on the current epoch t ($\alpha, \delta : \mathbb{N} \to \mathbb{R}$), and decrease across epochs either linearly or exponentially, to make the algorithm converge. It is important to notice that, for each training sample x, not only the winning reference is modified, but the adaptation to x affects all the weights w_j depending on the proximity of r_j to $b(x)$ with a step size that decreases with the distance between the units r_j and $b(x)$ in the lattice. This way neighboring units respond to similar input patterns and each data point close in the input space is mapped to same or nearby map neurons (inducing a topology-preserving property on the codebook). The weights of the neurons w_i are typically initialized either by randomly sampling the V data set or using the well-known Principal Components Analysis (PCA) technique.

A key difference between the SOM training algorithm and other vector quantization or clustering techniques is that, in the neighborhood function definition (3), the topological distance between a pair of units is declined as the Euclidean distance on the map and not in the data space. The formulation in (2) is called the *online update* rule, that is not suitable for a parallel implementation since each iteration directly depends on the one immediately before and only processes a single data sample at a time. Therefore, a *batch parallel* implementation has been proposed: instead of updating the neuron weights for each data sample, they are updated after a batch $B \subseteq V$ of N' data samples (in the following we will assume $N' = N$, for the sake of simplicity). Essentially, the term of (2) that depends for each $r_k \in \mathcal{L}$ on the input sample by $h(b(x), r_k, t)(x - w_k)$ is replaced by a weighted sum of the same terms computed in parallel for all samples in the batch, using the formula:

$$\frac{\sum_{x \in B} h(b(x), r_k, t)(x - w_k)}{\sum_{x \in B} h(b(x), r_k, t)} \quad \forall k \tag{4}$$

This way, one can compute in parallel all numerator and denominator parts (i.e., $h(b(x), r_k, t)(x - w_k)$ and $h(b(x), r_k, t)$, respectively) for each sample in each batch and then sum up all numerator and denominator parts and finally compute the weight update.

After the training is complete, the result is that the manifold data V is divided into a finite number of subregions:

$$V_i = \left\{ x \in V \mid \|x - w_i\|_2 \leq \|x - w_j\|_2 \quad \forall j \neq i \right\} \tag{5}$$

called Voronoi tessellation, in which each sample vector x is described by the corresponding weight of the BMU $w(b(x))$. It is important to point out that the update rule is fundamental to the formation of the topographically ordered map. In fact, the weights are not modified independently of each other but as topologically related subsets. For each step a subset of neurons is selected on the basis of the neighborhood of the current winning unit. Hence, topological information is supplied to the map because both the winning unit and its lattice neighbors receive similar weights updates that allow them, after learning, to respond to similar inputs. After the training phase, the map can be used to visualize different features of the codebook and of the represented data, such as (i) the density of the reference vectors (e.g., with a color scale proportional to neuron hits); (ii) likewise, the distances among reference vectors, where a dark color indicates a large distance between adjacent units, and a light color indicates a small distance (i.e., the so-called U-matrix); (iii) a plot of the reference vectors for each neuron, to see at a glance all the different behaviors detected in the training dataset.

A careful choice of the SOM hyper-parameters should be made in order to have a suitable trade-off in terms of quality of the clustering and computational performance. Some details on how the right hyper-parameters have been chosen for our analysis are given in Sect. 5. In order to mitigate the problem of having different neurons specializing on almost the same data samples (e.g., when the number of SOM neurons is large with respect to the data sample variability), we have applied an automated grouping technique over the SOM reference codebook, detailed in Sect. 5.4.

3.2   VMware vRealize Operations Manager

The vRealize Operations Manager (vROps)[1] – by VMware – is an enterprise-grade software used at Vodafone to operate the NFV infrastructure. Such framework can be deployed either on-premise or in the cloud and its main purpose is to support operations teams in automating and continuously improving their fundamental activities, also leveraging on data-driven methodologies. Indeed, the core of vROps consists of a pervasive monitoring infrastructure that collects system data at every level of the stack (e.g., physical hosts, virtual machines, networking components, etc.) and feed them to a powerful analytical engine that is able to provide useful insights and actionable feedback to the human operators, such that possible issues or anomalies can be early spotted and corrected. More than 300 system metrics, being them classical raw counters (e.g., cpu utilization, memory contention, network traffic, etc.) or more convoluted analytics computed by the engine, can be exported from the system, allowing also for the integration with third-party tools. Besides monitoring and alerting functionalities, vROps enables automated management of the VMs (or containers) that compose the deployed applications such that, for instance, the corresponding

---

[1] https://docs.vmware.com/en/vRealize-Operations/index.html.

workloads can be balanced according to the optimization of specified indicators (e.g., application KPIs, licensing costs, etc.).

4   Proposed Approach

In this paper, we propose the use of SOMs in order to perform a behavioral analysis of the VMs that implement VNFs within an NFV data center infrastructure. Our approach consists of the joint analysis of two classes of metrics that are usually collected and analyzed independently of one another: *system-level metrics*, reporting information related to the utilization of the underlying infrastructure, hereafter also referred to as *INFRA* metrics, which are usually available through the NFV infrastructure manager (e.g., the well-known VMware vRealize Operations Manager or others); and *application-level metrics*, i.e., KPIs of the individual virtualized services, collected through their own monitoring subsystems, which will be referred to as *VNF* metrics. Considering both types of metrics allows for gathering a comprehensive overview of the major behavioral patterns that characterize VMs and possibly identifying suspect (anomalous) behaviors.

The proposed technique relies on the capability of SOMs to preserve the topology in the projection from the input space to the SOM reference vector space. In other words, using SOMs similar input patterns are captured by same or nearby neurons (see Sect. 3.1 for details). A VM behavior can be monitored by considering the shift of its BMU, during the time horizon under analysis, so that any changes in a *suspect* BMU could be used to trigger an alarm.

4.1   Workflow

We realized a SOM-based clustering tool that is capable of detecting anomalies by clustering using a number of input metrics. In our experimentation, we have been applying this technique over individual monthly data available with a 5-min granularity (288 samples per day, per metric, per monitored VM or physical host), amounting to several GBs of data per month, for a specific region of the Vodafone network operator. Figure 1 summarizes the overall workflow that we applied to process the available input metrics. First, the raw data are preprocessed to address possible data-quality issues (e.g., missing values imputation and time-series detrendization) and to filter out the additional information that is not relevant for the analysis. The input samples to the SOM are constructed, for each VM, by dividing the time horizon under analysis according to a predefined period (i.e., 24 h) and merging the contributions of the individual metrics into a single vector. Then, such data are fed to the SOM that, after a training phase, infers for each VM the neuron capturing the most similar behavior and, thus, clusters on the various behavioral patterns of all the various VMs under analysis.

The input data are filtered – on the k specified metrics – and partitioned to have a sample (i.e., a time-series) for each metric, VM and period (usually a day) of the time horizon under analysis. Before being fed as input to the SOM training phase, samples are subject to a preprocessing phase, addressing possible issues such as (i) missing values and (ii) significant differences in the magnitude among the different metrics. On the one hand, to address (i), a data imputation strategy (i.e., a simple linear interpolation) is performed to mitigate the absence of data points within a sample and to retain as much data as possible for the analysis. However, in order to preserve the quality of the data set, the interpolation step has been designed not to be *aggressive*, such that a time-series can be discarded if it contains too much consecutive missing values. On the other hand, it is recommended to address (ii) when using SOM for multi-metric analysis since, due to the Euclidean distance being used as samples distance evaluation mechanism, metrics with significantly larger values (e.g., number of transmitted/received packets or bytes) tend to hide the contribution of other metrics which take on smaller values, for instance, being bounded by a predefined range that is much smaller (e.g., CPU utilization percentage). We have designed two possible strategies to tackle such problem. The first strategy, referred to as *normalized*, consists of computing the so-called *z-score*, i.e., scaling each time-series by subtracting its mean and dividing by its standard deviation. Using such a strategy hides any information regarding the magnitude of the original values and emphasizes differences in shapes. The second strategy, referred to as *non-normalized*, consists of scaling each time-series to the $[0, 1]$ range of values considering, for each metric, the historically observed minima and maxima values. Such a strategy retains information regarding the magnitude of the original values while keeping the data bounded in the same interval. However, this technique causes different metric patterns with very similar shape, but differing merely in their magnitude, to be grouped into different SOM neurons at a certain distance from each other (in the SOM grid topology). Depending on the chosen strategy, we obtain either an analysis focused on the shapes of the behavioral patterns, or we can also distinguish among the absolute values of the average levels of the metrics. In general, in the latter case one should expect more clusters to be outputted with respect to the former case, due to the possibility that the system could have

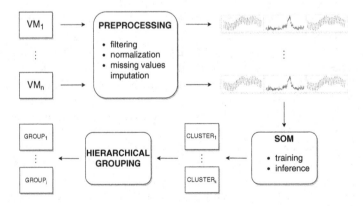

Fig. 1. Overview of the SOM-based clustering workflow.

experienced very diverse levels of load during its operation. Hence, one should take this possibility into account and increase the size of the SOM grid when performing a non-normalized analysis in order to avoid neurons *over-population* (i.e., too many patterns crowding within the same BMU), despite them being significantly distant from each other.

Each input sample to the SOM is constructed by concatenating k vectors (one for each of the k metrics under analysis), for each VM and period. Notice that, since INFRA metrics have been provided with a 5-min collection granularity, if a period of a day is considered, we typically have for each day 288 data points of each metric and for each VM. After the training phase, the SOM is used to infer the BMU for each input sample, i.e., the neuron that exhibits the least quantization error when compared with the considered input sample. Multiple VMs are expected to be associated to the same BMU and, thus, a number of different VM clusters can be derived from such process. Such an output can be used by a data center operator to visually inspect the behaviors assumed by the different VMs during the time horizon under analysis, in order to spot possible suspect/anomalous ones. Furthermore, since the individual input samples are related to the behavior of a specific VM at specific point in time, it is also possible to visualize the evolution of the VMs throughout the time horizon, to possibly detect interesting patterns in their behavioral changes.

On top of the clustering mechanism described above, we have devised an approach capable of detecting possible suspect behaviors without the need for a human operator to daily inspect the status of the SOM (these aspects are described in details in Sect. 4.4). Such additional feature consists of an alerting system that is triggered whenever an input sample is firstly associated to a group of similar neurons but in the following days a sudden group change takes place. Because of the considerable distance from the BMU (i.e., the *closest* neuron) of the neurons in the two different groups, such samples are likely to depict an uncommon behavior and, thus, an alert is raised to the operator. Besides the aforementioned support that such a tool can give to data center operators in their manual operations, this feature in particular enables the possibility to deploy a fully automated anomaly detection system.

4.2 SOM Implementation

To implement our anomaly detection tool we leveraged on an efficient open-source SOM implementation, namely Somoclu[2], which has been designed around the batch parallel SOM variant (see Sect. 3.1) to employ multi-core acceleration, as well as GPGPU hardware acceleration, to perform massively parallel computations [36]. Such accelerations have been proved to be necessary in order to reach a satisfactory performance when tackling the massive data set provided by Vodafone. In the future, we plan to switch to a new implementation we recently realized performing even better [23].

---

[2] https://github.com/peterwittek/somoclu.

4.3   Hierarchical Grouping

An interesting aspect that came to our attention during the development of the aforementioned SOM-based approach is that, whenever using relatively big SOM networks, the training phase ends up with many close-by SOM neurons catching behaviors that were very similar to each other. This is in line with the topology-preservation property of the SOMs, i.e., close-by input vectors in the input space are mapped to close-by neurons in the SOM grid. This phenomenon can be controlled to some extent by acting on the neighborhood radius. However, from the viewpoint of data center operators, a set of close-by neurons with relatively similar weight vectors needs to be considered as a single behavioral cluster/group. For this reason, after the SOM processing stage, we added a step consisting of a top-down clustering strategy, based on recursively separating weight-vector's sets whose diameter is higher than a given threshold. The principal aim of this technique is to offer the possibility of collapsing similar SOM neurons, according to the distances among their representative vectors, in order to decrease the possibility to raise an alarm when it is not needed (e.g., consider very frequent movements of a VM between two similar neurons over time) and to facilitate the human operators in interpreting the results and spotting anomalous behaviors. Indeed, as shown in Sect. 5.4, this led to the overall technique outputting a reduced and more comprehensible number of behavioral clusters.

Specifically, the aforementioned technique, known as *hierarchical clustering*, can be described as follows. Let ε be a fixed threshold which provides a bound for the maximum diameter of a group. The algorithm consists of the following steps:

1. **Initialization:** The set of the groups to process is initialized with a single group $\mathcal{G}_0$ containing all the neurons $\mathcal{G}_0 = \{n_1, \cdots, n_{H \times K}\}$, and the set of the final groups is initialized to be an empty set.
2. **Distance Measure:** A group $\mathcal{G}$ is removed from the set of groups to process and its diameter D is computed by finding the two farthest away neurons:

$$(n_S, n_N) \in \arg\max_{(n,m)\in\mathcal{G}} d(w(n), w(m)), \quad D = d(w(n_S), w(n_N))$$

   where $w(n)$ is the weight of neuron n. In the case that $\mathcal{G}$ contains just one neuron, its diameter D is defined as zero.
3. **Splitting:** If $D \leq \varepsilon$ (i.e., the diameter is within the specified threshold), then $\mathcal{G}$ is moved to the set of final groups. Otherwise, the group is split into two smaller (non-empty by construction) groups $\mathcal{G}_1$ and $\mathcal{G}_2$ defined as:

$$\mathcal{G}_1 := \{n \in \mathcal{G} : d(w(n), w(n_S)) \leq d(w(n), w(n_N))\}$$
$$\mathcal{G}_2 := \{n \in \mathcal{G} : d(w(n), w(n_S)) > d(w(n), w(n_N))\}$$

   that are added to the set of groups to process.
4. **Loop:** Steps 2,3 are repeatedly applied to all the elements in the set of groups to process, until it becomes empty, and the set of final groups contains only groups with a diameter lower than or equal to ε.

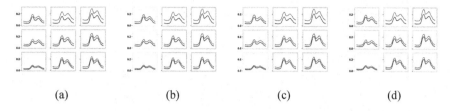

| (a) | (b) | (c) | (d) |

Fig. 2. Example of grouping steps: (a) initialization; (b) first split; (c) second split; (d) final split. Neurons with same border color belong to the same group.

Figure 2 reports a graphical representation of how the algorithm works on a real example. From left to right, we can see all the four steps of the algorithm that bring to the final result in which each group contains only neurons with a pair-wise distance smaller than the provided threshold.

As explained above, the kernel of the hierarchical clustering technique is the measure of the diameter of a set. This implies that the definition of the distance impacts on the final result.

Definition 1. *For each $p \in \mathbb{N}$, the function $d_p : \mathbb{R}^n \times \mathbb{R}^n \to \mathbb{R}_+$ defined as*

$$d_p(v, w) := \left(\sum_i |v_i - w_i|^p \right)^{\frac{1}{p}}$$

is the Minkowski distance of order p.

Note that, according to Definition 1, the Minkowski distance with $p = 2$ is the Euclidean distance, and that d_∞ degenerates into the Chebychev distance (maximum among the coordinates). Figure 3 shows that using $p = 4$, or in general a value higher than 2, allows for increasing the distance between neurons exhibiting a spike (i.e., neurons that are almost flat, except for an isolated huge value), so that we are able to isolate in a dedicated group such spiky neurons.

4.4 Alerting

A grouped SOM grid combined with a *calendar* representation of the VM behaviors can be used by an operator to spot possible anomalies. A calendar representation is a table containing for each couple (VM, DAY) a reference to the corresponding group. In addition, we designed a set of alerting systems based on heuristic methods, that can be used to simplify the inspection of such behaviors. We propose two main categories of alerting systems: the *calendar-view* alerting system, consisting of techniques that give a global view of the alerts over the entire period of interest, and the *dashboard-like* alerting system, consisting of techniques that give a detailed view of the behaviors that raise the alerts. In what follows, $V = \{v_1, v_2, \ldots, v_i, \ldots\}$ is the set of virtual machines under analysis, $D = \{d_1, d_2, \ldots, d_i, \ldots\}$ is the set of days that compose the time period

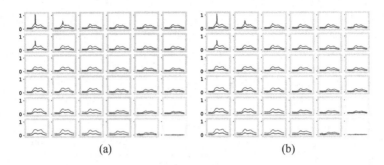

(a)   (b)

Fig. 3. Examples of grouping using different p values. Grouping with $p = 2$ (a) makes no distinction between spiky and smooth neurons, whereas grouping with $p = 4$ (b) clusters the spiky neuron on the top-left corner in a dedicated group.

under analysis and grp $: V \times D \to G$ is the function that associates to each couple (VM, DAY) the corresponding group.

Calendar-View Alerting System. This category contains those alerts that generate a calendar table in which each couple (VM, DAY) is associated with a value between 0 and 1, providing a level of alerting. In what follows, we denote with p the *period* and with m the *memory*, both expressed in days (i.e., $p = 7$ days, $m = 2$ weeks).

Definition 2 (Strong). *Given p, m, the Alert takes one VM v and one day d and returns a boolean value raising an alert if the VM v is classified into a different group in at least one day among the ones at most m periods apart:*

$$Alert_s(v, d) : \text{``}\exists j \in \{\pm 1, \cdots, \pm m\}, \quad grp(v, d) \neq grp(v, d - jp)\text{''} \qquad \text{(SAS)}$$

This alerting system is the most peaky (i.e., often producing false-positives) and, thus, performs the best when used in contexts where a few changes occur.

Definition 3 (Weak). *Given p, m, the Alert takes one VM v and one day d and returns a boolean value raising an alert if the VM v is classified into a different neuron in all the days among the ones at most m periods apart:*

$$Alert_w(v, d) : \text{``}\forall j \in \{\pm 1, \cdots, \pm m\}, \quad grp(v, d) \neq grp(v, d - jp)\text{''} \qquad \text{(WAS)}$$

This alerting system is more loose than the previous – sometimes producing false-negatives – and, thus, performs the best in chaotic contexts, where many random changes occur.

Definition 4 (Fuzzy). *Given p, the Alert takes one VM v and one day d and returns a real number, between 0 and 1, defined as follows:*

$$Alert_z(v, d) := \quad \#\{j \in \mathbb{Z} : grp(v, d) \neq grp(v, d - jp)\}/\#D(v, d) \qquad \text{(ZAS)}$$

where $D(v, d) = \{j \in \mathbb{Z} : \exists grp(v, d - jp)\}$ is the set of all the comparable days.

This alerting system, producing real values, can be used in a wide range of situations and could be useful to understand if a change in the behavior of a VM is common or infrequent.

Dashboard-Like Alerting System. The aim of a dashboard-like alerting system is to provide a detailed view of the behaviors which raise the alert, providing also further information on the geometrical distance between the actual and the expected behavior in terms of weight of the SOM or also a count of the frequency of VM/Days which are clustered into *rare* groups.

Definition 5 (Expected Behavior). *Let v be a VM for which an alert is raised at day d, i.e., $Alert(v, d) = 1$. Let $\tilde{d}$ be the nearest day, corresponding to the same weekday, for which the most common group is taken from v and for which $grp(v, d) \neq grp(\tilde{d})$ holds. Then, we define*

- GRP:$= grp(v, d)$
- NEU:$= neu(v, d)$
- E_GRP:$= grp(v, \tilde{d})$
- E_NEU:$= neu(v, \tilde{d})$
- DIST:$= \|w(\text{E\_NEU}) - w(\text{NEU})\|_2$

where the function $neu : V \times D \to \mathcal{L}$ returns the coordinates of the BMU associated to the behavior of a VM v during a day d and the function w, defined in Sect. 3.1, returns the weight of a neuron.

Such alerting system depends on the output of the calendar-like alerting system. Usually, we apply this method to the *weak* alerting system table (see Definition 3) in order to avoid false-positives alerts.

Definition 6 (Suspicious-day). *Given a parameter K, let $occ_d : G \to \mathbb{N}$ be the function that counts the occurrences of a group in the days.*

$$occ_d(g) := \#\{d \in D : \exists v \in V, grp(v, d) = g\}. \tag{6}$$

If a group g is such that $occ_d(g) \leq K$, then those VMs whose take the group g are stored in a table whose columns are DAY, VM, NEU, GRP, OCC_DAY, where OCC_DAY$= occ_d(g)$.

Such alerting system helps in catching days in which an infrequent group appears.

Definition 7 (Suspicious-VM). *Given a parameter K, let $occ_v : G \to \mathbb{N}$ be the function that counts the occurrences of a group in the VMs.*

$$occ_v(g) := \#\{v \in V : \exists d \in D, grp(v, d) = g\}. \tag{7}$$

If a group g is such that $occ_v(g) \leq K$, then those VMs whose take the group g are stored in a table whose columns are VM, DAY, NEU, GRP, OCC_VM, where OCC_VM$= occ_v(g)$.

Such alerting system helps to catch VMs that are clustered into an infrequent group.

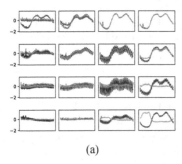
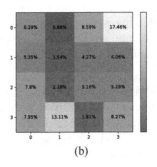

(a)   (b)

Fig. 4. (a) INFRA resource consumption clusters identified with the multi-metric analysis. The dark blue, green and light blue curves in each plot correspond to the cpu|usage_average, net|usage_average and cpu|capacity_contentionPct vROps metrics, respectively. (b) SOM grid showing the percentage of training samples captured by each neuron.

5   Experimental Results

In this section, we provide an overview of the results that can be obtained using the approach proposed in Sect. 4, that partially extend what has been already presented in our previous work [6]. For the analysis, we have relied on the experience of domain experts and focused our attention over a limited set of metrics that are considered the most relevant in this context, i.e., the ones related to the computational, networking and storage activity of VMs and VNFs of interest. Specifically, in the following, we highlight results obtained analyzing the following vROps metrics: cpu|capacity_contentionPct, cpu|usage_average, net|usage_average.

5.1   Multi-metric Analysis

The plots reported in Fig. 4 are examples of the results that can be obtained through the multi-metric SOM-based analysis presented in Sect. 4, applied over a month worth of system-level (INFRA) metrics, using the normalized strategy. The trained SOM network is visually represented in terms of the weights of its neurons. Indeed, each subplot reports the VMs daily behavior that the specific neuron specialized into. In order to simplify the representation, the weight vectors – jointly computed over the three metrics cpu|usage_average, net|usage_average and cpu|capacity_contentionPct – are overlapped but in different colors. For instance, one of the most recurrent patterns, occurring in 17.46% of the observations and depicted in Fig. 5a, is the one identified by the top-right neuron. Because of the standard data normalization performed during the preprocessing phase to discard the magnitude information in favor of enhancing the behavioral information of the input samples, the values on the Y axis can be negative. This means that VMs have been clustered based on the

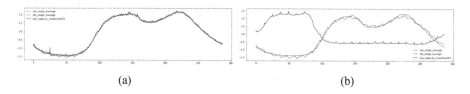

(a)   (b)

Fig. 5. (a) The most recurrent VM cluster of Fig. 4a and (b) a singular VM pattern captured by the bottom-right neuron of Fig. 4a (both appeared in [6]).

joint shape of their daily resource consumption patterns, not their absolute values. Notice that in this example we can observe a quite suspect output, since the cpu|capacity_contentionPct figure follows closely the daily traffic pattern on the involved VMs. In a normal condition of a healthy system, i.e., when VMs are provided with appropriate computational resources, we would have expected this metric to stay close to zero, or at least experience a slight increase only during the peak hours. A significantly different pattern is the one reported in Fig. 5b, corresponding to the bottom-right neuron in Fig. 4a. Such behavior represents the 8.27% of the observed daily patterns in the time period under analysis. As evident from the picture, there is a higher CPU contention during night, when the VM has lower traffic, than during the day.

An additional remark regarding the possible presence of anomalies can be done considering the fact that the VMs included in the analysis are guaranteed to have the same role in the corresponding VNFs, i.e., they manage traffic in load sharing-mode. While it was expected to obtain an identical output for all of them, the SOM-based analysis has pointed out that a subset of such VMs exhibits daily patterns very different to the expected ones instead. This could be interpreted by human operators as a warning, that requires further monitoring and analysis of the involved components of the infrastructure. In addition, it is worth noticing that asynchronous changes among the metrics included in such analysis could be indications of anomalous behavior of the NFV environment, and not necessarily of the VNF itself.

5.2   Hyper-parameters Grid Search

As mentioned in Sect. 4.1, different hyper-parameters lead to very different clusters after training. An extensive grid search has been conducted over the search space summarized in Table 1. A total of 1600 different configurations has been tested monitoring quantization error and readability of results. Figure 6 shows the effect of using a low σ value (0.1) in different map sizes. Using a low σ with a low learning rate gives the worst results with very few BMUs that capture more than 95% of data, resulting in higher quantization errors.

Table 1. The hyper-parameters values used for grid search (appeared in [6]).

Hyper-parameter	Space
SOM dimensions	8×8, 12×12, 16×16, 24×24, 32×32, 48×48
Learning rate	$0.1, 0.2, \ldots, 0.9, 1.0$
Neighborhood radius (σ)	$0.1, 0.2, \ldots, 0.9, 1.0$
Epochs	$5, 10, 20$

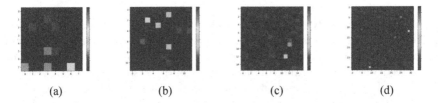

(a)   (b)   (c)   (d)

Fig. 6. SOMs with low σ values: (a) 8×8, σ: 0.1, lr: 0.2; (b) 12×12, σ: 0.1, lr: 0.2; (c) 16×16, σ: 0.1, lr: 0.9; (d) 32×32, σ: 0.1, lr: 0.8. For confidentiality reasons, the scale has been omitted (appeared in [6]).

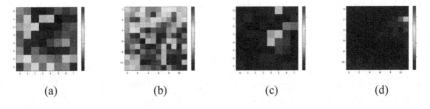

(a)   (b)   (c)   (d)

Fig. 7. SOMs with high σ values: (a) 8×8, σ: 0.6, lr: 0.2; (b) 12×12, σ: 0.6, lr: 0.2; (c) 8×8, σ: 0.6, lr: 0.9; (d) 12×12, σ: 0.6, lr: 0.9. For confidentiality reasons, the scale has been omitted (appeared in [6]).

SOM maps greater than 12×12 require very high σ (>0.8) and very low learning rate (<0.3) in order to have low quantization errors, but in these cases the results tend to become unreadable due to the fact that too many neurons specialize on similar patterns. In Fig. 7, the SOM maps reported in Fig. 7a and 7b are trained using high σ and low learning rate, while the ones reported in Fig. 7c and 7d are trained using high σ and high learning rate. Therefore, for our analysis the best combination of hyper-parameters are high values of σ (>0.6) and low values of learning rate (<0.6) with results that are better both in terms of quantization error and readability.

5.3   Per-VNF Analysis

Another interesting characterization we could perform applying the SOM-based analysis, is a study of how different VNFs behave in terms of their daily resource

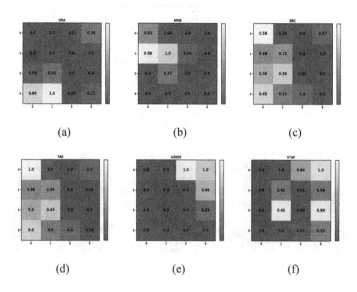

(a)　　　　　　　　(b)　　　　　　　　(c)

(d)　　　　　　　　(e)　　　　　　　　(f)

Fig. 8. SOM clusters and corresponding per-VNF hitmaps. For confidentiality reasons, the total number of hits in the hitmap cells has been rescaled to 1 (appeared in [6]).

consumption patterns. In this case, we produced hitmaps highlighting how many daily patterns of VMs of each given VNF map onto each SOM neuron. The result can be visualized as in Fig. 8. For example, by comparing such plots with the corresponding map reporting the captured behaviors (like the one in Fig. 4a, even though, in this case, the two figures are derived from different subsets of the available data), one can discover that both the SBC and the TAS VNFs have mostly the usual *"nightly/daily"* pattern, characterized by a low workload over nightly hours and a high workload over daily hours, with peaks around noon and 6pm. On the other hand, the DRA VNF exhibits the classical nightly/daily pattern for the cpu|capacity_contentionPct metric, and periodic peaks every 30 min for the other two metrics. Moreover, a consistent number of VTAP VMs are characterized by hourly periodic peaks.

5.4   Hierarchical Grouping

In this section, we report two examples of grouping/clustering technique described in Sect. 4.3, starting from another month of data, with respect to the experiments shown above. In the first example, we obtained the trained SOM whose weights are presented in Fig. 9a. By applying the distance-based grouping, with a group-distance threshold of 0.007, we obtained the clustering shown in the same figure, where neurons belonging to the same group have the same border color. Moreover, to facilitate a visual inspection of the behavior of each VM during the month, we produced a calendar view of the VMs, as shown in Fig. 9b, by associating to each couple (VM, DAY) the group of the BMU in

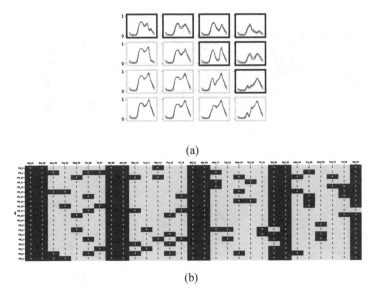

(a)

(b)

Fig. 9. (a) Distance-based grouping applied to a square SOM grid, 4 neurons per side. (b) VMs exhibiting common behaviors.

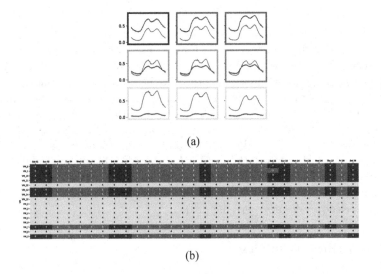

(a)

(b)

Fig. 10. (a) Distance-based grouping applied to a square SOM grid, 3 neurons per side. (b) VMs exhibiting anomalous behaviors.

the SOM grid. For instance, in this case we can notice a very common behavior: the majority of group changes take place during the week-end. The second example shows how the two outputs could be jointly used by a system operator to visually detect anomalies in the behavior of VMs. The grouped SOM grid in Fig. 10a highlights three main (i.e., more frequent) groups. In particular, the yellow group contains all the neurons within an almost flat VM metric. By inspecting the calendar in Fig. 10b, it is evident that these behaviors are associated to those VMs that have an anomalous *constant* course, without any variations during the week-end.

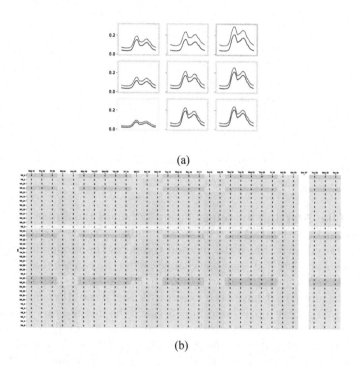

(a)

(b)

Fig. 11. (a) A SOM grid with neurons grouped in 5 behaviors. (b) Calendar view of the set of VMs involved in the analysis.

5.5 Alerting

In this section, we provide some examples of output of the two main kind of alerting systems. All the alerting systems are applied to the behaviors captured by the SOM grid in Fig. 11a. Notice the presence of two groups with a high working-level (red, orange); two groups with a low working-level (brown, green); one group with a unique almost flat neuron (gray). Figure 11b reports the behavioral evolution of the VMs whose data have been used to conduct this experiment. The reference time period is April 2020 and, in particular, on April 13th (Easter Monday) many VMs change behavior, passing from their usual high working-level group to a low working-level group.

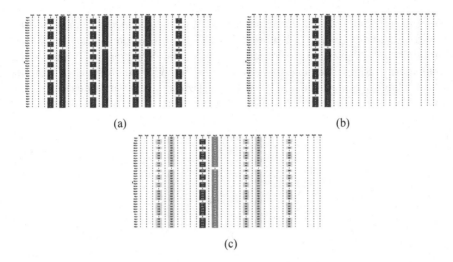

Fig. 12. (a) Strong Alerting System. (b) Weak Alerting System. (c) Fuzzy Alert System.

Calendar-Like Alerting Systems. Figure 12a shows the *Strong Alerting System* defined in Equation (SAS), with $m = 3$ and $p = 7$, where dark green cells stand for a raised alert. Since the method compares the groups in same week-days and raises an alert if at least one change occurs, we can see that many alerts have been raised (some of them are obviously false positives). In contrast, Fig. 12b shows the alerts that have been raised with the *Weak Alert System* defined in Equation (WAS), with $p = 7$ and $m = 3$. Since the method raises an alert if a group appears only once in same week-days, we can see that only a few behaviors raise an alert. The output from the *Fuzzy Alerting System* defined in Equation (ZAS), with $p = 7$, is shown in Fig. 12c. The higher the value (i.e., the darker the color), the higher the probability of an alert being significant. As expected, many of the *false-positives* reported by the *Strong Alerting System*, and not by the *Weak* one, are associated to a low value.

6   Conclusions

In this work, we focused on the problem of analysis and classification of the behavioral patterns of VM metrics in a NFV data center. We described the technique we realized, based on self-organizing maps, that is being used across the data centers of the Vodafone network operator. We described some results we obtained from its application, highlighting the capability of our technique to identify interesting points in space and time (i.e., precise VMs and hosts within the infrastructure, and precise days within the analyzed time range) with potentially anomalous behaviors, thus deserving further attention and investigations by data center operators. Also, we detailed a clustering technique applied over a trained SOM codebook in order to mitigate the problem of neuron over-representation, and an alerting system built atop the SOM-based clustering, improving the anomaly detection pipeline effectively reducing the number of false positives.

In our experimentation, we identified a variety of open questions that still need additional investigations. First, the proposed technique has a number of hyper-parameters (SOM grid size and parameters, and various thresholds as described in Sect. 4) that have to be decided. A grid search can be used for such purpose, but it requires a non-negligible processing time as possible configurations can easily grow in the range of tens or hundreds. In order to select the best SOM hyper-parameters, the various analysis runs should be compared with one another using an automated and quantitative assessment method. This cannot be simply done based on the SOM quantization error, as it would decrease increasing the SOM size, driving the choice towards excessively large networks. For example, we plan to use the average silhouette width to such purpose [29]. Finally, another promising path we plan to explore is the one to combine our approach with the use of Deep Learning (DL) for time-series classification [18,19,21]. An interesting approach could be using the SOM to produce a more compact and discrete representation of a time-series autoencoder, as explained in [9].

References

1. Van den Berg, F.D., et al.: Product uniformity control-a research collaboration of European steel industries to non-destructive evaluation of microstructure and mechanical properties. In: Electromagnetic Non-Destructive Evaluation (XXI), 6 September 2017 through 8 September 2017, pp. 120–129 (2018)
2. Bertero, C., Roy, M., Sauvanaud, C., Tredan, G.: Experience report: log mining using natural language processing and application to anomaly detection. In: 2017 IEEE 28th International Symposium on Software Reliability Engineering (ISSRE), pp. 351–360. IEEE, October 2017
3. Buczak, A.L., Guven, E.: A survey of data mining and machine learning methods for cyber security intrusion detection. IEEE Commun. Surv. Tutorials 18(2), 1153–1176 (2015)
4. Canetta, L., Cheikhrouhou, N., Glardon, R.: Applying two-stage SOM-based clustering approaches to industrial data analysis. Prod. Plann. Control 16(8), 774–784 (2005)
5. Chen, D.R., Chang, R.F., Huang, Y.L.: Breast cancer diagnosis using self-organizing map for sonography. Ultrasound Med. Biol. 26(3), 405–411 (2000)
6. Cucinotta, T., et al.: Behavioral analysis for virtualized network functions: a SOM-based approach. In: Proceedings of the 10th International Conference on Cloud Computing and Services Science. Prague, Czech Republic, May 2020
7. Díaz, I., Domínguez, M., Cuadrado, A.A., Fuertes, J.J.: A new approach to exploratory analysis of system dynamics using SOM. applications to industrial processes. Expert Syst. Appl. 34(4), 2953–2965 (2008)
8. Farshchi, M., Schneider, J.G., Weber, I., Grundy, J.: Metric selection and anomaly detection for cloud operations using log and metric correlation analysis. J. Syst. Softw. 137, 531–549 (2018)

9. Fortuin, V., Hüser, M., Locatello, F., Strathmann, H., Rätsch, G.: SOM-VAE: interpretable discrete representation learning on time series. In: International Conference on Learning Representations (2019)
10. Frey, C.W.: Monitoring of complex industrial processes based on self-organizing maps and watershed transformations. In: 2012 IEEE International Conference on Industrial Technology, pp. 1041–1046. IEEE (2012)
11. Fuertes, J.J., Domìnguez, M., Reguera, P., Prada, M.A., Dìaz, I., Cuadrado, A.A.: Visual dynamic model based on self-organizing maps for supervision and fault detection in industrial processes. Eng. Appl. Artif. Intell. **23**(1), 8–17 (2010)
12. Gulenko, A., Wallschlager, M., Schmidt, F., Kao, O., Liu, F.: Evaluating machine learning algorithms for anomaly detection in clouds. In: Proceeding of IEEE International Conference on Big Data, pp. 2716–2721. IEEE, December 2016
13. Gulenko, A., Wallschläger, M., Schmidt, F., Kao, O., Liu, F.: A system architecture for real-time anomaly detection in large-scale NFV systems. Procedia Comput. Sci. **94**, 491–496 (2016), the 11th International Conference on Future Networks and Communications (FNC 2016) / The 13th International Conference on Mobile Systems and Pervasive Computing (MobiSPC 2016) / Affiliated Workshops
14. Gupta, L., Samaka, M., Jain, R., Erbad, A., Bhamare, D., Chan, H.A.: Fault and performance management in multi-cloud based NFV using shallow and deep predictive structures. J. Reliable Intell. Environ. **3**(4), 21–231 (2017)
15. Harris, T.: A kohonen SOM based, machine health monitoring system which enables diagnosis of faults not seen in the training set. In: Proceedings of 1993 International Conference on Neural Networks, vol. 1, pp. 947–950. IEEE, Nagoya, Japan (1993)
16. Hawilo, H., Shami, A., Mirahmadi, M., Asal, R.: NFV: state of the art, challenges, and implementation in next generation mobile networks (vEPC). IEEE Netw. **28**(6), 18–26 (2014)
17. Haykin, S.: Neural Networks: A Comprehensive Foundation, 3rd edn. Prentice-Hall Inc, USA (2007)
18. Ismail Fawaz, H., Forestier, G., Weber, J., Idoumghar, L., Muller, P.-A.: Deep learning for time series classification: a review. Data Min. Knowl. Discov. **33**(4), 917–963 (2019). https://doi.org/10.1007/s10618-019-00619-1
19. Kashiparekh, K., Narwariya, J., Malhotra, P., Vig, L., Shroff, G.: ConvTimeNet: a pre-trained deep convolutional neural network for time series classification. In: International Joint Conference on Neural Networks, IJCNN 2019 Budapest, Hungary, 14–19 July 2019, pp. 1–8. IEEE (2019)
20. Le, L., Sinh, D., Lin, B.P., Tung, L.: Applying big data, machine learning, and SDN/NFV to 5G traffic clustering, forecasting, and management. In: 4th IEEE Conference on Network Softwarization and Workshops, pp. 168–176, June 2018
21. Malhotra, P., TV, V., Vig, L., Agarwal, P., Shroff, G.: TimeNet: pre-trained deep recurrent neural network for time series classification. In: 25th European Symposium on Artificial Neural Networks, Computational Intelligence and Machine Learning, 2017, Bruges, Belgium (2017)
22. Malini, N., Pushpa, M.: Analysis on credit card fraud identification techniques based on KNN and outlier detection. In: 2017 Third International Conference on Advances in Electrical, Electronics, Information, Communication and Bio-Informatics (AEEICB), pp. 255–258, February 2017
23. Mancini, R., Ritacco, A., Lanciano, G., Cucinotta, T.: XPySom: high-performance self-organizing maps. In: IEEE 32nd International Symposium on Computer Architecture and High Performance Computing (SBAC-PAD). Porto, Portugal (2020)

24. Miyazawa, M., Hayashi, M., Stadler, R.: VNMF: distributed fault detection using clustering approach for network function virtualization. In: IFIP/IEEE International Symposium on Integrated Network Management, pp. 640–645, May 2015
25. NFV Industry Specif. Group: Network Functions Virtualisation. Introductory White Paper (2012)
26. Niwa, T., Miyazawa, M., Hayashi, M., Stadler, R.: Universal fault detection for NFV using SOM-based clustering. In: 2015 17th Asia-Pacific Network Operations and Management Symposium (APNOMS), pp. 315–320, August 2015
27. Ostberg, P.O., et al.: Reliable capacity provisioning for distributed cloud/edge/fog computing applications. In: EuCNC 2017 - European Conference on Networks and Communications, pp. 1–6. IEEE, June 2017
28. Pitakrat, T., Okanović, D., van Hoorn, A., Grunske, L.: Hora: architecture-aware online failure prediction. J. Syst. Softw. **137**, 669–685 (2018)
29. Rousseeuw, P.J.: Silhouettes: a graphical aid to the interpretation and validation of cluster analysis. J. Comput. Appl. Math. **20**, 53–65 (1987)
30. Samrin, R., Vasumathi, D.: Review on anomaly based network intrusion detection system. In: 2017 International Conference on Electrical, Electronics, Communication, Computer, and Optimization Techniques, pp. 141–147, December 2017
31. Sauvanaud, C., Kaâniche, M., Kanoun, K., Lazri, K., Da Silva Silvestre, G.: Anomaly detection and diagnosis for cloud services: practical experiments and lessons learned. J. Syst. Softw. **139**, 84–106 (2018)
32. Van Gassen, S., et al.: FlowSOM: using self-organizing maps for visualization and interpretation of cytometry data. Cytometry A **87**(7), 636–645 (2015)
33. Vannucci, M., Colla, V.: Novel classification method for sensitive problems and uneven datasets based on neural networks and fuzzy logic. Appl. Soft Comput. **11**(2), 2383–2390 (2011)
34. Wallschläger, M., Gulenko, A., Schmidt, F., Kao, O., Liu, F.: Automated anomaly detection in virtualized services using deep packet inspection. Procedia Comput. Sci. **110**, 510–515 (2017)
35. Watanabe, Y., Otsuka, H., Sonoda, M., Kikuchi, S., Matsumoto, Y.: Online failure prediction in cloud datacenters by real-time message pattern learning. In: Cloud-Com 2012 - Proceedings: 2012 4th IEEE International Conference on Cloud Computing Technology and Science, pp. 504–511. IEEE, December 2012
36. Wittek, P., Gao, S.C., Lim, I.S., Zhao, L.: Somoclu: an efficient parallel library for self-organizing maps. J. Stat. Softw. **78**(9), June 2017

From DevOps to NoOps: Is It Worth It?

Anshul Jindal[✉][iD] and Michael Gerndt[iD]

Chair of Computer Architecture and Parallel Systems,
Technical University of Munich, Garching, Germany
anshul.jindal@tum.de, gerndt@in.tum.de

Abstract. With the rise of the adoption of microservice architecture
due to its agility, scalability, and resiliency for building the cloud-based
applications and their deployment using containerization, DevOps were
in demand for handling the development and operations together. However, nowadays serverless computing offers a new way of developing
and deploying cloud-native applications. Serverless computing also called
NoOps, offloads management and server configuration (operations work)
from the user to the cloud provider and lets the user focus only on the
product developments. Hence, there are debates regarding which deployment strategy to use.

This research provides a performance comparison of a cloud-native
web application along with three different function benchmarks in terms
of scalability, reliability, and latency when deployed using DevOps and
NoOps deployment strategy. NoOps deployment in this work is achieved
using Google Cloud Function and OpenWhisk, while DevOps is achieved
using the Kubernetes engine. This research shows that neither of the
deployment strategies fits all the scenarios. The experimental results
demonstrate that each type of deployment strategy has its advantages
under different scenarios. The DevOps deployment strategy has a huge
performance advantage (almost 72% lesser 90 percentile response time)
for simple web-based requests and requests accessing databases while
compute-intensive applications perform better with NoOps deployment.
Additionally, NoOps deployment provides better scaling-agility as compared to DevOps.

Keywords: Microservices · Serverless · DevOps · NoOps ·
Cloud-native applications · Cloud computing

1 Introduction

Cloud computing providing a "pay-as-you-go" model, enables cheap and easy
access to the data processing and storage resources. Nowadays most enterprises
have migrated or refactored their existing monolithic-based applications into
the microservices architecture and deployed it on the cloud [14]. Microservices
architecture offers higher agility since it decouples a big application service into
smaller microservices and each microservice is then deployed separately either

© Springer Nature Switzerland AG 2021
D. Ferguson et al. (Eds.): CLOSER 2020, CCIS 1399, pp. 178–202, 2021.
https://doi.org/10.1007/978-3-030-72369-9_8

on a virtual machine or in a container where the resources can be scaled on-demand. Developers are now not only assigned the task for the development of the microservices but also include the operations task like deployments, therefore are called *DevOps*. DevOps is the fusion of development and operations. It drives the services lifecycle, from the design to the delivery. Besides many advantages, microservices architecture also has some disadvantages in software development. For instance, each service communicates through the network via REST API endpoints, which can pose data security concerns during the communication. Also, network latency and load balancing do arise. Furthermore, research shows that the development team with a strong DevOps culture may get benefit from the microservices architecture, therefore the effort to establish DevOps culture is another consideration for adopting a microservices architecture [38].

On the other hand, serverless computing has gained higher popularity and more adoption in different fields since the launch of AWS Lambda in 2014 [19]. Serverless computing is a cloud computing model that abstracts server manage-ment and infrastructure decisions away from the users [43]. In this model, the allo-cation of resources is managed by the cloud service provider rather than by the team of application developers. In other words, DevOps are free from operations work and can purely focus on development and is therefore called *NoOps*. Also, in serverless computing cost is charged on the number of requests received to the functions and the time it takes for the code to execute [17]. This pricing model is much simpler as compared to the traditional instance pricing model which is based on the number of instances and their diverse types. Therefore, application owners in this model are also free from the decisions of choosing instance types and several instances. Function-as-a-Service (FaaS) is a key enabler of serverless computing [43]. In FaaS, an application is decomposed into simple, standalone functions that are uploaded to a FaaS platform for execution. These functions are stateless, i.e., the state is not kept across function invocations. Functions can be invoked by a user's HTTP request or by another type of event created within the FaaS platform. The FaaS platform is responsible for deploying and facili-tating resources to the application functions. Currently, there exist many open source and commercial FaaS platforms [31]. All of the large cloud providers have FaaS platforms available based on a *container orchestration platform* such as Kubernetes. In this work, we have used OpenWhisk and Google Cloud Function as the FaaS platforms for deploying application functions.

Both *DevOps* and *NoOps* methodologies have their advantages and disadvan-tages and the decision to adopt a design pattern depends on the team capability and project requirements. In this research, we have analyzed a cloud-native web application along with 3 function benchmarks refactored into both microser-vices and FaaS deployment models from the aspect of scalability, reliability, and latency. The experimental results demonstrate that the *DevOps* deployment strategy has a huge performance advantage (almost 72% lesser percentile-90 response time) for simple web-based requests and requests accessing databases while compute-intensive applications perform better with *NoOps* deployment.

Additionally, *NoOps* deployment provides better scaling-agility as compared to *DevOps*.

The main contribution of this paper are as follows:

- Performance comparison between *DevOps* and *NoOps* deployment methodologies using two different methods in terms of scalability, reliability, cost, and latency. In our previous work [16], we compared microservices to serverless using AWS Lambda as the FaaS platform and a native cloud web application but in this work, we have extended it by using OpenWhisk and Google Cloud Functions as FaaS platforms. Furthermore, we have added additional function benchmarks and an application for the evaluations.
- Performance comparison between OpenWhisk and Google Cloud Functions is presented as part of this work and we are the first one to do so.
- We highlight different use cases recommendations where *DevOps* and *NoOps* deployment methodologies can be used based on the type of load, scenario, and the amount of the requests.

The rest of this article is composed as follows. Section 2 discusses the background knowledge required for this paper in brief. Section 3 provides the overall methodology used for the evaluation including the different methods and load test settings. Section 4 showcase the results of the conducted analysis. Section 5 summarizes the discussion of the results and in Sect. 6 we describe some of the previous works in this domain. Lastly, Sect. 7 concludes the paper.

2   Background

In this section, we first present an overview of the *DevOps* and *NoOps* deployments cloud model. Following this, we describe the architecture and high-level workflow of the two FaaS platforms used in this work.

2.1   DevOps-Based Cloud Model

DevOps cloud model is based on the microservices architecture where the developers are responsible both for the development and operations task. Microservices consists of a suite of modules, and each module is dedicated to a specific business goal and communicates via a well-defined interface. The principle of *DevOps* cloud model architecture is loose-coupling, which requires multiple service instances for an application [36]. The deployment of *DevOps* cloud model can be achieved either by deploying each microservice on a separate virtual machine instance or deploying microservices per container or one can even combine multiple microservices per virtual machine and container. The containerization deployment benefits from the higher deployment speed, agility, and lower resources consumption [37]. This strategy also allows each microservice instance to run in isolation on a host. This enables the guaranteed quality of service for each microservice at the cost of idle resources. Container orchestration tools like

Kubernetes[1] and Google Kubernetes Engine (GKE)[2] can be used for managing the microservices containers.

The benefits of this model are improved fault tolerance, flexibility in using technologies and scalability, and speed up of the application [32]. However, there are also some disadvantages such as the increase of development and deployment complexity, implementing an inter-service communication mechanism, and challenging to conduct end-to-end testing [12].

2.2 NoOps-Based Cloud Model

NoOps cloud model is based on the serverless computing where Function-as-a-Service (FaaS) platform facilitates application development and the user does not have to worry about the infrastructure management, but only about the code being deployed. The pricing is charged based on the number of requests to the functions and the duration, the time it takes for the function code to execute [1]. The latter varies according to the number of resources such as memory and CPU cores allocated to the function, and are automatically adapted to deliver the best performance. Instead of developing application logic in the form of services and managing the required resources, the application developer implements fine-grained functions connected in an event-driven application and deploys them into the FaaS platform [43]. The platform is responsible for providing resources for function invocations and performs automatic scaling depending on the workload. The functions can be closely integrated with other services, e.g., cloud databases, authentication and authorization services, and messaging services. These services are called Backend-as-a-Service (BaaS). BaaS are the third-party services that replace a subset of functionality in a function and allow the users to only focus on the application logic [26]. In FaaS, function invocations are handled by using containers. Since functions are stateless, the state of the application is stored in databases. In comparison to *DevOps* model, *NoOps* has three advantages (1) no continuously running services are required, (2) functions are only charged when they are executed, and (3) the function abstraction increases the developer's productivity.

One of the biggest differences between other forms of cloud models and the *NoOps* model is scalability [22]. The application automatically scales up or down based on the resource usage (with scaling down to zero number of instances as well) and developers do not have to specify any scaling parameters. The infrastructure of the cloud service provider starts up ephemeral instances of each function on-demand. In general, the total cost of ownership decreases.

NoOps based functions can be invoked by a user's HTTP request or by another type of event created within a FaaS platform. The FaaS platform is responsible for providing resources for function invocations and performs automatic scaling. Currently, a significant number of open source and commercial FaaS platforms are available [31]. FaaS platforms implementations are based

---

[1] https://kubernetes.io/docs/.

[2] https://cloud.google.com/kubernetes-engine.

on starting containers for function invocations on top of a *container orchestration platform* such as Kubernetes. Applications are defined via a *deployment specification* that describes the functions, APIs, permissions, configurations, and events that make up a serverless application. The specification can be given via a command-line or web interface, or by using some frameworks like Serverless [39] and Architect [8].

We introduce in the following subsections two FaaS platforms which are used as part of this work.

OpenWhisk (OW). Apache OpenWhisk is a serverless open source cloud platform that was originally developed by a research group at IBM in 2015 and was released in December 2016. It was later donated to the Apache Software Foundation [33]. It powers IBM's serverless offering, IBM Cloud Functions, and implements FaaS on top of Kubernetes as the container orchestration platform. Functions in OpenWhisk are called actions and the execution of an action is called an invocation. Actions and rules can be created through the command-line interface (CLI) (`wsk` [6]), user interface (UI), or SDK. Created actions can then be invoked either manually through the same methods or by event triggers. Events can originate from multiple sources including timers, databases, message queues, or websites like Slack.

OpenWhisk consists of multiple components under the hood and all the components are packaged inside their individual docker containers when OpenWhisk is deployed [7]. Each function invocation is translated into an HTTP request to the Nginx server [35]. The Nginx server is a single point of entry and its main purpose is to implement the support for the HTTPS secure web protocol. On receiving a request, the Nginx server forwards it to the controller where the controller is responsible for authenticating and authorizing the requests. The controller keeps track of the availability of the invokers, i.e., the workers that run the code and chooses one of them for the invocation. The controller publishes the messages to Kafka addressed at a chosen invoker and once the message delivery is confirmed by the invoker, an HTTP request is sent back to the user with an *ActivationId*, which can be used for retrieving the results of this function call. Invokers set up a new docker container for each action, inject the code into them, execute the code, obtain the results, and then destroy it. These containers are run inside Kubernetes pods. There can be an invoker per Kubernetes worker node or an invoker can be responsible for managing multiple Kubernetes worker nodes. Functions can also be chained together into sequences where chained functions use the output of the preceding function as input.

Google Cloud Functions (GCF). Google Cloud Functions is a serverless execution environment for building and connecting services in a cloud-based application [2]. With Google Cloud Functions, developers do not need to provision any infrastructure or worry about managing any servers, the whole environment including infrastructure, operating systems, and runtime environments are managed by Google. Currently, Cloud Functions supports JavaScript, Python 3, Go, and Java runtimes. Cloud Functions are simple, single-purpose functions that are attached to events emitted from the cloud infrastructure and services. The function is triggered when an event being watched is fired. These events can be things like changes in a database, files added to a storage system, or a new virtual machine instance is created. A response to an event is created using a trigger which can then be attached to a function to capture and act on events.

Each Cloud Function runs in its own isolated secure execution context, scales automatically, and has a lifecycle independent from other functions [18]. Cloud Functions handles incoming requests by assigning them to instances of function. Depending on the volume of requests, as well as the number of existing function instances, Cloud Functions may assign a request to an existing instance or create a new one. Each instance of a function handles only one concurrent request at a time. Thus the original request can use the full amount of resources (CPU and memory) that you requested. In cases where inbound request volume exceeds the number of existing instances, Cloud Functions start multiple new instances to handle requests. This automatic scaling behavior allows Cloud Functions to handle many requests in parallel, each using a different instance of the function.

3   Methodology

For understanding the performance differences between the *DevOps* and *NoOps* deployment strategies, we consider a range of benchmarks. These benchmarks are evaluated for both the deployment strategies using two different methods in each case. In this section, we first present the details about the benchmarks used for evaluating the deployment strategies and then describe the four different deployments (Kubernetes hosted by Google Kubernetes Engine and self-hosted Kubernetes cluster for DevOps, and OpenWhisk based functions deployment and Google Cloud functions for NoOps) methods used in this work. We also present the load testing infrastructure and details used for the evaluation in this section.

3.1   Benchmarks

We have considered a microservices application matching with the real world applications along with 3 function benchmarks which include compute-intensive, simple API endpoint, and image processing functions for evaluating the deployment strategies. Below subsections present the details about the microservices application and the benchmarks.

Cinema Microservices Application. For demonstrating the performance differences between deployment of an application using the DevOps methodology (microservices-based deployment) and NoOps methodology (function-based deployment), we use an opensource microservices application: *cinema*[3], which

---

[3] https://github.com/umermansoor/microservices.

contains movies information, show timings of the movies, users information, and movie bookings made by the user. The overall architecture, its services, interaction between them, and the API endpoints in each of the services are shown in Fig. 1. All the data required by each service is stored inside the Mongo database. The application is developed in Python and consists of the following four services:

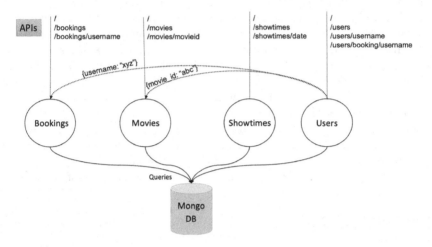

Fig. 1. Overall architecture of the microservices *cinema* application along with the interaction between its services and the API endpoints supported by each of its services.

- **Movies:** This service is responsible for accessing the movie's information (movie title, director, and rating) stored in the "movies" collection of MongoDB. It has two main API endpoints, 1) `/movies` to return all the movies information as JSON, and 2) `/movies/movieid` to return a movie information based on the specified `movieid` parameter.
- **Showtimes:** Movies show timings are managed by this service and are stored in the "showtimes" collection of MongoDB. It also has two main API endpoints, 1) `/showtimes` to return all the shows information for all the dates as JSON, and 2) `/showtimes/date` to return movie shows information for the specified `date`.
- **Bookings:** It manages the movie shows booked by the users and stores them into the "bookings" collection of MongoDB. It also has two main API endpoints, 1) `/bookings` to return all the bookings made by all the users as JSON, and 2) `/bookings/username` to return the movie bookings made by a particular user.
- **Users:** It manages the user information (full name, and address) stored in the "users" collection of MongoDB. It has three main endpoints: 1) `/users` to return all the users information as JSON, 2) `/users/username` to return user information based on the specified `username` parameter and 3) `/users/booking/username` to return the movie bookings information made by the user for the specified `username`; here the service first queries the *Bookings* service to provide the movie reservations made by the user and then

based on that information it queries the *Movies* service to get the movies information and return its JSON back to the user.

Additionally, for testing the *NoOps* deployment, the application services are decomposed into different functions. Each of the API endpoints is converted into a new function and therefore in total, there are 13 functions and 4 microservices. Summary of each of these functions and microservices is shown in the Table 1.

Table 1. Overview of the API endpoints, microservices containers, their ports and serverless functions in *cinema-application* and used in this work for evaluation.

Service	API endpoint	Microservices (container:port)	Serverless (function)
Movies	/ /movies /movies/movieid	movies:5001	movies-base movies-all movies-id
Bookings	/ /bookings /bookings/username	bookings:5003	bookings-base bookings-all bookings-username
Showtimes	/ /showtimes /showtimes/date	showtimes:5002	showtimes-base showtimes-all showtimes-date
Users	/ /users /users/username /users/booking/username	users:5000	users-base users-all users-id users-booking

Functions. To investigate further the performance differences of each deployment strategy, we used a subset of the benchmarks provided with the FaaSProfiler [40] and modified them for our use case. Furthermore, we developed microservices implementations of the chosen functions to enable their execution on the Kubernetes engine. The OpenWhisk action container generally includes code for the function along with its language runtime. OpenWhisk processes the incoming HTTP requests for the function invocation with any number of arguments and sends the results back to the user or caller. For most of the functions, we have used the default runtime environment provided by OpenWhisk depending on the language that the function is written in. If a function uses some extra packages which are not part of their default language runtimes, we created a Docker runtime for it based on their default docker runtime. While on google cloud functions the package requirements along with the code are specified. They automatically create a runtime environment based on it.

The functions used as part of this work are summarized in the Table 2 along with their description and language runtimes. The `nodeinfo` function exposes an HTTP endpoint and provides the user with basic information about the system such as hostname, underlying architecture, number of CPUs, etc. We utilize this function to test the general performance of each strategy and get an overall idea of their performance on a basic web application. The compute-intensive `primes-python` function is used for comparing their performances on compute-intensive applications and study the scalability aspects. Finally, for demonstrating the access latency each strategy adds up when accessing an object (in our work an image) stored on google cloud storage `image-processing` function is used where after getting the image basic operations like flipping, rotating, conversion to grayscale, and resize are performed.

Table 2. List of functions we developed or modified for demonstrating performance differences of each deployment strategy.

Function name	Description	Language runtime
nodeinfo	Gives basic characteristics of node like CPU count, architecture, uptime	Node.js
primes-python	Calculates prime numbers till 10000000	Python 3
image-processing	Reads an image from object storage (here google object storage) and performs basic operations	Python 3

3.2   Deployment Strategies

The above-presented application and function benchmarks are deployed using the two strategies: *DevOps* and *NoOps*. *DevOps* deployment is achieved by deploying the microservices on a Kubernetes cluster and configuring the scaling and other

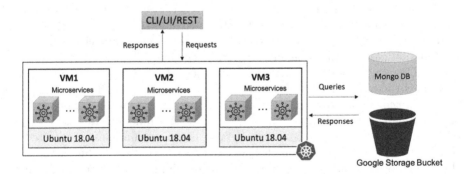

Fig. 2. Overall architecture of *DevOps-Deployment* model along with the interaction between its components using Kubernetes as the underneath container orchestration. The Kubernetes engine is created using the Google Kubernetes Engine (GKE) on Google Compute Platform (GCP).

parameters manually, whereas *NoOps* deployment is achieved by deploying the functions (of the applications and function benchmarks) on a FaaS platform. In this work, we have used our self hosted OpenWhisk platform and Google Cloud Functions as FaaS platforms. Additionally, we have hosted the mongo database externally therefore it remains common to all the methods along with the google storage bucket for the *image-processing* function.

DevOps. The *DevOps* deployment strategy is achieved by deploying the microservices on a Kubernetes cluster with a manual configuration of the scaling parameters. In this work, this is achieved using two methods:

1. **Google Cloud Platform hosted Kubernetes Engine (devops-gcp-hosted- kubernetes):** In this deployment method, a Google Kubernetes Engine (GKE) cluster is created with three nodes each with a configuration of 4 vCPU and 16 GB of memory. The Autoscaling of nodes is not enabled. Once the cluster is created then each of the microservices of the application and the converted microservices of the functions are deployed on it. Additionally, each of the microservices are exposed externally using a Load Balancer. Also, horizontal pod autoscaling is enabled for each of the microservices as well with the CPU utilization threshold set to 80%, and minimum replicas to 1 and maximum as 5. The overall deployment architecture is shown in Fig. 2. Clients through the command-line interface (CLI) or REST APIs send requests to the external addresses of the exposed microservices and get a response in return. Each of the microservices of the application can access the externally hosted mongo database and google storage bucket.

2. **Self-hosted Kubernetes Engine (devops-self-hosted-kubernetes):** In this deployment method, instead of using the Kubernetes engine hosted by GKE, we created our own using the kubeadm[4] tool with three nodes each with the same configuration as the previous method (4 vCPU and 16 GB memory). The cluster has three nodes with one master and two worker nodes but to have the same configuration as the one hosted by GKE we tainted the master node as well so as to allow the pods to be scheduled on it. Other configurations: deployment of the services, exposing them externally, and enabling autoscaling were done in a similar manner as the above method. Each of the service here also can access the externally hosted mongo database and google storage bucket. The overall deployment architecture is similar to the one shown in Fig. 2.

---

[4] https://kubernetes.io/docs/setup/production-environment/tools/kubeadm/create-cluster-kubeadm/.

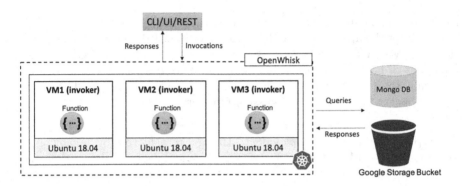

Fig. 3. Overall architecture of *NoOps-Deployment* model using OpenWhisk with Kubernetes as its container factory. The Kubernetes engine is created using the Google Kubernetes Engine (GKE) on Google Compute Platform (GCP).

NoOps. The *NoOps* deployment strategy is achieved by deploying the functions on a FaaS platform. Functions can then be invoked by a user's HTTP request or by another type of event created within the FaaS platform. The FaaS platform is responsible for providing resources for function invocations and performs automatic scaling. In this work, we have used two FaaS platforms for the evaluation:

1. **OpenWhisk (noops-openwhisk):** We started an OpenWhisk platform on top of a Kubernetes cluster hosted using Google Kubernetes Engine (GKE) with three nodes each with a configuration of 4 vCPU and 16 GB of memory. Additionally, we increased the default limits on the number of concurrent invocations and invocations per minute which can be served in OpenWhisk to 99999, and the memory allocated to the invoker is set to 2048 MiB. Once the OpenWhisk is deployed, then the *wsk* command-line interface is used for deploying the functions onto the OpenWhisk. Each function is allocated memory of 256 MB. The overall deployment architecture is shown in Fig. 3. Clients through the command-line interface (CLI) or REST APIs send function invocation requests to the exposed OpenWhsik Nginx external address and get responses in return.
2. **Google Cloud Functions (nops-google-cloud-functions):** In this deployment method, instead of using the self-hosted FaaS platform, we have used the Google Cloud Function for deploying the functions. As part of it, we only specified the function runtime and the python code of the functions. Google Cloud automatically handles the operational infrastructure. Each function is allocated memory of 256 MB along with Python 3.7 as the function runtime and used HTTP as the trigger type. Each of the function here is exposed externally and also access the externally hosted mongo database and google storage bucket. The overall deployment architecture is shown in the Fig. 4.

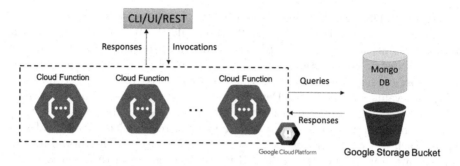

Fig. 4. Overall architecture of *NoOps-Deployment* model using Google Cloud Functions on Google Cloud Platform (GCP).

3.3 Load Test Settings and Infrastructure

Our evaluation strategy is implemented via a load testing tool - *k6* [3]. *k6* is a developer-centric open-source load and performance regression testing tool for testing the performance of the cloud-native backend infrastructure, including APIs, microservices, functions, containers, and websites. *k6* generates different patterns of the user workload to the deployed system. *k6* uses a script for running the tests where the HTTP(s) endpoint along with the request parameters are specified. HTTP(s) endpoint represents the deployed microservice or function endpoint. Two of the other k6 parameters which are configured as part of each test are:

- **Virtual Users (VUs):** Virtual Users (VUs) are the entities in k6 that execute the test and make HTTP(s) or websocket requests. VUs are concurrent and will continuously iterate through the request endpoint until the test ends.
- **Duration:** A string specifying the total duration a test will run. During this time each VU will execute the script in a loop.

The number of requests per second generated by k6 depends on the number of VUs and the time taken by each request to complete. For example, if there are 10 VUs with total test duration set to 10 min and each request from a VU took 30 s to complete, then from each VU, there will be 2 requests per minute and 20 requests per minute from 10 VUs with a total of roughly 200 requests completed in the whole duration.

k6 is deployed on the Google Compute Platform and the testing results from *k6* are ingested into the InfluxDB[5], which is an open-source time-series database. Additionally, Grafana[6], an open-source analytic & monitoring solution, visualizes the queried data from the InfluxDB and presents it in real-time in a user-defined dashboard style.

The performance for each deployed strategy is evaluated by calculating the HTTP-request-duration (90-percentile), and the number of total requests served

---

[5] https://docs.influxdata.com/influxdb/v1.7/.
[6] https://grafana.com/docs/grafana/latest/.

successfully. The response time for a HTTP request below which 90% of the response time values lie is called the 90-percentile (P90) response time, which means 90% of the requests are processed in a 90-percentile response time or less. This metric is important from the SLA point of view, where one wants to have most of the requests (90% in this case) completed before a certain time. We have evaluated each of the DevOps and NoOps strategies through different microservices and functions API endpoints across linearly increasing (continuously increasing) and random (random number of requests) user workload patterns. Each test of an API endpoint is executed for 30 min. The total duration for which the metrics data is collected is set to 31 min and the sampling rate is set to 10 s, i.e., metrics values are aggregated for 10 s. The term unit time refers to the sampling interval in Sect. 4.

4   Results

To compare the performance of both *DevOps* and *NoOps* strategies, we focused on the 90-percentile response time of requests along with the number of requests served. The x-axis for each of the graph represents the unit time duration (each point corresponds to aggregated value over 10 s). In the section, we present our findings from different tests across different deployment strategies.

4.1   Cinema Application

As part of this application, we only show the results from 2 API endpoints: 1) /movies, and 2) /users/booking/username for both the workload patterns, 2 deployment strategies and their 2 ways of achieving it. The rest of the API endpoints in this application are similar to /movies and hence are not presented.

/movies API Endpoint. The /movies API endpoint which is used to get all the movies stored in the Mongo database is used for demonstrating the evaluation. Figure 5 shows the comparison results for this API endpoint for different deployment strategies along with two different methods by which these two can be achieved on two workload patterns for two metrics: number of requests served and P90 response time. Overall *DevOps* strategy compared to *NoOps* showcased the best performance results. *devops-gcp-hosted-kubernetes* along with *devops-self-hosted-kubernetes* achieved almost the similar performance on both types of workloads showcasing approximately a response time of 4.1 ms and average number of requests served per second as 13.65 on linearly increasing workload and 3.77 ms on random workload pattern with serving 9.98 number of requests per second. However, in case of the *NoOps* strategy, *noops-openWhisk* showcased the worst performance with the P90 response time of *1322* ms for linearly increasing workload and 780 ms on random workload pattern. Also, *noops-google-cloud-functions* compared to *DevOps* methods has a huge performance drop but is better than the *noops-openWhisk-functions* showcasing approximately a response time of 344.74 ms and average number of requests served per second

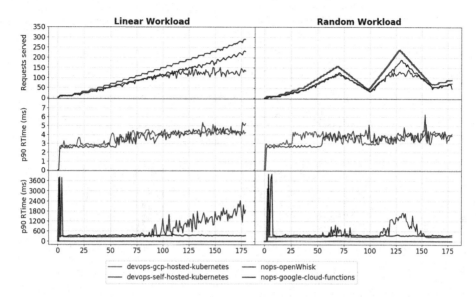

Fig. 5. /movies API endpoint performance comparison results for different deployment strategies along with two different methods by which these two can be achieved on two different workload patterns for two metrics: number of requests served and P90 response time.

as 10.52 on linearly increasing workload, and 339.94 ms on random workload pattern with serving 7.69 number of requests per second.

The high requests response times in the case of the *NoOps* strategy at the beginning of each test is due to the cold-start [30] problem but afterward, it becomes stable. The performance drop in *noops-openWhisk-functions* compared to *noops-google-cloud-functions* can be attributed to the no availability of the resources underneath as virtual machines scaling was not enabled which might be possible in google cloud functions. Furthermore, finding optimal configuration parameters for each workload is required. One potential explanation of the huge performance difference between *NoOps* and *DevOps* strategies can be due to the big virtualization stack (FaaS platform) added inside *NoOps* for decreasing the operational tasks, which does not exists in *DevOps*.

/users/bookings API Endpoint. /users/booking/username API endpoint returns the movie booking information made by the user. This service is querying two other services. It takes **username** as the parameter and first queries the /bookings/username API endpoint to get the movie reservations made by the user and then based on that information it queries the */movies/movieid* service to get the movies information and return its JSON to the user. Figure 6 shows the comparison results for this API endpoint for different deployment strategies along with two different methods by which these two can be achieved on two

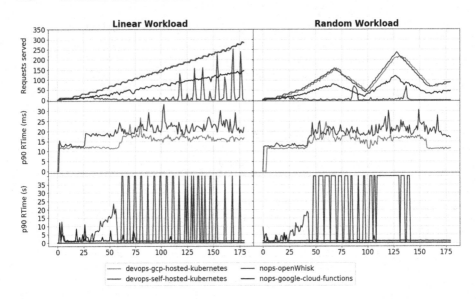

Fig. 6. /users/bookings API endpoint performance comparison results for different deployment strategies along with two different methods by which these two can be achieved on two different workload patterns for two metrics: number of requests served and P90 response time.

workload patterns. Overall as in the previous result, *DevOps* strategy compared to *NoOps* showcased the best performance results.

Although *devops-gcp-hosted-kubernetes* along with *devops-self-hosted-kubernetes* achieved almost the similar performance on both types of workloads but opposite to previous results they have a small difference of approximately **5 ms** (*devops-self-hosted-kubernetes* taking a longer time to process requests) between the P90 response times for both the workloads while serving an almost equal number of requests per second. On the other hand, *noops-openWhisk-functions* could not handle the load after a certain number of requests and start taking more than a minute to process the requests which can also be seen in the Fig. 6 (3rd row, 1st column). However, *noops-google-cloud-functions* showcased better performance than *noops-openWhisk* but again like previous results have a huge performance overhead almost having **72x** more P90 response time than *Devops* deployments. This again can be attributed to the huge virtualization stack embedded into FaaS platforms which increases up the response times of the requests. Also, *NoOps* deployments have some initial high response times due to the cold start problem and we can also in between the test *noops-google-cloud-functions* in the case of linear workload a few spikes which most probably are due to the more function replicas being getting created.

Summary results from both these APIs are showcased in the Table 3.

Table 3. Summary results for *cinema* application showcasing HTTP P90 response time and the average number of requests served successfully for all the deployments methods in *DevOps* and *NoOps* at two user workload patterns.

API	Metrics	P90 response time (ms)				Avg. RPS			
	Type	DGCP	DSELF	NOW	NGCF	DGCP	DSELF	NOW	NGCF
/movies	Linear	**4.15**	4.20	1322.21	**344.74**	13.65	**13.66**	8.58	**10.52**
	Random	**3.77**	3.77	780.7	**339.94**	9.98	**9.98**	7.29	**7.69**
/ub*	Linear	**16.47**	22.04	59999.12	**1192.89**	13.46	**13.46**	1.65	**6.53**
	Random	**16.44**	20.90	60021.0	**1167.74**	9.78	**9.85**	2.080	**4.83**

4.2 Primes-Python Function

This function calculates prime numbers till 10000000 and is used for demonstrating the behavior of each of the deployment strategies on a compute-intensive microservice and function. We have converted this function to a microservice as well using the Python Flask framework and deployed it to each of the Kubernetes clusters in case of *DevOps* strategy. Figure 7 shows the comparison results for this function for different deployment strategies. It is clear from the figure that there is no winner. In the case of *DevOps* strategy, *devops-gcp-hosted-kubernetes* initially performed better by serving more number of requests with lesser response time but with the increase in the number of requests the scaling of replicas kicks in and the requests start to take longer time to respond. *devops-self-hosted-kubernetes* is not able to cope up with the high requests and larger compute requirements for the microservice, hence not able to scale properly and the number of requests served is much lesser than the one completed by *devops-gcp-hosted-kubernetes*. This points towards the load balancing and traffic re-distribution problem for *devops-gcp-hosted-kubernetes*.

On the other hand, in the case of *NoOps* strategy, both of the deployments suffer from the cold start problem and hence have longer response times in the beginning. However, *noops-google-cloud-functions* shows a constant request response time even with the increase in the number of requests for the rest of the test duration in both the workload patterns. This indicates that the *NoOps* deployment is more agile in terms of scalability and can provide a constant response time baring the initial cold starts. Furthermore, with the increase in time *noops-google-cloud-functions* was able to serve more number of requests than any other deployment strategy for this compute-intensive function.

4.3 Image-Processing Function

For demonstrating the access latency each deployment strategy adds up when accessing an object (in our work an image) stored on google cloud storage, `image-processing` function is used. Google cloud storage is an object store in buckets, which can store unstructured data such as photos, videos, log files, backups, and container images. This function first gets an image from the bucket and

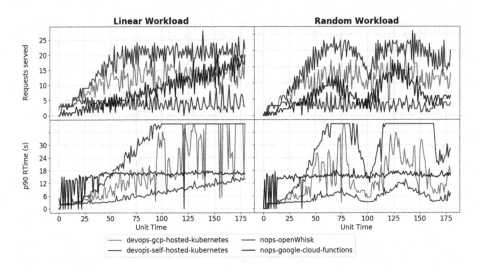

Fig. 7. `primes-python` function performance comparison results for different deployment strategies on two different workload patterns for two metrics: number of requests served and P90 response time.

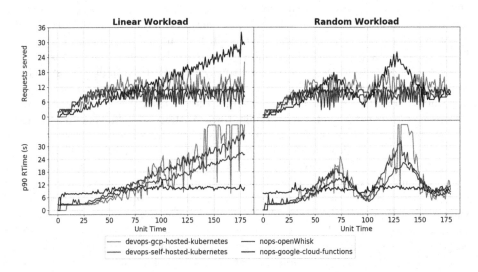

Fig. 8. `image-processing` function performance comparison results for different deployment strategies on two different workload patterns for two metrics: number of requests served and P90 response time.

then basic operations like flipping, rotating, conversion to grayscale, and resize are performed. Like the previous function, this function as well is converted to microservice for deployment on the Kubernetes engine. Figure 8 shows the comparison results for this function for different deployment strategies. *noops-google-cloud-functions* can serve a higher number of requests and at a lower response time for both the workloads therefore this deployment method is the clear winner in this case. *devops-gcp-hosted-kubernetes* has varied response times with the increase in the number of requests which again points towards the load balancing and traffic re-distribution problem in it. In the case of *devops-self-hosted-kubernetes*, the response time was continuously increasing with the number of requests which also suggests the scaling issues in it, while the *devops-gcp-hosted-kubernetes* can provide a constant requests response times even when the number of requests is increasing. This again indicates that the *NoOps* deployment is more agile in terms of scalability for this scenario as compared to *DevOps*. Therefore, *NoOps* deployment can be used for the applications requiring the constant requests latency. Though the *DevOps* strategy could also provide a constant request latency but finding the optimal scaling and configuration parameters is difficult and requires a prior load testing of the application.

4.4   Nodeinfo Function

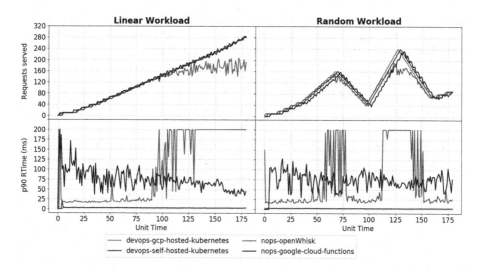

Fig. 9. nodeinfo function performance comparison results for different deployment strategies on two different workload patterns for two metrics: number of requests served and P90 response time.

The nodeinfo function is a function to replicate a simple HTTP server endpoint. We utilize this function to test the base performance of each strategy and get an estimate of their performance on a basic web application. Figure 9 shows the comparison results for this function for different deployment strategies.

Overall *DevOps* strategy compared to *NoOps* showcased the best performance results. *devops-gcp-hosted-kubernetes* along with *devops-self-hosted-kubernetes* achieved almost the similar performance on both types of workloads showcasing approximately a response time of **13ms** and average number of requests served per second as **13.46** on linearly increasing workload and **12ms** on random workload pattern with serving 10 number of requests per second. However, there is a big performance difference when the function is executed using *NoOps* strategies, taking longer time to process the requests. From the initial P90 response times of the requests for both the workloads, it can be inferred that *noops-google-cloud-functions* has a big virtualization stack in comparison to the our own hosted *noops-openWhisk* FaaS platform as the requests took times more time to complete when executed on *noops-google-cloud-functions* than on *noops-openWhisk*. However, when the number of requests increases, *noops-google-cloud-functions* is able to cope up with scalability better than *noops-openWhisk*, which can also be seen from the P90 response time of *noops-google-cloud-functions* as **66.9ms** as compared to **789.42ms** for *noops-openWhisk* in case of linear workload. Similar behaviour can also be seen for the random workload pattern.

Summary results from both the above-discussed functions evaluations are showcased in the Table 4 with the best ones highlighted.

Table 4. Summary results for function benchmarks showcasing HTTP P90 response time and the average number of requests served successfully for all the deployments methods in *DevOps* and *NoOps* at two user workload patterns.

Function	Metrics	P90 response time (ms)				Avg. RPS			
	Type	DGCP	DSELF	NOW	NGCF	DGCP	DSELF	NOW	NGCF
primes	Linear	26417.4	59999.2	**15810**	16810.8	1.13	0.38	**1.72**	0.84
	Random	21062.6	59999.12	**8590.0**	16299.5	1.06	0.32	**1.66**	0.65
imageP*	Linear	27694.4	29231.9	23650.1	**10429.8**	1.14	0.79	0.951	**1.38**
	Random	15710.0	21314.9	17570	**10123.1**	**1.05**	0.79	0.96	**1.15**
nodeinfo	Linear	**2.61**	2.92	789.42	66.9	**13.68**	13.67	11.29	13.24
	Random	**2.58**	2.64	260.45	72.7	**9.99**	**9.99**	9.19	9.66

5   Discussion

To summarize, we have drawn five points of discussion mentioned below.

NoOps Deployment Strategy Which Is based on Serverless Computing Suffers from the Cold-start Problem: From all the evaluations conducted above, one can see that in the case of *NoOps* whenever a function is triggered or invoked by a user request in the beginning there are always significant-high response times as compared to later. This problem is referred to as the *cold-start* problem. Whenever a function is invoked, it is deployed in a newly-initiated container and there is always a certain small period that a request needs to wait until the container is ready to serve. This wait is usually taken by the container to initialize the environment and pull the function source code which results in high response times. There already have been many kinds of research to decrease the cold start time like using pre-warmed containers [42], periodic warming consisting of submitting dummy requests periodically to induce a cloud service provider to keep containers warm [5] and pause containers [30]. Application developers need to keep this in consideration when deploying an application and decide based on the use case whether this deployment strategy is beneficial or not.

Google Cloud Functions Can Provide a Stable Latency Baring the Initial Cold-starts: From the evaluations conducted, it can be seen that even when the workload is constantly increasing or randomly increasing and decreasing Google Cloud Functions were able to provide a near-constant P90 response time for the requests while the others could not. This can useful for the applications which need constant latency. However, if the function instances are not invoked for a certain time period then they will scale down to zero and the new requests will suffer from a cold-start. To avoid that, a dummy application can be created which will just send dummy requests to the functions for keeping them always warm.

DevOps Deployment Strategy Outperforms When Fetching Simple Web-based and Database Query Requests: For the API calls where the requests are with the simple payload and invoked repetitively having the static or small size response then they should leverage a *DevOps* deployment due to high performance, cost advantages and no cold-start problem. In the evaluations, we can see the decrements in P90 response times to almost 72%. *NoOps* deployment has some minimum overhead due to either the virtualization stack or the different involved components which is much more than what these usecases need as a result for such cases *DevOps* deployment methods should be preferred.

DevOps Deployment Strategy Suffers from the Load Balancing and Traffic Re-distribution Problem: Despite the cold start problem in the *NoOps* deployment, it performed stably after the initial period. In contrast, microservices deployment had a high peak of duration scattered randomly during different tests. One potential explanation is that these are due to the scaling out or scaling in of the pods triggered by horizontal pod autoscaling which resulted in the increase in the response time. If one needs a stable latency over the whole time, then one could choose deployment using *NoOps* deployment method.

NoOps Deployment Is More Agile in Terms of Scalability: As we compare the scalability and agility of both the deployments, *NoOps* is better than *DevOps*. Since in the *DevOps* deployment, microservices starts to auto-scale only after the system has reached the defined criteria for at least one minute, there is always a delay of responsiveness to re-balance the current workload. As a result, there is an increase in response time with the increasing workload, then it drops after the new containers have been launched. Furthermore, if the underneath resources are not scaled than the requests will start to timeout as was in our evaluations. The granularity of the monitoring set can also limit the agility of the microservices scalability which is not the case with the *NoOps* deployment method. However, this disadvantage can be resolved by configuring a proper caching mechanism to store repetitive content but the user has to deal with more than what is required.

6   Related Work

We present here the related work in threefolds, firstly, on the performance evaluation of *DevOps* based microservices deployment, secondly on the performance evaluation of *NoOps* based serverless deployment and lastly on the architectural decisions on selecting *DevOps* or *NoOps* deployment.

In [9], they introduced a four-step approach for the quantitative assessment of microservice architecture deployment alternatives. They found that in autoscaling cloud environments, careful performance engineering activities should be executed before additional resources are added to the architecture deployment configuration otherwise can result in significant performance degradation. In [4], three microservices design patterns practiced in the software industry are evaluated from the aspects of query response time, efficient hardware usage, hosting costs, and packet loss rate. They concluded that there is no single microservices pattern that is better than the others. Each design pattern performs better in different scenarios. Casalicchio and Perciballi [13] analyze the effect of using relative and absolute metrics to assess the performance of autoscaling. They have deduced that for CPU intensive workloads, the use of absolute metrics can result in better scaling decisions. Jindal et al. [23] addressed the performance modeling of microservices by evaluation of a microservices web application. They identified a microservice's capacity in terms of the number of requests to find the appropriate resources needed for the microservices such that, the system would not violate the performance (response time, latency) requirements. Kozhirbayev and Sinnott [25] present the performance evaluation of microservice architectures in a cloud environment using different container solutions. They also reported on the experimental designs and the performance benchmarks used as part of this performance assessment.

NoOps based on serverless computing topic has been researched recently to a great extent [11,15,24,28]. Baldini et al. [11] presents the general features of serverless platforms and discuss open research problems in it. Lynn et al. [29] discuss the feature analysis of enterprise based serverless platforms, including AWS Lambda, Microsoft Azure Functions, Google Cloud Functions, and OpenWhisk. Lee et al. [27] evaluated the performance of public serverless platforms for CPU, memory, and disk-intensive functions. They concluded that AWS Lambda outperforms other public cloud solutions. Similarly, Mohanty et al. [31] compared the performance of open-source serverless platforms Kubeless, OpenFaaS, and OpenWhisk. They evaluated the performance of each in terms of the response time and success ratio for function when deployed in a Kubernetes cluster. Shillaker [41] evaluates the response latency on OpenWhisk at different levels of throughput and concurrent functions. They proposed a way for improving startup time in serverless frameworks by replacing containers with a new isolation mechanism in the runtime itself. Pinto et al. [34] showcased the use of serverless in the field of IoT by dynamically allocating the functions on the IoT devices. Furthermore, researchers have identified the limitations of current serverless platforms, such as no control over specifying additional hardware resources like the required number of CPUs, GPUs, or other types of accelerators for the functions [10,20].

With the rise of *NoOps* based on serverless computing, *DevOps* based on microservices architecture is not the only choice when developing an application. There are debates about architecting decisions when it comes to choosing between these two. Jambunathan et al. [21] elaborated on the aspects of architecture decisions on microservices and serverless. From the service deployment's perspective, serverless has infrastructure restrictions that need native cloud service support and must be hosted by cloud service providers. In contrast, a microservices architecture could deploy on either the private data center or public cloud. However, the benefits of auto-scaling without considering complex server configuration is a deployment advantage on serverless than microservices.

In our previous work [16], we have compared microservices to serverless using AWS Lambda as the FaaS platform and a native cloud-native web application from the aspects of scalability, reliability, cost, and latency. We showcased the use cases where each of the deployment strategies can be used. But in this work, we have extended it by using OpenWhisk and Google Cloud Functions as FaaS platforms. Furthermore, we have added additional function benchmarks and applications for concluding the decisions.

7 Conclusion

Based on the experimental evaluations for *DevOps* and *NoOps* deployments, it can be concluded that no single type of deployment can fit all kinds of applications. For example, a GET and POST request to API endpoints fetching a response body by querying a database has a huge overhead in *NoOps* as compared to *DevOps*. On the other side, compute-intensive functions invocations were well served *NoOps* deployments due to its scaling agility as compared to *DevOps* where the user has to find the optimal scaling parameters and can suffer from latency in auto-scaling execution. Also, *NoOps* strategy provides immediate scalability and prompt response when handling random traffic, by which it can offer a constant latency.

In the end, this research derived a future research direction towards optimizing the deployment in terms of cost, performance, and application domain by building a hybrid deployment environment consisting of both the *DevOps* and*NoOps* deployment strategies. A deployment strategy is selected dynamically based on the workload pattern or load-balanced between the two.

8   Availability

The used applications, functions and the conducted evaluations are publicly available on GitHub under the link https://github.com/ansjin/devops_to_noops.git.

Acknowledgements. This work was supported by the funding of the German Federal Ministry of Education and Research (BMBF) in the scope of the Software Campus program. Google Cloud credits were provided by the Google Cloud Platform research credits. The authors also thank the anonymous reviewers whose comments helped in improving this paper.

References

1. Aws lambda - pricing. https://aws.amazon.com/lambda/pricing/. Accessed 30 July 2020
2. Cloud functions overview. https://cloud.google.com/functions/docs/concepts/overview. Accessed 22 Aug 08 2020
3. What is k6? https://k6.io/docs/. Accessed 28 July 2020
4. Akbulut, A., Perros, H.G.: Performance analysis of microservice design patterns. IEEE Internet Comput. **23**(6), 19–27 (2019)
5. Şamdan, E.: Dealing with cold starts in AWS lambda (2018). https://medium.com/thundra/dealing-with-cold-starts-in-aws-lambda-a5e3aa8f532. Accessed 14 Feb 2020
6. Apache: Openwhisk cli (2017). https://github.com/apache/openwhisk/blob/master/docs/cli.md#openwhisk-cli
7. Apache: Openwhisk documentation (2017). https://openwhisk.apache.org/documentation.html
8. Architect: Project philosophy (2020). https://arc.codes/intro/philosophy. Accessed 4 Feb 2020
9. Avritzer, A., Ferme, V., Janes, A., Russo, B., Schulz, H., van Hoorn, A.: A quantitative approach for the assessment of microservice architecture deployment alternatives by automated performance testing. In: Cuesta, C.E., Garlan, D., Pérez, J. (eds.) ECSA 2018. LNCS, vol. 11048, pp. 159–174. Springer, Cham (2018). https://doi.org/10.1007/978-3-030-00761-4_11
10. Baldini, I., et al.: Serverless computing: current trends and open problems. In: Chaudhary, S., Somani, G., Buyya, R. (eds.) Research Advances in Cloud Computing, pp. 1–20. Springer, Singapore (2017). https://doi.org/10.1007/978-981-10-5026-8_1
11. Baldini, I., et al.: Serverless computing: current trends and open problems. CoRR abs/1706.03178 (2017). http://arxiv.org/abs/1706.03178
12. Bhojwani, R.: Design patterns for microservice-to-microservice communication - DZone microservices, December 2018. https://dzone.com/articles/design-patterns-for-microservice-communication
13. Casalicchio, E., Perciballi, V.: Auto-scaling of containers: the impact of relative and absolute metrics. In: 2017 IEEE 2nd International Workshops on Foundations and Applications of Self* Systems (FAS*W), pp. 207–214 (2017)
14. Di Francesco, P., Lago, P., Malavolta, I.: Migrating towards microservice architectures: an industrial survey. In: 2018 IEEE International Conference on Software Architecture (ICSA), pp. 29–38, April 2018. https://doi.org/10.1109/ICSA.2018.00012

15. Eivy, A.: Be wary of the economics of "serverless" cloud computing. IEEE Cloud Comput. **4**, 6–12 (2017)
16. Fan., C., Jindal., A., Gerndt., M.: Microservices vs serverless: a performance comparison on a cloud-native web application. In: Proceedings of the 10th International Conference on Cloud Computing and Services Science, CLOSER, vol. 1, pp. 204–215. INSTICC, SciTePress (2020). https://doi.org/10.5220/0009792702040215
17. Gancarz, R.: The economics of serverless computing: a real-world test (2017). https://techbeacon.com/enterprise-it/economics-serverless-computing-real-world-test. Accessed 23 Mar 2020
18. GoogleCloud: Cloud functions execution environment. https://cloud.google.com/functions/docs/concepts/exec. Accessed 22 Aug 2020
19. Handy, A.: Amazon introduces lambda, containers at AWS re:Invent (2014). https://sdtimes.com/amazon/amazon-introduces-lambda-containers/. Accessed 4 Feb 2020
20. Hendrickson, S., Sturdevant, S., Harter, T., Venkataramani, V., Arpaci-Dusseau, A.C., Arpaci-Dusseau, R.H.: Serverless computation with openlambda. In: 8th USENIX Workshop on Hot Topics in Cloud Computing (HotCloud 2016) (2016)
21. Jambunathan, B., Yoganathan, K.: Architecture decision on using microservices or serverless functions with containers. In: 2018 International Conference on Current Trends Towards Converging Technologies (ICCTCT), pp. 1–7, March 2018. https://doi.org/10.1109/ICCTCT.2018.8551035
22. Jamieson, F.: Losing the server? (2017). https://www.bcs.org/content-hub/losing-the-server/
23. Jindal, A., Podolskiy, V., Gerndt, M.: Performance modeling for cloud microservice applications. In: Proceedings of the 2019 ACM/SPEC International Conference on Performance Engineering, ICPE 2019, pp. 25–32. Association for Computing Machinery, New York (2019). https://doi.org/10.1145/3297663.3310309
24. Jonas, E., Pu, Q., Venkataraman, S., Stoica, I., Recht, B.: Occupy the cloud: distributed computing for the 99 cloud computing. In: SoCC 2017, pp. 445–451. Association for Computing Machinery, New York (2017). https://doi.org/10.1145/3127479.3128601
25. Kozhirbayev, Z., Sinnott, R.O.: A performance comparison of container-based technologies for the cloud. Future Gener. Comput. Syst. **68**, 175–182 (2017). https://doi.org/10.1016/j.future.2016.08.025. http://www.sciencedirect.com/science/article/pii/S0167739X16303041
26. Lane, K.: Overview of the backend as a service (baaS) space. API Evangelist (2015)
27. Lee, H., Satyam, K., Fox, G.: Evaluation of production serverless computing environments. In: 2018 IEEE 11th International Conference on Cloud Computing (CLOUD), pp. 442–450, July 2018. https://doi.org/10.1109/CLOUD.2018.00062
28. Lloyd, W., Ramesh, S., Chinthalapati, S., Ly, L., Pallickara, S.: Serverless computing: an investigation of factors influencing microservice performance. In: 2018 IEEE International Conference on Cloud Engineering (IC2E), pp. 159–169, April 2018. https://doi.org/10.1109/IC2E.2018.00039
29. Lynn, T., Rosati, P., Lejeune, A., Emeakaroha, V.: A preliminary review of enterprise serverless cloud computing (function-as-a-service) platforms. In: 2017 IEEE International Conference on Cloud Computing Technology and Science (CloudCom), pp. 162–169, December 2017. https://doi.org/10.1109/CloudCom.2017.15
30. Mohan, A., Sane, H., Doshi, K., Edupuganti, S., Nayak, N., Sukhomlinov, V.: Agile cold starts for scalable serverless. In: Proceedings of the 11th USENIX Conference on Hot Topics in Cloud Computing, HotCloud 2019, p. 21. USENIX Association (2019)

31. Mohanty, S.K., Premsankar, G., di Francesco, M.: An evaluation of open source serverless computing frameworks. In: 2018 IEEE International Conference on Cloud Computing Technology and Science (CloudCom), pp. 115–120, December 2018. https://doi.org/10.1109/CloudCom2018.2018.00033

32. Novoseltseva, E.: Benefits of microservices architecture implementation (2017). https://dzone.com/articles/benefits-amp-examples-of-microservices-architectur. Accessed 23 Mar 2020

33. Pierre-Louis, M.A.: OpenWhisk: a quick tech preview. DeveloperWorks Open, IBM, p. 7, 22 February 2016 (2016)

34. Pinto, D., Dias, J.P., Ferreira, H.S.: Dynamic allocation of serverless functions in IoT environments. In: 2018 IEEE 16th International Conference on Embedded and Ubiquitous Computing (EUC), pp. 1–8, October 2018. https://doi.org/10.1109/EUC.2018.00008

35. Reese, W.: Nginx: the high-performance web server and reverse proxy. Linux J. **2008**(173) (2008)

36. Richardson, C.: Introduction to microservices, May 2015. https://www.nginx.com/blog/introduction-to-microservices/. Accessed 25 Jan 2020

37. Richardson, C.: Microservices pattern: microservice architecture pattern, May 2019. https://microservices.io/patterns/microservices.html. Accessed 28 Jan 2020

38. Schneider, T.: Achieving cloud scalability with microservices and DevOps in the connected car domain. In: Software Engineering (2016)

39. Serverless: documentation (2020). https://serverless.com/framework/docs/. Accessed 4 Feb 2020

40. Shahrad, M., Balkind, J., Wentzlaff, D.: Architectural implications of function-as-a-service computing. In: Proceedings of the 52nd Annual IEEE/ACM International Symposium on Microarchitecture, pp. 1063–1075 (2019)

41. Shillaker, S., Pietzuch, P.R.: A provider-friendly serverless framework for latency-critical applications (2018)

42. Thömmes, M.: Squeezing the milliseconds: how to make serverless platforms blazing fast! (2017) https://medium.com/openwhisk/squeezing-the-milliseconds-how-to-make-serverless-platforms-blazing-fast-aea0e9951bd0. Accessed 14 Feb 2020

43. CNCF WG-Serverless: CNCF WG-Serverless whitepaper v1.0, March 2018. https://gw.alipayobjects.com/os/basement_prod/24ec4498-71d4-4a60-b785-fa530456c65b.pdf. Accessed 15 July 2020

Fuzzy Container Orchestration for Self-adaptive Edge Architectures

Fabian Gand, Ilenia Fronza, Nabil El Ioini, Hamid R. Barzegar,
Shelernaz Azimi, and Claus Pahl[(✉)]

Free University of Bozen-Bolzano, Bolzano, Italy
{fabian.gand,ilenia.fronza,nabil.ioini,hamidr.barzegar,
shelernaz.azimi,claus.pahl}@unibz.it

Abstract. The edge or edge computing refers to the computational
infrastructure between sensors and Internet-of-Things world on the one
side and centralised cloud data centres on the other. Edge clusters could
consist of small single-board devices, which are widely used in different
applications. This includes microcontrollers regulating an industrial process or controllers monitoring and managing traffic roadside. Although
generally hardware capabilities of devices are growing, resources at the
edge are often still limited, requiring an intelligent resource management. This can done through self-adaptive scaling mechanisms in these
clusters allowing to scale components of the application in the cluster.
We introduce here an auto-scalable cluster architecture for lightweight
container-based edge devices. A serverless architecture forms the core
of this architecture. The auto-scaling component is based on fuzzy logic
in order to better manage uncertainty problems arising in such contexts.
Our evaluations show that our platform architecture and the auto-scaling
functionality satisfy the need of lightweightness in edge architecture.

Keywords: Edge cloud · Container technology · Cluster ·
Self-adaptive system · Performance engineering · Auto-scaling · Fuzzy
logic

1 Introduction

Today, many processing tasks in distributed environments are executed directly
on nodes at the edge of a network rather than being send to central, but remote
processing hubs. This principle is often called Edge Computing [52]. The management of such edge systems often requires different concepts for scaling system
components dynamically in order to deal with changing resource requirements
in a constrained environment. Proposed solutions range from simple algorithms
that define scale values based on set thresholds [76] to systems using neural networks for decision making [42]. However, more work in the edge context [18] is
needed on auto-scaling algorithm.

Our objective is the evaluation of a serverless architecture managed by an
auto-scaling component. The goal is to provide a lightweight edge computing

© Springer Nature Switzerland AG 2021
D. Ferguson et al. (Eds.): CLOSER 2020, CCIS 1399, pp. 203–232, 2021.
https://doi.org/10.1007/978-3-030-72369-9_9

solution, which extends our previous work in [18] by focusing more on the architecture implementation here. At the core is a serverless approach that delegates the deploying, scaling and maintaining of software to the cloud/edge provider [6]. The experimental edge platform we use here is implemented using a cluster of eight single-board devices. Such small clusters have been evaluated in basic settings. We aim here to evaluate a complete system based on real-life requirements and constraints with dynamic scalability included that would for instance arise in automotive and mobility applications.

We deploy Raspberry Pis as single-board devices and evaluate under which conditions a cluster of these devices can support low latency needs, which are tightly constrained by given performance requirements. We use technologies and tools such as MQTT for inter-cluster communication, openFaas and Docker Swarm for the implementation of the serverless concept, also Prometheus for monitoring purposes. This is combined with fuzzy logic at the core the central auto-scaling component. We look at the performance of the system in a range of cases, aiming to detect bottlenecks. The implemented auto-scaling algorithm is evaluated experimentally.

In the remainder of this paper, relevant concepts, tools and technologies are introduced in Sect. 2. Then, Sect. 3 starts with a high-level architecture, followed by details of the auto-scaling mechanism in Sect. 4. In Sect. 5, we evaluate platform and auto-scaler. Then, related work on distributed edge systems and auto-scaling is reviewed, before concluding with a summary and ideas for future research.

2   Background Concepts and Technologies

Our contribution is a scalable platform architecture, for which central concepts and technologies shall be introduced first [54,56].

2.1   Platform and Architecture Concepts

Our platform architecture requires some background in architecture, deployment and self-adaptivity [13,30,35,53].

Edge Computing. Cloud computing is based on the idea of centralised data centers that can process large volumes of data [20,24,25,39,43]. With edge computing, the potential local processing power at the "Edge" network is meant to be used, remedying the often significantly increased latency of a centralised approach. Edge Computing leverages the processing power of local edge nodes. These nodes are an intermediate layer [39] that process data within the local network rather than handling this in the cloud remotely.

Microservice Architecture. Microservices is a recent architectural paradigm. Traditionally, architectures provide an application as a monolith, i.e., an application is bundled into one executable that is then deployed. When migrating to a microservice architecture, the monolith is split into different parts (the microservices) that run in independent processes [32,58,69].

Usually, there needs to be some kind of bus system that the services use for communication. Consequently, each microservice needs to expose an interface for receiving and sending data. Often, this is implemented using HTTP methods and resources. Fowler suggests that these services should be split according to business capabilities rather than separating them based on the technology layer [14]. The size of microservices is highly disputed and ranges from services that can be managed by a single person to services that are developed by a dozen developers. There are different approaches to microservice architecture. The Micro-SOA approach splits the monolith into services that are relatively small (a few hundred to a few thousand lines of code) and need to interact with each other frequently. The corresponding architecture is highly scalable, but the constant communication between the services results in a higher network latency [70]. The Distributed DDD (Domain-Driven-Design) Framework aims at providing microservices that are an order of a magnitude bigger than in the Mico-SOA approach and are separated based on logical boundaries. They should be able to process requests independently and therefore contain their own domain data. Important challenges that need to be addressed when implementing an architecture based on microservices are service discovery (enabling the services to find each other), load balancing (splitting the load among services) and routing (making sure the requests are relayed to the right service).

Serverless Computing. Serverless computing is an new concept for the deployment of cloud applications that has seen an increase in popularity since it was first introduced a couple of years ago [6]. It allows developers to focus on the application without having to consider the deployment servers, which is handled by the cloud provider. This allows for features such as fault-tolerance and auto-scaling to be centrally managed [6]. Serverless computing is related to the Functions-as-a-Service (FaaS) approach. Here, small chunks of functionality are deployed in the cloud and scaled dynamically by the cloud provider [40]. These functions are usually smaller than microservices, are short-lived and have clear input and output parameters. If the component to be deployed is more complex than a simple function and is supposed to stay active for a longer period of time, a stateless microservice is another option [12]. Managing and deploying these microservices is similar to serverless functions.

In addition to major cloud providers already offering serverless functionality as part of their cloud solutions, several open-source frameworks have been developed and released in recent years. These solutions usually involve having to self-host the serverless frameworks on own hardware instead of relying on hardware provided by third-party providers. Here, we will mainly focus on open source, self-hosted solutions.

Table 1. Comparison of open-source, Serverless frameworks [18].

Framework	Languages	Type	License	Vendor monitoring	Key components	Other features
openFaas	C#, Dockerfile, Go, Java, NodeJS, PHP, Python, Ruby	Complete framework	MIT	Community driven	Prometheus	Container (Docker), Prometheus, gateway API, GUI
OpenWhisk	NodeJS, Swift, Java, Go, Scala, Python, PHP, Ruby, Ballerina	Complete framework	Apache License 2.0	Apache	Kamon for system metrics, kafka events for user metrics	nginx Webserver, CouchDB, Kafka, Containers(Docker)
Kubeless [41]	Python, NodeJS, Ruby, PHP, Go, .NET, Java, Ballerina	Complete framework	Apache License 2.0	Community driven	Prometheus	Kubernetes (native)
Serverless (community version) [67]	Python, NodeJS, Java, Go, Scala, C#	CLI for building + deploying	MIT	Serverless, Inc	–	Deployment to providers: AWS, MS Azure etc.

Four open-source frameworks are compared in Table 1, which aids us in the selection of a suitable one.

2.2   Self-adaptiveness and Fuzziness Concepts

Self-adaptive systems [2,28,29] adapt their behavior dynamically to either preserve or enhance required quality attributes in the presence of uncertain operating conditions. The development of microservice applications as self-adaptive systems is still a challenge [48,62–64]. In practice, platforms such as Kubernetes container orchestration facilitate the deployment and management of microservice applications. However, Kubernetes natively only supports basic auto-scaling by changing the number of service instances automatically.

Fuzzy logic aims to bridge between machine and human reasoning. Computers traditionally work well for tasks that contain formal calculations. Human reasoning, however, is often more complex. Natural language is rarely precise in a way that it quantifies something as one thing or the other: words can have uncertain, ambiguous meanings [21]. Thus, human reasoning is fuzzy. Uncertainty also arises in edge environments through incomplete or potentially incorrect or conflicting observations.

Fuzzy logic has the objective of addressing this by mapping inputs (e.g., observations) to outputs (e.g., analyses or reactions) based on gradually changing functions and a set of rules rather than fixed thresholds. A so-called *membership function* is a function that represents a fuzzy set and decides to which degree an item belongs to a certain set. *Fuzzification* is a process that refers to input values

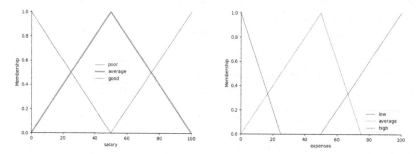

(a) Membership function for flexible salary [18].   (b) Membership functions for expected expenses.

Fig. 1. Membership functions for the two input values considered [18].

that are mapped to membership functions to derive the degree of membership in that set [46] – which is different from a binary approach where the element can either be part of a set or not. *Fuzzy rules* define how after fuzzification the values are matched against if-else rules. *Defuzzyfication* is the final step, where a numerical output value is generated.

An examples ahall illustrate this. A sample goal might be to calculate the money that should to be saved each month based on a flexible salary and the expected expenses. The amount of money that is to be saved in a long-term savings account will be returned by the fuzzy system. We illustrate the ingredients of a fuzzy system:

– Membership functions – The variables salary, expected expenses and the money that is suggested to be saved are visualized in Figs. 1a, 1b and 2. Each variable consists of three membership functions: low, high and medium.

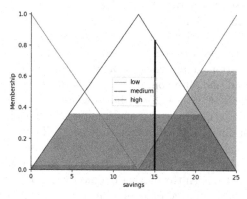

Fig. 2. Savings membership functions with final value [18].

These can represent, e.g., the degree to which a salary of 50 can be considered a low, high or average salary.

– *Rules* – The rules of the fuzzy system can be defined in the following way:

```
IF salary LOW OR expenses HIGH THEN savings LOW
IF salary AVERAGE THEN savings AVERAGE
IF salary HIGH OR expenses LOW THEN savings HIGH
```

– *System Input* – Savings are calculated based on a salary of 82 and expected expenses of 51.4.
– *Defuzzyfication* – After the final defuzzyfication step, a savings recommendation of 15.03 results.

2.3   Platform Tools and Technologies

The above abstract principles shall be complemented by the introduction of concrete infrastructure and software technologies used in the platform implementation.

Raspberry Pi. A *Raspberry Pi* is a widely used single-board computer based on an ARM-processor. Its original purpose was to introduce school children to programming [8,73,74]. Due to its low price and various use cases it has found its way into more industrial IT projects. Since the start of the project in 2012 there have been four major iterations of the Raspberry Pi platform. The version 2 B models that are used in this cluster include a 900 MHz quad-core ARM Cortex-A7 CPU and 1 GB of RAM [60]. The Raspberry Pi Model 3 B comes with a Quad Core 1.2 GHz Broadcom BCM2837 64 bit CPU. All (model B) Raspberry Pi versions include several GPIO Pins, a 100 Base Ethernet Port four USB Ports and an SD-Card slot.

Docker and Docker Swarm. *Docker* is software for containerization. Containerization is a virtualization technology that, instead of virtualizing hardware, separates processes from each other by utilizing certain features of the Linux kernel. It has been successfully used on Raspberry Pis [65,66]. Docker containers bundle an application along with all of its dependencies. Docker offers the ability to create, build and ship containers [11]. Compared to virtual machines, containers offer a far better use of the host resources while providing similar advantages of having a separate system. Images are the blueprints of docker containers. Each container is created from an image. The images, on the other hand, are built using Dockerfiles which describe the system to be constructed. Docker (specifically the Docker Engine) is based on a client-server architecture. The client communicates with the Docker daemon via a command-line interface. The docker daemon is in charge of managing the components and containers. Docker services represent the actual application logic of a container in production. Using services, a distributed web application could be split into one service for the front-end components, one for the database and another one for the content management system that is used to update the website. *Docker Swarm* is the cluster management tool that is integrated into the Docker Engine. Instead of running the given services and their corresponding containers on one host, they can be deployed on a cluster of nodes that is managed like a single, docker-based system. By setting the desired number of replicas of a service, basic scaling is also possible.

Hypriot OS and Related Tools. Hypriot OS is an operating system based on Debian that is specifically tailored towards using Docker Containerization technology on ARM devices such as the Raspberry Pi [22]. The OS comes prepackaged with the latest Docker version ready to be used. Hypriot OS also comes bundled with a few additional tools that we will use.

Clout Init – Clout init is a light-weight approach to creating templates of an operating system [9]. This can be used to ensure that two nodes are identical clones of each other. The instances are configured in .yml configuration files. These files can be used to set, for example, the hostname of the node or to execute certain commands at boot time.

Avahi – Avahi is a tool for simplifying networking by allowing nodes in a network to address each other with their hostnames without having to configure static IP addresses or rely on DHCP or DNS services [3]. If the hostname of the master node has been set in the cloud-init configuration file, all worker nodes are able to directly connect to the master node by addressing it by its hostname.

Ansible. Ansible is a tool for automating a variety of tedious tasks in a cluster and cloud environments such as individual node configuration or application deployment [1]. The nodes are usually connected using SSH. Ansible usually uses SSH keys for authorization [1]. The individual nodes need to be defined in a host configuration file. After defining the nodes, Ansible can be used to execute instructions on all nodes synchronously. These instructions can either be raw commands for simple cases or "playbooks", that contain a set of instructions for more complex tasks.

MQTT. *MQTT* is a network protocol that is primarily used for unreliable networks with limited bandwidth, thus it is suitable for Internet of Things applications. MQTT uses a publisher-subscriber approach. Clients establish a connection to a broker and subscribe to topics. Clients may also publish a message to a topic. When a message is published, the broker relays the message to all clients that are subscribed to the corresponding topic. If a message is flagged as a retained message it is kept by the broker after relaying it. Clients will receive the retained message as soon as they subscribe to the topic.

Prometheus. *Prometheus* is a monitoring tool used to gather and process application metrics. In contrast to other monitoring tools, it does not rely on the application delivering the metrics to the monitoring tool. Prometheus "scrapes" the metrics from a predetermined interface in a given interval. This means that the metrics are expected to be exposed by the application.

OpenFaaS. As a FaaS Functions-as-a-Service framework for containers, Open-Faas can be deployed on top of a Docker swarm or a Kubernetes cluster. When starting the openFaas framework a number of standard docker containers are deployed:

– Gateway: used as the central gateway for calling functions from anywhere in the cluster. Exposes a webinterface for managing functions.
– Prometheus: a simple Prometheus instance is running on this container. In addition, the Prometheus webinterface is also exposed.
– Alertmanager: reads Prometheus metrics and issues alerts to the gateway.

openFaas does provide a simple form of autoscaling [50] that leverages the default metrics aggregated by Prometheus and scales based on given thresholds.

Functions and serverless microservices can be written in a variety of different programming languages. Functions are usually created by using the faas-cli command line tool. An example for creating a function in python would be:

```
faas-cli new --prefix=examples --lang python3-armhf example-function
```

This command creates a directory structure as follows:

```
example-function
└─ example-function
   ├─ handler.py
   └─ requirements.txt
└─ example-function.yml
```

The *.yml* configuration file contains information such as the IP address of the gateway or the name of the docker image. The programming logic can be found

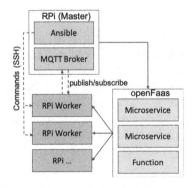

Fig. 3. Hardware and networking components [18].

within the *handler.py* file. It needs to contain a *handle* function that receives a request parameter and returns a response after executing its logic. The *requirements.txt* file contains the python-pip dependencies needed for the project. The corresponding pip install command is executed automatically once the function is built. The *–lang* parameter determines the language and architecture template that is used for this function. In the given case, a python function running on an ARM architecture is created. The *–prefix* parameter is used as a prefix for the resulting Docker image that is uploaded to the Docker hub. The Docker hub is used for distributing the images across the cluster. Stateless microservices can be built by using the *Dockerfile* template. In this case a Dockerfile has to be set up manually to create a container for the service to run in. Among the serverless frameworks compared in Table 1, we selected openFaas for the implementation of the application. The reasons are a wide array of supported languages, openFaas being a complete, all-in-one framework, Prometheus as an integrated, extendable monitoring solution, the simple set-up process and its out-of-the-box support for Docker Swarm. Other frameworks either lacked a simple monitoring solution (serverless), included more custom components that needed to be configured manually (openWhisk) or did not support Docker Swarm (Kubeless).

2.4 Towards a Lightweight Edge Platform

The architecture approach is decomposing the application into microservices and containerizing them, by utilizing the above technologies and allowing the hardware to be reallocated dynamically.

OpenFaas allows building and deploying services in the form of functions across a cluster. Some of its features, such as built-in Prometheus services or the gateway, can be extended to make openFaas the central building block [19]. An overview of the different technologies in the context of the given platform is presented in Fig. 3.

OpenFaaS also enables scaling the different parts of the application. Even though openFaas scaling is limited, we use it as a foundation for our self-adaption. We implement a more fine-grained scaling algorithm using the built-in monitoring options. As the reasoning foundation for scaling, we use fuzzy logic.

3 Platform and Controller Architecture

We introduce here the core elements of our architecture before covering low-level implementation details of the platform and its auto-scaling component in the next section. The proposed binding blocks of the application such as the a serverless and microservices-based architecture can be reused for different applications in different contexts. The scaling component is also usable in different applications by reconfiguring a few parameters.

We use a Traffic Management (TM) System as a sample application. We assume a constant exchange of messages between the traffic management and vehicle components that in our prototype implementation contains simulations of vehicles. A control system is used to scale the TM System based on the monitored and analysed data. While we investigate a specific case, transferability is given.

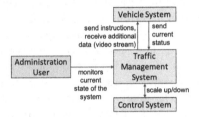

Fig. 4. Interaction between different systems [18].

We build on a three-layered architecture. The platform layer represents the hardware architecture of the cluster. The system layer comprises the central management components. On top of these, the controller layer scales the components of the platform. Figure 4 shows the interaction between system and controller layer and additional components.

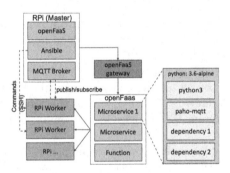

Fig. 5. Platform layer [18].

3.1   Platform and Cluster Configuration

The application is deployed on a cluster managed by Docker Swarm. The cluster includes one master node and an arbitrary number of worker nodes. Ansible is used to execute commands on all nodes without having to connect to each node individually. All nodes are able to connect to the MQTT broker that is running on the master device after startup. Using Docker swarm and openFaas, the RPIs can be connected so that they can be seen as one system. If a service is supposed to be deployed, openFaas will distribute it among the available nodes. There is no need to specify a specific node as this abstraction layer is hidden behind the openFaas framework. The services and functions are built and deployed using the openFaas command line interface. OpenFaas is also utilized to scale the services independently. Communication between the services is achieved by relying on the openFaas gateway as well as on the MQTT broker. These elements of the platform layer are shown in Fig. 5.

Cluster Setup. Our cluster architecture is comprised of eight Raspberry Pi 2 Model B connected to a mobile switch via 10/100 Mbit/s Ethernet that is powering the RPIs via PoE (Power over Ethernet). We have documented our solution on github. The system components are split into three repositories. The rpicluster repository[1] contains the clout-init configuration files for setting up the Raspberry Pis. The rpicluster-application repository[2] includes all the microservices and scripts that make up the application logic. The third repository[3] includes the openFaas repository in a modified form.

All nodes of the cluster run hypriot OS. Cloud-init is used to define the initial boot steps of the nodes. The master initiates the docker swarm. The only command that needs to be executed on the workers is the swarm join command. It can be distributed among the nodes by using Ansible. After this command is executed on each node, the swarm is fully set up. The worker nodes contain almost no additional dependencies since they are all included in the Docker containers. The only additional dependencies that are directly installed on the nodes are used to run a python script that monitors system metrics and publishes them to the metrics service.

The complete steps to set-up the system on the cluster are as follows:

1. Flash one master configuration of hypriot to an SD Card and insert it into the master RPI:

   ```
   flash --hostname master --userdata ./user-data-master.yml hypriotos.img
   ```

2. Flash n worker configurations of hypriot to SD Cards and insert them into worker RPIs.
3. Power up the cluster.
4. Wait for the predefined boot steps to download and set up the system. Logs can be inspected on the RPI nodes at: */var/logs/cloud-init-output.log*
5. On the master node:
   (a) Add the hostname of all workers to the *hosts* file in the root directory.
   (b) Use the ansible command line tool to execute the docker join command on all workers.
   (c) See if all nodes joined the swarm of the cluster: `docker node ls`
6. Git clone the modified openFaas repository:

---

[1] https://gitlab.com/gandfabian/rpicluster.git.

[2] https://gitlab.com/gandfabian/rpicluster-application.git.

[3] https://gitlab.com/gandfabian/rpicluster-faas.git.

```
https://gitlab.com/gandfabian/rpicluster-faas.git
```

7. Execute the openFaas setup script:

```
~/rpicluster-faas/deploy_stack.armhf.sh
```

8. Wait until the built-in openFaas services are started (can be checked by calling `docker service ls`). After startup is complete, the openFaas GUI (at `http://master:8080`) and the modified Prometheus, instances configured for use with custom metrics, (at `http://master:9090`) are accessible from the network.

The system can now be started from within the `rpicluster-application` folder by executing the `control.py` script that will use openFaas to start-up all application components and enable auto-scaling.

3.2   Platform Monitoring

Monitoring is done through the openFaas Prometheus instance, provides as one of the predefined containers.

Metrics Service. The metrics service is used to acquire metrics about the system, mainly by serving as a central hub that accumulates all cluster-wide metrics and by publishing those metrics via a flask HTTP endpoint. This endpoint is the central interface for Prometheus to scrape from. The Prometheus python API is used to implement the metrics. The metrics service exposes the number of messages, e.g., the number of active cars in our case as well as the cumulative memory and CPU usage. The number of messages is implemented as a counter which is continuously increasing. The CPU/memory usage, on the other hand, is realized by using a gauge which can be a set to an arbitrary number.

OpenFaas: Prometheus. This instance is used to store metrics and query them when needed. Prometheus provides a REST API along with a language called PromQL to aggregate and query metrics [59]. The aggregated data is returned in the JSON format. Before startup, Prometheus needs to be informed about the endpoints that metrics should be collected from. The Prometheus instance that is shipped with openFaas only scrapes metrics from the openFaas gateway since only metrics related to function execution are being monitored by default. Configuring the openFaas Prometheus instance to aggregate custom metrics of an application is not documented. Exploring this possibility and implementing it was a part of the scope of this thesis. In order to add a second endpoint for the additional metrics, the openFaas repository had to be forked and the `prometheus/prometheus.yml` configuration file had to be edited, adding the metrics endpoint to the file. The metrics microservice is accessible via the gateway. Therefore, it is possible to address the metrics endpoint by calling the gateway and there is no need to specify the static IP address of the node the metrics service is running on. Specifying the metrics path (`/appmetrics`) as well as the port (8080) is also mandatory.

4   A Fuzzy Auto-scaling Controller

The central component in our architecture that manages performance is the auto-scaling controller. A requirement for it is lightweightness. Consuming too many system resources such as storage space or CPU usage has to be avoided because the algorithm is meant to be deployed on the RPI cluster itself with most of the clusters resources being reserved for application components themselves.

At the core is fuzzy logic that is a good compromise between a powerful decision-making process and a limited resource consumption. The initial fuzzy knowledge base is, however, difficult to obtain. The following solution combines reactive and proactive configuration methods by initially anticipating demand in the calibration and configuration (proactive) and then continuously re-adjusting them if needed (reactive).

In order to set-up an initial fuzzy knowledge base, values of previous runs of the system are used. The reactive part of the algorithm continuously updates parts of the knowledge base dynamically.

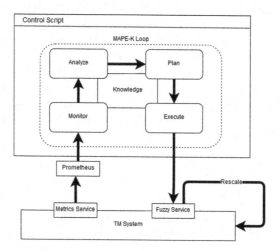

Fig. 6. MAPE-K loop for fuzzy auto-scaling controller [18].

4.1 Principles of Auto-scaling

The auto-scaling algorithm builds on the MAPE-K [38] controller loop for self-adaptive systems. The steps of this MAPE-K controller loop are *Monitor* the application and collect metrics, *Analyze* the gathered data, *Plan* actions accordingly in order to maintain objectives, and *Execute* the planned actions. The *Knowledge* component defines a shared, continuously updated knowledge base.

Scaling Configuration and Calibration: The scaling algorithm, based on the four main phases of the MAPE-K loop, is implemented in a python script (*control.py*). The script is run independently on a single cluster node. The algorithm starts by building the fuzzy membership functions, essentially calibrating them based on existing experience. The values used for constructing the functions are part of the MAPE-K knowledge base. These values are calculated by relying on metrics of previous runs of the system. Therefore, before starting the scaling algorithm effectively, the system needs have been run at least once to determine behaviour that can be anticipated. Based on the initial membership functions, a first global scale value is computed according to which the system is scaled. This forms the *proactive* part of the controller, which provides settings for future runs based on anticipated load and performance. The MAPE-K loop for the given system is presented in Fig. 6.

Continuous Scaling: The *reactive* part of the algorithm is executed as the default after start. It aims to adjust the current settings to specified requirements. The script receives current performance metrics from the Prometheus API. These metrics are evaluated against the allowed threshold values stored in the knowledge component. The knowledge component is implemented within the control script. Based on these computations, a plan is devised that involves updating the membership functions. The goal is to constantly update the membership function such that the fuzzy service provides optimal scale values for all load scenarios. Optimal is defined as a system that is scaled in order to meet the SLO without wasting unnecessary resources, i.e., the ultimate goal is to only scale up as much as necessary. The membership functions are passed to the fuzzy service that calculates a scale value. After scaling, the loop repeats by monitoring and analyzing the effects of the previous iteration. The definitions of the membership functions are also part of the knowledge component and are continuously updated (Fig. 7).

4.2 The Fuzzy Service

The task of the *fuzzy service* is to determine the scale value. Its rules are predefined. It uses the *membership functions as input.* Another parameter is the range of the scale values, which can be defined to set the minimum and maximum scale values that are considered acceptable. The services returns a *global scale value as output.*

The *calc* function is used to simulate a function that is called continuously. It is always scaled to the maximum. If there are only a few message processes by the system that the *calc* function is allowed to scale higher. When the number rises,

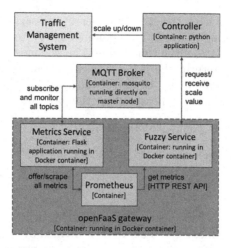

Fig. 7. Details of services providing scaling functionality [18].

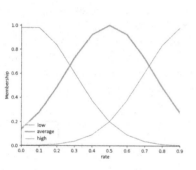

(a) Initial membership functions.

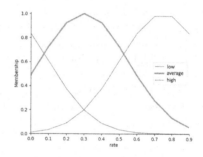

(b) Re-adjusted membership functions: the system can handle less messages than expected.

Fig. 8. Scaling service [18].

the allowed number of replicas will decrease. The minimal alpine distribution, which is used for the other images, could not be used in this case since *sk-fuzzy*, the python fuzzy module that was used, relies on the *numpy* module that requires a more complex OS. Therefore, the image of the *fuzzy service* is based on *ubuntu:18.04*.

4.3 Controller Calibration and Configuration

The metrics that are gathered during earlier system runs are used as the basis for calibrating the fuzzy membership functions in order to manage the anticipated demand better. The metric used here to measure the current load of the system is the number of exchanged messages in a given time frame. This metric, called *messages_total*, only defines the total number of messages the system has to process since monitoring started. This requires a way to measure how many messages are processed in a given time frame. This is done using the Prometheus *rate()* function, which returns the *per second rate of increase*.

The following example query is used throughout the application to return the per-second rate of increase measured for the past 20 s:

```
rate(messages_count_total[20s])
```

The increase rate r is then calculated as follows:

$$r = \frac{x_i - x_{i-t}}{t} \tag{1}$$

where x_{i-t} is the number of messages for t seconds in the past with x_i as the most recent number of messages. This value is divided by t, the time frame that is considered, since r is the per-second value. Based on the rate, the Prometheus query language is used to obtain three values: the global median, the global standard deviation and the global maximum. Global in this context refers to metrics that were calculated based on previous runs of the system. These values are used to create the initial membership functions of the rate of messages. In *sk-fuzzy*, Gaussian membership functions are created by defining their mean and their standard deviation. The Gaussian membership functions are simple to create and re-adjust. All membership functions set the previously obtained global standard deviation σ_g as their own standard deviation. The mean of the *average* membership function is placed at the global median:

$$median(a)_g \tag{2}$$

with a being a set of data, in this case the rate of messages. The mean of the *low* membership function is:

$$median(a)_g - \sigma_g \tag{3}$$

with σ_g again being the global standard deviation. The mean of the *high* membership function is thus:

$$median(a)_g + \sigma_g \tag{4}$$

The initial membership functions are shown in Fig. 8a.

The next step is the calculation of the three global variables. As an example, the following query provides the median value over all rates of messages (i.e., the rates covering a time span of 20 s each) of the last 90 days:

```
quantile_over_time(
  0.5, rate(messages_count_total[20s])[90d:20s] )
```

While Prometheus does not support a *median* function, the built-in *quantile* function can be used to calculate the median. A quantile splits a probability distribution into groups according to a given threshold. The 0.5 quantile equals the median. Generally, the median can be defined as:

$$Q_A(0.5) = median(a) \tag{5}$$

The standard deviation over time is calculated by using the corresponding *PromQL* function:

```
stddev_over_time(
  rate(messages_count_total[20s])[90d:20s]) )
```

This call returns the standard deviation of the rate of messages (covering a time span of 20 s each). The total time span that is considered are the last 90 days. The standard deviation for the given context is:

$$\sigma_g = \sqrt{\frac{1}{N} * \sum_{i=1}^{N} *(x_i - \mu)} \tag{6}$$

with N being the rates of messages considered while x_i is a single rate of messages and μ is the mean of all rates of messages. Finally, only the global maximum of the data set remains to be calculated:

```
max_over_time(
  rate(messages_count_total[20s])[90d:20s] )
```

4.4   Continuous Auto-scaling

Auto-scaling is based on the previous initial membership functions that are re-adjusted continuously. This reactive part is implemented as part of an infinite loop. After the initial configuration and calibration part is concluded, the initial membership functions are passed to the fuzzy service that returns a scale value that scales the relevant services:

$$s = round(D * G) \tag{7}$$

Here, s denotes the new scale value that a service is scaled to. D refers to the default value the service is scaled to at startup and G is the rounded global scale value that has been calculated by the fuzzy service and is used for all dynamically scaled components. The scalable components include the gatherer service and the decision function that were introduced earlier.

The Message Roundtrip Time MRT is calculated after a scaling action. This metric for the sample Traffic Management use case indicates the average time a vehicle needs to wait for a response from the gatherer after publishing its latest status. In the analysis phase, the MRT is compared to the maximum threshold that is defined in the SLA. If the average MRT is above the SLO, the membership functions need to be re-adjusted. The initial membership function shown in

Fig. 8a results in a scale value too low for the given load: the measured MRT after scaling was above the defined threshold. Therefore, the membership function need to be shifted to the left. The result of this shift can be seen in Fig. 8b. If we assume the current load to be 0.5 and compare the degree of membership in both figures, we find that in the initial figure a load value of 0.5 is considered an "average" load. Looking at the re-adjusted functions, a value of 0.5 is now seen as more of a "high" load. Since the fuzzy service classifies a value of 0.5 as a "higher" load now, it also maps it to a higher scale value. Consequently, the system now scales up at a load value of 0.5 where it had previously taken no action. Similarly, we need to consider a situation in which the MRT is well below the defined threshold. In this case, the functions need to be shifted to the right. The rate at which the functions are adjusted (shifted) in each iteration of the loop can be controlled by (manually) updating the adjustment factor. Hence, the membership functions for each iteration are determined in the following way:

- Membership function *low*: $median(a)_g - \sigma_g + A$
- Membership function *average* : $median(a)_g + A$
- Membership function *high*: $median(a)_g + \sigma_g + A$

Here, A is the adjustment factor for the functions. A is computed in each iteration. A positive re-adjustment factor results in a shift to the right, a negative one to the left. To avoid constantly moving the functions back and forth, shifting right is only allowed until a situation is encountered where the STO threshold is not met anymore. After completing the shifting process with the control script, the reactive part of the algorithm is started again, providing the fuzzy service with the re-adjusted membership functions.

Algorithm 1 outlines the continuous reactive scaling functionality explained above.

Algorithm 1. Reactive Autoscaling.

1: **function** SCALE(MEMBERSHIPFCTS)
2:     $sto \leftarrow$ STO threshold
3:     $scalevalue \leftarrow$
4:      getScaleValueFromFuzzyService(membershipFcts)
5:     $rescale(scalevalue)$
6:     $invocationtime \leftarrow$ get current invocation time
7:     **if** $invocationtime < slo$ **then**
8:         shift membership functions right
9:     **if** $invocationtime >= slo$ **then**
10:        shift membership functions left
11:     $Scale(membershipFcts)$

---

5   Controller Evaluation

Performance is the critical property. Thus, the evaluation shall focus on the performance of the proposed serverless architecture with the auto-scaling mechanism at the core and determine crucial bottlenecks.

5.1   Evaluation Objectives and Metrics

The auto-scaling approach needs to be evaluated in terms of its effectiveness as the core solution component. Being effective means that the auto-scaling algorithm is able to maintain the set SLO thresholds by re-adjusting the fuzzy membership functions. This would result in a smooth scaling process where the scalable components are gradually scaled up or down, avoiding sudden leaps of the scale value. For the given application, we also determined the maximum load, i.e., here the maximum number of vehicles the architecture (including the network it is operated in) can support[4].

The evaluation goals were analyzed for two different cluster set-ups. In order to obtain a first understanding of the system and the possible range of variables, a pilot calibration evaluation was conducted on a small cluster of three RPIs. As a second step, the evaluation procedure was repeated for a complete cluster (consisting of eight RPis).

For the evaluation, we report a range of performance metrics that indicate the effectiveness of the system or provide insight into an internal process.

- The Message Roundtrip Time (MRT) is the central variable of the system since it reports on the effectiveness of the application execution.
- Included in the MRT is the (openFaas) Function Invocation Time (FIT) that is listed separately in order to individually report on serverless performance aspects.

All MRT and FIT values are considered average values aggregated over the last 20 s after the previous scaling operation was completed. Here, the maximum scale value was unknown. In concrete scenarios, this value could be determined prior to execution. We use different MRT thresholds. In concrete settings, the maximum response time could be given in advance and would unlikely to be the subject of change. For all set-ups and iterations that were evaluated, the hardware workload was measured by computing the average CPU and memory usage over all nodes of the cluster.

5.2   Evaluation Setup

Some configurations were made to facilitate the evaluation. Prometheus is used to gather and aggregate the metrics for the evaluation. The cloud-init configuration was adjusted so that an additional python script is executed on each node.

---

[4] Note, that the vehicles referred to here could be replaced by other application components.

Table 2. Results for cluster of 3 RPIs. Scaling was active with variables set to values reported in Fig. 3 [18].

Vehicles	Memory	CPU	MRT	FIT
2	25.55	46.97	1.63	1.51
4	37.94	47.24	1.85	1.48
8	57.1	49.36	1.79	1.61
12	71.77	51.81	4.49	1.79
14	92.78	55.49	10.24	2.13

Table 3. Initial Calibration Scaling run for cluster of three RPIs with fixed number of 12 cars. Shift Left/Right reports on the direction the membership functions are shifted during an iteration. The number of scaled components is also reported. Manually set variables: Maximum Scale Value: 5, MRT Threshold: 2.0 s – FSV: Fuzzy Scale Value, IT: Invocation Time after scaling, Ga: Gatherer, DF: Decision Function [18].

Iteration	FSV	IT	Shift	# Ga	# DF
1	2.74	1.74	Right	10	5
2	2.63	2.5	Left	10	5
3	2.74	2.05	Left	10	5
4	2.95	1.9	Right	12	6

The script uses the *psutil* python module to record CPU and memory usage of the node and publish them to a specific MQTT topic. Additional functionality was also added to the metrics service: the service receives the CPU/memory metrics of all nodes and stores them internally. When the metrics are collected, the service calculates average CPU and memory usage across all nodes. Prometheus then processes these.

5.3   Evaluation Implementation

Pilot Calibration. An initial evaluation (calibration pilot) was conducted to obtain an initial idea of the system's capabilities and adjust the manually-tuned parameters accordingly. It was also used to evaluate whether the scaling functionality yields promising results before putting it to use in a bigger set-up. The evaluation was started with a cluster consisting of three RPIs: a master and two worker nodes. The maximum scale value was initially set to 5 in order to avoid scaling unreasonably high. Table 2 reports on the initial set of metrics for different numbers of vehicles. The scaling functionality was active when the metrics were monitored. Table 3 includes data of the scaling algorithm for an initial calibrating run.

Full Cluster. A cluster of eight RPIs was used. Here, the decision-making functionality is included in the gatherer service, which is now scaled independently. Hence, there is no longer the need to call the decision function for each message. Results for the auto-scaling algorithm can be found in Table 4.

Table 4. Scaling experiment for cluster of 8 RPIs. Manually set variables: Maximum Scale Value: 12, Number of cars: changing, MRT Threshold: 0.3 s – FSV: Fuzzy Scale Value, AF: Adjustment Factor [18].

Iteration	Cars	FCV	MRT	AF
1	25	4.77	Initial	0.0
2	25	6.94	0.03	2.58
3	25	7.79	0.04	0.0
4	25	8.80	0.03	−2.58
5	50	10.11	0.178	−7.74
6	50	10.82	0.44	−10.32
7	50	10.82	0.44	−10.32
8	75	11.06	0.09	−12.9
9	75	11.24	0.033	−18.06
10	75	11.3	3.95	−20.64
11	75	11.34	0.07	−23.22

The CPU usage started at 47% and showed a linear increase up to about 56% at 14 vehicles. The hardware does not seem to be the limiting factor. The inital setup, however, shows a MRT of about 1.6 s for only 2 vehicles. At 12 vehicles, a Roundtrip Time of 4.5 s is reached and at 14 vehicles the MRT is already above 10 s, which is clearly a value too high for many real-world scenario. However, based on these findings, an initial evaluation run of the auto-scaling algorithm was conducted with the Roundtrip Time threshold set to 2.0 s. Even though this is not realistic, it allows for testing the auto-scaling functionality.

The experimental runs yielded promising results and show that the algorithm is able to adaptively rescale the system: The MRT is initially below the predefined threshold at about 1.7 s. In the second iteration, the MRT value is recorded above the threshold at 2.5 s. The system reacts to this situation by slowly re-adjusting the membership function, resulting in a higher fuzzy scale value, which consequently scales the system up until the measured MRT drops below the threshold again.

5.4   Discussion of Results

We derived starting values for all variables using the calibration pilot on a smaller cluster set-up. The evaluation of the architecture indicated that serverless function calls should be restricted since they introduce network latency problems.

The bottleneck is here the network. The given set-up was not able to process more than 75 user processes at a time. The CPU and Memory usage numbers as well as the steady but slow increase of the MRT imply that the hardware itself is able process a higher number of vehicles. Future extensions should find different network set-ups that allow for a dependable solution overcoming the limits identified here.

Our fuzzy auto-scaling solution works as intended, i.e., it is able to scale the system in a balanced manner. After finding a SLO, usually given in the system specifications, only the maximum scale value and the adjustment factor are the values that need to be set manually.

We can conclude that the full version of our system architecture provides satisfactory results in terms of resource consumption and performance (MRT). Furthermore, we could demonstrate acceptable scalability of the system.

6   Related Work

The discussion of serverless technology in academia is still in its early beginnings as noted by Baldini et al. [6]. This is a stark contrast to the attention is has gotten from industry and the software engineering community. Baldini et al. go on to introduce several commercial implementations such as Amazon's AWS Lambda or Microsoft Azure Functions. The major advantages mentioned are the responsibility of managing servers and infrastructure that no longer rests with the developer. Another advantage is that the provider may offer additional services such as logging or monitoring to be used on top of the client's applications. Kritikos et al. review several serverless framework and report on challenges faced when designing and implementing an application leveraging serverless technology [40]. They report on the need for new methods for creating an architecture for applications that contain both serverless components like functions as well as "classic" components such as microservices running inside a Docker Container [71]. They also note that the decision on how the application components should scale is largely left to the developer and suggest further research into automating this process. Lastly, they add that monitoring could be improved. Especially the option to use and aggregate custom metrics is noted as "missing in most of the frameworks" [40].

Kiss et al. gather requirements for applications making use of Edge Computing [39]. Specifically in the context of combining them with the capabilities of the 5G standard. They mention that recently released single-board devices open up the possibility of processing some of the data at the edge of the cluster. This, however, goes along with the challenge of orchestrating the available processing power. The IoT system needs to be able to "reorganize itself" [39] based on changing conditions. In order to create such a system, they propose the following steps: In the discovery phase the granular parts of the system are identified and the application is split up accordingly. Based on the observations, a deployment plan is created. This is followed by the execution phase in which the parts of the application are deployed to their corresponding locations and the system is started. The system's performance is monitored at run-time and reconfiguration steps are taken if necessary. The cycle is concluded by the learning and predicting step. To make use of the data gathered at run-time, the system needs to be able to learn using AI from it in order to improve its reconfiguration steps.

There different examples of comparable IoT Systems that have been documented. In order to be comparable to the proposed solution in this thesis, the systems had to be comprised of different hardware nodes that needed to communicate with each other as well as with a central node. Tata et al. outline the state of the art as well as the challenges in modeling the application architecture of IoT Edge Applications [72]. One of the exemplary scenarios they introduce is a system for smart trains based on the principles of edge computing. The system is comprised of a set of different sensors attached to crucial components of a car. The data is gathered by a central unit for each car that sends its own data to the central processing unit of the train. This unit is then able to communicate with the cloud. The task of gathering and processing data is shifted to nodes at the edge of the network before passing it on the cloud. They go on to suggest further research in the field of finding the optimal balance between modeling an IoT application independently of its environment and designing it in a way that accurately represents the structure of the environment it is deployed in. Another issue they mention is the scalability of such applications since the number of cars and sensors on different trains can vary significantly. The modeling of the architecture should therefore consider a way to deploy some parts of the application only to a specific set of nodes.

The mentioned papers offer an overview over the requirements and create proposals for the architecture of distributed IoT Systems. They also offer guidance on where more research could be conducted. They remain, however, on an abstract level and do not implement a prototype of a corresponding applications. The work presented in this paper aims at making use of the proposed approaches to implement a concrete, distributed IoT System based on a real-life scenario that is executable, observable and analyzable. The task of leveraging custom application metrics to enable auto-configuration will also be addressed. The devised solution will be evaluated in a second step.

A system similar to ours in architectural terms as a Raspberry Pi-based implementation of an application system has been introduced in [68]. The authors introduce a containerized cluster based on single-board devices that is tailored towards applications that process and compute large amounts of data. They deploy this application, a weather forecast model, to the Raspberry Pi cluster and evaluate its performance. They note that the performance of the RPi cluster is within limits acceptable and could be a suitable option for comparable use cases, although networking performance of the Raspberry Pis has been identified as a bottleneck. We will address performance degradations here through auto-scaling.

There are a range of scalability approaches. [31] categorize them into reactive, proactive and hybrid approaches. Reactive approaches react to changes in the environment and take action accordingly. Proactive approaches predict the need for resources in advance. Hybrid systems combine both approaches, making use of previously collected data and resource provisioning at run time.

AI approaches can be used to improve the network response to certain environmental factors such as network traffic or threats to the system [45]. The authors propose a general architecture of smart 5G system that includes an independent AI controller that communicates with the components of the application. The controller obtains certain metrics from these interfaces, uses its own functionality (based on a cycle of sensing, mining, prediction and reasoning) to analyse results and sends these back to the system while adapting its own parameters dynamically to improve its accuracy. The paper categorizes machine learning, the subset of AI it focuses on, into three categories:

Examples of implementations of algorithms for auto-scaling and auto-configuration exist. [61] propose tuning configuration parameters using an evolutionary algorithm called Covariance-Matrix-Adaption. Using this approach, potential candidates for solving a problem are continuously evolved, evaluated and selected, guiding the subsequent generations towards a desired outcome. This algorithm does not rely on pre-existing information about the system and is therefore a black-box approach. The aim of the algorithm is to find an optimal set of parameters to "maximize throughput while keeping the response time below a threshold" [61]. This threshold is defined in a so called Service-Level-Agreement(SLA) [7,55,57].

Another paper introduces a Smart Hill Climbing Algorithm for finding the optimal configuration for a Web application [76]. The proposed solution is based on two phases: In the global search phase, they broadly scan the search space for a potential starting point of the local search phase. Another interesting approach aims at optimizing the configuration of Hadoop, a framework for distributed programming tasks [36]. This is an example of an offline, proactive tuning algorithm that does not reallocate resources at run-time, but tries to find the best configuration in advance. The proposed algorithm starts by computing a signature of the resource consumption. This signature is then compared against a database of signatures of other applications. This database maps the signature of the different applications to the predefined set of optimal parameters. The configuration parameters of the current application are then updated with the values of the application from the database it most closely resembles.

There are some proposals using fuzzy logic for auto-configuration. [31] introduce an elasticity controller that uses fuzzy logic to automatically reallocate resources in a cloud-based system. Time-series forecasting is used to obtain the estimated workload at a given time in the future. Based on this information, the elasticity controller calculates and returns the number of virtual machines that needs to be added to or removed from the system. The allocation of VMs is consequently carried out by the cloud platform. There, the rule base and membership functions are based on the experience of experts.

Reinforcement Learning in the form of Fuzzy Q-learning has been evaluated in this context [26,33]. The aim of these systems is to find the optimal configuration provisioning by interacting with the system. The controller, making use of the Q-learning algorithm, selects the scaling actions that yield the highest long-term reward. It will also keep updating the mapping of reward values to state-action pairs [26]. The idea of using supervised learning approaches and relying on training data has also been discussed. Yigitbasi et al. introduce an approach based on the Support-Vector-Regression Model [77]: a set of several machine-learning algorithms based on training-data that are used for classification and regression. Fuller introduces the idea of using Neural Networks for building and improving the fuzzy knowledge base [17]. Adaptive neuro-fuzzy inference systems (ANFIS), combining neural networks and fuzzy logic, are discussed in [34]. He states that neural networks excel at pattern recognition but it is usually difficult to follow their "reasoning" process. This process is easier to comprehend for fuzzy logic systems but they rely on a knowledge base that is not trivial to obtain. Fuzzy logic and neural networks are shown to complement each other in a hybrid system. Newer papers highlight a "self-adaptive neural fuzzy controller" for server provisioning [42]. The proposed architecture is making use of a neural network of four layers. The layers of the neural network represent the fuzzy membership function and rule base. The neural network will constantly learn and adapt itself. This will lead to the membership functions and rules being established and refined over time. It excels over a regular fuzzy controller based on manual tuning of the knowledge base.

Our work here focused on introducing a practical implementation approach for a lightweight auto-scaling controller based on fuzzy logic. So far, fuzzy auto-scaling for lightweight edge architectures has not been investigated in the literature.

7   Conclusions

At the core of our platform is a containerized architecture on a cluster of single-board devices. Combined with a fuzzy auto-scaler, this results overall in a reconfigurable, scalable and dependable system. The implementation is a proof-of-concept with the constraints of the environment playing a crucial factor in the implementation. We aimed at experimentally evaluating a self-adaptive autoscaler based on the openFaas framework and a microservices-based architecture. The evaluation of the system was carried out to analyze the performance. OpenFaas was used for inter-service communication as well as for monitoring. The auto-scaling algorithm was specifically designed to support dependable resource management for lightweight edge device clusters.

Using fuzzy logic, the auto-scaling controller can gradually scale the system. Previous examples of fuzzy auto-scalers that were deployed in large cloud infrastructures, the fuzzy scaling functionality in our case was constrained in its processing needs since it was deployed together with the main system components on the limited hardware cluster. Consequently, the algorithm was focused on using data and technologies that were already available within the cluster. This also applies for fuzzy systems based on neural networks. There are still parameters that need to be tuned manually to achieve the desired outcomes.

This leaves a certain degree of uncertainty when applying the algorithm on a black-box system.

In our use case scenarios. Our evaluation demonstrated that the set-up is only able to process up to 75 vehicles simultaneously. While our focus was on compute/storage resources, here network limitations emerge as the reason. Exploring these more deeply is part of future work. We shall also focus on improving the application management components towards more realistic behavior.

We discussed related work on Adaptive Neuro-Fuzzy Inference Systems (called ANFIS). Working examples of ANFIS are relatively uncommon. One example uses python and the machine-learning framework tensorflow to combine fuzzy logic and a neural network [10]. Relying on the ubuntu distribution used for the fuzzy service, it is possible to create an ANFIS service for our setting. Previously, compiling and running the tensorflow framework on hardware such as the Raspberry Pi was a challenging task. With release 1.9 of the framework, tensorflow officially started supporting the Raspberry Pi [75]. Pre-built packages for the platform can now be directly installed. This adds new possibilities for creating a lightweight ANFIS service for the given system. ANFISs rely on training data. This introduces the challenge of finding sample data that maps the rate of messages and a scale value to an indicator that classifies the performance as acceptable/not acceptable: *(rate of messages, scale value)* $\rightarrow$ *acceptable/not acceptable performance*. This dataset could be aggregated manually or in an automated manner to address the problems.

We also plan to address more complex architectures with multiple clusters to be coordinated [15,16]. We propose Particle Swarm Optimization (PSO) [4] here, which is a bio-inspired optimization methods suitable to coordinate between autonomous entities such as clusters in our case, combined with machine learning techniques for the construction of the controller [5]. PSO distinguishes personal (here local cluster) best fitness and global (here cross-cluster) best fitness in the allocation of load to clusters and their nodes. This shall be combined with the fuzzy scaling at cluster level.

Our abstract application scenarios, with cars just being simulated data providers, allows us to generalise the results beyond the concrete application case [23,27]. We considered at traffic management and coordinated cars, where traffic and car movement is captured and processed, maybe supplemented by infotainment information with image and video data. Another application domain is mobile learning that equally includes heavy use of multimedia content being delivered to mobile learners and their devices [37,44,47,49,51]. These systems also rely on close interaction with semantic processing of interactions in order to support cognitive learning processes. Some of these can be provided at edge layer to enable satisfactory user experience based on sufficient platform performance.

References

1. Ansible: Overview: How ansible works (2020). https://www.ansible.com/overview/how-ansible-works. Accessed 04 June 2020

2. Ardagna, C.A., Asal, R., Damiani, E., Dimitrakos, T., El Ioini, N., Pahl, C.: Certification-based cloud adaptation. IEEE Trans. Serv. Comput. **14**, 82–96 (2018)
3. Avahi - What is avahi? (2020). https://www.avahi.org/. Accessed 04 June 2020
4. Azimi, S., Pahl, C., Shirvani, M.H.: Particle swarm optimization for managing performance in multi-cluster IoT edge architectures (2020)
5. Azimi, S., Pahl, C.: Root cause analysis and remediation for quality and value improvement in machine learning driven information models. In: 22nd International Conference on Enterprise Information Systems ICEIS (2020)
6. Baldini, I., et al.: Serverless computing: current trends and open problems. CoRR, abs/1706.03178 (2017)
7. Barrett, R., Patcas, L.M., Pahl, C., Murphy, J.: Model driven distribution pattern design for dynamic web service compositions. In: Proceedings of the 6th International Conference on Web Engineering, pp. 129–136 (2006)
8. Belam, M.: The raspberry Pi: reviving the lost art of children's computer programming (2012). https://www.theguardian.com/commentisfree/2012/feb/29/rasperry-pi-childrens-programming. Accessed 04 June 2020
9. Cloud-Init: cloud-init: The standard for customising cloud instances (2020). https://cloud-init.io/. Accessed 04 June 2020
10. Cuervo, T.: TensorANFIS (2020). https://github.com/tiagoCuervo/TensorANFIS. Accessed 04 June 2020
11. Docker: What is docker? (2020). https://www.redhat.com/en/topics/containers/what-is-docker. Accessed 04 June 2020
12. Ellis, A.: Introducing stateless microservices for openfaas (2018). https://www.openfaas.com/blog/stateless-microservices/
13. Fang, D., Liu, X., Romdhani, I., Jamshidi, P., Pahl, C.: An agility-oriented and fuzziness-embedded semantic model for collaborative cloud service search, retrieval and recommendation. Future Gener. Comput. Syst. **56**, 11–26 (2016)
14. Fowler, M.: Microservices (2014). https://martinfowler.com/articles/microservices.html. Accessed 04 June 2020
15. Fowley, F., Pahl, C., Jamshidi, P., Fang, D., Liu, X.: A classification and comparison framework for cloud service brokerage architectures. IEEE Trans. Cloud Comput. **6**(2), 358–371 (2016)
16. Fowley, F., Pahl, C., Zhang, L.: A comparison framework and review of service brokerage solutions for cloud architectures. In: Lomuscio, A.R., Nepal, S., Patrizi, F., Benatallah, B., Brandić, I. (eds.) ICSOC 2013. LNCS, vol. 8377, pp. 137–149. Springer, Cham (2014). https://doi.org/10.1007/978-3-319-06859-6_13
17. Fuller, R.: Neural Fuzzy Systems (1998)
18. Gand, F., Fronza, I., El Ioini, N., Barzegar, H.R., Azimi, S., Pahl, C.: A fuzzy controller for self-adaptive lightweight edge container orchestration. In: 10th International Conference on Cloud Computing and Services Science CLOSER (2020)
19. Gand, F., Fronza, I., El Ioini, N., Barzegar, H.R., Pahl, C.: Serverless container cluster management for lightweight edge clouds. In: 10th International Conference on Cloud Computing and Services Science CLOSER (2020)
20. Gand, F., Fronza, I., El Ioini, N., Barzegar, H.R., Pahl, C.: A lightweight virtualisation platform for cooperative, connected and automated mobility. In: 6th International Conference on Vehicle Technology and Intelligent Transport Systems (VEHITS) (2020)
21. Hong, T.-P., Lee, C.-Y.: Induction of fuzzy rules and membership functions from training examples. Fuzzy Sets Syst. **84**(1), 33–47 (1996)
22. Hypriot: HypriotOS (2020). https://blog.hypriot.com/about/. Accessed 04 June 2020

23. El Ioini, N., Pahl, C.: A review of distributed ledger technologies (2018)
24. El Ioini, N., Pahl, C.: Trustworthy orchestration of container based edge computing using permissioned blockchain. In: International Conference on Internet of Things: Systems, Management and Security (IoTSMS) (2018)
25. El Ioini, N., Pahl, C., Helmer, S.: A decision framework for blockchain platforms for IoT and edge computing. In: IoTBDS 2018 (2018)
26. Ipek, E., Mutlu, O., Martinez, J.F., Caruana, R.: Self-optimizing memory controllers: a reinforcement learning approach. In: 2008 International Symposium on Computer Architecture, pp. 39–50 (2008)
27. Jamshidi, P., Pahl, C., Chinenyeze, S., Liu, X.: Cloud migration patterns: a multi-cloud service architecture perspective. In: Toumani, F., et al. (eds.) ICSOC 2014. LNCS, vol. 8954, pp. 6–19. Springer, Cham (2015). https://doi.org/10.1007/978-3-319-22885-3_2
28. Jamshidi, P., Sharifloo, A., Pahl, C., Arabnejad, H., Metzger, A., Estrada, G.: Fuzzy self-learning controllers for elasticity management in dynamic cloud architectures. In: International Conference on Quality of Software Architectures, pp. 70–79 (2016)
29. Jamshidi, P., Pahl, C., Mendonca, N.C.: Managing uncertainty in autonomic cloud elasticity controllers. IEEE Cloud Comput. **3**, 50–60 (2016)
30. Jamshidi, P., Pahl, C., Mendonca, N.C.: Pattern-based multi-cloud architecture migration. Softw. Pract. Exp. **47**(9), 1159–1184 (2017)
31. Jamshidi, P., Ahmad, A., Pahl, C.: Autonomic resource provisioning for cloud-based software. In: Proceedings of the 9th International Symposium on Software Engineering for Adaptive and Self-Managing Systems, SEAMS 2014 (2014)
32. Jamshidi, P., Pahl, C., Mendonca, N.C., Lewis, J., Tilkov, S.: Microservices: the journey so far and challenges ahead. IEEE Softw. **35**(3), 24–35 (2018)
33. Jamshidi, P., Sharifloo, A.M., Pahl, C., Metzger, A., Estrada, G.: Self-learning cloud controllers: fuzzy Q-learning for knowledge evolution. In: ICAC 2015, pp. 208–211 (2015)
34. Jang, J.S.R.: ANFIS: adaptive-network-based fuzzy inference system. IEEE Trans. Syst. Man Cybern. **23**(3), 665–685 (1993)
35. Javed, M., Abgaz, Y.M., Pahl, C.: Ontology change management and identification of change patterns. J. Data Semant. **2**(2–3), 119–143 (2013)
36. Kambatla, K., Pathak, A., Pucha, H.: Towards optimizing hadoop provisioning in the cloud. In: Conference on Hot Topics in Cloud Computing, HotCloud 2009 (2009)
37. Kenny, C., Pahl, C.: Automated tutoring for a database skills training environment. In: ACM SIGCSE Symposium 2005, pp. 58–64 (2005)
38. Kephart, J.O., Chess, D.M.: The vision of autonomic computing. Computer **36**(1), 41–50 (2003)
39. Kiss, P., Reale, A., Ferrari, C.J., Istenes, Z.: Deployment of IoT applications on 5G edge. In: 2018 IEEE International Conference on Future IoT Technologies (2018)
40. Kritikos, K., Skrzypek, P.: A review of serverless frameworks. In: 2018 IEEE/ACM UCC Companion (2018)
41. Kubeless: Kubeless: The kubernetes native serverless framework (2020). https://kubeless.io/. Accessed 04 June 2020
42. Lama, P., Zhou, X.: Autonomic provisioning with self-adaptive neural fuzzy control for end-to-end delay guarantee. In: International Symposium on Modeling, Analysis and Simulation of Computer and Telecom Systems (2010)

43. Le, V.T., Pahl, C., El Ioini, N.: Blockchain based service continuity in mobile edge computing. In: 6th International Conference on Internet of Things: Systems, Management and Security (2019)

44. Lei, X., Pahl, C., Donnellan, D.: An evaluation technique for content interaction in web-based teaching and learning environments. In: 3rd IEEE International Conference on Advanced Technologies, pp. 294–295 (2003)

45. Li, R., et al.: Intelligent 5G: when cellular networks meet artificial intelligence. IEEE Wirel. Commun. **24**(5), 175–183 (2017)

46. Lin, C.-T., Lee, C.S.G.: Neural-network-based fuzzy logic control and decision system. IEEE Trans. Comput. **40**(12), 1320–1336 (1991)

47. Melia, M., Pahl, C.: Constraint-based validation of adaptive e-learning courseware. IEEE Trans. Learn. Technol. **2**(1), 37–49 (2009)

48. Mendonca, N.C., Jamshidi, P., Garlan, D., Pahl, C.: Developing self-adaptive microservice systems: challenges and directions. IEEE Softw. **38**, 70–79 (2019)

49. Murray, S., Ryan, J., Pahl, C.: A tool-mediated cognitive apprenticeship approach for a computer engineering course. In: Proceedings 3rd IEEE International Conference on Advanced Technologies, pp2–6 (2003)

50. openFaaS: openfaas: Auto-scaling (2020). https://docs.openfaas.com/architecture/autoscaling/. Accessed 04 June 2020

51. Pahl, C., Barrett, R., Kenny, C.: Supporting active database learning and training through interactive multimedia. ACM SIGCSE Bull. **36**(3), 27–31 (2004)

52. Pahl, C., El Ioini, N., Helmer, S., Lee, B.: An architecture pattern for trusted orchestration in IoT edge clouds. In: International Conference on Fog and Mobile Edge Computing (2018)

53. Pahl, C., Jamshidi, P., Zimmermann, O.: Architectural principles for cloud software. ACM Trans. Internet Technol. (TOIT) **18**(2), 17 (2018)

54. Pahl, C.: An ontology for software component matching. In: Pezzè, M. (ed.) FASE 2003. LNCS, vol. 2621, pp. 6–21. Springer, Heidelberg (2003). https://doi.org/10.1007/3-540-36578-8_2

55. Pahl, C., Giesecke, S., Hasselbring, W.: An ontology-based approach for modelling architectural styles. In: Oquendo, F. (ed.) ECSA 2007. LNCS, vol. 4758, pp. 60–75. Springer, Heidelberg (2007). https://doi.org/10.1007/978-3-540-75132-8_6

56. Pahl, C., Fronza, I., El Ioini, N., Barzegar, H.R.: A review of architectural principles and patterns for distributed mobile information systems. In: 14th International Conference on Web Information Systems and Technologies (2019)

57. Pahl, C.: Layered ontological modelling for web service-oriented model-driven architecture. In: Hartman, A., Kreische, D. (eds.) ECMDA-FA 2005. LNCS, vol. 3748, pp. 88–102. Springer, Heidelberg (2005). https://doi.org/10.1007/11581741_8

58. Pahl, C., Jamshidi, P., Zimmermann, O.: Microservices and containers. In: Software Engineering SE 2020 (2020)

59. Prometheus: Prometheus: Querying (2020). https://prometheus.io/docs/prometheus/latest/querying/. Accessed 04 June 2020

60. Raspberry Pi: Raspberry pi: products (2020). https://www.raspberrypi.org/products/. Accessed 04 June 2020

61. Saboori, A., Jiang, G., Chen, H.: Autotuning configurations in distributed systems for performance improvements using evolutionary strategies. In: International Conference on Distributed Computing Systems (2008)

62. Samir, A., Pahl, C.: Anomaly detection and analysis for clustered cloud computing reliability. In: International Conference on Cloud Computing, GRIDs, and Virtualization, pp. 110–119 (2019)

63. Samir, A., Pahl, C.: A controller architecture for anomaly detection, root cause analysis and self-adaptation for cluster architectures. In: International Conference on Adaptive and Self-Adaptive Systems and Applications, pp. 75–83 (2019)

64. Samir, A., Pahl, C.: Detecting and localizing anomalies in container clusters using Markov models. Electronics **9**(1), 64 (2020)

65. Scolati, R., Fronza, I., Ioini, N.E., Samir, A., Pahl, C.: A containerized big data streaming architecture for edge cloud computing on clustered single-board devices. In: International Conference on Cloud Computing and Services Science CLOSER (2019)

66. Scolati, R., Fronza, I., El Ioini, N., Samir, A., Barzegar, H.R., Pahl, C.: A containerized edge cloud architecture for data stream processing. In: Ferguson, D., Méndez Muñoz, V., Pahl, C., Helfert, M. (eds.) CLOSER 2019. CCIS, vol. 1218, pp. 150–176. Springer, Cham (2020). https://doi.org/10.1007/978-3-030-49432-2_8

67. Serverless: Serverless framework (2020). https://serverless.com/. Accessed 04 June 2020

68. Steffenel, L., Schwertner Char, A., da Silva Alves, B.: A containerized tool to deploy scientific applications over Soc-based systems: the case of meteorological forecasting with WRF. In: CLOSER 2019 (2019)

69. Taibi, D., Lenarduzzi, V., Pahl, C.: Microservices anti-patterns: a taxonomy. Microservices, pp. 111–128. Springer, Cham (2020). https://doi.org/10.1007/978-3-030-31646-4_5

70. Taibi, D., Lenarduzzi, V., Pahl, C., Janes, A.: Microservices in agile software development: a workshop-based study into issues, advantages, and disadvantages. In: XP 2017 Scientific Workshops (2017)

71. Taibi, D., El Ioini, N., Pahl, C., Niederkofler J.R.S.: Patterns for serverless functions (Function-as-a Service): a multivocal literature review. In: Proceedings of the 10th International Conference on Cloud Computing and Services Science, CLOSER (2020)

72. Tata, S., Jain, R., Ludwig, H., Gopisetty, S.: Living in the cloud or on the edge: opportunities and challenges of IoT application architecture. In: 2017 IEEE International Conference on Services Computing (SCC), pp. 220–224

73. von Leon, D., Miori, L., Sanin, J., El Ioini, N., Helmer, S., Pahl, C.: A Performance exploration of architectural options for a middleware for decentralised lightweight edge cloud architectures. In: International Conference on Internet of Things, Big Data and Security (2018)

74. von Leon, D., Miori, L., Sanin, J., El Ioini, N., Helmer, S., Pahl, C.: A Lightweight Container Middleware for Edge Cloud Architectures. In: Fog and Edge Computing: Principles and Paradigms, pp. 145–170 (2019)

75. Warden, P.: Tensorflow 1.9 officially supports the raspberry Pi (2020). https://medium.com/tensorflow/tensorflow-1-9-officially-supports-the-raspberry-pi-b91669b0aa0. Accessed 04 June 2020

76. Xi, B., Xia, C.H., Liu, Z., Zhang, L., Raghavachari, M.: A smart hill-climbing algorithm for application server configuration. In: 13th International Conference on WWW (2004)

77. Yigitbasi, N., Willke, T.L., Liao, G., Epema, D.: Towards machine learning-based auto-tuning of mapreduce. In: IEEE 21st International Symposium on Modelling, Analysis and Simulation of Computer and Telecommunication Systems, pp. 11–20 (2013)

Performance Management in Clustered Edge Architectures Using Particle Swarm Optimization

Shelernaz Azimi[1]([⊠]), Claus Pahl[1], and Mirsaeid Hosseini Shirvani[2]([⊠])

[1] Free University of Bozen-Bolzano, Bolzano, Italy
{seyedehshelernaz.azimi,claus.pahl}@unibz.it
[2] Department of Computer Engineering, Sari Branch, Islamic Azad University, Sari, Iran

Abstract. Recently distributed computing capacities are brought to the edge of the Internet, permitting Internet-of-Things applications to process calculation all the more locally and subsequently more productively and this has brought a totally different scope of apparatuses and usefulness. This instrument can The most significant characterizing highlights of edge processing are low latency, location awareness, wide geographic distribution, versatility, support for countless nodes, etc. We want to likely limit the latency and delay in edge-based structures. We center around a progressed compositional setting that considers communication and processing delays and the management effort notwithstanding a real request execution time in an operational efficiency situation. Our design is based on multi-cluster edge layer with nearby autonomous edge node clusters. We will contend that particle swarm optimization as a bio-motivated optimization approach is a perfect candidate for distributed IoT load handling in self-managed edge clusters. By designing a controller and utilizing a particle swarm optimization algorithm, we show that delay and end-to-end latency can be reduced.

Keywords: Internet of Things · Edge computing · Cloud computing · Edge cluster · Particle swarm optimization · Latency · Delay · Performance

1 Introduction

With the growing internet, we are seeing also devices in our vicinity in many everyday activities. So far, the fundamental use of the internet has been the utilization by human individuals for a specific function. We are now seeing another type of internet known as the Internet of Things. The Internet of Things gives the capacity to associate items over internet-based connectivity.

The IoT is the foundation to convey energizing new services. A framework is needed without which there would be no service. We need to compare the Internet of Things and the traditional internet for a better comprehension of the problem. Has the internet alone presented to us a service? To tell the truth, the internet has given a stage to offer appealing types of services, for example, the web, email and online services by interfacing PCs, cell phones and other networkable equipment. So is the Internet of Things. By connecting items to the network, it gives a scope of appealing and helpful services,

© Springer Nature Switzerland AG 2021
D. Ferguson et al. (Eds.): CLOSER 2020, CCIS 1399, pp. 233–257, 2021.
https://doi.org/10.1007/978-3-030-72369-9_10

for example, remote control, reporting and alerting, accident prevention, cost reduction and smart automation noted. IoT alludes to a situation wherein everything, regardless of whether human, creature, or lifeless, has a unique identifier or Internet protocol fit for recognizing, controlling, transmitting, and transmitting information to each other and to the pertinent database. Information gathered from items will be visible through different apparatuses, for example, cell phones, kinds of PCs and tablets. When IoT is implemented, data can be moved between various entities. IoT is the consequence of the assembly and advancement of the three components of the Internet, wireless technology and microelectronic frameworks. The fundamental result of IoT is the interconnection of devices [17].

Edge computing gives a transitional layer to computation and storage at the 'edge' of the system, regularly between Internet-of-Things devices and centralized data center clouds [18,28]. Edge computing guarantees better performance through lower latency since calculation is drawn closer to where the application sits. Lessening the transfer of information by keeping away the exchange of huge volumes of information to distant clouds has likewise the side effect of reducing security risks. Localization here is the key standard. Edge computing is suitable for applications that require high response speed, low latency, and real time. All these studies show that resource sharing provides low latency, better scalability, distributed processing, better security, crash tolerance and privacy to provide better haze infrastructure.

Propagation delay refers to the amount of time it takes for the first bit to travel over a link between sender and receiver, whereas latency refers to the total amount of time it takes to send an entire message.

Execution and load management in edge architectures has been tended to in the past [5,22], yet frequently the structures alluded to do not mirror the regularly geographically distributed nature of edge computing. We extend here on works like [9,34] that have considered single autonomous clusters as it were. We propose here an answer for a multi-cluster arrangement, where each cluster works semi-independently, just being composed by an orchestrator that oversees load distribution. Another direction that we include is a sensible impression of performance concerns. In our performance model we consider delays cause by correspondence and queueing just as processing times of controllers and edge execution nodes into a comprehensive end-to-end latency idea that understands the response time from the requestor's point of view.

Accordingly, our methodology expands the state-of-the-art by joining an end-to-end latency optimization framework with a multi-cluster edge architecture. We propose Particle Swarm Optimization (PSO) for the optimization here which extends our previous work in [3]. PSO is a bio-motivated evolutionary optimization technique [30] reasonable to organize between autonomous elements, for example, edge clusters in our case. PSO recognizes individual (here local clusters) best fitness and global (here cross-cluster) best fitness in the distribution of load to clusters and their nodes - which we use to optimize latency. Our orchestrator takes local cluster computation, yet additionally, whenever required, incorporated cloud processing as choices on board. We extend earlier work in [3] by providing more technical implementation detail, the comparison with related work and broaden the evaluation.

We show the viability of our performance optimization by contrasting it and other normal load distribution systems and settings.

The paper is organized as follows. In Sect. 2, particle swarm optimization will be introduced. In Sect. 3, our method for multi-cluster performance optimization of load distribution will be presented. In Sect. 4, the implementation will be evaluated. In the following section, the related work will be discussed. Finally, conclusions and suggestions for future work will be presented.

2 Principles of Particle Swarm Optimization

Particle Swarm Optimization (PSO) is a bio-inspired concept that is at the core answer for our performance optimization technique. We introduce central PSO ideas as well as explicit tools and methods that we consolidated for our context.

2.1 Particle Swarm Optimization Basics

Particle swarm optimization is an optimization strategy that can manage issues whose solution is a point or surface in a n-dimensional space. In such a space, a basic speed is assigned to particles in the swarm, just as the channels of communication between particles. Firstly, particles in our research are edge nodes that provide computing resources. Secondly, velocity is linked to processing load and performance. These nodes then move through the response space and the results are calculated on the basis of a merit criterion after each time interval. Over time, nodes accelerate toward nodes of higher competence that are in the same communication group. Although each method works well in a range of problems, PSO has shown great success in solving continuous optimization problems. This algorithm is one of the optimization algorithms based on the random generation of the initial population. In this algorithm, it is constructed by modeling and simulating the group flight behavior of birds or group movement of fish. Each member in this group is defined by the velocity vector and the position vector in the search space. At each time iteration, the new position of the node is defined by the velocity vector and the position vector in the search space. At each iteration, the new node position is updated according to the current velocity vector, the best position found by that node, and the best position found by the best node in the group. This algorithm was originally defined for continuous parameters, but since in some applications we deal with discrete parameters, it is also extended to discrete parameters. The node swarm optimization algorithm is introduced with BPSO. In this algorithm, the position of each node is defined by a value of 1. In this algorithm, the position of each node is represented by a binary value of zero or one. In BPSO the value of each node can be changed from zero to one or from one to zero. The velocity of each node is also defined as the probability of each node changing to one value [33].

2.2 Basic Algorithm Definitions

We assume here a d-dimensional search space. The first node in this d-dimensional space for the position vector X_i is described in Eq. (1):

$$X_i = (x_{i_1}, x_{i_2}, x_{i_3}, ..., x_{i_d}) \tag{1}$$

The velocity vector i of the first node is also defined in Eq. (2) with the vector V_i:

$$V_i = (v_{i_1}, v_{i_2}, v_{i_3}, ..., v_{i_d}) \tag{2}$$

In Eq. (3), we define the best position that the i-node has with $P_{i.best}$:

$$P_{i.best} = (p_{i_1}, p_{i_2}, p_{i_3}, ..., p_{i_d}) \tag{3}$$

And we define the best position of the best node among all the nodes with $P_{g.best}$ as Eq. (4):

$$P_{g.best} = (p_{g_1}, p_{g_2}, p_{g_3}, ..., p_{g_d}) \tag{4}$$

In order to update the location of each node when moving through the response space, we define the following equations:

$$\begin{aligned} V_i(t) = w * v_i(t-1) + c_1 * rand_1 * (P_{i.best} - X_i(t-1)) \\ + c_2 * rand_2 * (P_{g.best} - X_i(t-1)) \end{aligned} \tag{5}$$

and

$$X_i = x_i(t-1) + V_i(t) \tag{6}$$

where w is the inertial weight coefficient (moving in its own direction) indicating the effect of the previous iteration velocity vector (V_i (t)) on the velocity vector in the current iteration ($V_i(T + 1)$). c_1 is the constant training coefficient (moving along the path of the best value of the node examined). c_2 is the constant training coefficient (moving along the path of the best node found among the whole population). $rand_1$, $rand_2$ are random numbers with uniform distribution in the range of 1 to 2. V_i (t − 1) is the velocity vector in iteration (t − 1). $X_i(t − 1)$ is the position vector in iteration (t − 1). To limit the velocity of a node moving from one location to another or diverting the velocity vector, we limit the velocity variations to the range V_{min} to V_{max}, that is. The upper and lower speed limits are determined by the type of problem.

Some domain issues have specific definitions for their parameters and only have a limited, logical, and defined value in this domain. In other words, if there are any constraints or constraints in the problem under consideration, they must be accounted for by a mechanism to prevent nodes from entering the unauthorized space. This mechanism is called space constraint. If these mechanisms are not used, the response found by the algorithm is incorrect or unreliable. For example, Eq. (7) for negative x values in most programming languages is an error.

$$f_x = \sum_{d=1}^{d} \sqrt{x} \tag{7}$$

The mechanism used to account for this constraint is as follows:

$$X = max(0, x) \tag{8}$$

Sometimes, there are differences in how the algorithm is executed, which means that the steps are referred to in more separate ways, sometimes combining two or more steps into one step. But this does not make any sense in the programming that is done because what is important is to execute the program steps in the following order, and how these steps can be separated. In some references, for example, they combine steps four and five, meaning the step of updating the node velocity and moving the nodes to new locations as one step. This change will not cause any problems in the implementation of the algorithm.

2.3 Population Generation

The starting point is the generation of an initial population. The arbitrary generation of the underlying population is just the random determination of the underlying location of the nodes by a uniform dispersion in the solution space (search space). The arbitrary population generation phase of the underlying population exists in practically all probabilistic optimization algorithms. In any case, in this algorithm, notwithstanding the underlying random location the nodes, a specific measure of initial node velocity is additionally allocated. The underlying proposed range for node velocity results from Eq. (9).

$$\frac{X_{min} - X_{max}}{2} \leq V \leq \frac{X_{max} - X_{min}}{2} \tag{9}$$

2.4 Selection of Primary Nodes

Expanding the quantity of essential nodes reduces the quantity of iterations required for the algorithm to converge. In any case, this reduction in the quantity of iterations doesn't mean reducing the runtime of the program to accomplish convergence. An increase in the number of primary nodes does results in a decrease in the number of repeats. The increase in the number of nodes causes the algorithm to spend more time in the node evaluation phase, which increases the time it takes to run the algorithm until it achieves convergence, despite decreasing the number of iterations. So, increasing the number of nodes cannot be used to reduce the execution time of the algorithm. Another misconception is that the number of nodes can be reduced to optimize the execution time of the algorithm. It should be noted that decreasing the number of nodes may cause local minima to fall and the algorithm fails to reach the original minimum. If we consider the convergence condition as the number of iterations, although decreasing the number of initial nodes decreases the execution time of the algorithm, the solution obtained would not be the optimal solution to the problem. Thus, the initial population size is determined by the problem. In general, the number of primary nodes is a compromise between the parameters involved in the problem. Experimentally selecting the initial population of nodes of 2 to 5 nodes is a good choice for almost all test problems.

2.5 Evaluation of the Objective Function

The objective functions is also called the cost or fitness calculation of nodes. We have to assess every node which represents an answer for the issue under investigation. Contingent upon this, the assessment strategy differs. For instance, in the event that it is conceivable to define a mathematical function for the purpose, essentially by setting the input parameters (extracted from the node position vector) into this mathematical function, it is anything but difficult to calculate the cost of the node. Note that every node contains total data about the input parameters of the issue that this data is extracted and targeted to.

Sometimes it is not realistic to expect to characterize a scientific function for node evaluation. This happens when we have linked the algorithm to another software or used the algorithm for experimental data. In such cases, information about software input or test parameters should be extracted from the node position vector and placed in the software associated with the algorithm or applied to the relevant test. Running software or performing tests and observing or measuring the results determines the cost of each node at the end.

2.6   Recording the Best Position

The best position needs to be determined for each node (Pi.best) and the best position among all nodes (Pg.best). There are two cases to consider: On the off chance that we are in the first iteration (t = 1), we think about the current position of every node as the best location for that node - see Eqs. (10) and (11).

$$P_{i.best} = X_i(t), i = 1, 2, 4, ..., d \tag{10}$$

and

$$cost(P_{i.bes}) = cost(X_j(t)) \tag{11}$$

Furthermore, in the other iterations, we compare the amount of cost for the nodes in Step 2 with the value of the best cost for each node. If this cost is less than the best recorded cost for this node, then the location and cost of this node replaces the previous one. Otherwise there is no change in the location and cost recorded for this node:

$$\begin{cases} \text{if } \; cost(X_i(t)) < cost(P_{i.best}) \\ \text{else } \; no \; change \end{cases}$$

$$\Rightarrow \tag{12}$$

$$\begin{cases} cost(P_{i.best}) = cost(X_j(t)) \quad\quad i = 1, 2, ..., d \\ P_{i.best} = x_i(t) \end{cases}$$

3   Performance Optimization for Clustered Architectures

The PSO technique can now be applied as to optimize processing times in our multi-cluster edge scenario. We present another approach to limit total delay and latency in edge-based clusters.

Our optimization method for clustered edge architectures has the following four main steps:

1. the edge cluster architecture is defined.

2. the edge controller is designed.
3. the optimization problem is defined
4. the PSO optimization algorithm is applied.

In the following, each of these steps will be explained in detail.

3.1   Edge Request Management

Three layers can be identified in our architecture: the things layer, where the objects and end users are found, the edge layer, where the edge nodes for processing are found, lastly the cloud layer, where the cloud servers are located [11]. We expect the edge nodes to be clustered. That is, there are various clusters of edge nodes, where each has a local coordinator.

A cloud server can consist of a number of processing units, such as a rack of physical servers or a server with multiple cores. In each layer, the nodes are divided into domains where the IoT-edge-cloud application is implemented. A range of IoT nodes can be objects from a smart home, a temperature sensor in a factory, or a soil moisture sensor in a farm, all objects around which they are considered to be part of a domain.

Both edge and Cloud computing provide users with storage, applications and data. But edge is closer to the end user and has a wider geographical distribution. The edge networking consists of a data page and a control page. For example, on a data page, cloud computing allows services to be at the edge of the network rather than in the data center [18]. Devices in the edge are known as nodes. Any device with network, computing, and storage connections can be up to one node. The reason is simple: when data collection is close, data analysis is also less delayed [24].

Node-Based Request Processing. The correspondence between IoT, edge and cloud nodes occurs as follows. IoT nodes can process demands locally or send them to the controller for processing in edge or cloud. Edge nodes can process approaching demands or, if inaccessible, pass them to another edge node or the controller. Cloud nodes process the dispensed demands and return the outcome to the IoT nodes.

The purpose for this investigation is to minimize total execution time for IoT nodes in a proposed framework based on edge computing. The edge layer is located between the things layer and the cloud so that it can cover the majority of requests from the IoT nodes to minimize service delays.

We first introduce latency minimization rules and then formulate the IoT delay so we can analyze the rules analytically [36].

Request Offloading in the Edge Layer. The concept and rules of computational discharge in moving vehicles have been studied in different researches and on different criteria such as energy consumption, response time, availability, and so on. In this proposed method, the load discharge decision is a request based on the response time of the nodes of the edge, which depends on different factors. These include the amount of processing required to execute a request, the status of the node queue, and the computational power of a node. A controller decides to which edge (or cloud) node to allocate a request. The transfer time and the waiting (e.g., queuing time) at the controller typically causes a delay in processing.

Definition 1. *A **delay** is the time spent by transferring a request to the next node and waiting there to be processed. Thus, we typically have controller delays D_C, edge node delays D_E and IoT node delays D_I. A **processing time** is the time for execution at a node, i.e., either a controller processing time P_C or an edge node processing time P_E.*

Definition 2. *The **response time** R for an IoT node is the time it takes to get a request processed, i.e., the time between sending a request for processing until receiving the result.*

$$RT = D_C + P_C + D_E + P_E + D_I$$

*This is also known as **end-to-end latency** in networked environments.*

The requests are produced by the IoT nodes with a specific deadline for handling and they are sent to the controller for allocation of processing nodes. The architectural framework of the edge-based system used in this study is shown in Fig. 1. The requests transferred from different IoT nodes get into a queue until they finally get to the controller. The controller will consider the total waiting time of all edge nodes from their availability tables with consideration of the request deadline and will then allocate the request to the best edge node with the lowest total waiting time.

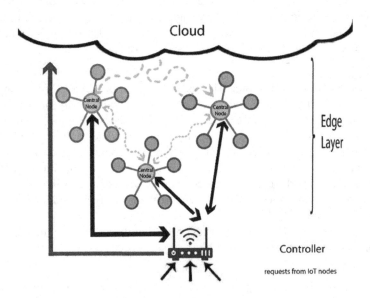

Fig. 1. The IoT-edge-cloud architecture [3].

3.2 Orchestration Controller Design

As a central component, the controller is inserted as an orchestrator between the things layer and the edge. All requests from the things layer will initially be moved to the controller and afterward sent to either the best edge node or directly to the cloud. As stated, the controller plays out the decision procedure based on the total waiting time of the entire request in various edge nodes. Upon receiving the new request, the controller determines the best node and allocates the request to that node according to the deadline of the request and the lowest total waiting time of all the edge nodes using the particle optimization algorithm PSO. The status of the selected node's queue and it's execution status are updated in the availability table. If no appropriate node is found in the edge layer for a received request, the controller sends the request directly to the cloud for backup processing.

Types of Cluster Interactions. We can identify two types of interaction for edge nodes that can be implemented [32]:

- coordinated, in which some dedicated nodes control the interactions of their surrounding nodes,
- distributed, in which each edge node interacts with the other node.

In the coordinated strategy, the edge layer is divided into smaller clusters, with a central coordinating node in every one of these clusters, which is directly cooperating with the controller and which controls other nodes in it's cluster. This coordinator is aware of the queue status of those nodes and stores all the information in the availability table. The central coordinating nodes are also processing nodes which aside from their processing responsibility, can manage the other nodes in their clusters too. These central coordinators have 3 different connections, 2 direct connections and 1 public connection. The central coordinators are directly connected to their cluster's nodes and the controller and they communicate with other central coordinators with public announces. When a request is sent to the controller, the cluster coordinators announce their best node in their area (personal best) as a publicly and support the lead controller in determining the best node in the layer (global best). This step was formalised in Eq. (6) presented earlier on.

3.3 Performance Optimization

PSO-based edge performance optimization is the concern of the third step. In our technique, the optimization issue has one main objective and one sub-objective so that the fulfillment of the sub-objective will lead to the satisfying of the main objective. In the following, each one of these objectives will be characterized.

- Primary objective: The main purpose is to minimize total response time R. In the proposed method, two elements, controller and the particle optimization algorithm have been used to accomplish this goal.
- Secondary objective: The secondary objective is to reduce delay D. Delay in each layer must be considered separately to calculate the total delay.

For our delay calculation, we adopt the solution presented in [37] in our cluster management setting.

Calculating Delay in the Things Layer. Note that thing nodes can both process requests themselves or send them to the edge or cloud for processing. On the off chance that an IoT node chooses to send their request to the edge or cloud for process, the request will be sent to the controller first. Considering the number of the IoT nodes and the number of the requests, the sent request will get into a queue before reaching the controller and after reaching the controller, the request should wait until the controller finds the best edge node for allocation. In other words, This is the delay before the allocation takes place.

Definition 3. *The delay in the IoT node i is represented by D_i and is calculated as follows:*

$$D_i := P_i^I \times (A_i) + P_i^F \times (X_{ij}^{IF} + Y_{ij}^{IF} + L_{ij}) + P_i^C \\ \times (X_{ik}^{IC} + Y_{ik}^{IC} + \overline{H}_k + X_{ki}^{CI} + Y_{ki}^{CI}) \tag{13}$$

where

- *P_i^I is the probability that the things node will process the request itself in the things layer, P_i^F is the probability of sending the request to the edge layer, and P_i^C is the probability of sending the request directly to the cloud; with $P_i^I + P_i^F + P_i^C = 1$.*
- *A_i is the average processing delay of node i when processing its request. X_{ij}^{IF} is the propagation delay from object node i to node jj, Y_{ij}^{IF} is the sum of all delays in linking from object node i to node j. Likewise, X_{ik}^{IC} delays propagation from object node i to cloud k server and $_{ki}^{CI}$ is the sum of all delays in sending a link from object node i to cloud server k. X_{ki}^{CI} and Y_{ki}^{CI} are broadcast and send delays from the k server to the node i. Delayed transmission from the cloud layer to the object layer will be considered in L_{ij}, as the request edge later be unloaded to another node in the edge layer. L_{ij} is the processing delay of the node i request in the edge layer or even the cloud layer, if it is unloaded from the edge node to the cloud server, so that the node j edge be the first node in the edge layer to which the node request of object i is sent. Note that the edge node j edge load the request for any reason to its best neighbor node or discharge cloud, and all similar delays occurring in L_{ij} are considered. $\overline{H}$ is the average delay for processing a request on the cloud server k, which includes the queue waiting time on the cloud server k plus the request processing time on the cloud server k.*

There is no specific distribution for $P_i^I, P_i^F, and P_i^C$, because their values will be defined by separate applications based on service quality requirements and rules. In other words, their values will be given as input to this framework.

Calculating Delay in Edge Layer. We now define a recursive function for the calculation of L_{ij}.

Definition 4. L_{ij} *is a delay for processing IoT node* i*'s requests in the edge layer. After allocation, the request will get into the chosen edge node's queue. This is the delay after allocation. Thus,* L_{ij} *is calculated from the equation below:*

$$
\begin{aligned}
L_{ij} &= P_j.(\overline{W_j} + X_{ji}^{FI} + Y_{ji}^{FI}) \\
&+ (1 + p_j.[[1 - \phi(x)][X_{jj'}^{FF} + Y_{jj'}^{FF} + L_{ij'}(x+1)] \\
&+ \phi(x)[X_{jk}^{FC} + Y_{jk}^{FC} + (\overline{H_k} + X_{ki}^{CT} + Y_{ki}^{CI}]] \\
&\quad j' = best(j), k = h(j)
\end{aligned}
\tag{14}
$$

$\overline{W}_j$ *refers here to the mean waiting time at node* j *and* $\phi(x)$ *is also a discharge function.*

3.4 PSO-Based Performance Optimization

In the fourth and final step, the actual performance optimization is carried out. The PSOalgorithm is utilized to take care of the optimization issue. This algorithms is comprised of a few stages, which will be discussed now.

Establish an Initial Population and Evaluate It. The particle swarm optimization algorithm starts with an initial random population matrix like many evolutionary algorithms, such as genetic algorithms. This algorithm, unlike genetic algorithms however, has no evolutionary operator such as a mutant. Each element of the population is called a node. In fact, the particle swarm optimization algorithm consists of a finite number of nodes that randomly take the initial value.

Here, the edge layer is divided into different clusters and in each cluster consists of a central coordinator node and its dependent nodes. For each node, two states of location and velocity are defined, which are modeled with a location vector and a velocity vector, respectively.

The Fitness Function. The fitness function is used for evaluating the initial population. Since the problem is a two-objective optimization, both goals must be considered in the fitness function.

- The first objective is to minimize the total response time in the edge-based architecture indicated by RT.
  To achieve the first goal, we define a metric called $T_E = P_E + D_E$ that represents the total execution time of the request at the edge node, which is the sum of the processing time P_E of the request and the waiting time D_E of the request in the edge node's queue. $TimeFinal$ (TF) is the maximum time T_E that is allowed for the execution at the edge node in other to meet the required deadline DL with

$$
TF = DL - (D_C + P_C + D_I)
\tag{15}
$$

  i.e., $Max(T_E) = TF$ or $T_E \in [0 \ldots TF]$.

– The second objective is to reduce the delay of the edge-based architecture D.

The second goal relates to the sum of the delays in the IoT layer and the delay in the edge layer:

$$D = D_C + D_E + D_I \qquad (16)$$

As is clear, both goals are defined as minimization.

Ultimately, fitness is calculated as follows:

$$Fitness = TF + D \qquad (17)$$

Determine the Best Personal Experience and the Best Collective Experience. The nodes move in the solution space at a dynamic rate based on the experience of the node itself and the experience of the neighbors. Unlike other evolutionary algorithms, particle swarm optimization does not use smoothing operators such as intersections in the frog algorithm. Thus, the answers remain in the search space to share their information and guide the search to the best position in the search space. So, here the coordinating nodes search for the best experience within their own and their neighbor's domain. To update the node's velocity and position, first the best position of each node and then the best position among all nodes in each step must be updated.

Location and Velocity Updates. The dimension of the problem space is equal to the number of parameters in the function to optimize. A memory is allocated to store the best position of each node in the past, and a memory is allocated to store the best position of all nodes. With the experience of these memories, the nodes decide how to move next. At each iteration, all the nodes move in the next n-dimensional space of the problem to find the general optimum point. The nodes update their velocities and their position according to the best absolute and local solutions. Here, the coordinating nodes read the availability table of their cluster nodes and publish their best nodes to the controller. In this way, they move towards the best node.

Check the Stop Condition. Finally, the stop condition is checked. If this condition is not met, we return to the stage of determining the best personal experience and the best collective experience.

There are several types of stopping conditions:

– Achieve an acceptable level of response,
– Reach a specified number of repetitions/time,
– Reach a certain number of iterations or time specified without seeing an improvement,
– Check a certain number of responses.

Here, the stop condition is to achieve an acceptable level of response.

3.5   Algorithm Definition (Pseudocode)

The proposed PSO Performance Optimization algorithm is presented in Algorithm 1.

Algorithm 1. PSO-based Edge Performance.

```
 1: function SCHEDULE(PSO,DAG)
 2:     Input: PSO and DAG characteristics
 3:     Output: Optimal Request Scheduling
 4:     Initial First Parameters
 5:     loop
 6:         Initial population
 7:         Calculate Fitness
 8:         if Fitness < PBest then
 9:             PBest ← Fitness
10:         GBest ← PBest
11:     loop
12:         Compute Velocity via Equation (1)
13:         Compute Position via Equation (2)
14:         Calculate Fitness via Equation (11)
15:         if Fitness < PBest then
16:             PBest ← Fitness
17:         GBest ← PBest
18:     Return: Optimal Schedule
```

4   Framework Implementation and Evaluation

The concept of IoT is to connect different devices through the Internet. With the help of IoT, different applications and devices can interact and talk to each other, even humans, via the Internet. For example, smart refrigerators that connect to the Internet tell you the inventory and expiry date of foods in the refrigerator. In fact, IoT enables you to remotely manage and control your used objects with the help of Internet infrastructure. IoT provides opportunities to integrate directly into the physical world and computer-based systems, such as smart cars, smart glaciers and smart homes, which are referred to these days in various discussions and conventions. And it is necessary to know that all of these devices fall under the category of Internet of Things. Edge is another layer of distributed environmental networks and is closely linked to cloud computing and IoT. Edge computing is the idea of a distributed network that connects the two environments. In the previous section, using a layer of edge, a method was proposed to reduce the amount of execution time and delay in executing IoT requests. In this section we will present the results of implementation. The main proposed method is to use the node swarm optimization algorithm in the controller but also to compare the bat algorithm in the controller.

4.1   Test Environment and Objectives

The overall objective here is to reduce the total response time, i.e., the end-to-end latency. We chose a comparative experimental approach to evaluate our framework.

The PSO particle swarm optimization algorithm and another bio-inspired, so-called BAT algorithm are utilized to build up the controller and compare. The BAT algorithm was picked because of its principle similarity to the particle swarm optimization.

Thus, it allows meaningful performance comparisons. Furthermore, its wide-spread use in different optimization situations make it a suitable benchmark. The BAT algorithm is an algorithm inspired by the collective behavior of bats in the natural environment proposed in [35]. This algorithm is based on the use of bats' reflection properties.

We used MATLAB software to evaluate the solution. The concepts presented earlier are fully coded and implemented in this software.

4.2   Definition of PSO and BAT Parameters

For better understanding, this algorithm is actualized with the double target evaluation function as indicated by Eq. (11) with 200 iterations. The underlying parameters indicated in this implementation are shown in Table 1.

Table 1. The initial parameters of the PSO Edge Performance Optimization [3].

Parameters	Amounts
Population number	50
Number of repeats	200
Value w	1
Decrease coefficient w	0.99
c1, c2, c3	2

4.3   Comparison of Fitness Values

Using the values in Table 1 as initialization, the particle swarm optimization algorithm is formed and the graph in Fig. 2 shows the result of the implementation of this algorithm.

As can be seen in Fig. 2, with the expansion of iterations, the results of the fitness evaluation function made for the two targets (runtime and delay) is decreased. Our PSO performance optimization algorithm is a two-target algorithm that decreases execution time and delay in execution of requests. The objective function value in the implementation of the particle swarm optimization algorithm is approximately 233. It should be noted that due to the random structure of the evolutionary algorithms, the results per run may be different from the previous ones.

So as to compare the proposed strategy, an evolutionary BAT algorithm has been actualized so as to contrast accurately and similar conditions. Thus, the BAT algorithm has been implemented with the same two-objective evaluation function and with 200 iterations as the particle optimization algorithm. The initial parameters specified in this implementation are shown in Table 2.

Utilizing the above qualities as the initialization, the BAT algorithm is formed and the diagram in Fig. 3 shows the aftereffect of the implementation of this algorithm.

In Fig. 3, the motion diagram of the BAT algorithm is shown. The conditions are the same for both particle swarm and bat optimization algorithms and the objective function in both algorithms has been implemented and evaluated with respect to both

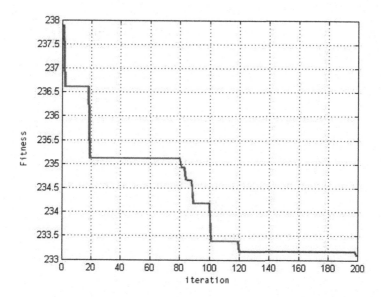

Fig. 2. Fitness results for the PSO algorithm [3].

Table 2. The initial parameters in bat [3].

Parameters	Amounts
Population number	50
Number of repeats	200
Minimum frequency	0
Maximum frequency	100
Sound intensity coefficient	0.1
Pulse rate coefficient	0.1

runtime and delay reduction. As can be seen, the BAT algorithm has reached the target function of 237.5, while in the particle swarm optimization algorithm this value is 233. These results indicate that the proposed algorithm is better than the evolutionary BAT algorithm.

4.4   Scenario-Based Comparison: Overview

In order to deepen the analysis, the proposed solution was tested across 3 different scenarios:

- once with different number of requests,
- once with different number of edge layer nodes,
- once with identical parameters, but in different iterations,

These will now be discussed in sequence.

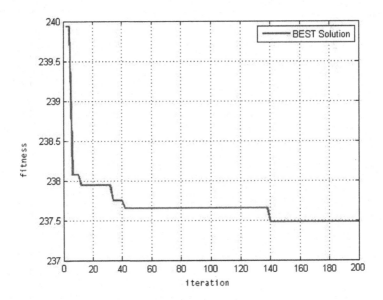

Fig. 3. Fitness results for the BAT algorithm [3].

Table 3. The initial parameters in first scenario [3].

Parameters	Amounts
Number of user requests	30/60/100/150/200/250
Number of edge layer nodes	20
Processing power of each edge node	4 G Ram/8 Mips Processor
Amount of time each user requests	Randomized in range [1, 20]
Amount of CPU per user request	Random in the interval [2, 8]

4.5 Scenario 1: Request Variation

In the first scenario, various requests and nodes in the edge layer are utilized to compare the outcomes. In this scenario, we fixed the quantity of edge layers nodes and assumed variable and incremental user requests. Table 3 shows the details of this scenario configuration.

Figure 4 shows the results of several different user requests with 20 nodes in the edge layer. In this scenario, the number of edge layer nodes is 20 and the number of user requests are 30, 50, 100, 150, 200 and 250. Equation (11) is used to calculate the fitness function.

As can be found in Fig. 4, our PSO-based optimization algorithm produces much better outcomes than the BAT algorithm. As the quantity of requests builds, the estimation of the target function (execution time + delay time) increments. Expanding the quantity of requests will build the execution time, just as increment the execution time,

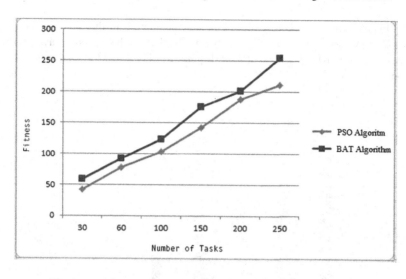

Fig. 4. Result of first scenario: fitness over number of requests [3].

as more nodes will be included. This expands the estimation of the target function, which is the sum of the execution time and delay. In all cases, our particle swarm optimization algorithm shows better results. Despite the increase in the objective function value in both algorithms, the growth rate of the objective function value in the particle swarm optimization algorithm is lower than the BAT algorithm, which means that this algorithm outperforms the BAT algorithm.

In order to make comparisons under different conditions, the next step is to increase the number of layer nodes in order to observe the effect of this increase in a graph.

4.6   Scenario 2: Edge Node Variation

In the second scenario, in contrast to the previous scenario, now the quantity of requests is fixed, yet the quantity of edge layer nodes is thought to be variable. Expanding the quantity of nodes has been done as an experimentation and no exceptional algorithm is utilized. Full details of the second scenario are given in Table 4.

Table 4. The initial parameters in the second scenario [3].

Parameters	Amounts
Number of user requests	100
Number of edge layer nodes	5/10/15/20/30/50
Processing power of each edge node	4 G Ram/8 Mips Processor
Amount of time each user requests	Randomized in range [1,20]
Amount of CPU per user request	Random in the interval [2,8]

For this experiment, 100 input requests are considered. In this scenario, the number of user requests is considered to be fixed, but the number of edge layer nodes is considered to be 5, 10, 15, 20, 30 and 50. Equation (11) is used to calculate the fitness function.

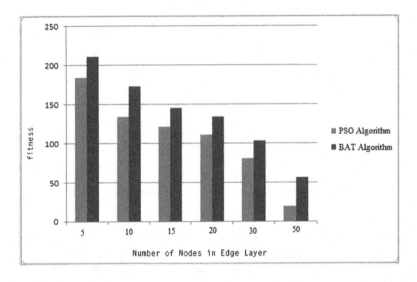

Fig. 5. Result of second scenario: fitness over number of requests [3].

By expanding the quantity of layer nodes in the edge, the fitness function diminishes because of the chance of executing requests on more nodes. The higher the quantity of edge layer nodes, the more probable it is that requests will be processed utilizing nodes whose latency is lower. In other words, with the increase in the number of edge layer nodes the controller's options for allocating more requests are increased and thus the chances of finding a suitable node with low latency increases. As the conditions change, the way in which requests are executed is also varied, which reduces execution time. For the particle optimization algorithm, the greater the number of edge layer nodes, the lower the objective function. Furthermore for PSO algorithm, the reduction of the target function is much faster than the BAT algorithm, which is evident in Fig. 5. Each algorithm was run multiple times to better compare the algorithms.

4.7 Scenario 3: Iteration Variation

In the third scenario, a number of iterations assume both the used requests and the quantity of nodes in the edge layer fixed. In this scenario, every algorithm was run multiple times with similar inputs and the outcomes were acquired. It ought to be noticed that in this investigation, the quantity of requests is 100 and the quantity of edge layer nodes is 50, which were steady at all 5 times. Equation (11) is used to calculate the fitness function. Table 5 shows the full configuration details of the third scenario.

Table 5. The initial parameters of the third scenario [3].

Parameters	Amounts
Number of user requests	100
Number of edge layer nodes	50
Processing power of each edge node	4 G Ram/8 Mips Processor
Amount of time each user requests	Randomized in range [1,20]
Amount of CPU per user request	Random in the interval [2,8]

According to Fig. 6, in different iterations we can see different results despite not changing the input values at each iteration. There are no identifiable rules or explanations detectable by analysing the outputs for the two different algorithms. For example, the value of the fitness function in the first step with one iteration is less than that of the BAT algorithm in the particle swarm optimization algorithm, and the value of this function in the second step with two iterations in both algorithms decreased while in the next step with three iterations, the value of this function is increased in both algorithms.

As a rule, it tends to be reasoned that the particle swarm optimization algorithm in executing requests utilizing the double fitness function (execution time + execution delay) yields essentially better outcomes over the evolutionary BAT algorithm. This is on the grounds that in many iterations, the target function value in the particle swarm optimization algorithm was lower than the BAT algorithm.

A feature of the particle swarm optimization algorithm is faster convergence. In addition, the particle swarm optimization algorithm yields overall good performance results that reduce orchestration and response time.

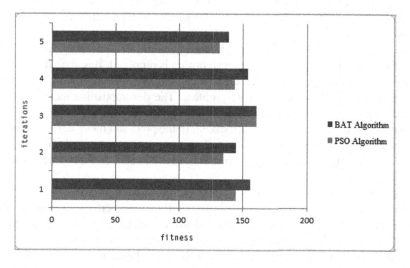

Fig. 6. Result of second scenario: fitness over number of requests [3].

5   Related Work

In this section, we review approaches to cloud and edge cluster management in general, but also look at how bio-inspired approaches such as PSO have been used. Regarding the first concern, [12] have studied the connection for the circulation of work and virtual machine task in cyber-physical frameworks based on edge computing standards. They looked at minimizing the final cost and satisfying service quality requirements. The quality needs of services provided by cyber-physical systems are challenged by unstable and delayed communication between data sources and devices. Processing resources at the edge of the network is introduced as a solution. The paper did not use realistic IoT and cloud scenarios. In [21], energy-delay computing is tended to in a task allocation setting. Given the significance of cost and energy in delay-delicate interactions for mentioning and giving processing resources, an ideal strategy for delay-sensitive associations was introduced. The plan looks to accomplish a energy-delay bargain at the edge of the cloud. The authors formalized the task allocation issue in a cloud-edge setting, and yet utilized basic models to plan energy loss and delay as the key indicators.

Another performance-centric view is [31], which also centers around demonstrating delay, energy loss and cost. In this examination, comparably to the past articles, delay and energy loss were detailed with fundamental models, and no laws were acquainted to minimize delay. Our aim is to use an evolutionary algorithm for edge orchestration and to obtain the optimal response times for the problem.

In a different direction, [4] proposes a human services framework. A server converts the perceptions and estimations to a far off server for future recovery of clinical experts over the Internet. In the proposed strategy, data and requests are sent over the Internet from the earliest starting point, in this way evading any potential delays because of the physical issues of the devices without adequate performance optimization. In [29], the solution is based on a wireless sensor network. The purpose of the proposed method is ultimately to identify the delays-sensitive requests and take action directly when the problem occurs.

We can also find PSO-specific solutions relevant to our context. In [10], a framework of the particle swarm optimization algorithm is proposed. Based on the proposed framework, a multi-objective discrete particle swarm optimization algorithm is proposed to solve the network clustering problem. The decomposition mechanism was adopted: A problem-specific population initialization method based on label propagation and a turbulence operator was introduced. In the proposed method, two evaluation objectives termed as kernel k-means and ratio cut were to be minimized. The clustering performances of the proposed algorithm have been validated on signed networks and unsigned networks.

In [1], a greedy discrete particle swarm optimization framework for large-scale social network clustering was suggested. To determine the performance of the algorithm, experiments on both synthetic and real-world social networks were carried out. The authors also compared the proposed algorithm with several state-of-the-art clustering methods for network settings. In [8], the authors developed an automated orchestration technique for clustered cloud architectures. An Autonomous Particle Swarm Optimization, called the A-PSO algorithm, was implemented that enabled an edge node, such as a remote storage, to work as part of a decentralized, self-adaptive intelligent task scheduling and load balancing agent between resources in distributed edge settings as one concrete example.

Often multi-objective optimisation is a concern. In [2], the authors model the task of complex network clustering as a multi-objective optimization problem and solve the problem with the quantum mechanism based particle swarm optimization algorithm, which is a parallel algorithm. Consequently, a quantum-behaved discrete multi-objective particle swarm optimization algorithm is proposed for complex network clustering. This algorithm has the ability to determine the number of clusters automatically, rather than setting the number of clusters in advance, which is very important for large scale network analysis. Here, since the network clustering is a discrete problem, the discrete PSO algorithm is adopted instead of the continuous one.

6 Conclusions and Future Work

In order to make the Internet-of-Things work, edge computing guarantees low latency because of more local processing. In any case, a more intensive look uncovers distributed and independently managed cluster of processing edge nodes that need be considered in a performance-oriented load allocation procedure. Moreover, delays do happen as the aftereffect of transmission processing and waiting times of requests at nodes that perform orchestration and processing tasks in the edge clusters.

We presented here a performance optimization framework, for which we utilized an orchestration algorithm based on particle swarm optimization, adapted to the multi-cluster requirements and concentrating on delay and end-to-end latency reduction, We compared our solution with a evolutionary BAT algorithm, another strategy to optimize and diminish the mean target function (delay and execution latency) of processing demands. Developmental algorithms are among the best optimization algorithms, and the particle swarm optimization algorithm we embraced here is less mind boggling than some other evolutionary algorithms. These advantages made our PSO-based technique an ideal orchestration strategy aiming to reduce execution time and delay as the key performance criteria.

Despite its general suitability here, particle swarm optimization algorithm has several characteristics and possible limitations that shall briefly be discussed here. In this algorithm, it is possible to place the node in local optimality. While the particle swarm optimization algorithm is faster than other evolutionary algorithms, it usually cannot offset the quality of the solution by increasing iterations. One of the reasons is that in this algorithm the nodes converge to a particular point, which is between the best general position and the best personal position. Due to this disadvantage, many changes have been made to the particle swarm optimization algorithm. Another disadvantage of this approach is its dependence on the problem. This dependence is usually the result of changes in the parameters of the algorithm. In general, one parameter cannot be used for all problems. The particle swarm optimization algorithm has several advantages over standard optimization methods:

– Particle swarm optimization algorithm is a population-based algorithm. This property makes it less likely to get caught in the local minimum.

- This algorithm operates on contingency rules, not definitive rules. Therefore, the node swarm optimization algorithm is a stochastic optimization algorithm that can search for uncertain and complex areas. This property makes the particle swarm optimization algorithm more flexible and robust than conventional methods.
- Particle swarm optimization algorithm deals with non-differential objective functions because the particle swarm optimization algorithm uses information output (efficiency index or objective function) to guide the search in the problem space.
- The quality of the proposed route response does not depend on the initial population. Starting at any point in the search space, the algorithm converges to the optimal solution.
- The particle swarm algorithm has a great deal of flexibility to control the balance between local and general search space. This unique property of the particle swarm optimization algorithm overcomes the problem of convergence in time and increases the search capacity that all of these properties make the particle swarm optimization algorithm different from Genetic Algorithm (GA) and other heuristic algorithms.

The results of this method show better suitability over some of the search optimization methods.

We have show a core solution that can be expanded in different ways. As a part of our future work, we intend to consider other algorithm bases, for example, the firefly algorithm rather than the particle swarm optimization algorithm for edge performance optimization. The firefly algorithm is a helpful and extremely common algorithm in optimization issues, yet it doesn't have the impediments of the genetic algorithm in how to choose the necessary parameters, which is the best decision for these two tasks. We could likewise consider the ant colony algorithm rather than PSO. This algorithm is extremely effective and is exceptionally utilized in routing issues. Aside from the algorithmic side, we additionally plan to refine the model by more exactly isolating starting points of delay in communication and buffering times. Likewise different coordination standards from completely centralized to peer-to-peer management can be thought of. Also, as a final plan, we mean to combine this with an auto-scaling controller [9], which we implemented so far just for a single cluster condition.

We provided a generic framework here. However, we aim to explore this in more concrete application settings. We consider here traffic management and coordinated cars as a concrete IoT and edge setting, where traffic and car movement is captured and processed, maybe combined by infotainment information with image and video data [6, 16, 20, 25]. This mobile setting would need to be supported by local clusters that act autonomously, but require some higher-level coordination [7, 14, 27].

Another application domain is mobile learning. This also relies on the extensive use of multimedia content being delivered to mobile learners, similar to the infotainment case above, and their devices [13, 23, 26]. These types of applications also need interaction with application-specific processing of interactions in order to support the required learning processes [15, 19]. In widely delivered course, particularly to mobile learners, these would need be provided at the edge to ensure sufficient platform performance for adequate user experience.

References

1. Cai, Q., Gong, M., Ma, L., Ruan, S., Yuan, F., Jiao, L.: Greedy discrete particle swarm optimization for large-scale social network clustering. Inf. Sci. **316**, 503–516 (2015). https://doi.org/10.1016/j.ins.2014.09.041. Nature-Inspired Algorithms for Large Scale Global Optimization

2. Li, L., Jiao, L., Zhao, J., Shang, R., Gong, M.: Quantum-behaved discrete multi-objective particle swarm optimization for complex network clustering. Pattern Recogn. **63**, 1–14 (2017). https://doi.org/10.1016/j.patcog.2016.09.013

3. Azimi, S., Pahl, C., Shirvani, M.H.: Particle swarm optimization for performance management in multi-cluster IoT edge architectures. In: International Conference on Cloud Computing and Services Science CLOSER. SciTePress (2020)

4. Babu, S., Chandini, M., Lavanya, P., Ganapathy, K., Vaidehi, V.: Cloud-enabled remote health monitoring system. In: 2013 International Conference on Recent Trends in Information Technology (ICRTIT), pp. 702–707, July 2013. https://doi.org/10.1109/ICRTIT.2013.6844286

5. Baktyan, A.A., Zahary, A.T.: A review on cloud and fog computing integration for IoT: platforms perspective. EAI Endorsed Trans. Internet Things **4**(14) (2018). https://doi.org/10.4108/eai.20-12-2018.156084

6. Barzegar, H.R., Ioini, N.E., Le, V.T., Pahl, C.: Wireless network evolution towards service continuity in 5G enabled mobile edge computing. In: 2020 Fifth International Conference on Fog and Mobile Edge Computing (FMEC), pp. 78–85 (2020)

7. El Ioini, N., Pahl, C., Helmer, S.: A decision framework for blockchain platforms for IoT and edge computing. SCITE Press (2018)

8. Faheem, H., Pahl, C.: Enhanced particle swarm optimisation and multi objective optimization for the orchestration of edge cloud clusters, September 2019

9. Gand, F., Fronza, I., Ioini, N.E., Barzegar, H.R., Azimi, S., Pahl, C.: A fuzzy controller for self-adaptive lightweight container orchestration. In: International Conference on Cloud Computing and Services Science CLOSER. SCITE Press (2020)

10. Gong, M., Cai, Q., Chen, X., Ma, L.: Complex network clustering by multiobjective discrete particle swarm optimization based on decomposition. IEEE Trans. Evol. Comput. **18**(1), 82–97 (2014)

11. González, L.M.V., Rodero-Merino, L.: Finding your way in the fog: towards a comprehensive definition of fog computing. Comput. Commun. Rev. **44**(5), 27–32 (2014)

12. Gu, L., Zeng, D., Guo, S., Barnawi, A., Xiang, Y.: Cost efficient resource management in fog computing supported medical cyber-physical system. IEEE Trans. Emerg. Top. Comput. **5**(1), 108–119 (2017). https://doi.org/10.1109/TETC.2015.2508382

13. Kenny, C., Pahl, C.: Automated Tutoring for a Database Skills Training Environment. Association for Computing Machinery, New York (2005)

14. Le, V., Pahl, C., El Ioini, N.: Blockchain based service continuity in mobile edge computing. In: 6th International Conference on Internet of Things: Systems, Management and Security (2019)

15. Lei, X., Pahl, C., Donnellan, D.: An evaluation technique for content interaction in web-based teaching and learning environments. In: Proceedings 3rd IEEE International Conference on Advanced Technologies, pp. 294–295 (2003)

16. von Leon, D., Miori, L., Sanin, J., Ioini, N.E., Helmer, S., Pahl, C.: A lightweight container middleware for edge cloud architectures, pp. 145–170 (2019)

17. Mahmoud, M.M.E., Rodrigues, J.J.P.C., Saleem, K., Al-Muhtadi, J., Kumar, N., Korotaev, V.: Towards energy-aware fog-enabled cloud of things for healthcare. Comput. Electr. Eng. **67**, 58–69 (2018)

18. Mahmud, R., Srirama, S.N., Ramamohanarao, K., Buyya, R.: Quality of experience (QoE)-aware placement of applications in fog computing environments. J. Parallel Distrib. Comput. **132**, 190–203 (2019)

19. Melia, M., Pahl, C.: Constraint-based validation of adaptive e-learning courseware. IEEE Trans. Learn. Technol. **2**(1), 37–49 (2009)

20. Mendonça, N.C., Jamshidi, P., Garlan, D., Pahl, C.: Developing self-adaptive microservice systems: challenges and directions. IEEE Softw. **38**, 70–79 (2019)

21. Meng, H., Zhu, Y., Deng, R.: Optimal computing resource management based on utility maximization in mobile crowdsourcing. Wirel. Commun. Mob. Comput. **2017**, 1–13 (2017)

22. Minh, Q.T., Nguyen, D.T., Le, V.A., Nguyen, D.H., Pham, T.V.: Task placement on fog computing made efficient for IoT application provision. Wirel. Commun. Mob. Comput. **2019**, 6215454:1–6215454:17 (2019)

23. Murray, S., Ryan, J., Pahl, C.: A tool-mediated cognitive apprenticeship approach for a computer engineering course. In: Proceedings 3rd IEEE International Conference on Advanced Technologies, pp. 2–6 (2003)

24. Mutlag, A.A., Ghani, M.K., Arunkumar, N.A., Mohammed, M.A., Mohd, O.: Enabling technologies for fog computing in healthcare IoT systems. Future Gener. Comput. Syst. **90**, 62–78 (2019)

25. Pahl, C., Ioini, N.E., Helmer, S., Lee, B.: An architecture pattern for trusted orchestration in IoT edge clouds. In: 2018 Third International Conference on Fog and Mobile Edge Computing (FMEC), pp. 63–70 (2018)

26. Pahl, C., Barrett, R., Kenny, C.: Supporting active database learning and training through interactive multimedia. ACM SIGCSE Bull. **36**(3), 27–31 (2004)

27. Pahl, C., Fronza, I., El Ioini, N., Barzegar, H.R.: A review of architectural principles and patterns for distributed mobile information systems. In: WEBIST, pp. 9–20 (2019)

28. Pahl, C., Jamshidi, P., Zimmermann, O.: Architectural principles for cloud software. ACM Trans. Internet Technol. (TOIT) **18**(2), 17 (2018)

29. Rolim, C.O., Koch, F.L., Westphall, C.B., Werner, J., Fracalossi, A., Salvador, G.S.: A cloud computing solution for patient's data collection in health care institutions. In: Finkelstein, J., Ossebaard, H.C., van Gemert-Pijnen, L. (eds.) eTELEMED, pp. 95–99. IEEE Computer Society

30. Saboori, A., Jiang, G., Chen, H.: Autotuning configurations in distributed systems for performance improvements using evolutionary strategies. In: 2008 The 28th International Conference on Distributed Computing Systems, pp. 769–776, June 2008. https://doi.org/10.1109/ICDCS.2008.11

31. Sarkar, S., Chatterjee, S., Misra, S.: Assessment of the suitability of fog computing in the context of internet of things. IEEE Trans. Cloud Comput. **6**(1), 46–59 (2018)

32. Shin, K.G., Chang, Y.: Load sharing in distributed real-time systems with state-change broadcasts. IEEE Trans. Comput. **38**(8), 1124–1142 (1989)

33. Sung, W., Chiang, Y.: Improved particle swarm optimization algorithm for android medical care IOT using modified parameters. J. Med. Syst. **36**(6), 3755–3763 (2012). https://doi.org/10.1007/s10916-012-9848-9

34. Tata, S., Jain, R., Ludwig, H., Gopisetty, S.: Living in the cloud or on the edge: opportunities and challenges of IoT application architecture. In: 2017 IEEE International Conference on Services Computing (SCC), pp. 220–224, June 2017. https://doi.org/10.1109/SCC.2017.35

35. Yang, X.S.: Bat algorithm for multi-objective optimisation. arXiv preprint arXiv:1203.6571 (2012)
36. Yi, S., Li, C., Li, Q.: a survey of fog computing: concepts, applications and issues. In: Proceedings of the 2015 Workshop on Mobile Big Data, Mobidata@MobiHoc 2015, Hangzhou, China, 21 June 2015, pp. 37–42 (2015)
37. Yousefpour, A., Ishigaki, G., Jue, J.P.: Fog computing: towards minimizing delay in the internet of things. In: IEEE International Conference on Edge Computing, EDGE 2017, Honolulu, HI, USA, 25–30 June 2017, pp. 17–24 (2017)

Investigating IoT Application Behaviour in Simulated Fog Environments

Andras Markus[✉] and Attila Kertesz

Department of Software Engineering, University of Szeged, Szeged, Hungary
{markusa,keratt}@inf.u-szeged.hu

Abstract. In the past decade novel paradigms appeared in distributed systems, such as Cloud Computing, Fog Computing and the Internet of Things (IoT). Sensors and devices of IoT applications need big data to be stored, processed and analysed, and cloud systems offer suitable and scalable solutions for them. Recently fog nodes are utilized to provide data management functionalities closer to users with enhanced privacy and quality, giving birth to the creation of IoT-Fog-Cloud systems. Such infrastructures are so complex that they need simulators for planning, designing and analysis. Though cloud simulation already has a large number of literature, the simulation of fog systems is still evolving. In this paper we plan to take a step forward in this direction by investigating current fog simulation approaches and compare two of them providing the broadest fog modeling features. We also perform evaluations of executing IoT applications in hybrid, Fog-Cloud architectures to show possible advantages of different setups matching different IoT behaviour.

Keywords: Fog computing · Internet of Things · Cloud computing · Simulation

1 Introduction

Parallel and distributed computing went through a rapid evolution in the past decade giving birth to cloud and fog technologies enabling virtualized service provisions. The appearance of small computational devices connected to the Internet has led to the Internet of Things (IoT) paradigm, which resulted in a vast amount of data generations requiring the assistance of cloud services for storage, processing and analysis. Cloud systems become good candidates to serve IoT applications, and their marriage created so-called smart systems [1]. One of their latest improvements addresses data locality meaning that data management operations are better placed close to their origins to reduce service latency. This idea created Fog Computing [2], which implied the appearance of IoT-Fog-Cloud systems with the highest complexity.

This research was supported by the Hungarian Government and the European Regional Development Fund under the grant number GINOP-2.3.2-15-2016-00037 (Internet of Living Things), and by the Hungarian Scientific Research Fund under the grant number OTKA FK 131793, and by the Hungarian Government under the grant number EFOP-3.6.1-16-2016-00008. This paper is a revised and extended version of the conference paper [14].

© Springer Nature Switzerland AG 2021
D. Ferguson et al. (Eds.): CLOSER 2020, CCIS 1399, pp. 258–276, 2021.
https://doi.org/10.1007/978-3-030-72369-9_11

These IoT-Fog-Cloud systems require significant investments in terms of design, development and operation, therefore the use of simulators for their investigation is inevitable. There are a large number of simulators addressing the analysis of parts of these systems, and we can find survey papers of cloud, IoT and fog simulators summarizing their basic capabilities and comparing them according to certain metrics, e.g. by [3]. These surveys highlight that fog modelling in simulators still needs further research, despite the promising approaches already capable of examining IoT-Fog-Cloud systems to some extent. In this paper we compare two of such simulators, namely the iFogSim and DISSECT-CF-Fog, which are able to model fogs, and found to be reliable and widespread enough by former surveys.

The main contributions of our paper are the comparison of the fog modelling capabilites offered by iFogSim and DISSECT-CF-Fog, and the evaluation of their features with a meteorological IoT application with three rounds of evaluations representing an increasing level of complexity. This paper is a revised and extended version of a conference paper [14]. We added new measurements and performance comparisons of the simulators.

The rest of the paper is structured as follows: Sect. 2 introduces the related literature in fog simulation. Section 3 presents a comparison of the fog modelling capabilities of the selected two simulators. Section 4 introduces the configurations for the experiments, while Sects. 5, 7 and 8 presents the evaluation rounds of an IoT application with different scenarios representing different complexity. Finally, Sect. 9 concludes our work.

2   Related Approaches in Fog-Cloud Simulation

We can find several survey papers in the field of Cloud Computing and Fog Computing of tools supporting modelling and simulation. Concerning the properties and modelling of Fog Computing, Puliafito et al. [3] presented a survey highlighting and categorizing the properties of Fog Computing, and investigated the benefits of applying fogs to support the needs of IoT applications. They introduced six IoT application groups exploiting fog capabilities, and gathered fog hardware and software platforms supporting the needs of these IoT applications. Markus et al. [11] focused on available cloud, IoT and fog simulators, and compared them according to several metrics such as software metrics and general characteristics. Concerning fog simulation, they introduced and classified 18 simulators.

Table 1. Comparison of fog simulators as partly shown in [14].

Simulator	Based on	Published	Type	Hits	Citations	Language
DISSECT-CF-Fog	DISSECT-CF	2019	Event-driven	82	79	Java
EdgeCloudSim	CloudSim	2019	Event-driven	183	127	Java
YAFS	–	2018	Event-driven	1	17	Python
FogNetSim++	OMNET++	2018	Network	3	37	C++
iFogSim	CloudSim	2017	Event-driven	851	664	Java
DockerSim	iCanCloud	2017	Network	10	6	C++
EmuFog	–	2017	Emulator	59	49	Java

We selected seven recent fog simulators, and briefly compared them in Table 1. We noted their base simulator, publication date and type for their categorization. The network type simulators usually focus on low-level network interaction between entities such as routers, switches and nodes, but less suitable for the higher level of abstraction (e.g. virtual machines), whilst event-driven type simulators are more general and usually lack implemented the network operations or only support minimal network traffic simulation, but they are easier to be used for accurate representation of higher level system components. We also summarized the number of literature search results (i.e. hits) performed in Google Scholar [16], and we summed the number of citations of the top five relevant hits. We also listed the applied programming language of the simulators.

DISSECT-CF-Fog is based on DISSECT-CF, and a direct extension of the DISSECT-CF-IoT simulator [13], also developed by the authors. The base simulator is able to model cloud environments and supports energy measurements of physical resources. The extended version supports the modelling of IoT systems and its communications. The whole software is fully configurable, and follows a hierarchical structure.

EdgeCloudSim [5] is a CloudSim extension with the main capabilities of network modelling, including extensions for WLAN, WAN and device mobility. The developers of this tool aimed to respond to the disadvantage of the simple network model of iFogSim by introducing network load management and content mobility to this simulator.

YAFS [6] simulator is proposed to investigate application deployment (i.e. module placement) on fog topology. It also supports the modelling of user mobility and dynamic failures of nodes and the implementation of different scheduling and routing algorithm of the IoT tasks.

The FogNetSim++ [7] is built on the OMNeT++ discrete event simulator, which focuses on network simulation. This extension provides configuration options for fog network management including node scheduling and selection. It is also able to model different communication protocols, such as MQTT or CoAP, and different mobility models.

One of the most applied and referred fog simulators is iFogSim [8], which is based on CloudSim. iFogSim can be used to simulate cloud and fog systems using the sensing, processing and actuating model. It is able to model cloud and fog devices with certain resource parameters. Sensors and actuators can also be managed represented by a Tuple. There are dedicated modules for processing and data-flows.

DockerSim [9] aims to support the analysis of container-based SaaS systems in simulated environments. It is based on the iCanCloud network simulator, this extension can model container behaviour, network, protocol and OS process scheduling behaviour.

EmuFog [10] emulator is dedicated to design fog infrastructures and investigate real application and workloads by emulation. EmuFog also handles its own network topology model and components (e.g. routers) and similarly to the DockerSim, it uses Docker containers for the application components deployed on fog nodes during the execution.

Though all of these simulators would be interesting to be further analysed, after performing a quick pre-evaluation we found that iFogSim and DISSECT-CF-Fog are the most mature and documented solutions, and we also took into account a literature search result and number of citations for our decision. We also considered numerous iFogSim extensions, which have appeared in the last few years, and the support for novel functions or properties of Fog Computing (as proposed by a recent survey in [11]). Unfortunately, only a few of those extensions were published with available source code, thus our goal was to make a comparison with the original version of iFogSim in a comprehensive way.

3   Fog Modelling in Two Simulators

The CloudSim-based extensions (e.g. iFogSim or EdgeCloudSim) are often used for investigating Cloud and Fog Computing approaches, and in general they are the most referred works in the literature. On the other hand, the DISSECT-CF simulator is proven to be much faster, scalable and reliable then CloudSim (see [4]). This work showed that the simulation time of DISSECT-CF is 2800 times faster than the CloudSim simulator for similar purely cloud use cases, therefore we have chosen to analyse their latest extensions to compare fog modelling. Next, we introduce the main properties of these simulators, and compare their fog modelling capabilities.

iFogSim is a Java-based simulator, its main physical components are the following: (i) fog devices (including cloud resources, fog resources, smart devices) with possibility to configure CPU, RAM, MIPS, uplink- and downlink bandwidth, busy and idle power values; (ii) actuators with geographic location and reference to the gateway connection; (iii) sensors, which generate data in the form of a Tuple representing information. The main logical components aim to model a distributed application: the AppModule, which is a processing element of iFogSim, and the AppEdge that realises the logical data-flow between the VMs. The main management components are: the Module Mapping that searches for a fog device to serve a VM – if no such device is found, the request is sent to an upper tier object; and the Controller is used to execute the application on a fog device. For simulating fog systems, first we have to define the physical components, then the logical components, finally the controller entity. Although numerous articles and online source codes are available for the usage of this simulator, there is a lack of source code comments for many methods, classes and variables. As a result, application modelling with this tool requires a relatively long learning curve, and its operations take valuable time to understand.

DISSECT-CF-Fog is an discrete event simulator for modelling Cloud, IoT and Fog environments, written in Java programming language. The main advantage of this tool is the detailed configuration possibilities across its low-level components: timer modules manage the simulation time and the events. The network layer can be used for simulating bandwidth and latency, and it models data transfers as well. The physical components are responsible for the creation of a physical infrastructure of any graph hierarchy with storage support for resource and file modelling. The sensor and smart device layer is responsible for modelling data generation with a certain frequency, measurement delays, geographical position and network connections, and sensor configurations. The application layer handles the physical topology, the task mapping for VMs, and the data-flow between the physical components. Finally, the support layer is capable of applying pricing models of real cloud providers to calculate resource usage costs for the experiments. These parameters could be easily edited through XML configuration files, thus large scale simulation experiments can be executed even without Java programming knowledge (for the predefined scenarios).

Table 2. Comparison of DISSECT-CF-Fog and iFogSim as partly shown in [14].

Property	DISSECT-CF-Fog	iFogSim
Unit of the simulation time	Tick	Millisecond
Unit of the processing	CPU core processing power	MIPS
Physical component	ComputingAppliance	FogNode
IoT model	Device and Sensor	Sensor
Logical component	Application	Application with AppModule and AppEdge
Task	ComputeTask on VM	Tuple
Architecture	Graph	Tree
Communication direction	Horizontal and vertical	Vertical
Data-flow	Implicit in physical connection	Separately in the AppEdge
Sensor	Processing depends on the size of the data generated	Predefined MIPS value
Cloud Pricing	Price per tick for each VM	Static cost for RAM, storage, bandwidth and CPU
IoT Pricing	Using real IoT providers' schemas	N.A.

iFogSim and DISSECT-CF-Fog are quite evolved and complex simulators, and follow different logic to model Fog Computing, as the previous paragraphs highlighted. This means that though they have similar components, we cannot match them easily. Based on [8], iFogSim was created to model resource management techniques in Fog environments, for what the DISSECT-CF-Fog can also be applicable [12]. To facilitate their comparison, we gathered and compared their properties and components closest to each other as it can be seen in Table 2. Its first column names a generic simulation property or entity, the second column shows how they are represented in DISSECT-CF-Fog, and the third summarizes their representation in iFogSim. As we can see, the biggest difference between them is the chosen unit for simulation time measurement. iFogSim measures time passing in the simulated environment in milliseconds, while DISSECT-CF-Fog has a specific naming for the smallest unit for simulation time called tick, which is related to the simulation events. The researcher using the simulator can set up the parameters and properties of a concrete simulation to associate a certain time interval (e.g. millisecond) for a tick. The measurement of processing power in the simulators can also be done with different approaches. iFogSim associates MIPS for every node, which represents the computational power and does not take into account the number of CPU cores. The number of CPU cores affects only the creation of virtual machines. In DISSECT-CF-Fog both physical machines (PM) and virtual machines (VM) have to be configured with CPU core processing values, which define how many instructions should be processed during one tick.

A physical component is represented by one dedicated class (see 3rd row of Table 2) in both simulators. To represent IoT components, iFogSim uses the Sensor class, while DISSECT-CF-Fog differentiate general IoT devices with computing and storage capacities and smaller sensors managed Device and Sensor classes. The logical components to define concrete applications are implemented with three classes defining processing elements and logical data-flow in iFogSim (Application, AppEdge, AppModule), which are not straightforward to configure. Besides, the ModuleMapping class is an important component, which is responsible for the mapping of the logical and physical entities based on a given strategy (e.g. cloud-aware, edge-aware). On the other hand, in DISSECT-CF-Fog the physical topology already defines data routes, so researchers can focus on setting up the required processing units (of the components placed in the topology). The representation of computational tasks is also different. In DISSECT-CF-Fog, researchers should define a ComputeTask with a certain number of instructions, also stating the number of instructions to be executed within a tick. In iFogSim, researchers should define a so-called Tuple for each task and state the number of MIPS required for its execution. In DISSECT-CF-Fog tasks can be dynamically created to process a certain amount of sensor-generated data, therefore the number of instructions will be proportional (to the available data) in the created tasks. In iFogSim a static MIPS value should be defined in the Tuple, hence it cannot respond to the actually generated data of a scenario. Concerning the communication among components, iFogSim orders components in a hierarchical way and supports only vertical communication among elements of its layers (by default), while DISSECT-CF-Fog supports communication to any direction among any components in the topology. To support cost calculations and pricing, in iFogSim static cost can be defined for CPU, bandwidth, storage and memory usage. DISSECT-CF-Fog has a more mature cost model, and it supports XML-based configuration for cloud and IoT side costs based on real provider pricing schemes.

To achieve fair comparison of the two simulators, we apply the following restrictions. We limit the configuration of DISSECT-CF-Fog by allowing only single core CPUs for the simulated resources. In case of DISSECT-CF-Fog, the speed of the task execution depends on the number of CPU cores and processing power of those, whilst in the iFogSim only the MIPS value of the task defines the time of task processing, as we mentioned before. The common parameters that can be set up in both simulators with similar values are the followings: simulation time, data generation frequency, processing power and configuration of the physical resources, count of instructions for the tasks, and finally the physical topology. Nevertheless, we cannot avoid introducing some different setups. In iFogsim, the devices have direct connections to the physical resources, while in DISSECT-CF-Fog, connection properties also include actual coordinates and distances to the corresponding physical resources.

We also have to deal with the issue that iFogSim does not take into account the size of the generated data in task creation, because the Sensors in iFogSim always create Tuples with the same MIPS value, hence the file size does not have an influence on that value. As a result, dynamically received sensor data on a fog node cannot be modelled, only static, predefined tasks have to be used. To allow fair comparison, we configured the scenarios in DISSECT-CF-Fog to always generate task with the same size. Concerning task forwarding, in iFogSim a fog device uses a method to forward a received (or generated) task to a higher-level device, if it cannot handle (i.e. process) it. In case of DISSECT-CF-Fog, every application module has a threshold value to handle task overloading, which defines the number of allowed waiting tasks. If this number exceeds the threshold (so more tasks arrive than it could be processed), the unhandled tasks will be forwarded to other available nodes (according to some selection algorithm). To match the default behavior of iFogSim, the topology defined in DISSECT-CF-Fog allowed only vertical forwarding among the available fog nodes (i.e. tasks are forwarded to upper nodes only).

4   IoT Application Scenarios and Architecture Configuration for the Evaluation

After applying the configuration restrictions for the two simulators discussed in the previous section, we define the IoT application scenarios to be used for comparison. Since meteorological applications are commonly used in IoT [13], we define our scenarios in this field. In our notion sensors are attached to IoT devices, which are weather stations that monitor weather conditions, and send the sensed data to fog or cloud resources for weather forecasting and analysis.

To perform the comparison, we defined four layers for the topology: (i) a cloud layer, (ii) an upper fog device layer with stronger resources, (iii) a lower fog device layer with weaker resources, and (iv) an IoT (smart) device layer. For the concrete resource parameters we defined one scenario with three different test cases:

– In the first test case we set up 20 IoT devices to generate data to be processed;
– in the second test case we initiated 40 IoT devices;
– while in the third test case we initiated 60 IoT devices for data generation (where each device had a single sensor).
– Concerning data processing we used the following resource parameters for the test cases: one cloud with 45 CPU cores and 45 GB RAM, 4 (stronger) fog nodes with 3 CPU cores and 3 GB RAM each, 20 (weaker) fog nodes with 1 CPU core and 1 GB RAM.

We did not use preset workloads for the experiments, only the started sensors generated data independently, thus in both simulators we executed so-called bag-of-tasks applications in fogs and clouds. In this work we refrain from distinguishing containers and traditional virtual machines, hence both considered simulators model virtual machines to serve application execution.

5   Results of the First Evaluation Round

To be as close to iFogSim as possible, we only used one type of Virtual Machine in DISSECT-CF-Fog, having 1 CPU core and 1 GB RAM. In case of iFogSim, the power of virtual machines was 1000 MIPS. The tasks to be executed in VMs were statically set to 2500 MIPS in both simulators. The simulation time was set to 10 000 s, and sensor readings were done every 5.1 s (i.e. the data generation frequency of the sensors). Each sensor generated 500 bytes of data during one iteration. The latency and bandwidth values were set equally in both simulators.

All the experiments were run on a PC having Intel Core i5-7300HQ 2.5 GHz, 8 GB RAM and running a 64-bit Windows 10 operating system. The results of executing the first round test cases with both simulators are shown in Table 3. We executed the same test cases five times with both simulators and counted their medium values to be stored in the table. To compare the use of the simulators, we only took into account the default outputs of the simulators and their execution time (e.g. cost calculations were neglected, hence they follow different logic in the simulators, and also do not really relevant for the performance comparisons).

According to these measurements, we can observe that the time needed for executing the simulation of the first test case was about ten times more with iFogSim, than with DISSECT-CF-Fog. In the second test case we doubled the number of IoT devices, and the runtime values increased with about 25% in case of DISSECT-CF-Fog and about 71% in case of iFogSim.

Comparing their runtime, DISSECT-CF-Fog is better suited for high-scale simulations, while iFogSim simulations become intolerably time consuming by modelling higher than a certain number of entities. In the third test case we could not even wait the measurements to finish (cancelled them after 1.5 h).

The application delay is the time within the simulation needed to process all remaining data in the system, after we stopped data generation by the IoT devices. The results in Table 3 show that this delay was longer in case of iFogSim, though the generated data sizes were equal for the same test cases in both simulators (hence the output results concerning the processed data were also equal). This is due to the different methods of task creation, scheduling and processing in the simulators (we could not eliminate all differences with the restrictions).

Finally, we used a simple source code metric to compare the implemented scenarios in the simulators. The so-called Lines of Code (LOC) is a common metric for analysing software quality. It is interesting to see that the same scenario could have been written three times shorter in case of DISSECT-CF-Fog, than in iFogSim. Of course, we tried to implement the code in both simulators with the least number of methods and constructs (in Java language). We also have to state that some configuration parameters had to be set at different parts of the software (this adds some lines in case of iFogSim, and around 20 lines of XML generation and configuration in case of DISSECT-CF-Fog). The considered iFogSim scenario is available online [17], while the DISSECT-CF-Fog scenarios are available here [18].

With this evaluation round we managed to model an IoT-Fog-Cloud environment with both simulators, and investigated a meteorological IoT application execution with different sensor and fog and cloud resource numbers. While DISSECT-CF-Fog dealt these simulations with ease, iFogSim struggled to simulate more than 65 entities of this complex system. Nevertheless, it is obvious that there are only a small number of real-world IoT applications that require only hundreds of sensors and fog or cloud resources; we need to be able to examine systems and applications composed of hundred thousands

Table 3. Comparison of the two simulators.

Property	DISSECT-CF-Fog			iFogSim		
Test case	I.	II.	III.	I.	II.	III.
Runtime (ms)	248.75	312.5	392.58	2260.33	3873.66	5400000*
Application delay (min)	3.41	4.33	4.33	14.89	17.52	N.A.
Generated data (byte)	19600000	39200000	58800000	19600000	39200000	N.A.
Lines of Code	50 lines + 6 XML files for detailed configuration			159 lines + 11 inline constants		

Table 4. Software metrics of the investigated simulators.

Metric	DISSECT-CF-Fog	iFogSim
Lines of Code	8.7k	28k
Duplication (%)	1.0	24.4
Code Smells	512	1.8k
Vulnerabilities	12	3
Bugs	37	139
Language	Java, XML	Java, XML
Files	108	291
Classes	160	306
Comments (%)	35.8	25.2
Cognitive Complexity	1.695	4.122

of these components. We continue our investigations in this direction, and we further raise the scale and analyse the behavior of DISSECT-CF-Fog, after we analyse thorough the system utilisation of the simulators in the next section.

6   Further Analysis of the Investigated Simulators

Since the result of the first scenario showed strong performance difference between the investigated simulators, we decided to perform further examinations on the source code of these simulators. To this end we used a static code analyzer tool and a performance profiler software, that helped us to point out implementation differences of the simulators. First, we used the SonarCloud tool [19] that provides static code metrics, security and code quality information, which are strongly related to the intuitive understanding of the code.

The results shown in Table 4 are based on the following information: Lines of Code refers to the number of lines in the source code of the software (empty lines are omitted), Duplication shows the percentage of the same lines in the code, Code Smells are defined as a maintainability-related component, which increases the time of changing the code (e.g. empty statements or readability of "switch-if" statements). Vulnerabilities are strongly connected to security issues (e.g. visibility of class members). Bugs refer to something wrong in the code, which require immediate fixes or corrections (e.g. variable casting or avoiding division by zero). Language shows the used programming and markup language, the Files and Classes represents the number of these elements in the code, respectively. Comments help the understanding of the source code and the software itself, thus it presents the ratio of the total lines (including empty lines) and lines containing comments. Finally, the Cognitive Complexity is an often used metric, which defines the understandability of methods. The higher the Cognitive Complexity is, the longer time and higher efforts are needed to understand the code and work with it.

Concerning the results, iFogSim contains about three-times more Lines of Code and about twice more Files and Classes, than DISSECT-CF-Fog. Except for the Vulnerabilities, the number of the Code Smells and Bugs are much higher in case of iFogSim, similarly to the Duplication ratio. These values show that there is a potentially higher chance to product malfunction during an iFogSim simulation. The Cognitive Complexity is about 2.5 smaller in case of DISSECT-CF-Fog, and it reaches better results in

Memory allocation call tree of iFogSim simulator:

```
100.0% - 12,140 kB - 296,526 alloc. org.fog.test.perfeval.DISSECT_To_iFogSim.main
  88.7% - 10,766 kB - 294,784 alloc. org.cloudbus.cloudsim.core.CloudSim.startSimulation
    88.7% - 10,766 kB - 294,784 alloc. org.cloudbus.cloudsim.core.CloudSim.run
      88.7% - 10,765 kB - 294,732 alloc. org.cloudbus.cloudsim.core.CloudSim.runClockTick
        85.6% - 10,387 kB - 283,380 alloc. org.cloudbus.cloudsim.core.SimEntity.run
        1.7% - 209 kB - 6,429 alloc. org.cloudbus.cloudsim.core.CloudSim.processEvent
        0.4% - 48,840 bytes - 1,402 alloc. org.cloudbus.cloudsim.core.FutureQueue.removeAll
        0.2% - 30,144 bytes - 991 alloc. java.util.ArrayList.add
        0.0% - 5,136 bytes - 170 alloc. org.cloudbus.cloudsim.core.FutureQueue.remove
        0.0% - 3,760 bytes - 126 alloc. org.cloudbus.cloudsim.core.FutureQueue.iterator
        0.0% - 1,792 bytes - 60 alloc. java.util.TreeMap$KeyIterator.next
      0.0% - 552 bytes - 14 alloc. org.cloudbus.cloudsim.core.CloudSim.runStart
  10.8% - 1,306 kB - 53 alloc. org.fog.test.perfeval.DISSECT_To_iFogSim.createApplication
  0.4% - 48,656 bytes - 1,168 alloc. java.util.Calendar.getInstance
  0.1% - 8,280 bytes - 244 alloc. org.fog.placement.ModulePlacementEdgewards.<init>
  0.0% - 5,808 bytes - 136 alloc. org.fog.test.perfeval.DISSECT_To_iFogSim.createCloud
  0.0% - 3,800 bytes - 120 alloc. org.fog.placement.Controller.<init>
  0.0% - 400 bytes - 11 alloc. org.cloudbus.cloudsim.core.CloudSim.init
  0.0% - 144 bytes - 6 alloc. org.fog.entities.FogBroker.<init>
0.0% - 40 bytes - 2 alloc. org.fog.test.perfeval.DISSECT_To_iFogSim.<clinit>
0.0% - 1,568 bytes - 30 alloc. direct calls to methods of unprofiled classes
```

Memory allocation call tree of DISSECT-CF-Fog simulator:

```
100.0% - 4,677 kB - 111,346 alloc. hu.u_szeged.inf.fog.simulator.demo.DISSECT_vs_iFogSim.main
  81.5% - 3,809 kB - 97,744 alloc. hu.mta.sztaki.lpds.cloud.simulator.Timed.simulateUntilLastEvent
    80.7% - 3,776 kB - 96,905 alloc. hu.mta.sztaki.lpds.cloud.simulator.Timed.fire
      27.6% - 1,289 kB - 33,200 alloc. hu.mta.sztaki.lpds.cloud.simulator.DeferredEvent$AggregatedEventDispatcher.tick
      27.3% - 1,276 kB - 32,771 alloc. hu.u_szeged.inf.fog.simulator.iot.Station.tick
      20.4% - 954 kB - 24,468 alloc. hu.mta.sztaki.lpds.cloud.simulator.iaas.resourcemodel.ResourceSpreader$FreqSyncer.tick
      3.2% - 149 kB - 3,781 alloc. hu.u_szeged.inf.fog.simulator.application.FogApp.tick
      2.1% - 97,824 bytes - 2,525 alloc. java.util.PriorityQueue.poll
  11.9% - 558 kB - 9,170 alloc. hu.u_szeged.inf.fog.simulator.physical.ComputingAppliance.loadAppliances
    5.4% - 252 kB - 4,013 alloc. hu.u_szeged.inf.fog.simulator.physical.ComputingAppliance.<init>
    5.3% - 248 kB - 4,340 alloc. hu.u_szeged.inf.fog.simulator.physical.ComputingAppliance.handleNullAppliancesWhenReading
    0.6% - 27,656 bytes - 491 alloc. hu.u_szeged.inf.fog.simulator.loaders.ApplianceModel.loadAppliancesXML
    0.6% - 26,912 bytes - 231 alloc. hu.u_szeged.inf.fog.simulator.physical.ComputingAppliance.createApplications
    0.1% - 3,288 bytes - 94 alloc. hu.mta.sztaki.lpds.cloud.simulator.Timed.<clinit>
  3.5% - 162 kB - 1,674 alloc. hu.u_szeged.inf.fog.simulator.providers.Instance.loadInstance
    3.4% - 160 kB - 1,630 alloc. hu.u_szeged.inf.fog.simulator.loaders.InstanceModel.loadInstanceXML
    0.0% - 1,968 bytes - 44 alloc. java.lang.ClassLoader.loadClass
  2.2% - 104 kB - 1,900 alloc. hu.u_szeged.inf.fog.simulator.iot.Station.loadDevice
    1.5% - 72,424 bytes - 1,370 alloc. hu.u_szeged.inf.fog.simulator.loaders.DeviceModel.loadDeviceXML
    0.7% - 32,352 bytes - 530 alloc. hu.u_szeged.inf.fog.simulator.iot.Station.<init>
  0.6% - 29,440 bytes - 646 alloc. hu.u_szeged.inf.fog.simulator.util.TimelineGenerator.generate
    0.3% - 14,576 bytes - 255 alloc. java.io.PrintWriter.println
    0.1% - 5,152 bytes - 72 alloc. java.text.SimpleDateFormat.<init>
  0.2% - 7,744 bytes - 148 alloc. hu.u_szeged.inf.fog.simulator.demo.ScenarioBase.printInformation
  0.1% - 3,760 bytes - 61 alloc. java.lang.ClassLoader.loadClass
0.0% - 128 bytes - 1 alloc. direct calls to methods of unprofiled classes
```

Fig. 1. Memory allocation call tree of the simulators.

the Comments as well. As a brief conclusion, according to the static code analysis, DISSECT-CF-Fog is more reliable and easy to use in the view of source code quality.

Next, we applied JProfiler [20], which is able to analyse Java-based applications considering threads, classes, instances, usage of the garbage collector, besides memory and CPU usage. We repeated the test cases defined for both simulators in the previous section focusing on these metrics and characteristics.

Concerning the results, first we looked at the memory allocation tree, and the aggregation level that was set to the methods. In case of iFogSim, the *startSimulation* method is responsible for starting the simulation and the *SimEntity* class represents entities, which handle events. In case of DISSECT-CF-Fog, the *SimulateUntilLastEvent* starts the simulation and *Timed* manages the inner clock of the simulator. Accordingly, a simulation in the iFogSim utilises 7.2 times higher memory, than DISSECT-CF-Fog, as shown in Fig. 1.

Telemetries of the iFogSim simulator:

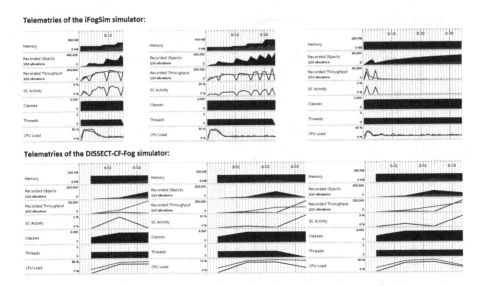

Telemetries of the DISSECT-CF-Fog simulator:

Fig. 2. Telemetries data of the investigated simulators during the 1st scenario. (Color figure online)

We also investigated the telemetries of the scenarios, as shown in Fig. 2. Each row presents the three test cases of first scenario in the corresponding simulator. The comparison is based on the following characteristics: Memory reflects the heap memory, the used size labeled by blue, whilst the free size of memory is labeled by green. Recorded Objects present the instantiated objects, blue refers to the number of arrays, green refers to the non-arrays objects. The Recorded Throughput shows the freed object per seconds using green colour, and blue represents created objects per second. The GC Activity presents the activity ratio of the garbage collector of the JVM, Thread presents the number of threads with runnable state, whilst the Classes shows the number of used classes during the evaluation. Finally, CPU Load reflects to the process load (by green) and the system load (by blue).

Interpreting the results, DISSECT-CF-Fog utilises less memory, and in all test cases the heap size stays less than 200 MBs, whilst in case of iFogSim the heap size of the second test case almost reaches the 400 MBs. The Recorded Object value is almost four-times higher during the evaluation with iFogSim, however DISSECT-CF-Fog uses almost 3000 Java classes for the evaluation (external libraries are considered by the JProfiler, as well). The iFogSim tool uses the CPU more intensively, than DISSECT-CF-Fog, the CPU Load almost reaches 90% in the first two test cases during the iFogSim simulations. The GC Activity and the Recorded Throughput metrics point out a possible malfunction in the third test case of iFogSim, because after about 5 s, these values are correlated showing no relevant operation occurrence.

The reason of this behaviour is the process starvation caused by the Java Finalizer thread. Similar issue is mentioned in [15], however this problem can strongly related to the negative code quality as well.

```
<?xml version="1.0"?>
<appliances>
  <appliance>
    <name>fog0</name>
    <xcoord>-38</xcoord>
    <ycoord>-11</ycoord>
    <parentApp>cloud2-app</parentApp>
    <file>fog_type1</file>
    <applications>
        <application tasksize="250000">
        <AppName>fog0-app</name>
        <freq>300000</freq>
        <instance>a1.xlarge</instance>
        </application>
    </applications>
    <neighbourAppliances>
      <device>
        <deviceName>fog11</deviceName>
      </device>
    </neighbourAppliances>
  </appliance>
</appliances>
```

Fig. 3. Sample XML description for the application model in DISSECT-CF-Fog as shown in [14].

7   The Second Evaluation Round

For the second round of evaluation we extend our investigation for larger IoT systems and applications, thus we increase the number of fog nodes to hundreds and smart devices to hundreds of thousands. We found DISSECT-CF-Fog more reliable for managing fog environments in our previous evaluation round, we continue its investigation with six additional test cases, in which we compare a cloud-centred solution to a fog-centred architecture, where additional fog nodes appear beside cloud resources.

As we mentioned before, DISSECT-CF-Fog uses an XML document structure to configure system parameters. To define the additional scenarios, we need to know this structure. Figure 3 presents an example of such description, which contains only one physical fog infrastructure (called *appliance*), but its tag can be used multiple times in the document. The *name* tag is the unique identifier of a fog device, and the *xcoord, ycoord* describes the exact location of this physical resource. In this case this XML describes a child fog node, since the *parentApp* refers to its parent node, which is a cloud apparently. The *file* tag contains the absolute path of another XML file, which present the configuration of physical machines this fog node should have. The *application* tag is also repeatable, it tells what kind of application this physical resource has

Table 5. Maximum number of created entities during the simulations in iFogSim and DISSECT-CF-Fog.

Scenario	DISSECT-CF-Fog			iFogSim		
	Cloud/Fog nodes	IoT devices	Sensors	Cloud/Fog nodes	IoT devices	Sensors
I/a	25	20	20	25	20	20
I/b	25	40	40	25	40	40
I/c	25	60	60	25	60	60
II/a	3	100 000	500 000	N.A.		
II/b	98	100 000	500 000			
II/c	113	100 000	500 000			
II/d	153	100 000	500 000			
II/e	208	100 000	500 000			
II/f	152	100 000	500 000			

(should execute). The *tasksize* attribute tells us how much data (in bytes) should be gathered to create a task (250 kB in this example). *appName* is the unique identifier of this application module. The application has a task creation frequency (called *freq*), which defines periodical intervals for task generation and data forwarding (in this case its value is 300000 ms, i.e. five minutes). The *instance* tag refers to a VM type this application should use. Finally, one can define possibly multiple neighbouring devices (by stating a formerly defined unique identifier of an infrastructure in the *device* tag), to which data or tasks may be forwarded. Possible advantages using XML files are to create simulation that researchers do not have to understand the tasks of low-level simulator components, XML schemas can secure more readable format to configure the system than a Java code.

In the current evaluation phase we introduced different VM types of flavors, to show some of the additional capabilities DISSECT-CF-Fog has. We used three real VM pricing and configuration types based on Amazon Web Services' offerings [21]: (i) a1.large VM (1 CPU cores, 2 GBs RAM with $0.051 hourly cost), (ii) a1.xlarge VM (2 CPU cores, 4 GBs RAM with $0.102 hourly cost) and the last one is (iii) a1.2xlarge VM (8 CPU cores, 16 GBs RAM with $0.204 hourly cost).

In this phase we enabled the dynamic task creation method that takes into account the size of the generated data. Our default configuration (for clouds) required every task to contain maximum 2 500 000 bytes of data (to be processed).

We defined IoT-Fog-Cloud systems using the same four layers as we used before: (i) a cloud layer, (ii) a stronger fog layer (called Fog Type 1 – T1), (iii) a weaker fog layer (called Fog Type 2 – T2), and (iv) an IoT device layer. In each layer we could define different number of cloud or fog infrastructures with different resources. We used the following configuration values for the computational infrastructures:

- a cloud contains 200 CPU cores and 400 GBs RAM, and all of its VMs are of type a1.2xlarge.
- a T1 fog contains 48 CPU cores and 112 GBs RAM, offering a1.xlarge VM type. It also redefines the default task size (to be executed in this node) to 1 250 000 bytes.
- a T2 fog contains 12 CPU cores and 24 GBs RAM, offering a1.large VM type. The task size in this infrastructure is set to 625 000 bytes.

We also changed the configuration of IoT devices (weather stations in the analogy) in this phase. Instead of containing a single sensor, we defined five sensors to be attached to an IoT device (so a weather station has five sensors to monitor temperature, humidity, pressure, rain, wind speed), all of them generating 100 bytes of data every minute (which is the data generation frequency).

In DISSECT-CF-Fog one can set the maximum number of tasks to be handled by a computational node. In this evaluation phase we set it to three, so if more data arrived to a node than what three tasks could process, the remaining data is forwarded (neighbouring) fog or cloud node to be processed. In case there is no available VM to execute a newly created task on a node, the VM managed tries to deploy a new one.

We used six different topologies for this second scenario: (a) three clouds, (b) three clouds with 15 Fog T1 and 80 Fog T2, (c) three clouds with 30 Fog T1 and 80 Fog T2, (d) three clouds with 30 Fog T1 and 120 Fog T2, (e) three clouds with 45 Fog T1 and 160 Fog T2 and the last (f) two clouds with 50 Fog T1 and 100 Fog T2.

To reach hundreds of thousands of simulated components we created eight test cases for each topology defined earlier. We investigated how the system behaves under serving an increased number of IoT devices. We defined 5 000 smart devices (weather stations) at the beginning, and we scaled them up to reach 10 000, 20 000, 30 000, 40 000, 50 000, 75 000, and finally in the last test case the total number of IoT devices were 100 000 (each of them run with five sensors, thus our simulator managed 500 000 entities). Table 5 summarizes the number of simulated components (entities) in each of the performed experiments.

8   Result of the Third Evaluation Round

Finally, for the third round of evaluations, we scaled up the simulation time to 24 h of weather forecasting, while we run the simulated data generation and processing for around 2.7 h in the former two rounds.

We present the evaluation results by comparing each scenario with the following metrics: the number of IoT devices managed in the simulations (we recall that each device had five sensors that generated data), the number of VMs needed to process the generated data, the total costs of operating the IoT devices and utilizing the VMs both in fogs and clouds, the application delay (or timeout) values that denoted the time passed after stopping the sensors (i.e. its data generation) till the end of the simulation, and finally the runtime (execution time) of the actual simulation. Detailed evaluation results are depicted in Figs. 4, 5, 6, 7 and 8.

Figure 4 shows an important characteristic of our simulated system. The configuration of larger task sizes in clouds led to the creation of a relatively small number of strong VMs (75 in the largest test case) to process these tasks. In case of fogs we had a much higher number of nodes executing a large number of weaker VMs (834 in the largest test case) to process the larger number of tasks (created to process less data than in clouds). We can also notice that after the fifth case (managing 40 000 IoT devices) the number of cloud VMs does not grow any more: we reached the maximum capacity of the available clouds (all physical resources are fully utilized). This means that in the purely cloud cases the infrastructure was heavily overloaded during managing

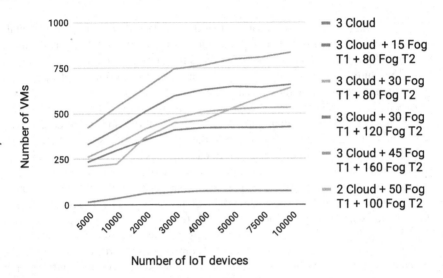

Fig. 4. Correlation of the number of VMs needed to process data and the number of IoT devices that generated the data in DISSECT-CF-Fog simulations.

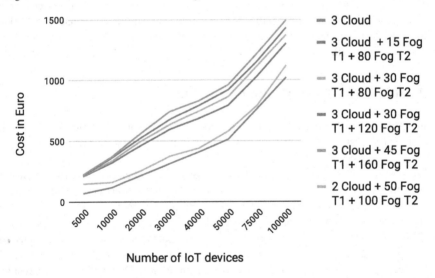

Fig. 5. Correlation of total operating costs of applications and the number of managed IoT devices in DISSECT-CF-Fog simulations.

more than 40 000 devices (weather stations). It can be also observed that the fog-aware topology *f*, which includes less cloud nodes but more Fog T1 nodes utilises less VMs in average (433.81) than the other fog topologies (516.57).

This issue was also approved by the results as it can be seen in Fig. 5, where we can observe the costs to be paid for hiring the management infrastructure. The purely clouds scenarios were the cheapest, where a small number of expensive VMs were

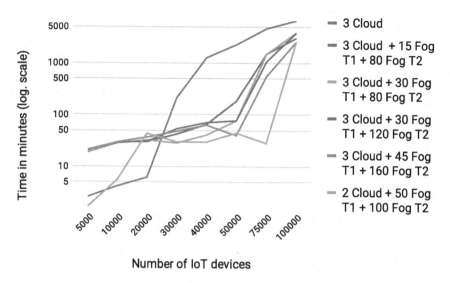

Fig. 6. Correlation of application delay and the number of managed IoT devices in DISSECT-CF-Fog simulations.

utilized (and overloaded most of the time). In general, with the configuration we used (based on Amazon pricing), hiring additional fog nodes resulted in higher costs, even if fog resources were cheaper (considering the total costs and the number of VMs utilized in the scenarios, a VM used in a fog topology costs 1.41 Euros, while a VM utilised in the purely cloud topology costs 7.15 Euros in average). It is also seen that the topology f performs with slightly higher cost than the purely cloud solution. Figure 8 further details the shares of fog and cloud utilization costs. Here we can see that the more fog nodes we introduce, the more they are preferred by the application. In case of 10 000 IoT devices, the Fog T2 layer serves the whole IoT application and there is no additional cloud and Fog T1 operating costs.

Figure 6 reveals additional interesting behavior. The f topology is slightly faster than the purely cloud topology in the first test case, but it then starts to increase, similarly to the other fog topologies. This figure also shows that in the purely cloud scenario the overloading started even after utilizing more than 20 000 IoT devices. So managing around 25 000 IoT devices (i.e. 125 000 sensors) we can see a trend break point: it is faster and cheaper to manage less number of devices with only clouds, while for a higher number of devices utilizing fogs can help to reduce the application delay (with higher costs). One can also observe that the f topology tries to keep the application delay as below as possible, the average delay is 347.0 min, while the average of the rest of the fog scenarios is 593.7 min.

For the test case having the highest scale, 6 591 min were needed for the application to terminate (after data generation of the sensors was stopped) in the purely cloud scenario, while utilizing the largest fog infrastructure needed only 2 574 min. By correlating this with their costs, we can conclude that we have to pay about 46% more for about 156% faster data processing.

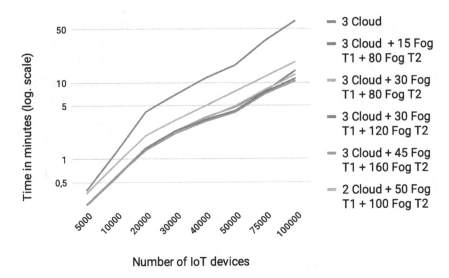

Fig. 7. Correlation of runtime of simulations and the number of managed IoT devices in DISSECT-CF-Fog.

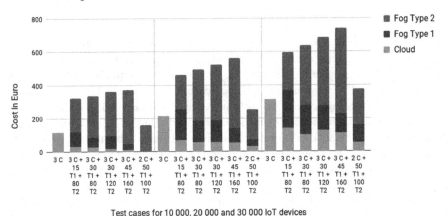

Fig. 8. Detailed cost values during DISSECT-CF-Fog simulations of 10 000 to 30 000 IoT devices.

Our last figure reveals how the simulator coped with the test cases of the scenarios. Figure 7 presents the elapsed real time (wall-clock time, or simply runtime) taken to execute the simulations of the test cases. It is also interesting to see that simulating a higher number of fog and cloud nodes and VMs took less time than a smaller number of cloud nodes and VMs. We can observe that runtime is in correlation with the application delay, so this is one of the reasons for this issue. The other explanation is that in the fog cases the higher number of smaller tasks (and their data) were better treated (processed) by the higher number of fog VMs, while in the purely cloud cases many bigger tasks (with larger amount of data) had to be waiting in queues for the overloaded VMs.

To summarize our evaluation, we can conclude that DISSECT-CF-Fog has a more detailed and fine-grained fog model than iFogSim as the comparative analysis shows us. It can also scale up to simulate hundreds of thousands of IoT-Fog-Cloud system components simultaneously with acceptable runtime. Our experiments also revealed that utilizing fogs beside clouds can be beneficial in terms of reducing the application execution time (and delay in our notion), though we had to pay more for them. Nevertheless, different pricing schemes for fogs (other than clouds) may also result in cost savings (e.g. own or a neighbor's fog device may be free to use in smart home applications).

9 Conclusions

The recent technological advances have transformed distributed systems and enabled the creation of complex environments called IoT-Fog-Cloud systems. The design, development and operation of these systems need simulation tools to save costs and time, therefore specialized simulators need to be created to provide means to investigate these processes.

In this paper we investigated the available solutions in this field, and compared two fog modelling approaches, namely iFogSim and DISSECT-CF-Fog, with detailed evaluations in three rounds of experiments representing an increasing level of complexity. The evaluations also showed how to create and execute simulated IoT scenarios using fog and cloud resources with these tools.

Our results highlight that DISSECT-CF-Fog can provide easier configurations and faster and more reliable simulations for higher scales, but the benefits of utilizing fog or cloud resources are highly dependent on the actual behaviour of the considered IoT application.

Our future work will investigate a more detailed representation and use of mobility features of IoT and fog devices.

References

1. Botta, A., de Donato, W., Persico, V., Pescapè, A.: Integration of cloud computing and Internet of Things: a survey. Future Gener. Comput. Syst. **56** (2016). https://doi.org/10.1016/j.future.2015.09.02

2. Dastjerdi, A.V., Buyya, R.: Fog computing: helping the Internet of Things realize its potential. Computer **49** (2016). https://doi.org/10.1109/MC.2016.245

3. Puliafito, C., Mingozzi, E., Longo, F., Puliafito, A., Rana, O.: Fog computing for the Internet of Things: a survey. ACM Trans. Internet Technol. **19** (2019). https://doi.org/10.1145/3301443

4. Mann, Z.A.: Cloud simulators in the implementation and evaluation of virtual machine placement algorithms. Softw. Pract. Exp. **48** (2018). https://doi.org/10.1002/spe.2579

5. Sonmez, C., Ozgovde, A., Ersoy, C.: EdgeCloudSim: an environment for performance evaluation of Edge Computing systems. In: Second International Conference on Fog and Mobile Edge Computing (FMEC) (2017). https://doi.org/10.1109/FMEC.2017.7946405

6. Lera, I., Guerrero, C., Juiz, C.: YAFS: a simulator for IoT scenarios in fog computing. IEEE Access **7** (2019). https://doi.org/10.1109/ACCESS.2019.2927895

7. Qayyum, T., Malik, A.W., Khan Khattak, M.A., Khalid, O., Khan, S.U.: FogNetSim++: a toolkit for modeling and simulation of distributed fog environment. IEEE Access **6** (2018). https://doi.org/10.1109/ACCESS.2018.2877696

8. Gupta, H., Dastjerdi, A.V., Ghosh, S.K., Buyya, R.: iFogSim: a toolkit for modeling and simulation of resource management techniques in the Internet of Things, edge and fog computing environments. Softw. Pract. Exp. **47** (2016). https://doi.org/10.1002/spe.2509

9. Nikdel, Z., Gao, B., Neville, S.W.: DockerSim: full-stack simulation of container-based software-as-a-service (SaaS) cloud deployments and environments. In: IEEE Pacific Rim Conference on Communications, Computers and Signal Processing (PACRIM) (2017). https://doi.org/10.1109/PACRIM.2017.8121898

10. Mayer, R., Graser, L., Gupta, H., Saurez, E., Ramachandran, U.: EmuFog: extensible and scalable emulation of large-scale fog computing infrastructures. IEEE Fog World Congr. (FWC) (2017). https://doi.org/10.1109/FWC.2017.8368525

11. Markus, A., Kertesz, A.: A survey and taxonomy of simulation environments modelling fog computing. Simul. Model. Pract. Theory **101** (2019). https://doi.org/10.1016/j.simpat.2019.102042

12. Kecskemeti, G.: DISSECT-CF: a simulator to foster energy-aware scheduling in infrastructure clouds. Simul. Model. Pract. Theory **58** (2015). https://doi.org/10.1016/j.simpat.2015.05.009

13. Markus, A., Kertesz, A., Kecskemeti, G.: Cost-aware IoT extension of DISSECT-CF. Future Internet **9** (2017). https://doi.org/10.3390/fi9030047

14. Markus, A., Gacsi, P., Kertesz, A.: Develop or dissipate fogs? Evaluating an IoT application in fog and cloud simulations. In: 10th International Conference on Cloud Computing and Services Science (CLOSER) (2020). https://doi.org/10.5220/0009590401930203

15. Abreu, D.P., Velasquez, K., Curado, M., Monteiro, E.: A comparative analysis of simulators for the cloud to fog continuum. Simul. Model. Pract. Theory **101** (2020). https://doi.org/10.1016/j.simpat.2019.102029

16. Google Scholar. https://scholar.google.com/. Accessed June 2020

17. iFogSim simulator. https://github.com/petergacsi/iFogSim/. Accessed September 2019

18. DISSECT-CF-Fog simulator. https://github.com/andrasmarkus/dissect-cf/tree/fog-extension/. Accessed June 2020

19. SonarCloud. https://sonarcloud.io/. Accessed June 2020

20. JProfiler. https://www.ej-technologies.com/products/jprofiler/overview.html. Accessed June 2020

21. AWS EC2 Instance Pricing. https://aws.amazon.com/ec2/pricing/on-demand/. Accessed September 2019

A Case for User-Defined Governance of Pure Edge Data-Driven Applications

João Mafra[✉], Francisco Brasileiro, and Raquel Lopes

Federal University of Campina Grande, Paraíba, Brazil
jvmafra@lsd.ufcg.edu.br,
{fubica,raquel}@computacao.ufcg.edu.br

Abstract. The increasing popularity of smartphones, associated with their capability to sense the environment, has allowed the creation of an increasing range of data-driven applications. In general, this type of application collects data from the environment using edge devices and sends them to a remote cloud to be processed. In this setting, the governance of the application and its data is, usually, unilaterally defined by the cloud-based application provider. We propose an architectural model which allows this kind of application to be governed solely by the community of users, instead. We consider members of a community who have some common problem to solve, and eliminate the dependence on an external cloud-based application provider by leveraging the capabilities of the devices sitting on the edge of the network. We combine the concepts of Participatory Sensing, Mobile Social Networks and Edge Computing, which allows data processing to be done closer to data sources. We define our model and then present a case study that aims to evaluate the feasibility of our proposal, and how its performance compares to that of other existing solutions (e.g. cloud-based architecture). The case study uses simulation experiments fed with real data from the public transport system of Curitiba city, in Brazil. The results show that the proposed approach is feasible, and can aggregate as much data as current approaches that use remote dedicated servers. Differently from the all-or-nothing sharing policy of current approaches, the approach proposed allows users to autonomously configure the trade-off between the sharing of private data, and the performance that the application can achieve.

Keywords: Edge-computing · Community · Analytics · Privacy

1 Introduction

Smartphones are now spread all over the world, being used by the most diverse people, following different cultures and lifestyles. According to statisa[1], we

---

This work was supported by the Innovation Center, Ericsson Telecomunicacoes S.A., Brazil and by EMBRAPII-CEEI.

[1] https://www.statista.com/statistics/330695/number-of-smartphone-users-worldwide/.

© Springer Nature Switzerland AG 2021
D. Ferguson et al. (Eds.): CLOSER 2020, CCIS 1399, pp. 277–300, 2021.
https://doi.org/10.1007/978-3-030-72369-9_12

reached in 2020 the mark of 3.5 billion smartphone users. Each smartphone comes with processing and networking capabilities, as well as a set of sensors (e.g. GPS - Global Positioning System, ambient light sensors and microphones). With these small computers around and online all the time, there is a great variety of applications already in place, leveraging their capabilities.

Many of these applications aim at getting sensoring information from the personal smartphones and other types of sensors in place and merging the collected data to extract new information on a larger scale. This technique known as participatory sensing has emerged in 2006 [5] and took a new dimension more recently when associated with Mobile Social Networks (MSN) [7]. Mobile Social Networks are virtual communities of individuals that have some common interests and keep in touch using their mobile devices. By considering the sensing capabilities of the users' devices, the users can share (their local) data and access the merged data to extract rich information to measure, map, analyze or estimate processes of common interest. For example, GreenGPS, relies on participatory sensing data to map fuel consumption on city streets, allowing drivers to find the most fuel efficient routes for their vehicles between arbitrary end-points [6]. Many applications like that came to life [13,18,19], all of them exploiting the participatory and opportunistic sensing capabilities of mobile devices.

At the heart of these applications are the users with a common goal. These users usually trade personal local data for global information that can be achieved just by collaboration. Only with the combined data collaboratively shared the users satisfy their common goal. It is common to see applications that are built, advertised and, after that, adopted by interested users, gathering data in a collaborative way and, eventually, using the applications to fulfill their own needs. These applications are commonly hosted in cloud infrastructures, requiring some sort of sponsorship, management and technical support to operate them. Many of these applications use machine learning and other artificial intelligence (AI) techniques to extract useful predictions/answers from raw data. This computational model usually centralizes the (collaboratively shared) data and processing to a central server (usually in the cloud), where the machine learning models are trained. Thus, the adoption of such a model boosts the need for external sponsorship and technical support.

Obviously, when the data shared by the users is sensitive there are privacy issues that must be considered. Federated Learning [3] has been proposed as a new architecture to build global machine learning models without data sharing. This architecture considers that AI models are built independently in the users' devices and then merged with the global model that is located in the cloud. Although data is not shared, the users themselves have no governance over the global model achieved, which is typically hosted in cloud providers.

In summary, participatory sensing, mobile social networks and federated learning are useful frameworks that allow shared knowledge to be extracted from raw data that is collaboratively gathered. However, they require a centralized hosting service where the back-end application runs, usually in the cloud. Keeping application governance in external hands may be inconvenient for a number of reasons. Just to start, we can mention that users are subject to unilateral changes on usage policies, decided by the provider. Yet more severe, providers can run out of business, or simply decide to stop supporting the applications, usually without any liabilities with respect to the users.

The fact that all data shared by the users is held by a single entity that governs the service gives opportunities to data misuse that can lead to privacy issues. In order to use the application, interested users (that have their local data to share) have to agree with a policy describing how sensitive data will be used. Despite leaving users aware of the use of their information, this data governance model might be risky. First, application providers can omit important details about how the data is used. An example of such a situation occurred recently, when Facebook was subject to a huge penalty from the government of the United States of America for misusing user data. Second, the use of the application is often conditional on acceptance of the terms of use which are established by the external sponsor, giving no chance for negotiation. Therefore, if the user does not agree with the policy, he/she may not be able to utilize the service. In other words, this is usually an all-or-nothing decision. Hereafter, we refer to all these issues discussed so far as *the problem of external governance*.

Central to this problem is the fact that external governance takes from the community the right of deciding how their data is shared, where it is stored, when and by whom it is used. Besides, there is a cost for maintaining such service in the cloud. In this chapter we present an approach that exploits the edge computing resources to provide a *community-governed service* as an alternative way to deliver analytics services to a community of users sharing a common goal.

Community-governed services involve data analysis, typically to help users to find better alternative answers to their common problem. Driven by their shared interest, they exchange data among themselves so they can make better decisions based on more information. For example, neighbors interested in finding the best spots to catch up outdoors can share air pollution related data they gather from the neighborhood to build a comprehensive report about the air quality in the neighborhood. Users indoors, such as a shopping mall, may be interested in the quietest places, and can resort to data collectively gathered to spot those places [21]. Members of a community may be interested in traffic conditions. Google maps does this by aggregating in a centralized environment data collected by users' smartphones to generate reports about traffic conditions.

The idea of community-governed services is to exploit the participatory sensing concept, but limiting the data exchange to the trusted partners in the social network, and eliminating the need of third party services such as cloud-based application providers. In order to do that, community-governed services follow a peer-to-peer (P2P) architecture: data is generated and processed at the edge of the network without the need to be transferred to the cloud to be processed. The community-governed services use the processing power of the edge devices themselves to gather, process and store the shared data. Of course, these devices are limited in terms of processing, storage and energy consumption, and some applications cannot be built that way, as we explore in Sect. 2.3.

Edge computing [23] is the core of the community-governed services, since the same (edge) devices that collect the data also store and process it. As expected, edge computing avoids data flooding in the cloud, saves bandwidth and reduces applications' latency, providing better user experience. But these are not the only benefits. By adopting community-governed services built on top of *pure* edge computing technology (not including fog servers, mobile edge computing servers [15] nor VM-based cloudlets [22]), we empower the data owners and service users to have their services the way the community desires. It is a pure P2P application built to unite the sensing and computing power of edge computing devices, driven and guided by those who feed and use the service.

Our previous work [14] shows a simplified evaluation of this service model, assuming that all members of the community trust each other when sharing data. Since this is impractical, in this chapter, in addition to revisiting the idea of community-governed service, we further analyze how trust relationships among community members impact the quality of the proposed solution.

The rest of the chapter discusses the architectural model of pure edge data-driven applications that allows for community-governed services. We discuss its components, application requirements, and limitations. We also present a use case that analyzes the trade-offs involved in using the proposed model from a service performance point of view.

2   Community-Governed Services Model

2.1   Definition

One of the main advantages of the *Community-Governed Services* is that it empowers users to jointly define the governance of the data that is manipulated by the service. Also, since the service is cooperatively implemented by the software running at the user's devices, failures or departure of users are likely to lead to a gentle degradation of the service, and not a complete disruption of the service. In this way, individuals have greater control over the use of their collected data, storing it locally and sharing only with those they trust. In addition, data processing can be done at the edge of the network, using the same devices that collect the information from the environment, avoiding the need for sponsorship to keep the application running in the cloud. To guarantee the governance to users, the proposed service has some fundamental principles:

- **Participatory Sensor:** Environment data collection using sensors installed on smartphones, smartwatches, bracelets, among other devices that are on the edge of the network. To guarantee the engagement of individuals, it is important that they have some **common goal** to be satisfied by the service as a form of motivation.
- **Data Sharing:** The users can communicate with each other using an **MSN** and share the collected data individually with their trusted peers. Taking advantage of the **mobility pattern** of individuals, this can be done at some point in which they are in a zone of local proximity.

- **Edge Processing:** Using Edge Computing paradigm, the collected data is processed on the users' own mobile devices.

Thus, a community of users has a common goal and harness the power of its own edge devices to collect and process the data collected. Between data collection and processing, users can share their data with trusted users in the same community. Since everything is done at the edge of the network, the need for a third party (logically) centralized server running at a cloud provider is obviated. It increases the robustness of the service by removing the dependency on a central entity represented by the server running in the cloud, eliminates the bottleneck in the communication with the centralized server, and most importantly, allows the community of users to jointly define and manage the governance of the service, which among other things mitigates privacy issues.

2.2 System Model

The system is composed by a number of personal devices running the community-governed service. The users utilize the service agent running in their devices to both collect and share data in a participatory sensing way, and query the service. The service agent that runs at each personal device is illustrated in Fig. 1. It consists of six modules: participatory sensor, community sensor, community data collector, community data filter, model builder and query dispatcher.

The *participatory sensor* component is responsible for collecting data in the vicinity of the device. The *community sensor* component takes care of discovering other members of the community. The *community data collector* contacts other members of the community in order to increase the amount of data that is available locally. The *community data filter* component regulates which data should be shared with other members of the community, in both directions, i.e. to whom local collected data can be shared, and from whom data should be requested. The *model builder* component is in charge of creating the service model from all the data collected. Finally, the *query dispatcher* provides the interface to the service.

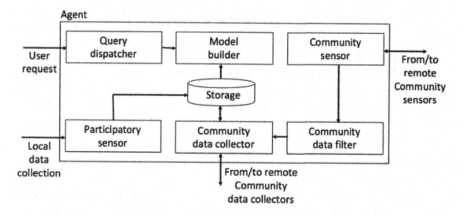

Fig. 1. Components of agent [14].

When a new request is received by the query dispatcher component, it uses the model generated by the model builder component in order to answer the request. Whenever a new data item is made available (either by the participatory sensor or the community data collector), the model builder assesses if a new model needs to be created. If this is the case, it uses all the data available to train the new model.

Periodically, the community sensor tries to identify members that are online. This information is passed to the community data filter that, in turn, decides to which members local data could be shared (upon request), and from which other members data could be requested. The community data collector contacts other community data collectors obeying the community data filter decision. Periodically, or upon the detection of an event of interest, the community data collector tries to collect data from the accepted members that are online. When contacted by an external member, the community data collector decides whether it should provide the data locally stored to the contacting member.

2.3 Application Requirements

First, the personal devices of the users must be able to collect data in a passive or active way. Second, the users share common service interests and form a community. So, at some point in time, these devices connect to each other through the formation of mobile social networks, a common local area network, or even a regular Internet connection. The creation of the community allows the users to share the collected data among the trusted peers (participatory sensing). Third, these services involve data analysis through analytical and/or machine learning models. We expect the quality of answers provided by the models to be proportional to the quantity and diversity of the data gathered. Thus, the more data is available to users, the more benefits they can get from the service.

The use of the edge devices to run the community-governed service, as well as to execute the sensing to collect data, limits these activities. In other words, the execution of the service, as well as the sensing activity must be lightweight, and ideally the battery consumption due to these activities should be acceptable to the user. Moreover, data storage consumption should also be low. There are a number of ways to mitigate the impact of these limitations. For instance, training machine-learning models tend to be a compute-intensive procedure. This could be executed only when the device is fully charged, and connected to the charger. Alternatively, simpler statistical models can be used to reduce the computation demand (in our case study we describe one example). Regarding data storage, in many cases a sliding-window approach can be used to release data that is old enough, and as a result less important.

3 Case Study

In order to shed some light on the feasibility of the community-governed service model we conducted a simulation-based case study in the area of public transportation. The choice of the application was based on the fact that it fits the features discussed above, and we have real data to feed our simulation model.

In many cities, urban bus schedules are made public and followed in a very strict way. In cities that use technology in an intensive way, buses can be equipped with sensors and tracked in real-time using a cloud-based service, or even using 5G-based solutions [11], so that unanticipated delays can be spotted, and alternative bus routes can be chosen. Nevertheless, in many places, especially in large cities of developing countries, knowing the actual time that a bus will leave a bus stop can be difficult. In these places, the timetables provided by the bus companies are rarely followed, due to many reasons, including traffic jams, unanticipated maintenance, etc. Not knowing the actual bus departure time can increase wait time at the bus stop, leading to wasted time and, in more serious situations, can make passengers more susceptible to urban violence. Our case study is focused on the latter scenario, and on a particular community of users: students in a big university campus.

A large number of college students use public transportation every week day, to get from home to the university and back. These students share a common interest regarding the bus transportation schedule. By forming a community, they can take advantage of their collective mobility pattern, which can be exploited by a community-governed service. Whenever they leave the university in a bus, they can collect information about which bus line was used, and what time the bus departed from the university. When students get back to the university, all the information they have previously collected is available in their devices. Thus, in this scenario, students that are online at the campus at the same time are able to share their collected data following the model described in Sect. 2.2. This data collected and shared is then processed and analyzed to satisfy common demands of this community.

With that in mind, the users' common goal in our case study is to estimate the departure time of buses in a bus line at a university campus, using only past travel data collected by the university community that uses this means of transportation, and evaluate how our proposed community-governed service behaves compared to other scenarios, like a typical cloud-based service.

4 Materials and Methods

4.1 Data Source

We have used public transportation data from Curitiba, a city in the South of Brazil with a population of around 2 million inhabitants. A brief characterization of the data and how it was collected can be seen in the work by Braz [17]. He used bus schedule data, raw GPS and smart card records to reconstruct trips at the passenger-level from the original data provided by Curitiba's Public Transport Department. In the trace rebuilt by Braz, each registry represents a bus travel made by a user. From it, we can get the bus stop that the bus departed, the time of departure, and the bus line associated to the bus. An example of an event in the trace might be a user whose id is 123456, who left bus stop 151 at 8:00 a.m on May 12 using bus line 500^2.

From the city map, we have selected the bus stops that are in the vicinity of our target university campus, in our case the Universidade Técnica Federal do Paraná (UTFPR), and considered only the trips that left or arrived from these bus stops. These trips, representing a set of arrival and departure events, were then arranged in chronological order.

Some adaptations to the trace and assumptions had to be made, so that we could somehow established the periods of time when a user was at the campus. These are signaled by both arrival and departure events in the trace. For each day and each user in the trace, there may be zero or more of such events. When an arrival event is followed by a departure event at the same day, then we assume that the user stayed at the campus for the period comprised between the arrival time and the departure time. However, if only a departure event is present, without an earlier arrival event at the same day, then we arbitrated that the user had arrived one hour before the time of the departure event. Similarly, if an arrival event is present with no later departure event, then we arbitrate that the user stayed at the campus for one hour since its arrival.

Our adapted trace has information about $74,907$ trips leaving $(45,346)$ or arriving $(29,561)$ at bus stops near the university campus, between May 2017 and July 2017, from $18,662$ different users.

4.2   Simulation Model

Every departure from the campus that appears in the trace considered generates a request to the service. Let t_d be the time of a departure logged in the trace. We assume that at some time t_r, prior to t_d, the user wants to know the estimated time he/she should leave the campus, if he/she prefers to take a particular bus line b. In other words, before leaving the campus at t_r, the user asks the service: "at what time should I go to the bus stop to get the next line b bus leaving the campus, so that I wait as little as possible at the bus stop?" We arbitrate the time t_r when the request is issued to the service as a time that is draw from a time interval that starts at most one hour before the actual time of the departure t_d, following a uniform distribution. This interval can be smaller than one hour if the last arrival event of the same user, say t_a, happened less than one hour before the departure time:

$$t_r = U(max(t_a, t_d - 1h), t_d). \tag{1}$$

A request that is made at time t_r asking the estimated time (t_e) to go to the bus stop in the vicinity of the campus in order to get the next bus of line b is denoted by $R_{t_r}^b$.

---

^{2} There are more attributes in the original data, but we just cite the data we use in our model.

Since t_d is not known to the service, given a request $R_{t_r}^b$, we use a prediction algorithm that is fed with the past data available to estimate the most appropriate time for the user to go to the bus stop to take a bus from line b. The objective of the prediction algorithm is to minimize the wait time at the bus stop. Since the goal of this work is not to provide the best solution for this problem, but rather to understand how the amount of available information impact the performance of a particular solution, we have chosen a quite simple algorithm, which is in line with the small footprint required for the service, as discussed in Sect. 2.3. We consider an algorithm that simply recommends the smallest departure time contained in the past data available (for any previous day) between time t_r, when the request was issued, and the next hour. So, if a user makes a request at 8:05 a.m, the algorithm will get from available historical data all trips between 8:05 a.m and 9:05 a.m, and recommend the earliest departure time as the most appropriate one. (To simplify, we do not take into account the time that the user needs to walk to the bus stop.)

The amount of historical data available to the prediction algorithm depends on how users are assumed to behave. We consider different configurations for that. In particular, we consider cases where users do not share data, neither among themselves, nor with centralized servers, cases where data is made available to centralized servers at different points in time, and cases where data is exchanged among users that are in the campus at the same time. As discussed before, data stored in the user device, directly sensed by the user him/herself or received from other users, is kept for some time. Our trace has a three-month duration, but the individual data units are quite small, thus, in our simulations we considered that all data gathered in the devices were kept until the end of the simulation. We present below the data sharing configurations evaluated in this proof of concept study:

- **Baseline.** The baseline configuration is as naive as possible. It does not use any historical data to estimate the time to go to the bus stop; it simply suggests the request time (t_r) as such time.
- **Offline.** In this configuration, the model is built using only trips collected by the user making the request; it represents the situation in which users never share their data with other members of the community.
- **Cloud.** Here all the collected data is made available at the very time the data is collected, since in this case the data is sent to a central cloud; all data available in the server can be considered by the prediction algorithm used to answer users' requests.
- **Cloudlet.** In this configuration we consider the existence of a local server in the university campus that is accessible only when the user is at the campus; data is made available to this server whenever a user arrives at the campus (and not at the time the data was collected, as in the previous configuration).

– **Community.** In this case, a user u that is at the campus at time t will share its data with a user u', provided that u' is also at the campus at time t, u is willing to share data with u', and u' trusts u as a data provider; in this case, all data that u has collected until that point in time (directly or indirectly) will be made available to u'; all data available at a user's device can be considered by the prediction algorithm used to answer queries.

Clearly, the amount of data used when processing a particular request in the offline configuration, except from unusual corner cases, is less than that used in the community configuration, which is, in turn, less than the amount used in the cloudlet configuration, which is less than what is used in the cloud configuration. The focus is to evaluate how feasible is to use just the data available for the community configuration, and also to compare the accuracy of the estimations done using these different levels of information available. Moreover, we consider different trust settings for the community configuration, which leads to different amounts of data available for performing predictions, as we describe in the following.

4.3 Defining Trust Relationship

We first consider that all users trust each other, so if two members of the community are at the campus at the same time, then they can exchange their data. This allows us to evaluate the best performance that the community approach can deliver. Then, we consider the case that all users in the trace have the same number m of other community members willing to share data with them, and evaluate the performance of the algorithm as the value of m varies from 10 to 80 (we refer to these configurations as community-m, $m \in \{10, 20, 30, 40, 50, 60, 70, 80\}$). The m data providers of a user u are randomly chosen from all members of the community. Clearly, this assumption is not realistic, but it helps to understand how the performance of the algorithm degrades, as the amount of information available diminishes. Finally, we consider the trust relationship in real social networks to arbitrate which members of the community trust each other, and evaluate the performance of the community-governed service in a more realistic setting.

For the last case described above, we took the following approach. We considered 100 social networks extracted from Facebook that connect students enrolled in universities in the United States of America [24]. We grouped these social networks considering several features, and selected one representative of each group. Then, for each social network graph considered, we randomly chose one member of the graph and started a Breadth First Search (BFS) from that node, until the number of nodes traversed in the graph was equal to the number of users in our trace. At this point, we built a new social network graph that contained only the nodes that have been traversed, and the connections that these nodes had with other nodes in the new graph. Finally, we randomly mapped each user in the trace to a different node in the graph. Users that were connected in the graph, trusted each other.

We used k-means [9] to group the 100 social networks in k groups, and both the silhouette [20] and the Within-cluster Sum of Squares (WSS) [8] methods to define an appropriate value for k (see Fig. 2 and Fig. 3). Based on the results achieved, we have chosen $k = 7$.

After grouping the 100 social networks in 7 groups, we chose the network which was closest to the centroid of each group as the social network that represented the group (we refer to this configurations as community-real-i, $i \in \{1, 2, 3, 4, 5, 6, 7\}$).

4.4   Experimental Design

The different users in our trace have quite different profiles. In particular, most users have just one departure event, and no arrival events, i.e. they never come back to share with others their unique trip collected. Thus, they can only share this information when the cloud configuration is used. Also, the distribution of "return-trips" performed by different users is quite skewed, as can be seen in Fig. 4. A lot of users have only one or two of such trips, but there are users with as many as 30.

Because of the skewness in the data, in addition to the whole trace, we considered two subsets of the trace, based on the users associated with the trips present in the trace: i) one that filtered out users that had no "return-trips"; and, ii) one that considered only the most active users of the community. For the latter, we computed the 90-percentile of the total trips that each user collected over time. This led us to consider only users who made available at least 9 trips over time. The summary of traces considered is presented in Table 1.

Table 1. Summary of the traces considered.

Name	Description	Number of users
All	Considers all users of the original trace	18,662
Contributors	Considers only users who made at least one "return-trip"	8,918
Most actives	Considers only users who made at least 9 "return-trips"	845

We have executed three simulation experiments, which differ on the values that we used for two factors: the trace, and the data sharing configuration. Only the first experiment considers the three traces defined, since the results of this experiment show that this factor has minimal impact on the results. In this experiment, it is assumed that all users trust each other (i.e. there are no restrictions on data sharing among them). This represents the best possible case of the community configuration in terms of the amount of information that can be shared and aggregated. This was the only experiment reported in our previous work [14].

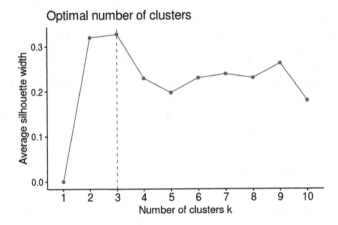

Fig. 2. Silhouette.

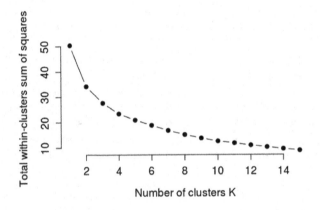

Fig. 3. WSS.

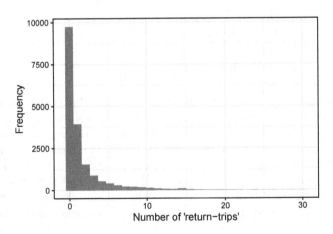

Fig. 4. Distribution of number of "return-trips".

In the other two experiments we have only used the trace with the most active users, since these are the users that would benefit most from the service. They consider the existence of social networks (synthetic or real), which limit the data sharing among users, as discussed in Sect. 4.3. The values considered for the factors in each experiment are summarized in Table 2.

Table 2. Summary of the experimental design.

Experiment	Trace	Data sharing configuration
I	All	Baseline
	Contributors	Offline
	Most actives	Cloudlet
		Cloud
		Community (all users trust each other)
II	Most actives	Community-m (every user trusts m other users)
III	Most actives	Community-real-i (trust based on friendship relations of 7 real social networks)

The community configurations in both Experiment II and Experiment III, have an stochastic behavior. In Experiment II, the m users that provide data to a particular user u are randomly drawn from the trace, while in Experiment III, the starting node for the BFS algorithm is randomly chosen from the social network, and after the new graph is generated, there is a random mapping of users in the trace to nodes in the new graph (see Sect. 4.3). Thus, for these settings, we replicated the execution of the experiments for a number of times that were enough to produce results with the required accuracy—50 for Experiment II, and 500 for Experiment III.

4.5   Evaluation Metrics

The focus of the evaluation of the proposed service model is on the quantity of data that users can aggregate and that will be used to make the predictions in each configuration. To do this, we have computed the amount of historical data used to answer each request, in addition to the proportion of requests that can be answered using some data from the past.

Despite the focus on data aggregation, we have also illustrated an example of a simple prediction algorithm (described in Sect. 4.2), in which greater data aggregation leads to the delivery of a better Quality of Service (QoS). To evaluate the QoS of the service, we have collected the wait time at the bus stop and the percentage of requests for which users could not catch a bus.

The relationship between the amount of data obtained and the quality of the predictions can vary depending on the niche of the application, the characteristics of the collected data and the prediction algorithm used. As already stated, our goal is not to find the best solution to the problem of estimating bus departure times, but to show that the proposed model is feasible, and to assess the trade-off between the amount of data that users share, and the amount of data that they can aggregate. The metrics introduced are further detailed below:

- **Proportion of Requests $R_{t_r}^b$ that Can Be Predicted using Past Data (PP).** As described earlier, the prediction algorithm uses data from past trips to infer when the next bus of line b will leave the bus stop. However, there are cases in which no data is available for the time interval associated with the request ($[t_r - 1h, t_r]$)—in this case, the baseline strategy is used, instead. This metric aims at measuring the proportion of requests whose predictions are done based on past data, and not on the baseline strategy.
- **Data Amount used to Perform Prediction (DA).** This metric indicates how many past trips were used to answer a given request. It is measured in number of trips.
- **Wait Time at the Bus Stop (WT).** This metric measures the amount of time that the user waits in the bus stop, until the next bus arrives. We note that this bus does not need to be the same whose departure (at t_a), registered in the trace, triggered the request in the first place. This is because the time the user gets to the bus stop (t_e, estimated by the prediction algorithm) can be both earlier than t_a—in which case the user might get another bus from the same line b that left the bus stop after t_e and before t_a —, or later than t_a—in which case it is not even guaranteed that there will be a bus from line b departing at a time later than t_a. To avoid having the user waiting indefinitely, we assume that if the bus does not arrive in as much as one hour after t_e, then the user gives up waiting, and we register the wait time as 1 h.
- **Missing Rate (MR).** This metric indicates the percentage of requests for which users could not catch a bus. In other words, the percentage of requests $R_{t_r}^b$, such that there is no bus of line b departing at a time t_d, $t_e \leq t_d \leq t_e + 1h$.

The PP and the MR metrics are computed only for Experiment I, and reported as the computed value for the single simulation run executed for each scenario. The other two metrics are computed in all three experiments. The DA metric is reported as the mean value for all the requests processed in the single run simulations. For the replicated experiments, we compute the mean value of each execution, and report the mean of these means, together with its associated 95% confidence interval. The WT metric is reported similarly, but using the median, instead of the mean. We use the median as the statistic to assess WT because its distribution is not symmetric, and the mean may be affected by extreme values.

5   Results and Discussion

5.1   Best Case Analysis: No Restrictions on Data Sharing

Table 3 shows results for DA, PP, MR and WT for each configuration. In general, the community configuration is able to aggregate as much data as in the cloudlet

Table 3. Summary of all metrics [14].

Trace	Configuration	DA	PP	MR	WT
All	Baseline	0.0	0.0%	0.008%	5.48 min
	Offline	1.3	39.8%	0.366%	5.13 min
	Community	51.9	92.6%	0.602%	3.65 min
	Cloudlet	53.7	96.0%	0.965%	3.35 min
	Cloud	57.1	97.7%	0.882%	3.30 min
Contributors	Baseline	0.0	0.0%	0.005%	5.40 min
	Offline	1.6	50.7%	0.460%	4.81 min
	Community	54.0	94.5%	0.547%	3.33 min
	Cloudlet	55.6	96.7%	0.744%	3.21 min
	Cloud	57.1	97.7%	0.747%	3.33 min
Most actives	Baseline	0.0	0.0%	0.008%	5.36 min
	Offline	3.6	75.8%	0.239%	4.46 min
	Community	53.4	96.0%	0.168%	3.16 min
	Cloudlet	53.9	96.5%	0.186%	3.16 min
	Cloud	54.4	97.0%	0.195%	3.13 min

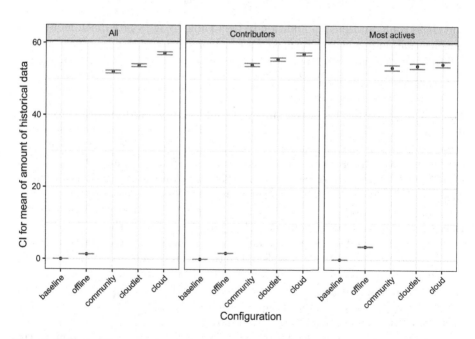

Fig. 5. 95% confidence intervals for mean of amount of historical data used in each scenario.

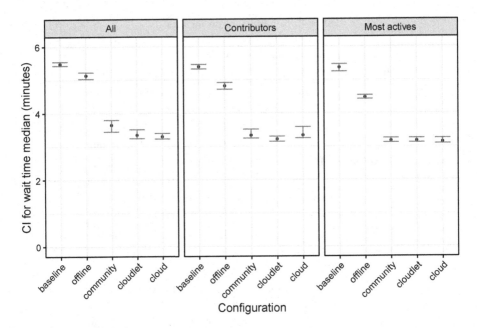

Fig. 6. 95% confidence intervals for the wait time median in each scenario.

and cloud configurations, in addition to being able to aggregate much more data than a situation in which there is no data exchange between community members (offline configuration). Moreover, in general, the more data is available, the better the prediction algorithm performs.

Data Aggregation. From the amount of information used in each of the predictions (accumulated locally on the user's device or aggregated in a centralized server, depending on the simulated configuration), we have calculated the 95% confidence interval for mean. As we can see in Fig. 5, the community configuration showed results very close to the cloudlet and cloud configurations, in which there is a central server that aggregates the data. On average, these configurations use between 52 and 57 historical data to generate the prediction model that serves the requests, considering all traces. Considering the "Most actives" trace, the difference from the community configuration to the other two is even smaller, and the confidence intervals of the three configurations overlap. In addition, in the community configuration it is possible to aggregate much more data than in the offline configuration, where there is no data sharing among users. In the "Most actives" trace, for example, on average, only 3 data items from the past are used to generate the prediction model.

The only configuration that is substantially affected by the different traces used is the offline one, specifically in the PP metric. This is expected, since the average amount of information that each user has is the main difference between the three traces. When the offline configuration and the "All" trace are used, only 40% of requests are answered based on the past data collected by the user

(PP). The other 60% of requests resort to the baseline strategy due to lack of data. This is because in this trace, half of users make only one request, and there is no past data collected by them. The value of PP increases to 75.8% when the offline configuration is used with the "Most actives" trace. Since in this trace all users traveled and collected data at least 9 times, as previously mentioned, when users make a service request, there is a high probability that they have already collected some information in the past that is stored on their smartphone locally and that can be used by the prediction model.

Still considering the PP metric, we also note that the difference between the community configuration and the cloud configuration, which is the best possible configuration regarding the amount of data available, is no more than 5% on the "All" trace. In the "Most actives" trace, this difference is even lower (1%).

Quality of Predictions. As discussed before, each request has a wait time (WT) associated and we have calculated the median for each scenario. Figure 6 shows the confidence intervals of the median in each scenario, with a confidence level of 95%. As we can see, in scenarios where more data is available, the wait time is shorter overall. The biggest evolution occurs when we move from the offline configuration to the community configuration. In cloudlet and cloud configurations there is a decrease in wait times, but it is not substantial. The Wilcoxon-rank-sum test confirms that, on average, there is only significant statistical differences between the configurations whose confidence intervals do not overlap. Considering the "All" trace, the wait times measured for the community configuration is less than the offline configuration and greater than the wait times of the cloudlet and cloud configurations. For the other two traces, there is no statistical difference between the wait times of the community configuration and the cloudlet and cloud ones. These results indicate that the community

Table 4. Comparison of wait times between baseline and the other configurations [14].

Trace	Configuration	Better	Worse	Equals
All	Offline	23.4%	16.4%	60.2%
	Community	77.7%	13.7%	8.6%
	Cloudlet	81.0%	13.8%	5.2%
	Cloud	83.8%	12.6%	3.6%
Contributors	Offline	29.9%	20.8%	49.3%
	Community	79.8%	13.6%	6.6%
	Cloudlet	82.1%	13.3%	4.6%
	Cloud	83.2%	13.2%	3.6%
Most actives	Offline	46.0%	29.8%	24.2%
	Community	82.0%	12.8%	5.2%
	Cloudlet	82.5%	12.8%	4.7%
	Cloud	82.9%	12.9%	4.2%

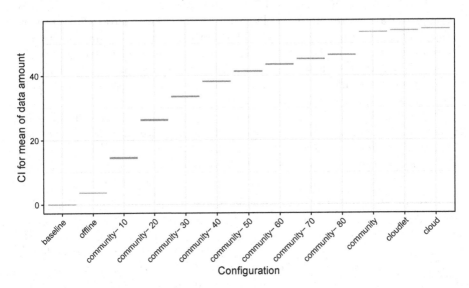

Fig. 7. 95% confidence interval for the mean of the data amount (DA) per configuration. (Color figure online)

network that is formed by the online users is, in general, as good as the case in which there is a central server to aggregate all the collected data.

Also, the missing rate for all scenarios simulated is very small, peaking at 0.96%, and smaller than 0.24% for all scenarios that considered the "Most actives" trace (see Table 3).

We also measured the difference between the baseline and all the other configurations. To measure this difference we pair the same requests in each configuration. Table 4 shows the proportion of requests in which the wait time was better (i.e. shorter), worse (i.e. greater) and equal to the baseline configuration.

In configurations with more data available for prediction, the proportion of requests in which the result was better than the baseline increases. Again, the main difference between traces is in the offline configuration. As said before, the baseline strategy is used in 60% of the requests of the offline configuration for the "All" trace. This means that for these cases, the offline configuration results are the same as the baseline. In only 23% of cases we see better results for the offline configuration. In the "Most actives" trace, this proportion increases to 46%. The community configuration had shorter wait times for more than 77% of the requests. Cloudlet and cloud configurations are better than the baseline in more than 80% of the cases.

In Experiment I, we did not take privacy issues into account, and considered that all users trust each other. In the next two experiments, we assess how the performance of the community-governed service is impacted by trust relationships among users.

5.2 Analysis of Data Sharing Using Synthetic Social Network Restrictions

In this experiment we consider the scenario where each user in the trace can receive information from exactly m other users. Figure 7 and Fig. 8 show, respectively, the 95% confidence interval for the mean of DA and the median for WT, for all configurations simulated in Experiment I (red), plus a number of configurations for community-m, simulated in Experiment II (blue).

As expected, as m increases, so does the mean amount of information used per prediction. As a result, the median of WT decreases as m increases. Moreover, for m as low as 20, the data amount used to make the predictions is already, on average, much better than that obtained in the offline configuration (26.2×3.6).

The analysis applies to the WT metric. The WT achieved is much better than that attained when the offline configuration is used—while the community-20 configuration increases WT by 24.3% when compared to the cloud configuration, for the offline configuration the increase on WT is of 42.5% (see Table 5). Allowing the user to receive information from other 80 users (community-80), the result is already very close to the community configuration, where all users trust each other, both for the data amount and the wait time at the bus stop.

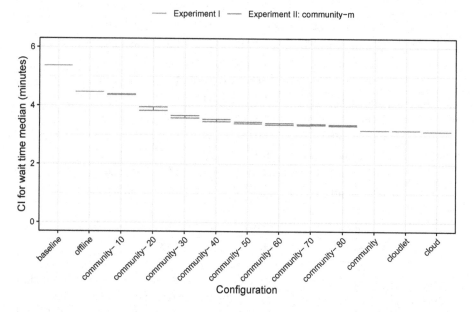

Fig. 8. 95% confidence interval for the median of the wait time (WT) per configuration. (Color figure online)

5.3   Analysis of Data Sharing Using Real Social Network Restrictions

We now consider the more realistic scenario where real trust relationships are used to inform the simulation model about which data can be shared (see Sect. 4.4). For comparison reasons, we use some results from Experiment I and Experiment II. Table 5 shows results for a single experiment execution (Baseline, Offline, Community, Cloudlet and Cloud), results for replicated experiment executions (community-m and community-real-i), and a result that aggregates all the replicated simulations involving real networks (community-real-all). The columns DA and WT represent, respectively, the mean of the amount of data available and the median of the wait time for the cases where a single experiment is executed, and the mean of the means, and mean of the medians for the cases where replicated experiments are executed. For the latter the table also shows the 95% confidence intervals (columns $DA(C.I.)$ and $WT(C.I.)$).

Table 5. Summary of metrics DA and WT (in minutes).

Configuration	DA	DA (C.I.)	WT	WT (C.I.)
Baseline	0.0	–	5.36	–
Offline	3.6	–	4.46	–
Community-20	26.2	[26.0, 26.3]	3.89	[3.83, 3.95]
Community-real-1	27.9	[27.4, 28.4]	3.91	[3.88, 3.93]
Community-real-2	30.4	[30.2, 30.6]	3.80	[3.78, 3.81]
Community-real-3	33.6	[33.1, 34.0]	3.71	[3.69, 3.73]
Community-real-4	34.3	[34.1, 34.5]	3.67	[3.66, 3.69]
Community-real-5	35.3	[35.2, 35.3]	3.63	[3.62, 3.65]
Community-real-6	38.0	[37.7, 38.3]	3.54	[3.52, 3.55]
Community-real-7	38.4	[38.3, 38.6]	3.53	[3.51, 3.54]
Community-real-all	34.0	[33.8, 34.1]	3.68	[3.67, 3.69]
Community-40	38.1	[38.0, 38.2]	3.50	[3.46, 3.53]
Community	53.4	–	3.16	–
Cloudlet	53.9	–	3.16	–
Cloud	54.4	–	3.13	–

From the simulation results we can conclude that the trust relationship existent in the real social networks makes the system perform at a level that is between the configurations community-20 and community-40. As mentioned before, results for the configuration community-20 are already much better than the offline configuration, both for the aggregated amount of data and for the quality of predictions made. On the other hand, when compared to the performance of the cloudlet and cloud configurations, the average WT of the community-governed service (community-real-all) is, respectively, 16.5% and 17.6% larger.

In our study, this is the average price that needs to be paid to limit data exposure. We note that if privacy is not a concern, then the community-governed service is able to aggregate more data and provide a service that performs as well as the cloudlet and cloud configurations, but without the external governance limitations that come with the need for a centralized provider.

6 Related Work

Community-governed services take advantage of mobile phone sensor capabilities to collect data from the environment and use it for some purpose in the future. This feature is known as participatory sensing, and its seminal idea is well described by Burke et al. [5]. Mobile crowd sensing is an extension of participatory sensing, which in addition to using data collected from users' devices, also uses data made available by other users from MSN services [7].

A wide variety of applications can be built by taking advantage of the features described above [6,13,18,19,26]. All of these applications provide a service for the good of a community of users who share a common goal, which is another important pillar of our idea. However, in currently available applications, all data gathered by users and used to provide the service for the community of users is sent to a remote cloud infrastructure to be processed. Our solution aims at giving the complete power to the users who collect, process and, most importantly, govern their data and applications without the need for relying on a single service provider entity, typically hosting the service in a cloud provider.

The works by Bonomi et al. [4] and Shi et al. [23] address a new paradigm named Edge Computing. It extends the cloud paradigm by considering resources that reside between end users and the central cloud, and that provide compute and network services close to users. VM-based cloudlets [22], smart gateways [1] and servers installed in shopping centers and bus stations [12] are some examples of technologies, cited in the literature, deployed closer to data sources to perform computational tasks. Our proposed service uses a completely distributed version of the edge computing paradigm, in which processing is done on the devices themselves, which also act as data sources, with no centralized component.

Community-governed services assume users can meet and share data with whom they trust, thus forming an MSN [16], coupled with a P2P architecture that allows users' devices to be both data consumers (clients) and data providers (servers) [25].

The idea proposed by Bellavista et al. [2] combines some of the characteristics mentioned above, like crowd sensing and edge computing paradigm, but it focuses on forming an *ad hoc* network with the devices of users of a community in an opportunistic way. The application monitors regions and detects points whose concentration of people is sufficient to form a network. However, it does not investigate the feasibility of building the type of services that we propose in this work.

Kuendig et al. [10] suggest a community-driven architecture that gets together devices within a zone of local proximity to form a collaborative edge computing environment in a dynamic mesh topology. Our proposal, in addition to using community users' devices to process tasks, also addresses the collection and sharing of data among these users, who have some common goal to be achieved.

In order to check the feasibility and efficacy of the community-governed services on the edge, we carried out a simulation-based case study fed with real data. This application aims at estimating the actual departure times of urban buses using past data collected by users. A similar application can be seen in the work by Zhou et al. [26], where users of a community have a common goal of anticipating the bus arrival time. For this purpose they use their mobiles phones to collect information while on the move, and thus help in performing predictions. In addition to past information, they also use real-time information. However, the application defined in that work uses a remote cloud as the back-end, while our proposal is based purely upon edge computing principles.

7 Conclusions

In this work, we have proposed an architecture in which individuals can define the governance of a service they are interested by using principles of Participatory sensing, Mobile Social Networks and Edge Computing. The idea is that members of the community will use resources at the edge of the network, i.e. the sensing and processing capabilities of their mobile devices, to gather data, share it with other members and then process it without having to send it to a remote cloud. This obviates the need for external governance, i.e. a cloud application provider that manages the life of the application and the data used. In this way, the proposed architecture provides more control to users over who has direct access to the data collected.

To evaluate the feasibility of the proposed model, we elaborated a case study in which university students want to know the departure time of the first bus of a particular bus line in the vicinity of the campus. We performed simulations, fed with real data from the Curitiba city public transportation system, to compare the community-governed service approach to other data sharing approaches, such as the state-of-the-practice approach where a server hosted on a cloud provider aggregates all data. The results show that it is possible to aggregate enough data from the community members to make good predictions. Moreover, the amount of data aggregated is far more than what a single user could collect. When privacy is not a concern, the aggregated amount of data is close to the approaches where a central server is needed, without facing the risks associated with the need for external governance. When users limit the exposure of their data, sharing only with whom they trust, the aggregated amount of data and the quality of predictions are impacted, but yet proving reasonable results. Thus, the model allows for a more flexible way to establish a trade-off between increased performance, and reduced data exposure.

References

1. Aazam, M., Huh, E.: Fog computing and smart gateway based communication for cloud of things. In: 2014 International Conference on Future Internet of Things and Cloud, pp. 464–470, August 2014. https://doi.org/10.1109/FiCloud.2014.83
2. Bellavista, P., Chessa, S., Foschini, L., Gioia, L., Girolami, M.: Human-enabled edge computing: exploiting the crowd as a dynamic extension of mobile edge computing. IEEE Commun. Mag. **56**(1), 145–155 (2018). https://doi.org/10.1109/MCOM.2017.1700385
3. Bonawitz, K., et al.: Towards federated learning at scale: system design. CoRR abs/1902.01046 (2019). http://arxiv.org/abs/1902.01046
4. Bonomi, F., Milito, R., Zhu, J., Addepalli, S.: Fog computing and its role in the Internet of Things. In: Proceedings of the First Edition of the MCC Workshop on Mobile Cloud Computing, MCC 2012, pp. 13–16. ACM, New York (2012). https://doi.org/10.1145/2342509.2342513, https://doi.org/10.1145/2342509.2342513
5. Burke, J., et al.: Participatory sensing. In: Workshop on World-Sensor-Web (WSW 2006): Mobile Device Centric Sensor Networks and Applications, pp. 117–134 (2006)
6. Ganti, R.K., Pham, N., Ahmadi, H., Nangia, S., Abdelzaher, T.F.: GreenGPS: a participatory sensing fuel-efficient maps application. In: Proceedings of the 8th International Conference on Mobile Systems, Applications, and Services, MobiSys 2010, pp. 151–164. ACM, New York (2010). https://doi.org/10.1145/1814433.1814450, https://doi.org/10.1145/1814433.1814450
7. Guo, B., Yu, Z., Zhou, X., Zhang, D.: From participatory sensing to mobile crowd sensing. In: 2014 IEEE International Conference on Pervasive Computing and Communication Workshops (PERCOM WORKSHOPS), pp. 593–598, March 2014. https://doi.org/10.1109/PerComW.2014.6815273
8. Hartigan, J.A., Wong, M.A.: Algorithm as 136: a k-means clustering algorithm. J. Roy. Stat. Soc. Ser. C (Appl. Stat.) **28**(1), 100–108 (1979). http://www.jstor.org/stable/2346830
9. Hartigan, J.A.: Clustering Algorithms, 99th edn. Wiley, New York (1975)
10. Kuendig, S.J., Rolim, J., Angelopoulos, K.M., Hosseini, M.: Crowdsourced edge: a novel networking paradigm for the collaborative community. Technical report (2019). https://archive-ouverte.unige.ch/unige:114607. ID: unige:114607; Paper submitted for publication at the Global IoT Summit 2019
11. Lohmar, T., Zaidi, A., Olofsson, H., Boberg, C.: Driving transformation in the automotive and road transport ecosystem with 5G. Ericsson Technology Review (2019)
12. Luan, T.H., Gao, L., Li, Z., Xiang, Y., Sun, L.: Fog computing: focusing on mobile users at the edge. CoRR abs/1502.01815 (2015), http://arxiv.org/abs/1502.01815
13. Ludwig, T., Reuter, C., Siebigteroth, T., Pipek, V.: CrowdMonitor: mobile crowd sensing for assessing physical and digital activities of citizens during emergencies. In: Proceedings of the 33rd Annual ACM Conference on Human Factors in Computing Systems, CHI 2015, pp. 4083–4092. ACM, New York (2015). https://doi.org/10.1145/2702123.2702265, https://doi.org/10.1145/2702123.2702265
14. Mafra, J., Brasileiro, F.V., Lopes, R.V.: Community-governed services on the edge. In: Ferguson, D., Helfert, M., Pahl, C. (eds.) Proceedings of the 10th International Conference on Cloud Computing and Services Science, CLOSER 2020, Prague, Czech Republic, 7–9 May 2020, pp. 498–505. SCITEPRESS (2020). https://doi.org/10.5220/0009765804980505

15. Mao, Y., You, C., Zhang, J., Huang, K., Letaief, K.B.: A survey on mobile edge computing: the communication perspective. IEEE Commun. Surv. Tutorials **19**(4), 2322–2358 (2017). https://doi.org/10.1109/COMST.2017.2745201. Fourthquarter

16. Miluzzo, E., et al.: Sensing meets mobile social networks: the design, implementation and evaluation of the CenceMe application. In: Proceedings of the 6th ACM Conference on Embedded Network Sensor Systems, SenSys 2008, pp. 337–350. ACM, New York (2008). https://doi.org/10.1145/1460412.1460445, https://doi.org/10.1145/1460412.1460445

17. de Oliveira Filho, T.B.: Inferring passenger-level bus trip traces from schedule, positioning and ticketing data: methods and applications. Master dissertation, Universidade Federal de Campina Grande, Paraíba, Brasil (2019)

18. Predić, B., Yan, Z., Eberle, J., Stojanovic, D., Aberer, K.: ExposureSense: integrating daily activities with air quality using mobile participatory sensing. In: 2013 IEEE International Conference on Pervasive Computing and Communications Workshops (PERCOM Workshops), pp. 303–305, March 2013. https://doi.org/10.1109/PerComW.2013.6529500

19. Reddy, S., Shilton, K., Denisov, G., Cenizal, C., Estrin, D., Srivastava, M.: Biketastic: sensing and mapping for better biking. In: Proceedings of the SIGCHI Conference on Human Factors in Computing Systems, CHI 2010, pp. 1817–1820. ACM, New York (2010). https://doi.org/10.1145/1753326.1753598, https://doi.org/10.1145/1753326.1753598

20. Rousseeuw, P.J.: Silhouettes: a graphical aid to the interpretation and validation of cluster analysis. J. Comput. Appl. Math. **20**, 53–65 (1987). https://doi.org/10.1016/0377-0427(87)90125-7, http://www.sciencedirect.com/science/article/pii/0377042787901257

21. Ruge, L., Altakrouri, B., Schrader, A.: SoundOfTheCity - continuous noise monitoring for a healthy city. In: 2013 IEEE International Conference on Pervasive Computing and Communications Workshops (PERCOM Workshops), pp. 670–675, March 2013. https://doi.org/10.1109/PerComW.2013.6529577

22. Satyanarayanan, M., Bahl, V., Caceres, R., Davies, N.: The case for VM-based cloudlets in mobile computing. IEEE Pervasive Comput. **8**, 14–23 (2009)

23. Shi, W., Cao, J., Zhang, Q., Li, Y., Xu, L.: Edge computing: vision and challenges. IEEE Internet Things J. **3**(5), 637–646 (2016). https://doi.org/10.1109/JIOT.2016.2579198

24. Traud, A.L., Mucha, P.J., Porter, M.A.: Social structure of Facebook networks. Phys. A **391**(16), 4165–4180 (2012)

25. Tsai, F.S., Han, W., Xu, J., Chua, H.C.: Design and development of a mobile peer-to-peer social networking application. Expert Syst. Appl. **36**(8), 11077–11087 (2009). https://doi.org/10.1016/j.eswa.2009.02.093, http://www.sciencedirect.com/science/article/pii/S0957417409002498

26. Zhou, P., Zheng, Y., Li, M.: How long to wait? Predicting bus arrival time with mobile phone based participatory sensing. IEEE Trans. Mob. Comput. **13**(6), 1228–1241 (2014). https://doi.org/10.1109/TMC.2013.136

Cluster-Agnostic Orchestration
of Containerised Applications

Domenico Calcaterra$^{(\boxtimes)}$, Giuseppe Di Modica, Pietro Mazzaglia,
and Orazio Tomarchio

Department of Electrical, Electronic and Computer Engineering,
University of Catania, V.le A. Doria 6, 95125 Catania, Italy
{domenico.calcaterra,giuseppe.dimodica,orazio.tomarchio}@unict.it

Abstract. The complexity of managing cloud applications' life-cycle
increases with the widening of the cloud landscape, as new IT players
gain market share. Cloud orchestration frameworks promise to handle
such complexity offering user-friendly management tools that help customers to transparently deal with portability and interoperability issues,
by hiding away the heterogeneity of the cloud providers' proprietary
interfaces. Regarding the provisioning of cloud-enabled applications, the
containerisation paradigm, along with the related micro-services technology, has managed to deliver the portability promise. While most of cloud
orchestration frameworks support container-based cluster technologies,
a standard-based approach to describe containerised applications still
lacks. In this work, we propose TORCH, a TOSCA-based cloud orchestrator capable of interfacing to theoretically any container run-time
software by leveraging a standard-aligned and easy-to-use language to
describe application requirements. Validation tests run on a small-scale
test-bed prove the viability of the proposed solution.

Keywords: Containerised applications · Deployment orchestration ·
Cloud provisioning · TOSCA · BPMN

1 Introduction

Nowadays, due to several benefits in terms of availability, scalability and costs,
more and more applications are deployed in a cloud environment. However, the
deployment and management of complex applications, which are built out of
many components with different technical dependencies and constraints and
make use of different platform components, has become a complicated and error-
prone task [11]. Several tools help to simplify this task but, in a scenario moving
towards multi-cloud environments, the lack of interoperability between different tools and platforms is a major limitation [31]. Thus, the need to describe
the topology and life-cycle management tasks of cloud applications at a higher
abstraction level , by using standardised formats, becomes a fundamental capability of a modern cloud orchestration tool [36]. In this context, the OASIS

© Springer Nature Switzerland AG 2021
D. Ferguson et al. (Eds.): CLOSER 2020, CCIS 1399, pp. 301–324, 2021.
https://doi.org/10.1007/978-3-030-72369-9_13

consortium has proposed TOSCA (Topology and Orchestration Specification for Cloud Applications) [25], a specification that aims to standardise the definition of application topologies for cloud orchestration. As such, it enables customers to define the topology of their cloud applications in a reusable manner and deploy them on TOSCA compliant clouds [4].

In this scenario, over the course of the past few years, several cloud platforms have shifted from managing VMs to managing more fine-grained units of work, from containers and services, through microservices and even "functions" (FaaS paradigm) [10,33]. Containers, in particular, can be either run as standalone services or organised in swarm services. Swarm services increase the flexibility of containers, allowing them to run on clusters of resources. This approach combines well with the Cloud Computing paradigm, providing faster management operations while granting all the advantages of cloud services.

Therefore, modern orchestrators should also take into account these new types of resources and services while providing their management tasks [35]. Our work just addresses this scenario: in this paper , we extend the work presented in [13] where we proposed TORCH, a framework for the deployment and orchestration of containerised applications. TORCH provides several desirable features, such as the possibility to describe the application using standard languages, a fault-aware orchestration system built on business-process models, compatibility with the main cloud providers, and integration with different container-based cluster technologies. In this work, we provide further details about the prototype implementation and some performance results obtained from running the framework prototype on a small-scale test-bed.

The remainder of the paper is structured as follows. In Sect. 2, we provide a brief background about container technologies, along with related works concerning container orchestration. In Sect. 3, the TOSCA specification is briefly presented. In Sect. 4, we analyse cluster orchestrators from the interoperability point of view, while in Sect. 5 we present our approach to describe containerised applications in order to operate on top of multiple cluster platforms. In Sect. 6, the design and a prototype implementation of TORCH are presented. Section 7 shows preliminary results of some experiments run on a small-scale testbed. Finally, Sect. 8 concludes the work.

2   Related Work

In this section, first, we provide a more in-depth background on containers and, then, we present a few business-oriented and research projects exploiting the TOSCA standard for container orchestration.

In the container landscape, Docker [16] represents the leading technology for container runtimes [34]. It provides a set of technologies for building and running containerised applications. Furthermore, Docker Hub[1] offers a catalogue of ready-to-deploy Docker images, which allows users to share their work. Among

---

[1] https://hub.docker.com/.

competitors, containerd [14], CRI-O [15], and Containerizer [3] are worth mentioning.

Recently, container-based cluster solutions have gained increasing popularity for deploying containers. Some of these solutions further support the orchestration of containers, providing greater scalability, improved reliability, and a sophisticated management interface. Kubernetes [20] currently represents the most widespread ecosystem to manage containerised workloads , which facilitates both declarative configuration and automation of container clusters. Docker Swarm [17] offers a native solution for cluster management to be integrated into Docker. Mesos [2] is an open-source project to manage computer clusters backed by the Apache Software Foundation. It natively supports Docker containers and may be used in conjunction with Marathon [23], a platform for container orchestration.

Some of the most renowned cloud providers, such as Amazon AWS, Microsoft Azure, and Google Cloud have built-in services to operate containers and clusters. In most cases, these built-in services are just ad-hoc implementations of the former cluster technologies. OpenStack [28] represents an open-source alternative to control large pools of resources. In order to support container orchestration, it uses the *Heat* [29] and *Magnum* [30] components. The first is a service to orchestrate composite cloud applications, while the second allows clustered container platforms (i.e., Kubernetes, Mesos, Swarm) to interoperate with other OpenStack components, through differentiated APIs.

The wide choice of technologies and providers gives developers many options in terms of flexibility, reliability, and costs. However, all these services are neither interchangeable nor interoperable. Switching from a service (or a platform) to another requires several manual operations to be performed, and the learning curve might be non-trivial. These shortcomings have led to the development of systems to automate deployment and management operations, able to manage the interface with multiple container technologies, clusters and cloud providers.

Cloudify [19] delivers container orchestration integrating multiple technologies and providers. While it offers graphical tools for sketching and modelling an application, its data format is based on the TOSCA standard. Alien4Cloud [18] is an open-source platform providing a TOSCA nearly-normative set of types for Docker support, where Kubernetes and Mesos orchestrators are available through additional plugins. Both Cloudify and Alien4Cloud achieve interoperability between different clusters and providers by defining complex sets of TOSCA non-normative nodes, which are specific to the technologies used. Their TOSCA implementations reckon on Domain-Specific Languages that, despite sharing the TOSCA template structure, diverge from the node type hierarchy defined in the standard. With respect to them, TORCH focuses on TOSCA-compliant application descriptions, making no prior assumptions regarding the technology stack to be established.

Apache ARIA TOSCA [1] is an open-source framework offering an implementation of the TOSCA Simple Profile v1.0 specification. Unlike Cloudify and Alien4Cloud, it provides an extension of TOSCA normative types for Docker.

Compared to TORCH, the derived node types lack the possibility to use role-specific containers and no cluster orchestrator is natively supported.

In [22] the authors present MiCADO, an orchestration framework that guarantees out-of-the-box reliable orchestration by working closely with Swarm and Kubernetes. Unlike the precedent approaches, MiCADO does not overturn the TOSCA standard nodes. However, the cluster container platform is still hard-coded in the *Interface* section of each node of the topology.

TosKer [9] presents an approach that leverages the TOSCA standard for the deployment of Docker-based applications. TosKer approach is very different from the one proposed in this paper: it does not provide any automatic provisioning of the deployment plan and it is based on the redefinition of several nodes of the TOSCA standard. Clustered scenarios are also out of the picture, even though some recent work [6] has been done to deploy applications on top of existing Docker-based container orchestrators.

In [21], the authors propose a two-phase deployment method based on the TOSCA standard. They provide a good integration with Mesos and Marathon, but they do not either support other containerised clusters or furnish automation for the deployment of the cluster.

Other approaches worth mentioning are OpenTOSCA [5], Indigo-DataClouds [11,32], and SeaClouds [7,8]. OpenTOSCA is a famous open-source runtime environment for deploying and managing TOSCA applications. Despite supporting the orchestration of Docker containers, it was designed to work with a former, XML-based version of TOSCA [25]. Although authors have provided a converter[2] to work with TOSCA Simple Profile, only a few YAML elements are supported thereby limiting the description of application components.

INDIGO-DataCloud is an open-source data and computing platform for the automatic distribution of applications and/or services over a hybrid and heterogeneous set of IaaS infrastructures. It adopts an extension of TOSCA for describing applications and services, and leverages Docker containers as the preferred underlying technology to encapsulate user applications. INDIGO-DataCloud also provides a good integration with Mesos and Marathon/Chronos, but no support for other containerised clusters is provided.

SeaClouds is an open-source middleware solution for deploying and managing multi-component applications on heterogeneous clouds. While SeaClouds fully supports TOSCA, it lacks support for Docker containers making it not suitable for orchestrating multi-component applications including Docker containers.

In summary, all the current works achieve container cluster interoperability, or partial interoperability, by either associating platform-specific information to the nodes of the topology template or by redefining the TOSCA standard nodes. In order to work with such frameworks, it is necessary to know in advance both the technological stack and the framework-specific nodes to use.

The work we propose differentiates from all existing works in its goals, which are: enabling high interoperability between different technologies and providers; providing a standard-compliant approach, with no overturning of the standard-

---

[2] https://github.com/CloudCycle2/YAML_Transformer.

defined types and no prior assumptions about the technology stack to be established; and adopting the principle of separation of concerns between the topology of the application and its orchestration.

3   The TOSCA Specification

Research community has focused on approaches using standardised languages to specify the topology and management plans for cloud applications. In this regard, TOSCA represents a notable contribution to the development of cloud standards, since it allows to describe multi-tier applications and their life-cycle management in a modular and portable fashion [4].

TOSCA is a standard designed by OASIS to enable the portability of cloud applications and the related IT services [25]. This specification permits to describe the structure of a cloud application as a *service template*, which is composed of a topology template and the types needed to build such a template.

The topology template is a typed directed graph, whose nodes (called *node templates*) model the application components, and edges (called *relationship templates*) model the relations occurring among such components. Each node of a topology can also contain some information such as the corresponding component's *requirements*, the operations to manage it (*interfaces*), the *attributes* and the *properties* it features, the *capabilities* it provides, the software *artifacts* it uses, and the *policies* applied to it. Inter-node dependencies associate the requirements of a node with the capabilities featured by other nodes.

TOSCA supports the deployment and management of applications in two different flavours: *imperative processing* and *declarative processing*. The imperative processing requires that all needed management logic is contained in the Cloud Service ARchive (CSAR). Management plans are typically implemented using workflow languages, such as BPMN [27] or BPEL [24] . The declarative processing shifts management logic from plans to runtime. TOSCA runtime engines automatically infer the corresponding logic by interpreting the application topology template. This requires a precise definition of the semantics of nodes and relations based on well-defined *Node Types* and *Relationship Types*. The set of provided management functionalities depends on the corresponding runtime and is not standardised by the TOSCA specification.

TOSCA Simple Profile is an isomorphic rendering of a subset of the TOSCA specification in the YAML language [26]. It defines a few normative workflows that are used to operate a topology and specifies how they are declaratively generated: deploy, undeploy, scaling-workflows and auto-healing workflows. Imperative workflows can still be used for complex use-cases that cannot be solved in declarative workflows. However, they provide less reusability as they are defined for a specific topology rather than being dynamically generated based on the topology content.

```
tosca_definitions_version: tosca_simple_yaml_1_0

description: Template for deploying MySQL and database content.

topology_template:
  inputs:
    # omitted here for brevity

  node_templates:
    my_db:
      type: tosca.nodes.Database.MySQL
      properties:
        # omitted here for brevity
      artifacts:
        db_content:
          file: files/my_db_content.txt
          type: tosca.artifacts.File
      requirements:
        - host: mysql
      interfaces:
        Standard:
          create:
            implementation: db_create.sh
            inputs:
              db_data: { get_artifact: [ SELF, db_content ] }

    mysql:
      type: tosca.nodes.DBMS.MySQL
      properties:
        # omitted here for brevity
      requirements:
        - host: db_server

    db_server:
      type: tosca.nodes.Compute
      capabilities:
        # omitted here for brevity
```

Listing 1.1. TOSCA sample template - YAML.

By way of illustration, Listing 1.1 shows a sample template to deploy a MySQL DBMS on a server and create a custom database content on top of it. The *mysql* node template (of type *tosca.nodes.DBMS.MySQL*) is related to the *db_server* node template (of type *tosca.nodes.Compute*) via the requirements section to indicate which compute resource (of type *tosca.nodes.Compute*) MySQL is to be hosted on. Specifically, the *host* requirement is fulfilled by referencing the *db_server* node template. The *my_db* node template (of type *tosca.nodes.Database.MySQL*) represents an actual MySQL database instance managed by a MySQL DBMS installation. The requirements section of the *my_db* node template stresses that the database is to be hosted on a MySQL DBMS node template named *mysql*. In the artifacts section of the *my_db* node template, there is an artifact definition named *db_content*, representing a text file that will be used to add content to the database as part of the *create* life-cycle operation. The logical diagram for this sample template is depicted in Fig. 1.

The work described in this paper grounds on the TOSCA standard and, specifically, on TOSCA Simple Profile which provides convenient definitions for container nodes. The *tosca.nodes.Container.Runtime* type represents the virtualised environment where containers run. The *tosca.nodes.Container.Application* type represents an application that uses container-level virtualisation.

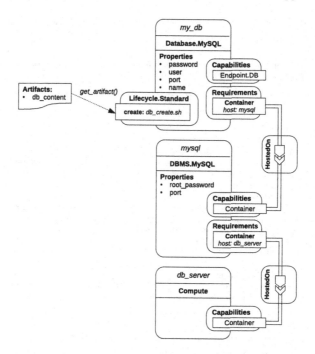

Fig. 1. TOSCA sample template - Diagram.

Besides container types, the TOSCA Simple Profile specification provides other useful resources for the description of containerised applications, such as the *Repository Definition*, which can be exploited to define internal or external repositories for pulling container images, the non-normative *tosca.artifacts.Deployment.Image.Container.Docker* type for Docker images, and the *Configure* step in *Standard interface* node life-cycle, which allows to define post-deployment configuration operations or scripts to execute.

4 Analysis of Cluster Orchestrators

In this section, we analyse existing swarm services to provide interoperability between multiple container cluster technologies. To operate on top of different cluster platforms, a common specification model, compatible across diverse technologies, is required. To develop such a model, we analysed three of the most popular cluster orchestrators: Docker Swarm, Kubernetes and Mesos + Marathon.

Our analysis focused on highlighting similarities and differences within the aspects that affect the deployment of containers. We found that all the three platforms implement the main features for container orchestration in a similar fashion. For instance, some entities and services represent identical concepts, even though they are named differently. The results of the comparison are available in Table 1.

Table 1. A comparison of how features are implemented in Docker Swarm, Kubernetes and Mesos + Marathon [13].

	Docker Swarm	Kubernetes	Mesos + Marathon
Application specification	Docker Compose YAML	YAML format	JSON format
Deployment unit	Service	Pod	Pod
Container	Container	Container	Task
Cluster	Swarm	Cluster	Cluster
Volume management	Volumes can be attached to Services or be automatically created according to the volume specification on the service	PersistentVolumes can be directly attached to Pods or may be automatically provisioned.	The appropriate amount of disk space is implicitly reserved, according to specification
Networking management	Overlay networks manage communications among the Docker daemons participating in the swarm	Services provide networking, granting a way to access Pods	Containers of each pod instance can share a network namespace, and communicate over a VLAN or private network
Configuration operations	It is possible to execute commands directly on the service (e.g. *docker exec*)	It is possible to execute commands directly on the container (e.g. *kubectl exec*)	It is possible to execute commands directly on the task (e.g. *dcos task exec*)

The field *Application Specification* indicates the method to describe the scenario to deploy, i.e. specification formats and languages. *Deployment Unit* refers to the atomic deployable entity, which is managed by the cluster in terms of scalability and availability. *Container* and *Cluster* indicate the names used for container entities and for clusters of physical machines. *Volume Management* describes the strategies to manage the attachment of storage entities and *Networking Management* illustrates how to establish internal and external connections. *Configuration Operations* present methods to execute post-deployment configuration operations on containers.

Firstly, we identified the most important features for deploying and initialising containerised applications. Then, for each of these features, we found strategies leading to similar results in all the analysed orchestrators. This information can be found in the rows of the Table.

From this analysis, many similarities emerged between the three platforms. All of them allow to specify the desired application using a tree-like data model within portable formats, such as JSON and YAML. Furthermore, all the orchestrators map resources for deployment units, containers, and clusters in a similar manner, where the main difference is given by the naming conventions.

With regard to volume and networking management, different platforms implement different strategies. However, all the volume management approaches share the possibility to delegate the provisioning of volumes to the platform, taking for granted that volume properties are indicated in the application specification. As for networking, each of the software grants accessibility to deployment units and containers, both within and outside the cluster, although they manage it in different ways. Finally, all the platforms allow to execute configuration commands on the deployed instances, by accessing them directly.

The analysis of container cluster interoperability laid the groundwork for a unified approach. This is further explored in the next section, where the common specification format and the interfaces to the different cluster orchestrators are discussed.

5   Achieving Cluster Interoperability

In this section, we present the strategy adopted to describe the topology of containerised applications operating on top of multiple cluster platforms, which leverages the TOSCA standard.

As discussed in Sect. 3, TOSCA Simple Profile includes several node types for container-based application topologies. According to the analysis in Table 1, we mapped TOSCA Container Runtime to Deployment Unit entities and TOSCA Container Application to containers. This allows to easily describe containerised applications within a cluster in terms of nodes. However, we found that using the plain TOSCA Container Application would flatten the node hierarchy present in the specification, removing the possibility to assign meaningful roles to each node in the topology (e.g. Database, WebServer).

```
tosca.nodes.Container.Application:
  derived_from: tosca.nodes.Root
  requirements:
    - host:
        capability: tosca.capabilities.Compute
        node: tosca.nodes.Container.Runtime
        relationship: tosca.relationships.HostedOn
    - storage:
        capability: tosca.capabilities.Storage
    - network:
        capability: tosca.capabilities.Endpoint
```

Listing 1.2. TOSCA Container Application node [13].

For the sake of clarity, Listing 1.2 shows the TOSCA Container Application node which represents a generic container-based application. Apart from hosting, storage and network requirements, no properties are defined. Besides, it directly derives from the root node as all other TOSCA base node types do. On the one hand, this allows to have consistent definitions for basic requirements, capabilities and life-cycle interfaces; on the other hand, customisation is only viable by type extension.

As a result, we extended the TOSCA Simple Profile hierarchy for containers, by deriving from the TOSCA Container Application type and defining the same properties and capabilities that are present in each of the corresponding TOSCA node types in the standard. Listing 1.3 and Listing 1.4 further explain our methodology, describing, by way of example, the TOSCA Database node and the TOSCA Container Database node respectively.

```
tosca.nodes.Database:
  derived_from: tosca.nodes.Root
  properties:
    name:
      type: string
      description: the logical name of the database
    port:
      type: integer
      description: >
        the port the underlying database service
        will listen to for data
    user:
      type: string
      description: >
        the user account name for DB administration
      required: false
    password:
      type: string
      description: >
        the password for the DB user account
      required: false
  requirements:
  - host:
      capability: tosca.capabilities.Compute
      node: tosca.nodes.DBMS
      relationship: tosca.relationships.HostedOn
  capabilities:
    database_endpoint:
      type: tosca.capabilities.Endpoint.Database
```

Listing 1.3. TOSCA Database node [13].

```
tosca.nodes.Container.Database:
    derived_from: tosca.nodes.Container.Application
    description: >
      TOSCA Container for Databases which employs
      the same capabilities and properties of the
      tosca.nodes.Database but which extends from
      the Container.Application node_type
    properties:
      user:
        required: false
        type: string
        description: >
          User account name for DB administration
      port:
        required: false
        type: integer
        description: >
          The port the database service will use
          to listen for incoming data and requests.
      name:
        required: false
        type: string
        description: >
          The name of the database.
      password:
        required: false
        type: string
        description: >
          The password for the DB user account
    capabilities:
      database_endpoint:
        type: tosca.capabilities.Endpoint.Database
```

Listing 1.4. TOSCA Container Database node [13].

While using the plain TOSCA Container Application type would still allow to deploy a scenario in our framework, we believe that preserving a node typing system would make the specification more descriptive. Moreover, this choice enables the use of the standard-defined typed relationships (i.e. ConnectsTo, DependsOn, HostedOn, ...) between different types of container nodes.

Another resource mapping was required for managing Volumes. TOSCA Simple Profile provides useful Storage node types for representing storage resources, such as *tosca.nodes.Storage.BlockStorage*. We mapped TOSCA Block Storage nodes to volumes. Each volume should be connected to the respective container using the standard-defined relationship *tosca.relationships.AttachesTo*. TOSCA AttachesTo already defines the *location* property which is of primary importance for containers, since it allows to define the mount path of a volume.

Networking management did not need any additional specification. Cluster networks may be arranged using the *port* property of a node and analysing its relationships with the other nodes in the topology.

6 System Design and Implementation

The aim of this work is to design and implement a TOSCA Orchestrator for the deployment of containerised applications on clusters. The Orchestrator should also be able to interface with several cloud providers and a variety of container technologies. The main features of the framework are described further in the following subsections.

6.1 Framework Architecture

Starting from the cloud application description, the framework is capable of devising and orchestrating the workflow of the provisioning operations to execute. Along with the application description, several application properties can be provided using the *Dashboard* tool. This is the main endpoint to interact with the framework, since it allows to configure and start the deployment process.

Firstly, the Dashboard allows users to either sketch the topology of their desired applications, using graphical modelling tools, or upload and validate previously worked application descriptions. Then, it is possible to deploy the uploaded applications, providing many configuration parameters, such as the target cloud provider or the cluster technology to use for containers. At a later stage, the Dashboard can also be used to display information about the deployment status and debug information.

We have designed and implemented a TOSCA Orchestrator which transforms the YAML model into an equivalent BPMN model, which is fed to a *BPMN engine* that instantiates and coordinates the related process. The process puts in force all the provisioning activities needed to build up the application stack. The overall provisioning scenario is depicted in Fig. 2.

For each framework service, multiple implementations can be provided for the supported cloud providers. All the services are offered within the framework through an Enterprise Service Bus (ESB). Three categories of provisioning services are provided: *Cloud Resource Services*, *Packet-based Services*, and *Container Cluster Services*. The latter include functionalities to deploy applications on cluster platforms.

In order to integrate such services in the ESB, we deploy a layer of *Service Connectors* which are responsible for connecting requests coming from the Provisioning Tasks with the Provisioning Services. Service Connectors allow to achieve service location transparency and loose coupling between Provisioning BPMN plans (orchestrated by the BPMN Engine) and Provisioning Services. The *Service Registry* is responsible for the registration and discovery of Connectors. The *Service Broker* is in charge of taking care of the requests coming from the Provisioning Tasks.

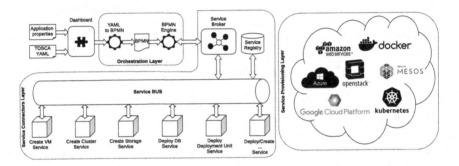

Fig. 2. Overview of the provisioning scenario, showing the different layers of the framework [13].

In this work we focus on container-based applications that use container cluster technologies. The TOSCA operations for container orchestration are different from resource and package operations, and cluster technologies frequently perform management operations that are relieved from the framework. The orchestration process for Deployment Units will be discussed later in this paper.

6.2   YAML Parsing

In our framework, the first step towards the deployment orchestration is the YAML processing. The Parser is the software component in charge of processing the TOSCA Template of an application and outputting the necessary information for the deployment of the application.

The Parser is able to deconstruct the complexity of the application scenario by analysing the nodes and the relationships present, acquiring the relevant configuration settings for the deployment, and compressing them into a format that can be processed by the framework.

In order to analyse a Deployment Unit, a bottom-up approach has been adopted. Starting from a Container Runtime, the Parser identifies the Deployment Unit and recursively finds all the containers stacked upon it and their dependencies, making a clear distinction between volume dependencies, which bind a storage volume to a container, and external dependencies, which bind a container to another container.

Each volume must be linked to its corresponding container using the "AttachesTo" relationship. It is important to specify the *location* parameter, which would serve as the mount path for the volume. This allows the Parser to correctly associate each volume to its container. External dependencies are identified and output by the Parser, since they would be used to setup Networking for each Deployment Unit.

Finally, the Parser produces BPMN data objects which are provided as data inputs for the BPMN plans.

6.3   BPMN Plans

The BPMN plans in our platform rework the strategy adopted in [12]. In Fig. 3, the overall service provision workflow is depicted. The diagram is composed of a parallel multi-instance sub-process, i.e., a set of sub-processes (called "Instantiate Node") each processing a TOSCA node in a parallel fashion. Originally, a TOSCA node was either a cloud resource or a software package. We expanded the BPMN Plans for our purpose, modelling a workflow path for deployment unit nodes.

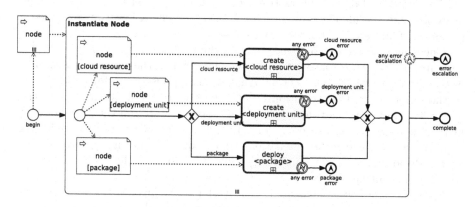

Fig. 3. Instantiate node overall workflow [13].

In Fig. 4, the detailed workflow for a deployment unit node is depicted. The creation of a deployment unit starts with a task that awaits notifications coming from the preceding sub-processes, which may consist of the "create cloud resource" sub-process for the creation of the cluster, in case this was not instantiated before, or other "create deployment unit" sub-processes. A service task will then trigger the actual instantiation by invoking the appropriate Connector on the ESB. If a fault occurs, it is immediately caught and the entire sub-process is

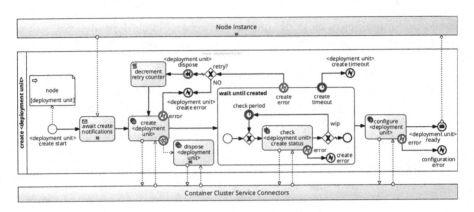

Fig. 4. Node deployment unit workflow [13].

cancelled. Following the path up to the parent process, an escalation is engaged. If the creation step is successful, a "wait-until-created" sub-process is activated.

Checks on the status are iterated until the cluster platform returns an "healthy status" for the deployed instance. The "check deployment unit create status" service task invokes the Connector on the ESB to check the status on the selected swarm service. The deployment unit's status is strongly dependent on the hosted containers' status. However, container cluster platforms automatically manage the life-cycle of containers, then the check is executed to detect errors which are strictly related to deployment units' resources.

Checking periods are configurable, so is the timeout put on the boundary of the sub-process. An error event is thrown either when the timeout has expired or when an explicit error has been signalled in response to a status check call. In the former case, the escalation is immediately triggered; in the latter case, an external loop will lead the system to autonomously re-run the whole deployment unit creation sub-process a configurable number of times, before yielding and eventually triggering an escalation event. Moreover, a compensation mechanism ("dispose deployment unit" task) allows to dispose of the deployment unit, whenever a fault has occurred.

Then the "configure deployment unit" task may be invoked to execute potential configuration operations on the deployed containers. When the workflow successfully reaches the end, a notification is sent. Otherwise, the occurred faults are caught and handled via escalation.

6.4   Service Connectors

Service Connectors are software modules that include the logic to provision a specific resource or service, interacting with the external providers.

Cloud Service Connectors implement interactions with cloud providers for the allocation of computational, networking and storage resources. *Container Cluster Connectors* concern the deployment of containerised units on different container cluster platforms. *Packet-based Connectors* implement interactions with all service providers that provide packet-based applications.

Cloud Service Connectors and Container Cluster Connectors contribute to the cause of container orchestration in our framework. The first category contains the services related to the different cloud providers. In particular, the cluster for deploying the scenario should be provisioned and the parameters for authenticating on the cluster should be provided to the ESB for future operations. The *Instantiate Cluster* connector interface provides an endpoint to deploy different kinds of container clusters on the cloud. All concrete Connectors to real cloud services (AWS, OpenStack, Azure, etc.) should implement the Instantiate Cluster interface.

The second category is related to the container cluster platforms, namely Docker Swarm, Kubernetes and Mesos. After creating the cluster, the ESB should be able to authenticate and communicate with the cluster for starting the operations that realise the deployment of the scenario. The *Instantiate DU* connector interface contains methods to interpret, deploy and configure a Deployment Unit on specific container-management platforms . All concrete Connectors to container cluster services should implement the Instantiate DU interface. These connectors perform a translation from the parsed topology to the specific format of the container cluster platform and communicate with the cluster to operate the deployment.

6.5   Prototype Implementation

In this subsection, we discuss the implementation of the framework.

The Dashboard is a web application, which has been implemented using the Vue.js framework[3], for the front-end user interface, and the PHP-based Laravel framework[4], for the back-end. The users' data, such as personal information, custom settings and deployments, are stored in an SQL database. The visualisation of an application's deployment graph as well as the tool to sketch a TOSCA template have been developed using the Cytoscape.js library[5], which is a JavaScript tool for networks' visualisation and analysis.

The Parser software component is widely based on the OpenStack parser[6] for TOSCA Simple Profile , a Python project licensed under Apache 2.0. The Parser builds an in-memory graph which keeps track of all nodes and dependency relationships between them in the TOSCA template.

We extended the Parser features to adapt it for containerised applications. The new module developed for the Parser is able to identify, analyse and output Deployment Units specification in a format that allows to integrate it into the BPMN plans.

---

[3] https://vuejs.org/.

[4] https://laravel.com/.

[5] https://js.cytoscape.org/.

[6] https://wiki.openstack.org/wiki/TOSCA-Parser.

We used Flowable[7], which is a Java based open-source business process engine, for the implementation of the BPMN workflow processing. Flowable includes several different components, such as Flowable Modeller, a module which allows to design new BPMN plans, and Flowable API, which represents a REST endpoint to the Flowable BPMN Engine. In our work, we used the Modeller to sketch the BPMN plans and the API module to integrate the Flowable Engine in our framework.

Finally, we implemented four Service Connectors: two OpenStack connectors, for the creation of either a Kubernetes cluster or a Docker Swarm cluster, one Kubernetes connector and one Docker Swarm connector, for the deployment of the DUs. The implementation has been done complementing Eclipse Vert.x[8], a Java toolkit for event-driven applications, with the OpenStack4J[9] library, for the creation of the clusters, and with the official Kubernetes Java client[10] and the Spotify Docker client[11], for the deployment of the DUs.

Overall, the implementation of TORCH is strongly *loosely-coupled*. The communication between the different components of the framework mainly builds upon web-based approaches, such as the adoption of REST APIs or CRUD services. The heterogeneity of the languages and the libraries used, along with the possibility to utilise different clients for the Service Connectors, provides a tangible proof of the extensibility of the framework.

7   Experiments

In this section, we assess the performance of our framework within two use cases: the first one is a simple Wordpress (WP) scenario, while the second one is a load test scenario, containing 20 Deployment Units (DU) in total, which represent ten instances of the original WP scenario. Our testbed consists of a machine running the full framework, along with the monitoring tools to collect some metrics about the system performance.

7.1   Use Case

We corroborate the working behaviour of our software with a test on a simple real-world scenario. This is a containerised version of a WP application including two DUs, MySQL and Wordpress, which are both stacked with a Volume and a Container. The scenario is depicted in Fig. 5, by using the TOSCA Simple Profile standard notation.

In the WP scenario, container images are Docker images that need to be pulled from the Docker Hub repository, as specified in the template. The TOSCA Artifact image fills the *implementation* parameter for the Create step in the

---

[7] https://www.flowable.org/.

[8] https://vertx.io/.

[9] http://www.openstack4j.com/.

[10] https://github.com/kubernetes-client/java.

[11] https://github.com/spotify/docker-client.

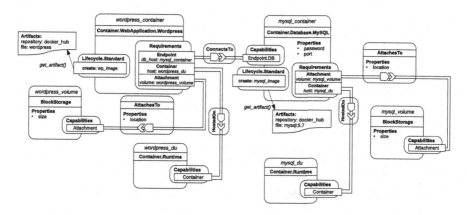

Fig. 5. The Wordpress scenario, described using TOSCA notation [13].

container life-cycle. Any environment variable for the Docker image should be given as an input of the implementation in the Create section of the container. For being correctly parsed, the environment variables have the same names that are indicated in the Docker Hub instructions for the image. Another parameter that can be specified in the Create inputs is the port. Otherwise, a port would be automatically chosen for the service by the container orchestrator.

In Listing 1.5, the TOSCA Simple Profile description of the types and the templates used for the MySQL deployment unit is exemplary provided. The description is drafted according to the principles defined in Sect. 5.

```
node_types:
  tosca.nodes.Container.Database.MySQL:
    description: >
      MySQL container from the Docker Hub repository
    derived_from: tosca.nodes.Container.Database
    requirements:
    - volume:
        capability: tosca.capabilities.Attachment
        relationship: tosca.relationships.AttachesTo

relationship_templates:
  tosca.relationships.MySQLAttachesToVolume:
    type: tosca.relationships.AttachesTo
    properties:
      location: { get_input: mysql_location }

node_templates:
  mysql_container:
    type: tosca.nodes.Container.Database.MySQL
    requirements:
    - host: mysql_deployment_unit
    - volume:
        node: mysql_volume
        relationship: tosca.relationships.MySQLAttachesToVolume
    artifacts:
      mysql_image:
        file: mysql:5.7
        type: tosca.artifacts.Deployment.Image.Container.Docker
        repository: docker_hub
    properties:
```

```
port: { get_input: mysql_port }
password: { get_input: mysql_root_pwd }
interfaces:
   Standard:
      create:
         implementation: mysql_image
         inputs:
            port: {get_property:[SELF,port]}
            mysql_root_password: {get_property:[SELF,password]}
mysql_volume:
   type: tosca.nodes.BlockStorage
   properties:
      size: { get_input: mysql_volume_size}
mysql_deployment_unit:
   type: tosca.nodes.Container.Runtime
```

Listing 1.5. MySQL deployment unit specification [13].

7.2 Performance Evaluation

We used the Prometheus[12] toolkit together with the Node Exporter[13] metrics collector to monitor the CPU, the memory and the network usage of the system. The machine used for the tests is equipped with an Intel(R) Core(TM) i7–4770 processor, 16 GB RAM, a 1 TB hard-drive and a 128 GB SSD, and it runs the Ubuntu 16.04 × 86–64 Linux distribution.

Table 2. Steady-state resource statistics about the testing system.

	CPU avg	MEM avg	NET IN avg	NET OUT avg
w/o Framework	0.39%	1.53 GiB	32.9 kbps	0 kbps
with Framework	0.94%	4.89 GiB	33.4 kbps	0 kbps

Table 2 displays the average values for the metrics when the machine is found in a steady state with and without the framework running. The metrics have been collected on a 5-min time frame and averaged over time, to prevent occasional system processes from interfering with our analysis. The table shows that the framework has a major impact on the RAM of the system, with around 3.45 GiB employed, a small impact on the CPU, with an increase of about 0.55% usage, and almost no impact on the network traffic. This is due to the absence of incoming network requests when the machine is in a steady state.

Overall, our tests utilise the framework in an end-to-end fashion. The testbed machine, hosting the whole framework, is accessed to upload the TOSCA scenario and provide any deployment properties, by using the Dashboard. Then, at the provisioning stage, the framework communicates with an OpenStack cluster to accomplish the deployment of the scenario.

---

[12] https://prometheus.io/.
[13] https://github.com/prometheus/node_exporter.

The OpenStack cluster is deployed on local machines and it consists of two computers: a Controller node and a Compute node. The Controller is equipped with an Intel(R) Core(TM) i7-4770S, 8 GB RAM and a 1 TB hard drive, and it also runs the Heat and Magnum services. The Compute is equipped with an Intel(R) Core(TM) i5–4460, 8 GB RAM, a 128 GB SSD and a 1 TB hard drive. Both nodes run the Ubuntu Server 18.04 × 86–64 Linux distribution.

Table 3. Deployment average times - WP single instance.

	Google Kubernetes		Docker Swarm	
	Value	Percentage	Value	Percentage
Create cluster	5min 41s ± 19s	65.58%	4min 4s ± 17s	71.13%
Create du	2min 59s ± 16s	34.42%	1min 39s ± 13s	28.87%
Total	8min 40s ± 20s	100%	5min 43s ± 16s	100%

Table 4. Deployment average times - WP multiple instances.

	Google Kubernetes		Docker Swarm	
	Value	Percentage	Value	Percentage
Create cluster	5min 54s ± 18s	54.29%	4min 7s ± 19s	61.60%
Create du	4min 58s ± 25s	45.71%	2min 34s ± 11s	38.4%
Total	10min 52s ± 40s	100%	6min 41s ± 2s	100%

Both the simple WP scenario and the load test scenario have been correctly deployed on Kubernetes and Swarm. The deployment times are shown in Table 3 and Table 4. The tables display the average times ± the standard deviation of ten deployment trials. Data is provided about the total amount of time needed to complete the deployment, but we also distinguish the necessary time to create the container cluster from the time employed to deploy all the DUs.

In general terms, the deployments are faster on the Swarm platform. This applies to both the cluster and the DU deployments, and it is likely due to the major resource requirements to run the Google's container cluster platform. As expected, the deployment times are longer for the load test scenario.

We detail the testbed machine resource usage in Fig. 6 and Fig. 7. The plots show the CPU, memory and network traffic states over time, for Kubernetes and Swarm deployment trials. We highlight the presence of three operational stages in the plots: the setup, the cluster creation and the DU creation. Overall, the performance of the testbed is very similar for the two container cluster platforms tested, across all the phases. However, we observe a difference in the CPU usage between the single WP and the load test scenarios, with the latter having a higher CPU usage.

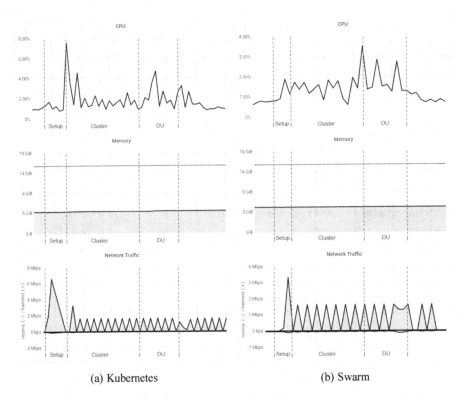

(a) Kubernetes   (b) Swarm

Fig. 6. WP single instance - resource monitoring.

The setup stage consists of the pre-deployment operations that are required to start the orchestration process, such as the communication of the application description to the orchestrator and the check of provisioning services that are adequate for the deployment. As for the plots, this stage implies an increase in the CPU usage, which reaches peaks of 6–7% usage for Kubernetes and 2–3% for Swarm . We also observe the largest peak in the network transmitted traffic, with the network usage being higher for the load test scenario. This is because the application specification file has a bigger size and there are more BPMN workflows to transfer, due to the higher number of DUs.

The cluster creation phase entails a steady usage of the CPU, with a value that is higher than the steady-state CPU usage but lower than in the other two phases. There are no heavy network transfers, but frequent spikes are present in the network plots because of the requests sent by the orchestrator monitoring the resources' provisioning status and by the Dashboard monitoring the deployment state of the DUs.

Finally, in the DU creation stage, it occurs another CPU increase. This is mainly due to the parallelism capabilities of the framework, which is able to deploy multiple DUs at the same time, exploiting the resource availability of

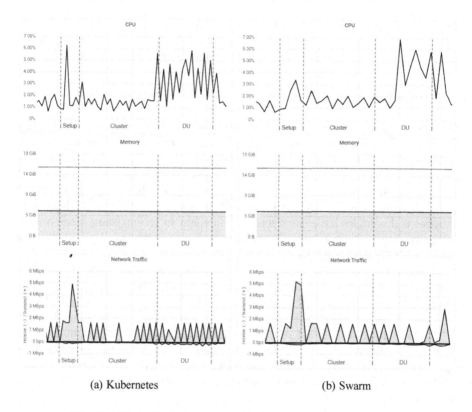

(a) Kubernetes   (b) Swarm

Fig. 7. WP multiple instances - load test resource monitoring.

the testbed machine. The network traffic is mainly busy with the transmission of monitoring information, even though we can notice a small increase in the received traffic, likely due to the numerous parallel incoming connections, communicating information about the DU deployment status.

During the DU creation stage, we observe the most significant difference between the single WP scenario and the load test scenario deployments: for the first, the CPU usage has its highest peaks at 4%, while for the second the highest peaks reach 7% of usage.

The results of our tests show that the framework is computationally inexpensive. In our evaluation, the CPU usage rarely goes beyond the 5% threshold and we often find the value to be lower than 3%. From a memory perspective, the framework requires a few GiB of RAM for being setup but, then, at the provisioning stage, the framework is parsimonious in the memory management and does not require substantial additional resources. Moreover, we noticed a regular network usage during all the provisioning phases.

Finally, we could not find tremendous differences between the deployment of a simple two-DU WP scenario and a twenty-DU load test scenario. This implies that the framework might have good scalability capabilities, although tests with multiple clusters should be performed to corroborate this hypothesis. Unfortunately, we were not able to deploy multiple clusters because of hardware constraints, but extensive scalability tests will be part of future work.

8 Conclusion

The ever-growing interest in cloud computing on the part of both academia and industry has promoted a business scenario where several cloud providers offer similar services and contend for an extremely lucrative market. One of the keys to competitive cloud providers is the automated provisioning of complex cloud applications. As a result, a number of orchestration tools have appeared in order to simplify the entire life-cycle management of cloud applications. Additionally, container technologies have come into the limelight in recent years, since organisations package applications in containers and orchestrate multiple containers across multiple cloud providers.

In this paper, we introduced a TOSCA-enabled framework for the deployment and orchestration of cloud applications across multiple providers, with special focus on containerised applications operating on top of multiple cluster platforms. A prototype implementation of the framework was developed and a few experiments were carried out on a small-scale test-bed. Preliminary tests corroborated the viability of the approach and showed promising results with regard to scalability. In the future, more experiments will be performed on top of different container-based cluster platforms to assess the maturity of the system on a large scale.

References

1. Apache Software Foundation: ARIA TOSCA. https://ariatosca.incubator.apache.org/. Accessed 10 July 2020
2. Apache Software Foundation: Mesos. http://mesos.apache.org/. Accessed 10 July 2020
3. Apache Software Foundation: Mesos Containerizer. http://mesos.apache.org/documentation/latest/mesos-containerizer/. Accessed 10 July 2020
4. Bellendorf, J., Mann, Z.Á.: Cloud topology and orchestration using TOSCA: a systematic literature review. In: Kritikos, K., Plebani, P., de Paoli, F. (eds.) ESOCC 2018. LNCS, vol. 11116, pp. 207–215. Springer, Cham (2018). https://doi.org/10.1007/978-3-319-99819-0_16
5. Binz, T., et al.: OpenTOSCA – a runtime for TOSCA-based cloud applications. In: Basu, S., Pautasso, C., Zhang, L., Fu, X. (eds.) ICSOC 2013. LNCS, vol. 8274, pp. 692–695. Springer, Heidelberg (2013). https://doi.org/10.1007/978-3-642-45005-1_62
6. Bogo, M., Soldani, J., Neri, D., Brogi, A.: Component-aware orchestration of cloud-based enterprise applications, from TOSCA to Docker and Kubernetes. Softw. Pract. Experience **50**(9), 1793–1821 (2020). https://doi.org/10.1002/spe.2848
7. Brogi, A., et al.: SeaClouds: seamless adaptive multi-cloud management of service-based applications. In: 17th Conferencia Iberoamericana en Software Engineering (CIbSE 2014), pp. 95–108 (2014)

8. Brogi, A., et al.: Adaptive management of applications across multiple clouds: the SeaClouds Approach. CLEI Electron. J. **18**, 2–2 (2015). https://doi.org/10.19153/cleiej.18.1.1

9. Brogi, A., Rinaldi, L., Soldani, J.: TosKer: a synergy between TOSCA and Docker for orchestrating multicomponent applications. Softw. Pract. Experience **48**(11), 2061–2079 (2018). https://doi.org/10.1002/spe.2625

10. Buyya, R., et al.: A manifesto for future generation cloud computing: research directions for the next decade. ACM Comput. Surv. **51**(5), 105:1–105:38 (2018). https://doi.org/10.1145/3241737

11. Caballer, M., Zala, S., García, Á.L., Moltó, G., Fernández, P.O., Velten, M.: Orchestrating complex application architectures in heterogeneous clouds. J. Grid Comput. **16**(1), 3–18 (2018). https://doi.org/10.1007/s10723-017-9418-y

12. Calcaterra, D., Cartelli, V., Di Modica, G., Tomarchio, O.: Exploiting BPMN features to design a fault-aware TOSCA orchestrator. In: Proceedings of the 8th International Conference on Cloud Computing and Services Science (CLOSER 2018), pp. 533–540. Funchal-Madeira (Portugal), March 2018. https://doi.org/10.5220/0006775605330540

13. Calcaterra, D., Di Modica, G., Mazzaglia, P., Tomarchio, O.: Enabling container cluster interoperability using a TOSCA orchestration framework. In: Proceedings of the 10th International Conference on Cloud Computing and Services Science (CLOSER 2020), pp. 127–137, May 2020. https://doi.org/10.5220/0009410701270137

14. Cloud Native Computing Foundation: containerd. https://containerd.io/. Accessed 10 July 2020

15. Cloud Native Computing Foundation: CRI-O. https://cri-o.io/. Accessed 10 July 2020

16. Docker Inc.: Docker. https://www.docker.com/. Accessed 10 July 2020

17. Docker Inc.: Docker Swarm. https://docs.docker.com/engine/swarm/. Accessed 10 July 2020

18. FastConnect: Alien4Cloud. https://alien4cloud.github.io/. Accessed 10 July 2020

19. GigaSpaces Technologies: Cloudify. https://cloudify.co/. Accessed 10 July 2020

20. Google: Google Kubernetes. https://kubernetes.io/. Accessed 10 July 2020

21. Kehrer, S., Blochinger, W.: TOSCA-based container orchestration on Mesos. Comput. Sci. Res. Dev. **33**(3), 305–316 (2018). https://doi.org/10.1007/s00450-017-0385-0

22. Kiss, T., et al.: MiCADO–microservice-based cloud application-level dynamic orchestrator. Future Gener. Comput. Syst. **94**, 937–946 (2019). https://doi.org/10.1016/j.future.2017.09.050

23. Mesosphere Inc.: Marathon. https://mesosphere.github.io/marathon/. Accessed 10 July 2020

24. OASIS: Web Services Business Process Execution Language Version 2.0, April 2007. http://docs.oasis-open.org/wsbpel/2.0/OS/wsbpel-v2.0-OS.html. Accessed 10 July 2020

25. OASIS: Topology and Orchestration Specification for Cloud Applications Version 1.0, November 2013. http://docs.oasis-open.org/tosca/TOSCA/v1.0/os/TOSCA-v1.0-os.html. Accessed 23 Dec 2020

26. OASIS: TOSCA Simple Profile in YAML Version 1.2 (2019). https://docs.oasis-open.org/tosca/TOSCA-Simple-Profile-YAML/v1.2/TOSCA-Simple-Profile-YAML-v1.2.html. Accessed 23 Dec 2019

27. OMG: Business Process Model and Notation (BPMN 2.0), January 2011. http://www.omg.org/spec/BPMN/2.0/. Accessed 10 July 2020

28. OpenStack: Build the future of open infrastructure. https://www.openstack.org/. Accessed 10 July 2020

29. OpenStack: Heat. https://wiki.openstack.org/wiki/Heat. Accessed 10 July 2020

30. OpenStack: Magnum. https://wiki.openstack.org/wiki/Magnum. Accessed 10 July 2020

31. Petcu, D., Vasilakos, A.: Portability in clouds: approaches and research opportunities. Scalable Comput. Pract. Experience **15**(3), 251–270 (2014). https://doi.org/10.12694/scpe.v15i3.1019

32. Salomoni, D., Campos, I., Gaido, L., et al.: INDIGO-DataCloud: a platform to facilitate seamless access to E-Infrastructures. J. Grid Comput. **16**(3), 381–408 (2018). https://doi.org/10.1007/s10723-018-9453-3

33. Singh, S., Singh, N.: Containers & Docker: emerging roles & future of Cloud technology. In: 2nd International Conference on Applied and Theoretical Computing and Communication Technology (iCATccT), pp. 804–807, July 2016. https://doi.org/10.1109/ICATCCT.2016.7912109

34. Sysdig: Sysdig 2019 container usage report (2019). https://sysdig.com/blog/sysdig-2019-container-usage-report/. Accessed 23 Dec 2019

35. Tosatto, A., Ruiu, P., Attanasio, A.: Container-based orchestration in cloud: state of the art and challenges. In: 9th International Conference on Complex, Intelligent, and Software Intensive Systems, (CISIS 2015), pp. 70–75 (2015)

36. Weerasiri, D., Barukh, M.C., Benatallah, B., Sheng, Q.Z., Ranjan, R.: A taxonomy and survey of cloud resource orchestration techniques. ACM Comput. Surv. **50**(2), 26:1–26:41 (2017). https://doi.org/10.1145/3054177

Self-healing in the Scope of Software-Based Computer and Mobile Networks

Natal Vieira de Souza Neto$^{(\boxtimes)}$, Daniel Ricardo Cunha Oliveira,
Maurício Amaral Gonçalves, Flávio de Oliveira Silva,
and Pedro Frosi Rosa

Faculty of Computing (FACOM), Federal University of Uberlândia (UFU),
Uberlândia, Brazil
{natalneto,drcoliveira,mauricioamaralg,flavio,pfrosi}@ufu.br
https://sonar.facom.ufu.br/

Abstract. Self-healing is an autonomic computing fundamental well-disseminated in standalone computer systems. In distributed systems, e.g. computer networks or mobile networks, the introduction of self-healing capabilities poses some challenges, mainly when software-based networks, e.g. Software-Defined Networking (SDN) and Network Functions Virtualisation (NFV), are involved. Such networks impose new control and management layers, and the adoption of self-healing functions means that all layers must be considered. In this paper, we present the challenges of self-healing in the scope of SDN and NFV, by revising the self-healing concept in computer and mobile networks, and by presenting the thorough difference between a system that applies fault tolerance from one that applies self-healing functions. We also introduce a framework for solving these challenges, by describing four use cases of self-healing, considering control, management, and data layers. The use cases focus on maintaining the health of the network at run-time, considering control, management, and infrastructure layers. Our framework is a novel Operations, Administration, and Maintenance (OAM) tool, based on a self-management network architecture that was introduced in our previous works.

Keywords: Self-management · Self-healing · Fault tolerance · OAM · SDN · NFV

1 Introduction

Future computer and mobile networks must simultaneously support diverging network requirements, e.g. low-latency, high-throughput, reliability, etc. Software-Defined Networking (SDN) and Network Functions Virtualisation (NFV)

This study was financed in part by the Coordenação de Aperfeiçoamento de Pessoal de Nível Superior - Brasil (Capes) - Finance Code 001.

© Springer Nature Switzerland AG 2021
D. Ferguson et al. (Eds.): CLOSER 2020, CCIS 1399, pp. 325–344, 2021.
https://doi.org/10.1007/978-3-030-72369-9_14

(NFV) are key enablers for this supporting, as these technologies facilitate network automation, virtualisation, and service composition [22], which are crucial for delivering dynamic allocation and reallocation of resources for critical requirements. Although the advances in specifications and implementations for these technologies in the last years, SDN and NFV have unresolved problems associated with network healthiness, which are discussed in this paper, e.g. controller channel maintenance, bugs and crashes in network applications, distributed resources management, and so on [3,8].

Before SDN and NFV, distributed protocols running inside the network infrastructure were responsible for network health maintenance. Such distributed protocols, like Open Shortest Path First (OSPF), resolve the network impairments that lead the network to the unhealthy state, e.g. link congestion, network overload, and inconsistency routing rules [16]. SDN and NFV approaches bring new network layers or planes, i.e. the control plane and management plane, with software components for operating in the environment. Such new network planes operate over the data plane, for ensuring the provisioning and maintenance of network resources, including routes in multi-path topologies, compute resources, e.g. storage, memory and processing power, and radio resources. Common SDN and NFV components, e.g. SDN Controller (SDNC) and Virtualised Infrastructure Manager (VIM), conveniently have mechanisms for supporting data plane failures; however, the communication maintenance between the data plane and control/management planes as well as the resilience of control/management components are open issues [17].

In this paper, which is an extended version of our previous work [20], we discuss the autonomic fundamental of self-healing applied to softwarised and virtualised networks. By using SDN and NFV technologies we propose a self-healing framework capable of acting on data, control, and management planes, and we add new use cases for self-healing in comparison to the original paper. To the best of the authors' knowledge, our framework is the first solution that addresses fault issues in all network layers for these technologies. The main objective of our solution is to ensure the network health even with unexpected behaviours in any network planes. The framework acts as an Operations, Administration, and Maintenance (OAM) tool, autonomously applying monitoring and recovery functions.

Autonomic computing fundamentals, e.g. self-healing, self-configuration, and self-optimisation, empower the self-management of computer and mobile networks, which is considered the future of the Network Management (NM) [18]. By the self-healing fundamental, the network must recover itself from faults that can culminate in a degraded or broken performance. This concept allows the network to maintain the Quality of Service (QoS) of applications running in the environment, avoiding these applications to achieve a degraded or broken state. Our framework covers different autonomic computing fundamentals, well-known as self-* – self-optimisation, self-configuration, self-protection, etc. – and, in this work, we chose the self-healing as the start point to evaluate the solution.

The remainder of the paper is structured as follows. In Sect. 2, we discuss the fault tolerance principle in data, control, and management planes; and position our contribution with some related works. In Sect. 3, we present our framework with technical details. In Sect. 4, we describe some use cases of our framework in an SDN/NFV environment and discuss them concerning the QoS point of view. Finally, in Sect. 5, we pose our concluding remarks and suggest some directions for future work.

2 Background

In computer science, a system that applies the self-healing concept can detect or predict faults that lead the system to a nonoperational state [9]. The system usually notices the fault and recovers itself before a completely broken state. In computer networks, this self-healing capability is complex due to the number of diverging nodes – which are Network Elements (NEs), including routers, switches, gateways, proxies, firewalls, etc. – running simultaneously in the network topology [21]. As every NE has its particularities and diverse protocols run in the environment, the detection and recovery of failures are more complex in computer networks than in standalone systems.

A computer network is a graph with NEs representing the nodes and links between the NEs representing the edges. Additionally, nodes can represent hosts or User Equipment (UE) that are connected in the NEs. In traditional architectures, before network softwarisation and virtualisation, the network is healthy when the communication between hosts and UE has no problems. However, some impairments can deteriorate the network health, such as broken/congested links, hardware/software failures, bugs in network applications, etc. [16]. In the current and future computer and mobile networks, the network is unhealthy if QoS requirements are not satisfied, even if the communication is established. Moreover, considering SDN and NFV, new graphs are abstracted in the environment, representing the topologies between the data plane with control and management planes. Such QoS requirements in the data plane and the new graphs pose more complexity in the environment, which requires autonomic functions as self-healing. In this section, we detail the complexity in data, control and management planes, and discuss the self-healing fundamental in these layers.

2.1 Fault Tolerance in the Data Plane

In an SDN topology, the data plane is the layer in which the NEs are placed. For NFV, the compute nodes where network functions run represent the data plane. Considering Fig. 1 as an example, NE_1, NE_2, ..., NE_8 are SDN NEs whilst Compute $Node_1$ and Compute $Node_2$ abstract the representation of NFV data layer components. The network functions running inside the compute nodes are connected by the NEs. In current mobile networks, Network Slices (NSs) [4] are abstracted by the components shown in the Data plane. The $SDNC_1$ provides the connections between different nodes in the data plane, applying routes inside the

NEs. Such routes are defined and created by SDN Applications running on the top of $SDNC_1$, through the Northbound Interface (NBI). The network functions running inside the compute nodes, e.g. Virtual Network Functions (VNFs), are instantiated by management components, e.g. OAM_1.

From the fault tolerance point of view, data plane issues are well-solved by current solutions because the control plane components are responsible for the operation of the data plane. It means that if NE_7, shown in Fig. 1, presents failures, the $SDNC_1$ will recalculate and apply routes avoiding such NE. Analogously, if the Compute $Node_1$ is overloaded, the OAM_1 will recreate new network functions into the Compute $Node_2$, and it will even migrate current network functions that are presenting problems. As the most known components found in the literature already have mechanisms for dealing with the data plane components, the focus in our framework is associated with QoS.

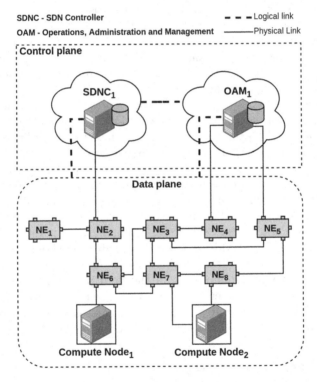

Fig. 1. A layered SDN and NFV typical environment. The Control plane contains operational and management components, represented by $SDNC_1$ and OAM_1, and the Data plane contains network components and computational infrastructure elements, represented by NEs and Compute Nodes respectively.

Even with solutions for fault tolerance in the data plane, applications with particular QoS attributes require specific fault tolerance actions. For example, Ultra-Reliable and Low Latency Communications (URLLC) applications demand strict latency during the whole service lifecycle [7]. In this situation, the applications require different attributes: one application can require 1 ms of latency, while another can require 10 ms. If the communications between such applications and end-users are using the same network link and this link has a delay of 5 ms, the first application is not running properly, but the former application has no problem. It means that services and applications with specific QoS requirements, e.g. reliability, low-latency, or high-throughput, are healthy if the network is delivering such requirements.

For future computer and mobile networks, e.g. 5G, Mobile Network Operators (MNOs) will probably share their infrastructure in several logical networks, named NSs [23]. In this approach, network orchestrators are responsible for provisioning each NS throughout the different network segments, e.g. Core Network (CN) and Radio Access Network (RAN). The orchestrators have information about the available resources and orchestrate such resources in a better way, ensuring that the required QoS will be delivered. The OAM tools ensure the continuous delivery of the services with the required QoS. In this way, the data plane must be monitored during the run-time and resource reallocation and network reconfiguration must be performed when the network pass through health problems, i.e. network impairments, such as network overload, is affecting the QoS of some NSs.

In this paper, the network self-healing framework, defined in Sect. 3, takes into account the QoS requirements from NSs for guaranteeing the QoS during the NS entire lifecycle. On the other hand, for fault tolerance of data plane components, e.g. link failures, the framework has no actions, because it is assumed that the SDN and NFV components are capable to deal with infrastructure impairments. Besides the data plane, the control and management layers are under academic investigation, since SDN and NFV were not designed with intrinsic management functions for fault tolerance of the control and management layer themselves [17].

2.2 Fault Tolerance in the Control and Management Planes

Former computer network architectures contain distributed protocols that are responsible for real-time operation; such protocols are responsible for fault tolerance in the data plane. In such architectures, network functions are performed in the same layer in which the data traffic is carried out, as there is no separation between control, management, and data planes. As an example, if a link between two NEs is having problems, the routing protocols, e.g. OSPF, modify the routes to avoid degradation of the link. In SDN, the routing function is performed by SDN Applications that run on top of the SDNC. In this way, the routing application ensures the modification of data plane routes. As pointed in Subsect. 2.1, this mechanism avoids or mitigates data plane failures. However, the integration between the data plane and the control plane, in which the SDN Controller and Applications are placed, requires an uninterrupted communication channel [17].

Figure 1 shows an SDN Controller, i.e. $SDNC_1$, controlling some NEs, i.e. NE_1, NE_2, ... NE_8; it is assumed that some SDN Applications are running on top of $SDNC_1$. As the $SDNC_1$ controls the NEs from the data plane, it has logical connections, represented by the dashed lines, with all these NEs. However, it has a physical connection, represented by the continuous lines, only with NE_2. The communication between $SDNC_1$ and NE_7 occurs through the paths $SDNC_1$-NE_2-NE_6-NE_7, $SDNC_1$-NE_2-NE_6-NE_3-NE_7, or $SDNC_1$-NE_2-NE_6-NE_3-NE_5-NE_8-NE_7. Considering the topology in Fig. 1, if NE_2 has a problem, or the link $SDNC_1$-NE_2 is broken or degraded, the entire data plane will be nonoperational since the decisions of routing and forwarding are made by $SDNC_1$ and its applications. As stated, an SDN environment requires fault tolerance actions for the communication inter-layers. For self-healing purposes, as the network must recover itself from problems, it must be able to recover from data, control, and management issues.

The aforementioned inter-layer communication is the first aspect of the self-healing of the control plane. The second aspect is associated with the control components. The $SDNC_1$ and its applications are software modules and can present bugs and crashes [8]. For achieving the self-healing fundamental, the network must recover these components from bugs or crashes, as well as increase the computing capability when the network presents overload. The auto-scale of control components is essential. Nonetheless, the auto-scale of data plane components (NEs) is another requirement if such elements are virtual switches (which is not the exemplification of Fig. 1).

From the NFV perspective, the communication between management and data planes components is similar to the aforementioned SDN approach. In Fig. 1, the OAM_1 could represent a VIM Controller, and the infrastructure where the virtual machines are deployed is on the represented compute nodes. Following the previous analogy, OAM_1 has logical connections with the Compute Node$_1$ and Compute Node$_2$, but the physical connection is made by the links from the data plane topology. It means that any overload in the NE_6 can compromise the communication between the OAM_1 and its managed virtual machines. The figure does not represent all NFV components, but the connectivity between the controllers/orchestrators is similar: a VNF Manager (VNFM) requires uninterrupted communication with its managed VNFs; a VIM controller requires uninterrupted communication with the compute nodes in the NFV Infrastructure (NFVI); etc.

In addition to the communication aspect, self-healing in an NFV environment must act over software and hardware problems. As an example, VIM tools commonly used in industry, e.g. Openstack [15] or Kubernetes [11], have mechanisms for self-healing and auto-scale of the containers and virtual machines previously instantiated. However, the VIM tool itself usually has no mechanisms for healing from problems. It means that a problem in the OAM_1 will leave Compute Node$_1$ and Compute Node$_2$ without management.

To achieve the self-healing fundamental, the network must also consider the placement of components. The $SDNC_1$ can run on virtual machines and, in this situation, it can be instantiated in different places in the topology. In Fig. 1, if the control traffic is bigger in NE_7, maybe the $SDNC_1$ could be instantiated inside the Compute Node$_2$. As stated in this section, the self-healing functions must consider communication, bugs and crashes in software and hardware, and components placement. Additionally, the number of aspects is not exhaustive and, for this reason, we designed a framework capable of deal with the three exemplified aspects, but also architectural capable of deal with new aspects in the future. In Subsect. 2.3 we position our contribution concerning other frameworks.

2.3   Related Work

SDN and NFV technologies bring many advantages for network and infrastructure operation [22]; nonetheless, there are some unresolved problems in these technologies, mainly associated with network and service management [16]. SDN transfers the operation over the data plane for the control and application layers, whilst the management of such layers is not standardised. NFV introduces new components for the management of virtual functions, whilst the management of the components themselves are not standardised as well. Besides the framework proposed in this paper has mechanisms to act in all layers, the focus is on the control and management layers.

The first unresolved problem in SDN and NFV is associated with the controller channel reliability, i.e. the communication between controllers and their controlled elements [16,17]. In SDN, the SDNC controls all the NE in the domain. In NFV, management components handle various virtual functions, including creating, maintaining and decommissioning such functions. For these reasons, the network must ensure the connectivity between the SDNC and the NEs, as well as the communication between NFV components and compute nodes in which the VNFs are placed. The Southbound Interface (SBI) protocol, i.e. the protocol for the communication between the control and data planes, e.g. Open-Flow [13], usually have procedures to create the paths between all NEs and the SDNC when every NE starts. The problem is when routes on such paths are not available: management functions must reroute previous paths. In the NFV, there are no default paths, hence the routes are dynamically defined at run-time, which means that network overload can compromise the control and management communication.

In literature, there are some works for solving the controller channel reliability in SDN, such as [5] and [6]. The first presents some functions for monitoring and recovery of control paths, i.e. paths between the NEs and the SDNC. The former introduces a control path migration protocol for virtualized environments, focused on control paths as well. To the best of our knowledge, there are no works considering other control and management components instead of the SDNC, such as the SDN Applications and NFV controllers and orchestrators. Our solution aims to build a catalogue of control and management entities, relating them to their controlled/managed elements. In this way, the network can achieve the self-healing fundamental, as the catalogue has information about what are the management relations in the environment.

Another challenge in SDN and NFV environments is the definition of control, management, and data components. In general, virtual environments allow the deploying of control/management components in the same infrastructure of data components. As an example, the Compute Node$_1$ in Fig. 1 can have a virtual instance, e.g. a Virtual Machine (VM), used for data processing, as well as the controller or orchestrator managing this VM. From the network topology point of view, even with the separation between control and data, as proposed by the SDN approach, the traffic of control and data primitives utilises the same NEs. It means that the control primitives are not processed by the NEs, but the traffic of such primitives is in-band, i.e. the same NEs used for forwarding data primitives are used for forwarding control primitives [19]. The deploy of out-of-band topology for control and management is not feasible as it is expensive and complex [19], and hence, a self-management solution must consider that data and control will share the same infrastructure. The key is the identification of control and management traffic and components, and prioritisation of them. The catalogue proposed in this paper is a novel solution for this achievement.

A third unresolved problem in the software/virtual-based network environments is the QoS of End-to-End (E2E) applications. In general, the projects found in the literature are considering Network Slicing as a Service (NSaaS) [23] as a key enabler for the acceptation of SDN and NFV technologies. In this way, the management functions are responsible for provisioning and maintenance of NSs that contain strict QoS attributes. There is not any unique solution for the operation of these NSs during the entire NS lifecycle. From the maintenance at run-time perspective, a 3GPP working group defined self-healing as essential [2].

The number of unresolved problems in software and virtual networks is not exhaustive, as management aspects are usually not considered at the design step in network solutions. For this reason, we use a self-management architecture as the starting point to build a framework capable of dealing with the problems described in this section, which are under investigation in other research groups, as well as future problems that future applications will pose.

3   Self-healing Framework

For applying self-healing in SDN and NFV environments, we built a framework based on Self-Organising Networks Architecture (SONAr) [10], which is an architecture for self-management of computer and mobile networks inspired by Self-Organising Networks (SON) [1] concepts. In this section, we first describe the framework architecture and show the placement of the self-* functions; we next detail the monitoring functions of our solution, followed by the recovery functions details; and finally, we present the Management Catalog and discuss some use cases.

3.1   Framework Architecture

In this section, we present some technical details about the project we have developed from our previous position paper. The SONAr has capabilities for self-configuration, self-protection, self-optimisation, and so son; however, we focus on the self-healing fundamental in this paper. Figure 2 shows a layered vision of our framework. In SDN and NFV, the Infrastructure Layer contains NEs, e.g. switches, and compute elements, e.g. servers. The Control Layer has the SDN components, e.g. controller and applications, and NFV elements, e.g. controller and orchestrators. Separated from the Control Layer, we present the Management Layer, in which our framework operates.

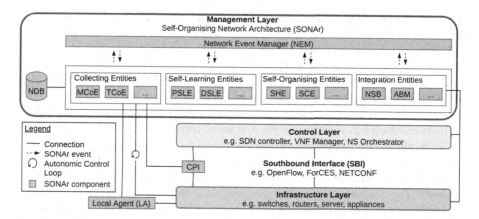

Fig. 2. The framework insight-architecture, i.e. SONAr. The Control and Infrastructure layers are monitored by the Management Layer. The collected data is transformed into events and the modules for self-management, i.e. SLE, SOE, and IE, address such events for real-time and prediction-based recovery.

From the self-healing aspect, the operation in any network topology is commonly performed by OAM systems and divided into two phases: (i) monitoring and (ii) recovery. In (i), the OAM framework, e.g. SONAr, retrieves information from the infrastructure. In (ii), the retrieved information is analysed for detecting or predicting failures and actions are executed for recovering from these potential/eventual failures.

3.2 Monitoring of Different Network Layers

SONAr applies three different monitoring techniques, as summarised as follows:

- Autonomic Control Loop (ACL): Every Collecting Entities (CoE) applies ACL for retrieving information from both Control Layer and Infrastructure Layer periodically, e.g. the Metrics CoE (MCoE), responsible for collecting metrics, can collect statistic usage from NEs' ports in the Infrastructure Layer or memory usage from an SDN application in the Control Layer.
- Local Agents (LAs): The LAs are placed inside the NEs in the Infrastructure Layer, for summarising information and sending it to the CoEs. This technique avoids the high cost of control loops and flooding.

– Interception of primitives in the SBI: an entity named Control Primitives Interceptor (CPI) is deployed as a proxy between the data and control planes. The CPI intercepts control primitives and send them to the CoEs. If the primitives are malicious or cause a crash in the destination (control components), SONAr can recover the destination.

Each aforementioned technique has advantages and disadvantages. According to our experience, ACL and LA techniques are sufficient to monitor the entire SDN and NFV environment. Additionally, the CPI is a novel contribution from SONAr and enables the recovery of crashes and bugs caused by control/management primitives.

The CoEs transform the collected/received information in events that are published in the Network Event Manager (NEM) publisher/subscriber platform. NEM works with topics and each event is categorised in a specific topic, e.g. the collected metrics are published in the topic named 'metric', and any other entity in the framework can subscribe to one or more topics. In this way, the collected events or the generated events, which are created by SONAr's components, are sent and received by any entity. From the self-healing point of view, the Self-Healing Entity (SHE) and Self-Learning Entities (SLEs) are essential for network recovery. The first has algorithms for real-time analysis and recovery actions, whilst the former has Artificial Intelligence (AI) algorithms for prediction actions that can avoid or mitigate future failures.

3.3   Recovery by Detection and Prediction

The recovery in SONAr is based on the analysis of every event travelling in the framework. For some events, the framework has no immediate actions, and such events are just stored in a distributed structure, i.e. Network Database (NDB). The SLEs performs analysis and Machine Learning (ML) algorithms using the stored information. For other events, urgent actions are necessary, e.g. a link down event. The SHE, which is a group of microservices for network healing, treats the real-time events. The basic microservices in this entity are summarised as follows: the topology microservice, which is subscribed to topology information topics, is responsible for building the network topology and logical control/management topology between data plane NEs and control/management components; the catalogue microservice, which creates a catalogue containing the information about the NEs and the components responsible for the management of such elements; the path engine microservice, which run routing algorithms to define the paths between every NEs and virtual function and their control/management components; the metric microservice, which analysis every collected metric to define whether such metric represents a failure (or a possible failure); and finally, the recovery microservice, which is responsible to build necessary commands to recover from a failure.

After the aforementioned analysis, the SHE has a list of commands that will be requested to control and manage components primarily, or to infrastructure elements directly, when control and management components are not available.

As an example, if a control primitive containing a link down warning is intercepted by the CPI, the CPI sends the primitive to the Topology CoE (TCoE), which transforms this primitive into an event and publish it into a topic 'topology' in NEM. SHE microservices, subscribed to the topic 'topology', receive the event. The topology microservice can decide whether this primitive will affect the communication between the SDNC and some NEs. In a positive situation, the recovery microservice builds new commands, which are placed into new events. Such new events are published into NEM, in a topic named 'recovery commands'. The events are received by all microservice from any entity that is subscribed to the topic 'recovery commands'. The Network Service Broker (NSB), responsible for the integration between SONAr and the components into Control and Infrastructure Layers, receives the events and builds command requests that are sent to the bottom layers. In the current example, a telnet command is necessary to modify the control paths between the affected NE and the SDNC.

The Self-Organising Entities (SOEs), divided into SHE, Self-Protection Entity (SPE), Self-Optimisation Entity (SOPE), and Self-Configuration Entity (SCE), focus on real-time actions. For fault tolerance, a real-time action means detection of failures in a reactive perspective, i.e. the failure already occurred and will be treated. However, for critical applications and services, e.g. URLLC or Enhanced Vehicular to Everything (eV2X), the time for detection and recovery can not be enough for maintaining the QoS of such applications. For this reason, SONAr has specified the SLEs, responsible for analysing the information stored into NDB to find behaviours that can implicate in future failures. If a future failure is predicted, the framework can mitigate or, in most cases, avoid such failure. A common example of this situation is the congestion. Since the LAs, ACL, and CPI provide information about metrics, a link usage metric is commonly stored into the NDB. In this scenario, if a link has a linear growth, it is possible to determine when the link will be congested.

The reason for the division between SOEs and SLEs is associated with the computing cost of AI algorithms. As some failures require immediate recovery actions, the SOEs need high performance for analysing and processing recovery actions as soon as possible. On the other hand, AI algorithms, e.g. ML procedures, can spend high processing; therefore, the SLEs are separated to not interfere in real-time actions from SOEs. Any entity listed in Fig. 2 can communicate with any other by events. Besides the SHE, which groups the healing microservices, other entities can also participate in the recovery process. As an example, if the SHE defines that a reboot is necessary for some NEs, the SHE will publish the recovery event into NEM. This event will be received by the SCE, which has the best strategies for network bootstrapping. The SCE can generate a new event, which will be received by the Auto-Boot Manager (ABM). The ABM has particular bootstrapping procedures and will send the necessary commands to Control and Infrastructure Layers.

3.4   The Network Database

The NDB is a NoSQL database that contains operational information used by SONAr and the events that are collected and generated by the framework. Additionally, the Management Catalog is stored in this structure and requires some details. First, SONAr CoEs retrieve the information about the topology and stores in NDB. Then, the ABM and NSB retrieve meta-information from controllers and orchestrators running in the environment. Such information allows the identification of a controller and its controlled NEs, as well as the identification of an orchestrator and its managed resources. This meta-information is important because enable the SHE and SLEs to detect and predict failures.

As an example of the Management Catalog, an SDNC, e.g. $SDNC_1$, controlling a topology with four NEs, e.g. NE_1, NE_2, NE_3, and NE_4 is considered, in addition to another SDNC, e.g. $SDNC_2$, controlling another topology with two NEs, e.g. NE_5, NE_6. In the catalogue, some rows are indicating what are the controllers and their managed elements. As the catalogue is a 2-tuple, the example is a set as follows: $\{(SDNC_1, NE_1), (SDNC_1, NE_2), (SDNC_1, NE_3), (SDNC_1, NE_4), (SDNC_2, NE_5), (SDNC_2, NE_6)\}$. For NFV components, SONAr keeps the information inside the catalogue as well. For example, a VNFM, e.g. $VNFM_1$, that had instantiated two VNFs, e.g. VNF_1 and VNF_2, is stored in the catalogue as follows: $\{(VNFM_1, VNF_1), (VNFM_1, VNF_2)\}$. The 2-tuple is the key from the catalogue rows, but the column families have many meta-information, indicating the logical addresses, type of NFV components, type of SDNC, vendors, versions, and so on.

The catalogue also stores properties information, which enables that SHE recovery microservice to build recovery commands. As an example, an Open Network Operating System (ONOS) controller has an open rest-Application Programming Interface (API) different from the OpenDaylight (ODL) controller [14]. With the properties information, the SHE can build the proper commands to request the open APIs from different SDNCs and different NFV components as well.

4   Use Cases

As exposed in the last section, we provided a self-management framework based on SONAr specification, allowing the implementation of different self-healing functions. The modular and flexible characteristics of the framework enable the monitoring and recovery of several scenarios of failures. In this section, we present four use cases focused on the control and management connectivity, showing the framework capacity. Nevertheless, there is a non-exhaustive number of use cases that the framework can treat, as the reference model allows the creation of new microservices on demand.

4.1   Control Paths Use Case

The Control Paths use case is associated with the logical connection between NEs, placed in the data plane, and the SDNC and its applications, placed in the control plane, i.e. the SBI connectivity. Figure 3a shows a basic SDN multi-path topology with four NEs connected, NE_1, NE_2, NE_3, and NE_4, and an SDNC, i.e. C_1. In this topology, C_1 has a single link connection with NE_1, which means that the communication between C_1 with NE_2, NE_3, and NE_4 is not directly, e.g. the control primitives sent from C_1 to NE_4 will follow by one of the routes NE_1-NE_4, NE_1-NE_2-NE_4, or NE_1-NE_3-NE_4. The OpenFlow protocol, which is a well-known SBI protocol in literature, has procedures for creating the initial flow rules between a NE and the controller at the initialisation time (bootstrapping). In the current example, the initial paths are represented as dashed lines in Fig. 3b. As the initial path from C_1 to NE_4 is C_1-NE_1-NE_4, all control primitives from NE_4 to the SDNC will follow throughout the path NE_4-NE_1-C_1; the other NE have analogous behaviours.

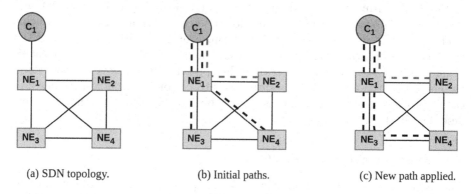

(a) SDN topology.   (b) Initial paths.   (c) New path applied.

Fig. 3. SDN control paths use case. At bootstrapping time, the SBI protocol has procedures for creating the initial logical paths from the controller to every NE, as shown in (b). If a degradation/failure in a link happens, e.g. in the link NE_1-NE_4, SONAr framework recalculates and applies a new logical control path, avoiding the degraded/broken link as shown in (c). Adapted from [20].

As the OpenFlow protocol defines the initial control paths, SONAr does not interfere in the NE bootstrapping in this situation. When the network is operational, SONAr retrieves the topology and logical paths information by using the SDNC open APIs: the NSB requests a service to the SDNC and stores the information, received in the response, in NDB. If the topology changes, the TCoE receives the changing information and updates the NDB. At this point, the SHE path engine microservice calculates all possible paths between C_1 and every NE. The CoEs, LAs, and CPI keep monitoring the data, control, and management planes. If a link degradation/broken is recognised by the SHE topology microservice, the SHE recovery microservice creates recovery commands for applying an alternative path. This situation is shown in Fig. 3b and c, in which the link NE_1-NE_4 presents a degradation. The NSB receives the recovery command events and applies flow rule modifications in the NE_1 and NE_4, and add flow rules in NE_3. Figure 3c shows the new logical path applied, avoiding the link NE_1-NE_4.

This use case has other scenarios that we can explore. A second scenario is overload or congestion. If the link NE_1-NE_4 is not broken, it could be congested at some time, caused by an overloading of NE_1 or NE_4, or even high traffic in this link, caused by data plane communication. As the MCoE keeps monitoring metrics such as link usage, the Prediction SLE (PSLE) keeps analysing such metrics at run-time. If by any reason the PSLE predicts congestion in any link, e.g. NE_1-NE_4, it publishes an event in NEM, then SHE receives this event and the SHE recovery microservice proactively defines recovery actions. In this situation, the logical control path between C_1 and NE_4 is modified before the congestion begins.

Diverse other scenarios are possible in the control path use case. The SOE must ensure uninterrupted communication between the SDNC and its controlled NE, as well as between SDN applications and the SDNC, which is not represented in Fig. 3. To ensure the availability of the paths, it is important that SONAr microservices first apply the flow rules for the new paths, and then remove the old flow rules. In this case, NEs duplicate some control primitives and the SDNC can receive both primitives. Assuming that the SDNC discards the duplicated primitives, this procedure is better than the opposite (first remove old flow rules to then create the new ones), because no control information is lost. Other use cases considering the control paths are enabled by SONAr, but they are not described in this document.

4.2   Management Paths Use Case

Another use case we selected is the management paths example. The control path use case applies to routes between the SDNC and its controlled NEs. However, in NFV there are other control/management components that we named OAM in this paper, e.g. a VNFM provisions and manages diverse virtual functions, i.e. VNFs. As SONAr primarily focuses on management traffic, any OAM requires uninterrupted communication with its managed resources. Figure 4a shows the network topology with four NEs, and additionally, a VNFM, i.e. V_1, managing two VNFs previously created, i.e. VNF_1 and VNF_2. In this scenario, the complete topology must consider the NEs topology and the NFV topology, which has different available logical paths connecting V_1 with VNF_1 and VNF_2.

Unlike the Control Paths use case, in the Management Paths use case there are no initial paths. The communication routes between V_1 with its VNFs are defined at run-time, by the routing application running on the top of the SDNC, or by the distributed routing algorithms placed inside the routers in traditional architectures. At first, there is no problem with this real-time routing mechanism. However, SONAr is prepared to provide functions to configure static and primarily routes. The highest priority is given to management routes, i.e. the routes for communication between the management components and their managed resources. For this, there are two additional functions performed by SONAr entities: (i) the creation of the catalogue containing the management components and their managed resources; and (ii) the definition and application

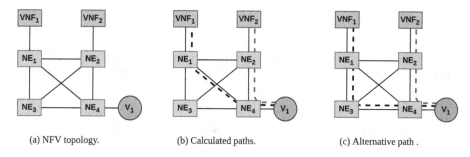

(a) NFV topology.   (b) Calculated paths.   (c) Alternative path .

Fig. 4. NFV management paths use case. A VNFM component has instantiated two VNFs and manages them. SONAr retrieves the information about the current VNFs and applies static routes between V_1 and VNF_1, as well as between V_1 and VNF_2, as shown in (b). If a degradation or failure happens in the link NE_1-NE_4, SONAr applies an alternative route, avoiding the degraded/broken link as shown in (c). Adapted from [20].

of initial paths between the components in the catalogue. After such functions, the initial paths are applied in the NEs, as shown in Fig. 4b.

We assume that the failures in network and infrastructure resources, managed by NFV components, are solved by such components. For example, failures in VNF_1 and VNF_2 are normally solved by V_1. Common failures include hardware and software problems, which demand re-instantiating the VNFs; an overload of a virtual function, demanding the increasing of VNFs; and problems inside the VNFM itself. SONAr must perform algorithms for ensuring the communication between V_1 and the VNFs, and to solve problems inside V_1. Analogous to the control path use case, if a problem occurs in a link utilised by the management paths, e.g. link NE_1-NE_4 in Fig. 4b, SONAr must apply an alternative path, as shown in 4c. The initial path calculated and applied by v microservices was V_1-NE_4-NE_1-VNF_1. After a detected/predicted degradation in the link NE_1-NE_4, the alternative path applied was V_1-NE_4-NE_3-NE_1-VNF_1.

4.3 SDN Controller Migration Use Case

Considering a cloud environment, with SDN and NFV components running over VMs or containers, it is reasonable that such components can modify the virtual locations. The migration of these components is expected in SONAr since it is necessary for recovery from some failures. In Fig. 5a, the same network topology used in the previous detailed use cases is shown. Assuming that compute nodes are available and physically connected with all NEs, the initial SDNC placement is in NE_1. The control traffic between C_1 with any NE obligatorily passes throughout NE_1.

The SONAr can operate to solve some failures that can occur after some specific impairments associated with the SDNC placement. The first one is associated with the issues that occur in the NEs directly associated with the SDNC, e.g. NE_1 in Fig. 5a. An overload or crash in NE_1 can culminate in a non-operational

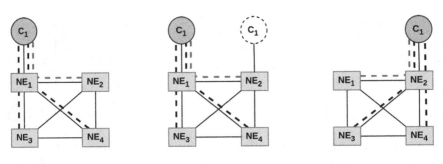

(a) Initial SDNC placement.   (b) New SDNC instantiation.   (c) Control paths migration.

Fig. 5. Migration of an SDN controller use case. SONAr can determine the best SDN controller placement based on failure identification or network traffic. If a controller is initially plugged in a NE, e.g. NE_1 as shown in (a), but the highest traffic of SBI control primitives is in another part of the topology, e.g. NE_2, SONAr migrates the controller, which is usually running on a VM, to another NE, as shown in (c).

data plane. As SONArs has procedures, in the SHE and SLEs, for failure detection or prediction respectively such impairments, recovery actions are possible if the C_1 runs over a VM or container. Assuming that NE_2 has a compute node directly connected with it, SONAr can instantiate a new VM and start C_1 inside this VM, as shown in Fig. 5b. For this, SONAr works as follows: CoEs collected information accusing the failure; SHE recovery microservice analyses the information and creates new events containing the solution, i.e. commands to instantiate a new controller instance; the new events reach the NSB, which transforms such events in the necessary commands; NSB requests the creation of a new VM to a VIM running in the environment; and finally, the NSB copies C_1 settings to the new VM, then it starts the applications, and finally it copies the current state from C_1. At the final, the new VM has the same configuration of C_1 running in the old VM. For avoiding loss of information, the ideal procedure is to maintain C_1 state in a structure shared by the old VM and the new VM until the final of the migration.

At the moment that the new C_1 VM is ready to assume the traffic, SONAr configures every NEs with flow rules to send the control traffic to the new VM, i.e. that one plugged on NE_2. This step is represented in Fig. 5c. The final step from SONAr is to turn down the old VM. The described situation shows the failure in the NEs where the C_1 was placed. However, other situations demand real-time controller migration. One of them is the high-traffic in some part of the network topology. As an example, the topology shown in Fig. 5 has the C_1 connected with the NE_1 at the beginning; however, if the control traffic is higher in NE_2, the controller can be migrated to NE_2, avoiding control traffic flooding in the network. SONAr is capable to work with this situation because SLEs have algorithms for dealing with metrics indicating the heat map of the topology, i.e. the part of the topology graph where the control/management traffic is higher. Besides that, Fig. 5 shows a basic four-node topology. In different topologies, there is the option to allocate the SDNC next to the NEs that demands more control traffic.

4.4   SDN Controller Instantiating Use Case

The SDNC Instantiating use case is similar to the migration use case. However, in this new use case, both SDNCs operate at the same time. Usually, an SDNC controls a segment inside a domain. In Fig. 6a, the C_1 controls a domain with four NEs in the topology, meaning that the domain has just one segment. This basic four-nodes topology will probably not have overload or performance problems, but it is enough to illustrate this use case. In this particular topology, NE_1, NE_2, NE_3, and NE_4 send control primitives to C_1 logical address, e.g. IPv4 or IPv6. For exemplifying, NE_3 will send all its control primitives to NE_1, which will send such primitives to C_1. When C_1 needs to send a request/response control primitive to NE_3, it will send the primitive to NE_1; NE_1 has flow rules configured to forward primitives with destination 'NE_3' to NE_3.

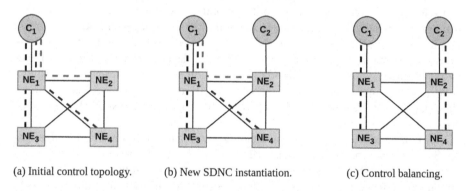

(a) Initial control topology.   (b) New SDNC instantiation.   (c) Control balancing.

Fig. 6. Control traffic balancing use case. Some current SDN controllers allow the distribution of controller instances. In this use case, SONAr identifies a high-traffic of control primitives to a unique instance as shown in (a). Next, SONAr instantiates a new controller instance, as shown in (b), and then migrates the control paths, balancing the control traffic as shown in (c).

Mainly for performance reasons, SONAr can assume that traffic balancing is necessary to maintain the high performance of the control primitives traffic. In this situation, it is necessary to instantiate a new SDNC instance and split the traffic. For this, the first step is to create a new instance as shown in Fig. 6b. Notice that, differently from the migration use case – Fig. 5b shows only one active C_1 node at a moment – in this use case the new instantiated SDNC is an additional instance as shown in Fig. 6b: there are two SDNC active instances, i.e. C_1 and C_2. Once the new instance is created and configured, SONAr integrates C_1 and C_2 in a way that they start to share the same state. It is crucial to mention that the procedures described in this section just work with SDNC prepared to work with a horizontal scale-up, e.g. the ONOS controller [12].

Since C_1 and C_2 are operational as shown in Fig. 6b, SONAr starts the migration of NEs to the new instance. SONAr defines the NEs that will be migrated to C_2 and modifies the flow rules inside such NEs. In the example shown in Fig. 6c, SONAr kept NE_1 and NE_2 logically connected with C_1; and modified NE_3 and NE_4 to send control primitives to C_2. The balancing algorithms performed by SONAr uses basic equations of traffic distribution to determine the number of new instances to be created and the distribution of NEs to these new instances. If more than one SDNC instance is available in the topology, the balancing use case is possible as detailed in this section. Additionally, it means that the use case related in Subsect. 4.3 is optimised, as the steps to instantiate new instances are not necessary.

5   Concluding Remarks and Future Work

In this paper, we introduced a new framework to apply self-healing functions on SDN and NFV environments. The framework is based on SONAr, which is a reference architecture for computer/mobile networks self-management. Our framework runs on the Management Layer and has procedures for autonomously monitoring the other layers. The difference between SONAr and other projects in literature is in the system placement: SONAr places at the Management Layer and it is entirely application-based. The common computer and telecommunications protocols are developed at SONAr, and its modular characteristic enables the adoption of SONAr even in environments in which SDN, NFV, or legacy NEs are already deployed.

We exploited the self-healing autonomic computing fundamental for illustrating SONAr's capabilities. There is a thorough difference between a fault tolerance system and a self-healing system. The first is a system capable to deal with faults, i.e. the system tolerates failures, which means that the system will continue to work because the components have backups or are partially distributed. The former means that the system has the notion that some of its parts are degraded or broken, and therefore it can self-recover itself. Considering a computer or mobile network, the entire network is the system, i.e. the graph representing the topology with nodes (NEs) and edges (links). In an SDN and NFV environment, the system is the infrastructure topology and the control/management layers. In this way, an SDN/NFV environment achieves the self-healing characteristic by considering all layers, i.e. Control, Management, and Infrastructure layers.

For implementing all self-healing functions for current and future applications, we decided to build a framework with an extensible flavour. Hence, the basic self-management procedures are built at the beginning, but new procedures can be introduced in the future without modification in the initial ones. For demonstrating this, we choose four use cases focused on control plane connectivity: (i) the first use case shows an SDN topology with degraded/broken links, and a real-time or preventive migration of control paths to avoid such links; (ii) the second use case shows the same scenario, but considering an NFV topology, in which static routes are necessary to ensure the connectivity between NFV components and their managed resources; (iii) the third use case illustrates a live migration of an SDN controller; and finally, (iv) the fourth use case illustrates an instantiating of a new SDN controller and the control traffic balancing.

The aforementioned use cases have proven the efficiency of SONAr for dealing with common problems that are found in control and management planes. For the best of our knowledge, SONAr is the first work to allow the implementation of these procedures in a flexible model, enabling diverse use cases. At this moment, we have the implementation of the basic SONAr components, which means that new researchers from our group can start the implementation of different microservices for the healing of mobile/computer networks. The self-healing was chosen in this paper as a study case, but the platform is prepared for self-configuration, self-optimisation, self-protection, and so on. As future work, we long for presenting the performance experiments of SONAr considering the four use cases just presented, as well as new self-* use cases.

References

1. 3GPP: Telecommunication management; Self-Organizing Networks (SON); Concepts and requirements. Technical Specification (TS) 32.500, 3rd Generation Partnership Project (3GPP) (2018). http://www.3gpp.org/-DynaReport/-32500.htm
2. 3GPP: Telecommunication management; Study on management and orchestration of network slicing for next generation network. Technical Report (TR) 28.801, 3rd Generation Partnership Project (3GPP), January 2018. http://www.3gpp.org/DynaReport/28801.htm, version 15.1.0
3. Abdelsalam, M.A.: Network Application Design Challenges and Solutions in SDN. Ph.D. thesis, Carleton University (2018)
4. Afolabi, I., Taleb, T., Samdanis, K., Ksentini, A., Flinck, H.: Network slicing and softwarization: a survey on principles, enabling technologies, and solutions. IEEE Commun. Surv. Tutor. **20**(3), 2429–2453 (2018). https://doi.org/10.1109/COMST.2018.2815638
5. Basta, A., Blenk, A., Belhaj Hassine, H., Kellerer, W.: Towards a dynamic SDN virtualization layer: Control path migration protocol. In: 2015 11th International Conference on Network and Service Management (CNSM), pp. 354–359, November 2015. https://doi.org/10.1109/CNSM.2015.7367382
6. Canini, M., Salem, I., Schiff, L., Schiller, E.M., Schmid, S.: A self-organizing distributed and in-band SDN control plane. In: 2017 IEEE 37th International Conference on Distributed Computing Systems (ICDCS), pp. 2656–2657, June 2017. https://doi.org/10.1109/ICDCS.2017.328
7. Chen, H., Abbas, R., Cheng, P., Shirvanimoghaddam, M., Hardjawana, W., Bao, W., Li, Y., Vucetic, B.: Ultra-reliable low latency cellular networks: Use cases, challenges and approaches. IEEE Commun. Mag. **56**(12), 119–125 (2018). https://doi.org/10.1109/MCOM.2018.1701178
8. Cox, J.H., et al.: Advancing software-defined networks: a survey. IEEE Access **5**, 25487–25526 (2017). https://doi.org/10.1109/ACCESS.2017.2762291
9. Ganek, A.G., Corbi, T.A.: The dawning of the autonomic computing era. IBM Syst. J. **42**(1), 5–18 (2003)

10. GonÇalves., M.A., de Souza Neto., N.V., Oliveira., D.R.C., de Oliveira Silva., F., Rosa., P.F.: Bootstrapping and plug-and-play operations on software defined networks: a case study on self-configuration using the sonar architecture. In: Proceedings of the 10th International Conference on Cloud Computing and Services Science - Volume 1: CLOSER, pp. 103–114. INSTICC, SciTePress (2020). https:// doi.org/10.5220/0009406901030114
11. Kubernetes: Kubernetes (2020). https://kubernetes.io/
12. ONOS: ONOS (2020). https://wiki.onosproject.org/
13. Open Networking Foundation: OpenFlow Switch Specification Version 1.5.1 (Protocol version 0x06) (2020). https://www.opennetworking.org/wp-content/ uploads/2014/10/openflow-switch-v1.5.1.pdf
14. OpenDaylight: OpenDaylight (2020). https://www.opendaylight.org/
15. Openstack: Openstack (2020). https://www.openstack.org/
16. Fonseca, P.C., Mota, E.S.: A survey on fault management in software-defined networks. IEEE Commun. Surv. Tutor. **19**(4), 2284–2321 (2017). https://doi.org/10. 1109/COMST.2017.2719862
17. Rehman, A.U., Aguiar, R.L., Barraca, J.P.: Fault-tolerance in the scope of software-defined networking (SDN). IEEE Access **7**, 124474–124490 (2019). https://doi.org/ 10.1109/ACCESS.2019.2939115
18. Sanchez, J., Yahia, I.G.B., Crespi, N., Rasheed, T., Siracusa, D.: Softwarized 5G networks resiliency with self-healing. In: 1st International Conference on 5G for Ubiquitous Connectivity, pp. 229–233, November 2014. https://doi.org/10.4108/ icst.5gu.2014.258123
19. Schiff, L., Schmid, S., Canini, M.: Ground control to major faults: towards a fault tolerant and adaptive SDN control network. In: 2016 46th Annual IEEE/IFIP International Conference on Dependable Systems and Networks Workshop (DSN-W), pp. 90–96, June 2016. https://doi.org/10.1109/DSN-W.2016.48
20. de Souza Neto., N.V., Oliveira., D.R.C., GonÇalves., M.A., de Oliveira Silva., F., Rosa., P.F.: A self-healing platform for the control and management planes communication in softwarized and virtualized networks. In: Proceedings of the 10th International Conference on Cloud Computing and Services Science - Volume 1: CLOSER, pp. 415–422. INSTICC, SciTePress (2020). https://doi.org/10.5220/ 0009465204150422
21. Thorat, P., Raza, S.M., Nguyen, D.T., Im, G., Choo, H., Kim, D.S.: Optimized self-healing framework for software defined networks. In: Proceedings of the 9th International Conference on Ubiquitous Information Management and Communication,. pp. 1–6 (2015)
22. Yousaf, F.Z., Bredel, M., Schaller, S., Schneider, F.: NFV and SDN–key technology enablers for 5G networks. IEEE J. Sel. Areas Commun. **35**(11), 2468–2478 (2017). https://doi.org/10.1109/JSAC.2017.2760418
23. Zhou, X., Li, R., Chen, T., Zhang, H.: Network slicing as a service: enabling enterprises' own software-defined cellular networks. IEEE Commun. Mag. **54**(7), 146–153 (2016). https://doi.org/10.1109/MCOM.2016.7509393

Author Index

Printed in the United States
by Baker & Taylor Publisher Services